From Rights to Needs

From Rights to Needs
A History of Family Allowances in Canada, 1929-92

Raymond B. Blake

UBCPress · Vancouver · Toronto

16 15 14 13 12 11 10 09   5 4 3 2 1

Printed in Canada with vegetable-based inks on FSC-certified ancient-forest-free paper (100% post-consumer recycled) that is processed chlorine- and acid-free.

Library and Archives Canada Cataloguing in Publication

Blake, Raymond B. (Raymond Benjamin)
  From rights to needs : a history of family allowances in Canada, 1929-92 / by Raymond Blake.

Includes bibliographical references and index.
ISBN 978-0-7748-1572-7

  1. Family allowances – Canada – History – 20th century. I. Title.

HD4925.5.C3B58 2008   362.82'820971   C2008-903381-7

Canadä

UBC Press gratefully acknowledges the financial support for our publishing program of the Government of Canada through the Book Publishing Industry Development Program (BPIDP), and of the Canada Council for the Arts, and the British Columbia Arts Council.

This book has been published with the help of a grant from the Canadian Federation for the Humanities and Social Sciences, through the Aid to Scholarly Publications Programme, using funds provided by the Social Sciences and Humanities Research Council of Canada.

UBC Press
The University of British Columbia
2029 West Mall
Vancouver, BC V6T 1Z2
604-822-5959 / Fax: 604-822-6083
www.ubcpress.ca

For Mary and Raymond Francis
who never forget the importance of family

Contents

Illustrations

Tables

Figures

Acknowledgments

THIS BOOK EXAMINES the history of family allowances in Canada from the time the subject was first raised in the House of Commons in the late 1920s to the demise of the program in 1992, when the government of Prime Minister Brian Mulroney decided that the funds committed to all Canadian families with children could be more effectively targeted to low-income Canadian families. The book argues that we can see the interplay of politics and policy through the prism of the family allowance program. It shows that social policy in Canada is not simply about creating a kinder, gentler, and more compassionate nation. Rather, public policy decisions in the field of social policy have been influenced by many considerations – economic conditions, politics, federal-provincial relations, constitutional negotiations, and international trends in public policy – as well as a desire to make good social policy.

I began research on this project more than a decade ago, and clearly this book has been too long in the making. Administrative tasks and other books and projects have pushed this work aside at various times, but my interest in the subject remained strong. I have benefited from the advice and support of friends and colleagues since I began work on this project. At St. Thomas University, there was great support and friendship, particularly from Juergen Doerr, who passed away in 2002, and Dan Gleason. The Centre for Canadian Studies at Mount Allison was a busy place and a great environment in which to write about Canada. Both colleagues and students there were great to work with; I wish to especially thank Stephanie Shattilla for research assistance and Eugene Goodrich for his support and encouragement. I first learned about public policy at the Saskatchewan Institute of Public Policy, and I believe this book is better as a result of having worked with people such as John Allan, John Whyte, and others who not only studied public policy but helped make it as well. Also at SIPP and the University of Regina, Erna Pearson was always a joy to work with, and I must acknowledge Marilyn Bickford for her assistance with copying and getting the manuscript ready for publication. Along the way, Jack Granatstein, Robert Wardhaugh, and Ken Leyton-Brown read all or parts of this book and offered valuable advice. Mark Anderson took more time and offered more sage advice on the manuscript than I had any reason to suspect he might or should. Various archivists at Library and Archives Canada provided useful advice with sources; Jill Delaney helped with arranging photographs that are included in the book. Melissa Pitts at UBC Press encouraged this project along and offered invaluable guidance when I needed it most. Stephanie VanderMeulen has made many editorial suggestions and has greatly improved the book in the process and Ann Macklem has demonstrated great patience and professionalism in shepherding this book through the publication process. This book is also much improved because of advice I received from anonymous reviewers. Last, but not least, I wish to acknowledge the financial support of the Social Science and Humanities Research Council for a Standard Research Grant, the Canadian Studies Directorate at Canadian Heritage for their generous support, and the Humanities Research Institute at the University of Regina.

I owe my greatest gratitude and thanks to my family. When I began this project, I had not realized the importance family allowances held for my own mother. Only as I talked with her about her monthly cheques did I appreciate how important a source of income they were to her. Without such payments, which did not begin in Newfoundland until 1949, her life would have been that much more difficult. Family allowance benefits made an important difference for her and for my family, but unfortunately she did not live to see the final product of my research. Wanda and our two boys, Robert and Ben, have always been a source of love and inspiration; without them this book could never have been done.

From Rights to Needs

Introduction

THE WELFARE STATE could be considered one of the greatest achievements of the 20th century. Especially in the generation during the Second World War, there emerged a collective commitment to improving the lives of all citizens. Nation-states everywhere, including Canada, accepted the notion of state responsibility for the social well-being of its citizens. Many of Canada's modern social welfare initiatives had their genesis as part of the comprehensive planning that began during that period. It would take several decades for federal and provincial governments to implement many of the social security measures discussed at that time. In the generation that followed, social expenditure consumed a large portion of government revenues. Although Canada failed to provide sufficient social protection for all of its citizens, the social security policies enacted by federal, provincial, and later First Nations governments became a hallmark of Canadian society. In the final decades of the last century, however, the welfare state in Canada, and in most other Western democracies, came under intense scrutiny as politicians, public commentators, and citizens alike raised serious questions about the nature and purpose of the welfare state. Many Canadians questioned the efficacy of the existing programs and demanded major reforms to make social spending more effective. Others called for major retrenchment, and still others for a more generous and expansive welfare state. Out of this dialogue that began in the 1970s, Canada's welfare state embarked on a long period of reform and reorientation, but it was not dismantled. Government expenditure on social programs remained relatively stable for decades, and though the welfare state was considerably transformed, Canada remains one of a few nations in the world where its citizens consider their social security programs a defining national characteristic.

Family allowances began as a universal social program under Prime Minister William Lyon Mackenzie King in 1945. One can only wonder if he realized the long-term impact of his initiative. However, we are able to glimpse in his diary some of his thoughts on the topic. One such moment comes from an entry on 17 July 1945 as he travelled to the constituency of Glengarry, a safe Liberal seat in southeastern Ontario that he hoped would return him to the House of Commons. He had lost his Saskatchewan riding in the general election earlier that

June along with fifty-five other incumbent Liberals, although his government had managed to hang on with a slim majority of just five members. The election had been bittersweet for him; after leading Canada successfully through the war, he and his government had promised Canadians a new social order and a better peace-time society. The new Family Allowances Act fulfilled one of his promises, but clearly voters were not terribly impressed with either him or his government. If he was disappointed that more Canadians had not voted Liberal or if he harboured any doubts about the family allowance program, he did not show it as his train pulled into the quaint Ontario town of Alexandria. Quite the contrary. After passing the home of a young mother who had three or four young children playing in her yard, he wrote in his diary that he "thought of the family allowances and all of the comfort and joy it would bring to that little home and what it would mean to them for the future of their lives – and not to them only but to the children of all Canada." He noted, "It is a great reform."[1]

King would retire three years after the introduction of family allowances, but he was clearly in control of the government when the program was established. Although he was Canada's longest serving prime minister, his was the politics of compromise, delay, and obfuscation, and perhaps for that reason he remains very much an enigma in Canadian history. It might also explain why he has not received the recognition he deserves for many of the public policy accomplishments during his twenty-two years as prime minister. This is certainly the case with the family allowance program. It has rarely been regarded as a major policy innovation; rather, scholars have long argued that King used family allowances to stymie the surging socialist movement in the Co-operative Commonwealth Federation (CCF) in 1943; to maintain the government's strict wage control system that was put in place in 1941 to control wartime inflation; to maintain consumer demand and avoid a postwar depression; to forestall the full development of a social security state in Canada; and to encourage women to return home after the Second World War. Granted, family allowances, like so many other effective and popular public policy initiatives, served a variety of interests, but no one can deny that it was also one of Canada's most innovative public policies in the postwar period. It was widely supported both inside and outside the government.

This book offers an examination of the family allowance program, one of the country's most important social security programs and its first universal one. From 1945 to 1992, the family allowance program paid benefits to all families with children. By tracing how one instrument of social security policy was introduced in Canada, how it evolved after 1945 onward, and how, too, a series of events led to its demise in 1992, this history will help us better understand in general the development of the welfare state in Canada. The broader aim of this study, then, is to examine the forces that lay behind the evolution of the family allowance policy at the national level and to do so in the context of the wider social, economic, ideological, and political changes occurring at the same time in Canada. As such, this book offers a national perspective on the history of social security policy in Canada. The focus on the national level is not to argue that the provinces did not play an important role in the evolution of family allowances. They did, particularly when Premier George Drew of Ontario opposed the introduction of a federal (rather than provincial) program in 1945, and when Quebec Premier Robert Bourassa linked the family allowance program to constitutional reform in the early 1970s. However, the focus here remains on the national decision-making process. It will be left to others to tell the corresponding story from the provincial perspective, as Dominique Marshall has done so well for Quebec.[2]

This is the first full book-length treatment of the history of family allowances in Canada, and it is my hope that it provides a nuanced and complete explanation for the origins and development of the program. This is possible because the study attempts to examine the whole panoply of primary sources available to help us understand the complex world in which family allowances originated and evolved; government records, the personal papers of most of the major participants and political parties, records of labour and social organizations, parliamentary debates, and newspapers and magazine articles were consulted. Using this extensive research as the basis for my history of family allowances, I address and engage many of the arguments made by other scholars who have discussed the subject. It is my hope this work will contribute to the wider discussion on the intriguing question of the origins and the subsequent development of the welfare state in Canada and, more broadly, to the wider discourse on the creation of Canadian public policy.

The literature on this subject is enormous, and much of it has focused on the period since the Great Depression of the 1930s and especially since the end of the Second World War. As I began work on this book, I was immediately struck by the insistence among many historians and other social scientists of a single explanation for the emergence of the welfare state in Canada. This study shows above all else that rarely can historical developments like the origins of a welfare state – and the origins and demise of the family allowance program – be explained by a single factor however hard we might try to prove that is the case. Few public policy decisions are ever the result of a single interest group and hardly ever the result of a single factor; social policy making in Canada is complex and it emanates from a variety of forces. A particular social policy usually becomes law when it serves a conjunction of interests.

Take the widely accepted argument, for example, that family allowances were introduced to maintain the government's strict wage control system that was put in place at the beginning of the war to control inflation. Building on the work of other scholars like Brigitte Kitchen, Jane Ursel argues in *Private Lives, Public Policy: 100 Years of State Intervention in the Family* that the King government introduced family allowances to maintain industrial harmony in Canada.[3] Ursel contends that by offering a dissatisfied and increasingly radicalized labour movement a program of family allowances in 1943, the government and its business allies were able to buy peace with labour for the duration of the war. Extending this argument, she describes the Family Allowances Act as "a Wage Subsidy Program." However, she asserts that when King announced his new labour policy in December 1943 to address growing worker unrest across Canada, he did not mention family allowances because to do so would forever link family allowances to wage rates; the government clearly did not wish to do that. Brigitte Kitchen makes a similar argument.[4]

There is a very good reason why Mackenzie King did not link family allowances to the government's labour policy that he announced on 4 December 1943: he and his Cabinet had not fully considered family allowances at that point, and would not do so until mid-January 1944. There had been no decision by the King government on whether or not there would be a family allowance program. There had been little discussion on what a family allowance program might pay to parents, and certainly no indication of when such a program would begin even if the government decided to launch such an initiative. And, of course, a family allowance program would not benefit single workers or workers without dependent children. It should also be pointed out that an angry labour movement – and workers themselves – would not likely be appeased by a promise of some indefinite and vague future payment for the children of workers, from a government that it had come to distrust by 1943. After all, there had been more labour disputes in that year than at any other time in Canadian history. It was also a period of remarkable and rapid growth in union membership, and labour had become increasingly dissatisfied with the Liberal government during the war. King reached an arrangement with labour in 1943 when his government amended its wage control policy and implemented a new code of labour relations in P.C. 1003, which established, for the first time in Canada, the right of workers to collective bargaining and required employers to negotiate with labour.[5] King did not buy labour peace in 1943 by offering a radicalized and angry labour movement a promise of family allowance two years down the road as Kitchen and Ursel have argued.

While I contend that the role of family allowances in King's 1943 labour policy has been exaggerated, there had indeed been some discussion in Canada about family allowances and meeting the demands of labour. The National War Labour Board (NWLB), appointed to investigate wartime labour issues, had noted in its report completed in August 1943 that a program of family allowances might meet the needs of workers demanding higher wages. However, simply because the NWLB made the suggestion does not mean the government accepted it. Kitchen assumes that it did, but she does not provide any evidence from government records to support that assumption. Ursel also discusses the NWLB report written by C.P. McTague, noting, "While it is not indicated in the memos [she found in the archives], it is likely they [Norman] Robertson and [W.C.] Clark [two high-ranking government officials] ... probably" told McTague that family allowances would be a way to solve the labour problem.[6] Yet there is no hard evidence to support this claim. Ursel describes the history of family allowances as a "research puzzle," noting that when she visited Library and Archives Canada to begin research on the origins of family allowance, she discovered there was no archival evidence concerning the beginnings of the program in the Department of National Health and Welfare, the department that was ultimately responsible for administering the program. This is not surprising since the department had not been created when the discussion of a family allowance program began; it was created, in part, to implement the family allowance program. Ursel highlights the fact that the records for the origins of family allowances were found in the NWLB and the Department of Finance. She writes, "The more sensitive the material the more likely its history is sealed in confidential government documents. The history of the Family Allowances Act is an excellent case in point." However, I contend that since the family allowance program was a new initiative, the paper trail for the origins of the program are perforce scattered through the government records for the period and in the papers of bureaucrats, politicians, social organizations, and numerous other collections in Library and Archives Canada. It would be most unusual, given the large financial cost of family allowances, if the Department of Finance had *not* played a key role in the discussions surrounding the introduction of the program. The fuller the breadth of research, the more apparent it becomes that many forces and rationales led to the creation of the family allowance program and that the one-theory approach is limited by one-theory research.[7]

Too often, I believe, Canadian scholars also limit explanations for government public policies, like family allowances, to single *Canadian* events. One example of this is the argument that the King government embraced family allowances solely to stifle the growing political threat to the Liberals from the CCF on the left.[8] As I suggest in Chapter 2, Canadian scholars might have exaggerated the political strength of the CCF in the mid-1940s. True, the CCF squeaked ahead of the Liberals in a 1943 public opinion poll, and Tommy Douglas led his CCF

Party to victory in Saskatchewan, but it was the Progressive Conservatives that unseated the provincial Liberals in vote-rich Ontario in 1943 and won a majority there in 1945. There was no subsequent breakthrough nationally for the CCF in the 1945 federal election; it captured only twenty-eight seats, eighteen of which came from Tommy Douglas' Saskatchewan. Still, many scholars remain steadfast in insisting that the CCF can take the credit for forcing the government to implement the family allowance program even though the Conservatives also supported family allowances and other social legislation and were the major political threat to the Liberal government in the mid-1940s.[9] Of course, in an electoral democracy, as James Rice and Michael Prince have pointed out, many social policy issues came about as a way of solving an immediate political problem. This is particularly true of the introduction of the old age program in 1927, but it might be more true of family allowances during the minority government of Pierre Trudeau from 1972 to 1974 than in the government of Mackenzie King in the 1940s.[10]

Canadian circumstances are important but it is imperative that we, as historians, be aware of international trends or international history even as we invariably find explanatory factors within our own borders to understand Canadian developments. As we consider the origins and evolution of family allowances, we cannot ignore the simple fact that many nations around the world embraced social security measures – and even family allowances – at the same time Canada did. Family allowances were introduced after the Second World War in several industrialized countries, and by 1950, they had become commonplace in seventeen countries. When Canada reformed its social welfare policies after the 1970s, other nations were doing precisely the same thing. As this book demonstrates, political expediency or electioneering was not the motivating factor leading to family allowances in Canada, although Mackenzie King and his political advisers certainly realized there was political advantage in any program that delivered monthly support cheques to virtually every family with children. That this particular social security measure and a wider discussion of a new welfare state came at the end of the Second World War seems to suggest – as Karl Polanyi said of an earlier period and social policy in general – that communities come together in times of change and uncertainty to produce policies that offer their citizens a measure of protection from that uncertainty and fear.[11]

The origins of the welfare state in Canada and elsewhere pre-date the 1930s, but many scholars have focused their attention on the postwar period and have offered a wide range of voices and interpretations. Canadian scholars have contributed to the discourse primarily by examining the Canadian experiment through the theoretical perspectives developed elsewhere. Some of the earlier interpretations saw the development of particular welfare policies as an act of enlightened government and societies, and as a logical and inevitable response to the forces of industrialization. This Fabian approach to the study of the welfare state saw the state progressively and gradually adopt policies to ensure greater equity among citizens to improve the lives of ordinary people. Much of this research has been associated with the work of such scholars as Harold L. Wilensky and Richard Titmuss. Wilensky argues that the welfare state emerged as a function of the modern industrial society.[12] During the process of industrialization and urbanization that was marked by the emergence of the wage earner without the traditional supports associated with rural and agrarian economies, the rise of modern and complex bureaucracies within the state eventually provided a range of basic social security measures. These were particularly in response to pressure for protective welfare policies to avoid the degradation of workers and citizens the poor laws entailed. As societies became more industrial, the extent of state support for citizens also improved.

Richard Titmuss of the London School of Economics adopted a similar approach when he attempted to explain the interest from both the state and its citizenry in a variety of new social policy initiatives that began in the latter stages of the Second World War. He finds the explanation for the development of the welfare state in national wartime management.[13] He argues that social policy had emerged as an important imperative in the immediate postwar period because nations had fought the Second World War on the concept of "total war." From 1939 to 1945, nations such as the United Kingdom and Canada had sought the involvement of the whole society and even looked to marginalized groups such as labour and women to participate in the national effort to defeat totalitarianism. The promise of a new social order after the war became part of the strategy of winning the war and ensuring lasting peace. Once victory was certain, the enlightened state finally moved to implement a variety of social welfare measures as it assumed greater responsibility for the health and well-being of all its citizens.

However, these interpretations could not explain the timing of the development of the welfare state throughout the industrial nations, as the level and extent of the welfare state varied enormously from one country to another. Some industrial societies developed comprehensive social security programs, while others provided only minimal social support for its citizens. Scholars such as Louis Hartz and Roy Lubove explained the timing of the origins and development of social welfare by exploring the values and beliefs of individual nation-states.[14] Those states that espoused the sanctity of individual rights saw little value in collective social programs, but those that placed greater emphasis on shared responsibility and the importance of communities were much more likely to develop comprehensive programs to protect the less fortunate citizens stricken with illness, unemployment, and other challenges of living. Yet this approach does not explain why in Britain, for instance, the government intro- duced a series of social welfare measures between 1906 and 1911 and none before that period and few again until the 1940s. Similarly, the United States saw a number of initiatives in the 1930s, but virtually none before that time, and very few after. Most provinces in Canada had some programs, such as workers' compensation and mother's allowance, before 1920 but virtually no programs at the national level until after the Second World War.

Whiggish interpretations of the welfare state – those that saw the state re- sponding progressively to the social ills in a changing society as an outcome of an enlightened state – have been replaced by what social scientists now term as either state-centred or society-centred approaches to the origins and develop- ment of social welfare policy. The question for these social scientists revolves around whether the impetus for the creation of and subsequent reforms to social programs emanated from inside the state itself or because of the influence of various actors outside the state. I realize, however, that such categorizing does not adequately reflect the nuances and complexities of the scholarship I consider in the following paragraphs. It should be noted, too, that these various inter- pretations have given a "voice" in the scholarly debate to several traditionally marginalized groups.

There are several interpretations of the welfare state that might be grouped within the society-centred model. One of the most persuasive is the Marxist and neo-Marxist approach. It takes as its starting point the conflict between capital and labour in the economic system, and sees the welfare state as essen- tially an instrument of the state to ensure social control and buy peace with labour. This approach maintains that political and economic pressure from labour and their working-class supporters has, through the state and welfare legislation, forced elites to make concessions. However, these legislative initia- tives have been achieved in a way that involves the minimum redistribution of wealth and political power. Proponents of the Marxist analysis maintain that social programs have provided social stability and at the same time served to legitimize the capitalist social structure. The Marxist interpretation also insists that the state adopt policies with the full support of business interests at times when labour needs to be pacified and the working class has become rife with discontent.[15]

This is the approach embraced by Dominique Marshall, who has written about family allowances and Quebec. Marshall claims that the family allowance program "begins with the workers' movement, which, in exceptional circum- stances due to the war, was given unparalleled power of negotiation." She contends that King's close ties with the economic elite gave him the opportunity to solicit the support of employers who have always been willing to provide "minimal policies towards workers in order to conserve the legitimacy of their power."[16] Yet, as James Struthers has argued, "interpretations of the welfare state which concentrate exclusively on the degree of labour's industrial and political mobilization present an overly simplified framework for understanding why and how social policy gets made."[17] Some recent gendered analysis of the origins of the welfare state has argued that rather than creating a more pliant women's movement, women used the support offered through the welfare state to become more independent. It might be reasonable, then, to assume that state expenditures for social welfare initiatives would have encouraged further discontent among labour and created a demand for further expansion of the welfare state rather than silencing labour. As Joel F. Handler and Yeheskel Hasenfeld have pointed out for the American experience, welfare policy has not been a very effective mechanism of social control; it has tended to fail quite often in regulating the poor.[18]

Much of the society-centred approach seems to focus on the legislative programs designed for a particular group. Cynthia R. Comacchio, author of *"Nations Are Built of Babies": Saving Ontario's Mothers and Children, 1900-1940*, uses a Marxist-feminist model that argues that a national campaign led by Ontario physicians to reduce infant and maternal mortality was part of a "conscious plan to modernize Canada to meet the ideological imperatives of industrial capitalism."[19] Carl Cuneo and Alvin Finkel have made similar arguments about unemployment insurance. However, this approach that seeks to explain social welfare outcomes as a struggle between capitalists and workers ignores other socioeconomic forces such as women, agricultural interests, constitutional imperatives, the role of the state, and political parties. In a debate over changes to Canada's unemployment insurance schemes in the 1970s, for instance, Leslie Pal rejected the Marxist analysis as an explanatory tool. He argued that the growing concern over the effective management of labour and fiscal constraint determined the course of reforms to the unemployment insurance program. Pal contends that fiscal constraint is "a factor internal to political logic and not one that is immediately governed by social forces." Pal has suggested that different forces have driven reforms at different times. The generous 1971 reforms to unemployment insurance did not emerge out of social tensions, but were the "result of a long bureaucratic gestation over the 1960s" and came at a time when the social service state was in full bloom and governments were not hampered by any notion of fiscal constraints. That came later. The 1978 changes to unemployment insurance that made the program much less generous emanated almost entirely within or between governments, and there was little consultation with the private sector or with labour. The pressures on government in that period of fiscal constraint, Pal argues, were "specific to the political level, they [did] not simply reflect external social forces."[20] This book argues that the fiscal strength of the state is an important explanatory factor in the origins and evolution of the welfare state in Canada. There have rarely been strong policy differences between the two leading national parties in federal politics.

Still, institutions are never neutral, a point forcefully and effectively made by feminist and gender analysis, another important society-centred approach that emerged in the 1980s. This approach radically changed the way scholars have viewed the origins and development of social welfare. Feminist and gender analysis embraces some of the concerns of Marxists, but it has looked primarily at sexual inequalities and the role of the state to explain why women have been systematically disadvantaged in society. Some scholars, such as Mimi Abramovitz and Jane Ursel, argue that social policy was designed to force women and children to remain dependent on the primary male breadwinner and to perpetuate the traditional role of women as mothers and caregivers.[21] They argue that many of the social welfare benefits were given to women not as citizens but as mothers. Scholars who have adopted this model of analysis see the welfare state as the successful effort of a patriarchal state to devalue and control women and ensure the maintenance of a patriarchal society. Abramovitz posits that the state used social policy to marginalize women's issues. Such policy initiatives even concealed the gender issue by attaching gender neutral terms like "family" to some social programs. For these scholars, the Keynesian welfare consensus that made state-sponsored social programs possible emerged from a male-dominated society and a state premised on the notion of a male breadwinner model that saw the husband in the paid labour force and the mother at home caring for the family. Ursel, who examines the Canadian experiment, argues that the postwar developments in social policy moved Canadian society from "familial patriarchal" to "social patriarchal" as the welfare state extended its control over women and children.

Gender analysis has become the major interpretation for sociologists and other social scientists who study social welfare policy, as illustrated by Maureen Baker and David Tippen's recent book, *Poverty, Social Assistance and the Employability of Mothers: Restructuring Welfare States*. They maintain that family allowances acknowledged the importance of marriage and reproduction. They also argue that since the Second World War, government policies have encouraged heterosexual marriage and stable nuclear families, and have attempted to promote reproduction and childbearing. The state has encouraged parents to

contribute to the continuity of a nation by bearing and raising children, reproducing a future population – labour, taxpayers, and consumers – necessary for
continuance of the capitalist society. Moreover, mothers typically provide most
of the physical and emotional care, and parents offer the discipline needed to
enable family members to contribute to society and remain independent of
state support.[22] Similar arguments have been made by Wendy McKeen. She
suggests that Canadian social policy "has established women's access to social
benefits on the basis of their status as wives and mothers, not individuals in
their own right."[23]

Historians have also contributed to this paradigm shift in the analysis. Nancy
Christie offers one of the best examples in her recent writings.[24] She downplays
the importance of class in her analysis, and argues that Canadian governments
"framed social welfare legislation in ways that would enforce the norm of nuclear
families dependent for sustenance on a male breadwinner whose income came
almost exclusively from employment earnings." Following the lead of many
British and American scholars, Christie found that the family allowance legislation was insensitive to the economic independence of women, to the well-being
of children, and to allowing the working class to rise out of poverty. Christie
asserts that family allowances were supported by the government because it
facilitated the employment of men by removing women from the workplace
after the end of the Second World War. Government spending in the form of
monthly payments for children would assist the economic transition from war
to peacetime production. Moreover, Christie saw such measures as family allowances not as the beginning of a modern social security system but as an
ideological link to an earlier era. She refutes the notion that the Canadian welfare
state emerged as a response to political pressure from either the left through
the power of organized labour or the right through the power of big business.
She correctly surmises that the King government was extremely worried about
the possibility of family breakdown during the Second World War and wanted
– as did society generally – to strengthen the traditional family in the postwar
period.

This book attempts to build on Christie's argument. It also contends that security and stability emerged as important issues during the Second World War
and in the postwar period, and that policy makers saw families as one of the
most important stabilizing institutions in society. As governments and political
parties engaged in postwar planning, they realized that the state would have to
play a major role to ensure security and stability, and to that end eventually
undertook a number of initiatives. The state immediately recognized the importance of cultivating and encouraging strong families, and saw an important

role for mothers in that process. Rather than being insensitive to the plight of women as Christie suggests, the government saw an important role for women, but it was undoubtedly one in keeping with the cultural-historical moment of the period. Ruth Roach Pierson has argued, however, that silence on women's issues simply meant priority was given to those of men.[25] Perhaps. As this study reveals, women across Canada welcomed the government's new public policy initiatives, particularly family allowances. For many parents, especially mothers, the family allowance program was seen as the state's recognition – finally – of its commitment and responsibility to the family. As Christie and others have argued, such policies created a particular role for women, but the primary concern of policy makers in the postwar reconstruction planning period was to bolster the overall role of Canadian families in creating a new social order, one that inculcated a measure of security and improved well-being for all Canadian citizens. Yet this was designed, as Jane Lewis argues, to conform to the male breadwinner model that was, by the middle of the 19th century, "built into the fabric of society."[26]

The origins of family allowances in the mid-1940s were not primarily about gender and neither were the major reforms to family allowances in the period after the 1960s. While gendered analysis has had an important impact on the study of social programs, the historical perspective of the approach needs to be strengthened. Nancy Christie supports her analysis primarily with the records of the Dependents' Allowances Board in Library and Archives Canada and the Cyril James and Harry Cassidy Papers. She asserts that the family allowance program was the "offspring of Principal F. Cyril James, who headed the Committee on Reconstruction, his research director Leonard Marsh, and experts within the powerful Economic Advisory Committee." None of the principals she identifies were responding to the pressure for economic emancipation of women, though they all might have wanted to provide a measure of support to the family in which a male breadwinner was the norm. Closely related to this argument is the notion presented by many scholars that family allowances was an incentive provided to women to return home after being in the paid workforce during the war. One political scientist has called family allowances an "indirect salary" for women to accept motherhood as a career. However, Jeffrey A. Keshen has recently argued that it would be a gross misrepresentation to imply that all working women who returned to domesticity were forced back home.[27]

The role of the state itself has been important in understanding the origins and development of social security policy. Explanations that place emphasis on the role of the state as an independent actor (the new institutionalism) have been explored by Theda Skocpol. She argues for a state-centred rather than society-centred approach to social policy development. She contends that "politicians and administrators must be taken seriously. Not merely as agents of other interests, they are actors in their own right, enabled and constrained by the political organizations within which they operate."[28] This study shows that many bureaucrats within the state played a major role in both the origins and subsequent development of public policy on family issues. This is true of the early history of family allowances, but it is also true in the reforms that came in the 1970s. Officials with the Department of National Health and Welfare, the government department responsible for administering family allowances, realized by the late 1960s that the program, as it then existed, was not particularly effective in helping low-income families raise their children. It is well known within the policy community that policy debates are informed by ideas on how to make existing programs more effective and how to correct the imperfections of earlier choices. Although the officials in Ottawa advocated for major revisions to the universal program in the 1960s and 1970s to get greater resources into the hands of families most in need, the reforms to family allowances came only very slowly. In this case, the officials were the ones advocating reform, but they discovered early on that their political masters were quite reluctant to make changes to a program that had become an important part of the Canadian identity. The social security bureaucracy played a significant role in shaping welfare policy, and in the 1960s the major push for reform came from liberal-minded professionals within the federal government.[29]

In a diverse and increasingly multinational state like Canada, where the lines of cleavage have always been particularly strong, the social security system has been seen as one way of maintaining national cohesion. This interpretation builds on the 1950 scholarship of T.H. Marshall and others who argued that the expansion of social rights became an important aspect of 20th-century citizenship.[30] Keith Banting and Janine Brodie have argued, for example, that for a multinational and multicultural society like Canada, where powerful and cohesive national symbols have been lacking, social programs have become instruments of statecraft to maintain national unity. Banting contends that the postwar blueprint for Canada was premised on the assumptions that citizens faced a common set of social needs, and "that a common set of programs could respond equitably for populations as a whole," providing health care and a range of other social benefits.[31] Social rights shared by and available to all citizens would enhance a wider sense of community and social cohesion. Because of the redistributive nature inherent in some of these social programs, they would strengthen the level of attachment to the nation and encourage citizens to see themselves as members of a single community, enjoying a common set of rights and sharing a common set of obligations. Hence, in Canada and other Western states, the development and expansion of social programs in the postwar period encouraged a sense of social citizenship. In Gosta Esping-Andersen's view, social citizenship constitutes the core of any welfare state. This study confirms that the family allowance program was seen by the federal government as one instrument of nation building in the postwar period.

Brodie is more direct in her analysis.[32] She argues that during the postwar period the federal government responded to the tensions within the country by "deliberately and strategically offer[ing] the promise of a pan-Canadian social citizenship as a remedy" for the challenges to national unity caused by First Nations and Quebec. She also believes that *social Canada* was accomplished through the language of universality rather than selectivity and the targeting of social welfare to those deemed to be in greatest need. Given the changes that have occurred in family allowances and other social welfare programs in the latter decades of the 20th century, Brodie wonders what the long-term implications are for Canada of the unravelling of the postwar social fabric. She maintains that the 1990s, in particular, witnessed the de-legitimization of social programs as the right of all Canadian citizens, as the nation witnessed a shift from *social* to *economic Canada* and the invention of new Canadian values.

However, Janet Siltanen points out that the "golden age" of Keynesian welfare state has been exaggerated. She contends that those who have associated social programs with social citizenship have ignored how little equality the various programs brought to those Canadians who were outside the hegemonic ideal of male, white, and middle class. Moreover, Siltanen refuses to describe recent reforms to social welfare as a move away from social citizenship to neo-liberalism; she notes that the notion that the "market" is opposed to a wide range of equality-seeking strategies is based on pure ideology conjecture.[33] Social Canada might best be achieved within the market itself; it was not achieved within Keynesian welfare state. It might be interesting to point out that in the 1980s, when the Mulroney government reformed some of Canada's social welfare programs, including family allowances, incomes became more equally distributed and poverty actually declined.[34]

In a federal system like Canada, scholars have also asked what role federalism plays in the origins and development of social programs. There are different views on this question. It has been suggested that federalism has had a negative impact on the development of the welfare state as it represents a form of institutional fragmentation; a federalism system has meant limited and even weak government.[35] Anthony Birch has argued that in countries that have federal systems of government, the development of social legislation has been inhibited,[36] while Pierre Trudeau has argued that federalism actually encouraged the growth of the state. In Trudeau's view, innovative policies were usually more acceptable in some parts of the country than in others, and innovative policies, once introduced in one region, would soon become popular in others.[37] Keith Banting has argued that the fragmentation inherent in a federal system like Canada's constrains the pace of change, specifically in the case of the development of Canadian pensions. He sees federalism as a conservative force in tempering the reformist tendencies of governments.[38]

This study also considers how the federal system impacted the development of family allowances and finds that conflict between the central government and the provinces was important in bringing about major changes to the family allowance programs. Quebec was instrumental in forcing Ottawa to introduce reforms to family allowances that would satisfy the province's constitutional objectives and the province's demands for greater autonomy within the Canadian federation.[39]

In addition, this book suggests that we need to reconsider some of the ideas Canadian scholars hold about the welfare state in the 1980s and 1990s. It is widely argued that the Brian Mulroney government dismantled the welfare state. Perhaps James P. Mulvale captures this sentiment best: he argues that the welfare state project emanated from "the values and activism of social democrats and organized labour" in the postwar period, but the global power of transnational corporations and global capital brought an end to the social democratic welfare state project in Canada. He begins his study of Canadian social welfare with the assertion that "the social welfare state that once prevailed in Canada is no more."[40] In *The Quick and the Dead: Brian Mulroney, Big Business and the Seduction of Canada,* Linda McQuaig attempts to show that Prime Minister Mulroney followed in the footsteps of Reagan and Thatcher and introduced a pro-business conservatism in Canada, but did so in an underhanded way by blatantly reducing social spending without the support and knowledge of Canadians.[41] Reginald Whitaker notes that the Canadian new right of the 1980s was not able to reshape the welfare state as quickly or radically as its British and American counterparts.[42] This may be because it was never the intent of the Mulroney Conservatives to do so. Granted, the welfare state was changed during that period and after, but per capita spending on social welfare programs actually increased. Between 1980 and 1995, social policy expenditure of all governments in Canada increased not only in absolute terms but also as a share of total program spending and as a share of GDP. In 1980, governments expended $73.3 billion on social policy spending, which accounted for 64.1% of all program spending and 23.7% of GDP. A decade and a half later, social policy expenditure reached $215.6 billion, which accounted for 75.1% of consolidated government spending and 28.8% of GDP.[43] As I show below, programs like family allowances changed considerably as the citizenry's view of social welfare evolved and as citizens demonstrated a greater interest in protecting health care and public pensions, for instance, than in preserving universal family allowances. Gosta Esping-Andersen acknowledges that, with the exception of Britain and New Zealand, the welfare state has not been dismantled in any of the industrialized countries and the reforms have been "modest." The right, he points out, accepted some level of safety social net that the social security policies provided, but it was one that was more residual and targeted than the social security system established in the postwar generation provided.[44]

A period of political consensus emerged in Canada in the 1940s when family allowances were introduced and again in the period beginning in the 1970s when the program underwent a long series of reforms. In the 1940s, family allowances gained support among all political parties because the program was seen as one deal to bring a measure of equality to all Canadian children; in the period when family allowances were changed and eventually replaced, the reforms were accomplished again when the public agenda supported such developments and there emerged a political consensus that existing programs were no longer effective. That consensus was driven by the realization of all of the major political parties in Canada that the fiscal and economic crises in the 1970s and 1980s meant that there had to be a reconsideration of state priorities in all policy areas, including social policy. This fact, as I demonstrate below, suggests that we cannot ignore the key role of the fiscal capacity of the state in the policy-making process.

The national family allowance program remained essentially unchanged for virtually two decades after it was introduced in 1945. One of the reasons for this is that family allowances was seen by all of the national political parties as an instrument of nation building and as one way for fostering a sense of pan-Canadian citizenship. When the program began its radical transformation in the late 1970s into an income-tested child tax benefit, there were other social policy programs to accomplish these nation building objectives, such as medicare. Perhaps because of this, no other Canadian social program over the past quarter century has undergone such a complete transformation from a "rights" to a "needs" based approach as family allowances. What is clear, however, is that the program began and changed significantly only during periods of considerable upheaval and uncertainty. We might note that a political crisis marked each of these periods in Canada.

Family allowances began as a response to the fear and uncertainty generated among politicians and citizens of what problems the end of the war might bring. Family allowances were introduced as the Second World War was coming to an end, in large part to deal with that insecurity and instability policy makers feared might come with peace; the policies and programs were part of the response to that political crisis, and played an important part in creating a new social order that would see the state with a greater role in many aspects of Canadians' lives in order to preclude the problems that occurred after the First World War. After the chaos and instability wrought by nearly two decades of economic depression and war, the Canadian government and the governments of other Allied nations were concerned about stability and security in the postwar world. Nothing worried King more; he realized that the family, one of the most important institutions in Canada, had endured tremendous stress during the Great Depression and the Second World War, and it had to be protected and strengthened. During and immediately following the Second World War, family allowances also became popular as a large number of other nations embraced similar social security programs to deal with their own insecurity and fear in the postwar period.

Once the legislation was enacted and benefits were paid, the federal government essentially left the program alone, even though there were groups across Canada that wanted the government to peg the benefits to the inflation rate. In the 1950s, when the number of immigrants to Canada dropped sharply, Ottawa changed the family allowance program to include payments of a special family allowance to immigrants immediately on their arrival in Canada, as was the case in the United Kingdom and Australia. This policy was intended to keep Canada competitive with other countries as an attractive destination for immigrants.

Despite the heavy expenditure on social security, it was clear by the 1960s that Canada's social security system had not delivered the intended results. A series of investigations from governmental and non-governmental agencies reported that poverty continued to be a serious problem in Canadian society. In fact, there was a new-found consciousness of poverty throughout North America. Not unexpectedly, questions were raised about the efficacy of government expenditure on social security, especially among those in the policy branches of the Department of National Health and Welfare.

At the same time, there emerged considerable pressure on Ottawa, particularly from the province of Quebec, to align social spending to develop an integrated strategy to fight poverty. Politicians, like Quebec's welfare minister René Lévesque, believed that poverty could only be addressed adequately through an approach that integrated all of the social spending within Quebec regardless of the source of the expenditure. Moreover, this approach should combine provincial and federal financial resources. A nationalist Quebec believed that it knew better than Ottawa what the province needed. Quebec demanded that Ottawa withdraw from the social policy field, including family allowances, and transfer instead monies expended on such programs to the provinces. Not surprisingly, then, family allowances eventually moved from the realm of sectoral politics, or "low politics," to "high politics" and became intricately involved in the mine-field of Canadian intergovernmental relations and constitutionalism, which was largely a first ministers' agenda.[45] Family allowances had rarely been the stuff of high politics after they were introduced, but in the 1970s they became something of a political football. At that time, they were a central issue in Canadian constitutionalism when the program was used by the federal government to try and resolve the tensions with Quebec for greater autonomy with the Canadian federation.

Yet family allowances were one of the few programs shared by all Canadian families, and as such they were one of the means of building social cohesion across Canada and maintaining the links between the Canadian state and its citizenry; Ottawa was not about to allow the provinces control over such an important national program and initially refused the entreaties from Quebec for greater provincial control. By the early 1970s, however, Prime Minister Trudeau was willing to make changes to the family allowance program as a means of enticing Quebec Premier Robert Bourassa to amend the British North America Act and allow the prime minister to achieve his constitutional objective. Although Bourassa eventually rejected the proposed constitutional changes hammered out at the Victoria Constitutional Conference, the Trudeau Cabinet authorized additional funding for family allowances and ceded a large measure of provincial control over the program in the hope of having Quebec sign on to the changes proposed in Victoria in June 1971. Still, Trudeau's government, like that of Mackenzie King a generation earlier, insisted that family allowances had to reinforce the linkages between the federal government and individual Canadian citizens in various regions but most importantly in Quebec. In the end, Bourassa did not support the constitutional amendments, but Quebec received a measure of control it had long desired over family allowances. And the federal government maintained its authority to disburse family allowance cheques, ensuring that "Government of Canada/Gouvernement du Canada" was embossed on each cheque sent to families each month in Quebec and throughout the rest of the country. Even reformed family allowance benefits would remain a tool of nation building by the federal government to help foster a pan-Canadian citizenship and attachment to the federal government.

Some of the bureaucrats in Ottawa had realized much earlier than 1973, when the first major reforms to the program occurred, that family allowances had decreased as a percentage of family income since the mid-1940s and that the monthly benefit no longer had the impact it once had for many families. The program was badly in need of reform then. Officials in the Department of National Health and Welfare soon realized that there might never be sufficient new funds to make the universal family allowance program as effective as it originally was; any reforms to the program, they soon realized, would have to be funded out of the existing expenditures for the program. In fact, throughout their existence in Canada, family allowances – and social policy initiatives, generally – have been impacted by the prevailing economic conditions, or what Tom Courchene has called "economic" Canada.[46] Family allowance was an expensive program, and government officials and politicians alike realized that they could not afford to simply increase benefits for all recipients. Building selectivity into the program was one possible option, but by the 1970s many Canadians had come to regard family allowances as a right simply by virtue of their Canadian citizenship. Although the Liberal government of Prime Minister Trudeau favoured selectivity rather than universality in family allowances, his ministers, other politicians, and even civil servants had come to realize that universal family allowances had become a part of the Canadian identity. As a result, change would be difficult and politically dangerous. The Liberals discovered just how much so in the election held on 30 October 1972, when the government saw its huge majority from the 1968 Trudeaumania election reduced to a minority position in the House of Commons. From that point on, the Liberals refused to tamper with the concept of universality that had been the family allowance program's hallmark since 1945, even though almost everyone agreed the program was then doing little to deal with issues of poverty or help Canada's working poor. It seems Canadian social policy had ceased being about protecting and helping the less fortunate and became more about protecting political positions since politicians were never willing to risk alienating themselves from powerful constituencies that had become attached to programs they had grown up with.

Even when the Liberals introduced a measure of selectivity into family allowances, they did so without eliminating universal benefits for the middle class. It has been argued in the scholarship on the history of social policy in Canada that the middle class sought to impose their values on the recipients of state support in the first decades of the 20th century. With the family allowance program in the 1970s and 1980s, it had become clear that the main concern of the middle class was to protect the cash benefits it received from the state. Equality in family allowances had come to mean the same treatment for everyone. Still, the reforms to family allowances that were introduced in the late 1970s marked the beginning of the end of universality, despite protests from the middle class. As new benefits targeted those in greatest need, there was recognition among many Canadians that income security programs, or cash transfers to individuals, such as family allowances, should take account of the recipients' level of income.

The economic situation created by high inflation in the late 1970s, as well as a crushing debt and deficit in the 1980s, also served as the catalyst for major reforms to the family allowance program. In the late 1970s, during a period of rampant inflation, the Trudeau government avoided tampering with the universality of family allowances months before an expected federal election, even though it realized that low-income Canadians needed additional assistance. What the government opted for was essentially a two-tier family support mechanism that left the universal program unchanged while introducing a new income-tested family credit for low-income families.

It was left to the Progressive Conservative government of Prime Minister Mulroney, during a political crisis created by the mushrooming deficit and debt, to implement the reforms that officials in the Department of National Health and Welfare had been advocating since the late 1960s. The Conservatives also wrestled for several years with the political implications of ending the universal nature of family allowances. There was a fierce debate in the Mulroney government over the issue of entitlement, since Canadians had come to regard social programs as part of their sacred social contract with the state. Only very warily and incrementally did the Conservatives move to a selective program that eliminated most of the benefits for high-income families with children while substantially increasing the benefits for low-income families. At this point, with the deficit reaching dangerous levels, the government effectively used the rationale of a political crisis and the necessity of economic rationalism to reform the family allowance system.

The budgetary process and the limited fiscal capacity of the state exerted a strong influence over the policy-making process, suggesting another way that the state itself plays a crucial role in the social policy field, especially when the government is faced with limited resources. The government argued that it had little political choice but to use its limited financial resources more effectively to help those in greatest need. There were some who wanted to dismantle the welfare state, some who wanted to redesign and remodel it to make it more effective, and some who simply wanted to leave it as it was. Each generation establishes its goals for social policy as it fashions its own vision of the welfare state. In time, most social policy commentators applauded the changes introduced under Mulroney, which were continued and enhanced during the time Jean Chrétien's Liberals held office as federal expenditure on family allowances and children's benefits continued to grow into the 1990s and beyond, as demonstrated by Table 1.

What this study suggests, then, is that the family allowance program was introduced at a time when the government was worried about the state of affairs in Canada and believed that universal payments to families might help prevent

Table 1

Family allowances and child benefits: payments, families, and children, 1946-2002

Fiscal year	Total payments ($000)	Average number of families	Average number of children receiving benefits
1946	172,632	1,477,600	3,429,600
1950[1]	297,514	1,818,100	4,116,200
1954	350,114	2,081,700	4,840,800
1958	437,887	2,366,900	5,682,700
1962	520,781	2,630,100	6,491,000
1966	551,735	2,766,800	6,843,700
1970	560,050	2,960,300	6,867,700
1974[2]	946,246	3,178,700	6,768,279
1978	2,093,020	3,602,601	7,066,129
1982	2,230,595	3,641,715	6,696,435
1986	2,534,420	3,651,183	6,584,481
1990	2,736,016	3,722,950	6,700,683
1994[3]	5,091,499	3,382,370	5,640,420
1998	5,703,302	3,187,990	5,480,880
2002	7,740,546	3,047,517	5,547,344

1 Newfoundland is included beginning in 1950.
2 The 1944 Family Allowances Act was revised in January 1974, and the figures include children formerly covered under Youth Allowance and Family Assistance programs.
3 New Child Tax Benefits/Canada Tax Benefits/Total Benefits.
Source: Canada, Statistics Canada, *Historical Statistics of Canada,* Series C1-13, C14-26, C27-39, http://www.statcan.ca/english/freepub/11-516-XIE/sectionc/sectionc.htm#Federal%20Income; Canada, Human Resources and Social Development Canada, *Social Security Statistics Canada and Provinces 1978-79 to 2002-03,* Child Tax Benefit, 1993-94 to 2002-03, http://www.hrsdc.gc.ca/en/cs/sp/sdc/socpol/tables/page02.shtml.

a crisis after the end of the Second World War. Subsequent changes to the program also came when successive governments believed that those changes would help resolve other crises within the Canadian state, whether the result of a dramatic decline in immigration or a constitutional impasse with Quebec, or during a period of difficulty in Canada's public finances. It would seem, therefore, that family allowances were an instrument used by the state to help resolve national crises. Underlying all of this was the governmental recognition that state support to families was important, perhaps crucial, in postwar Canada, but as this book shows, family allowances moved from a perceived right of all Canadians to one that was based solely on financial need.

In sum, this book argues that there is no simple or single explanation that allows us to understand the origins and development of family allowances in Canada. As James J. Rice and Michael Prince[47] have argued for social policy generally, we can understand the development of family allowances in Canada only by examining the interplay of several forces. Each phase of the program was shaped by different needs, different interest groups, and different political, economic, constitutional, and social consideration. Throughout each phase, the influence of individual government departments, the ministers and deputies within the Canadian government, as well as the relationship between various government departments – especially between the Department of National Health and Welfare and the Department of Finance – was of distinct importance. The state of federal-provincial relations was also a factor at times, as was the fiscal health of the nation, and the international context governing the rise of social welfare programs. The question of national unity has also never been far below the surface in the history of social programs. Each phase of family allowances was an attempt by the state to recognize the issues important to the nation at the time and to reflect the values of Canadians, especially as they related to the role of the social security system in the lives of the citizens. What becomes clear from this wide-ranging and archivally rich study is that the influences on Canada's social programs – specifically in this case, family allowances – changed dramatically over time, but only when there was a conjunction of interests.

1

The Dawning of a New Era in Social Security, 1929-43

THE DEBATE ON FAMILY allowances in Canada began in a parliamentary committee. J.E. Letellier, the Liberal member from the Quebec constituency of Compton, rose in the House of Commons on 13 February 1929 and proposed that the Select Standing Committee on Industrial and International Relations begin a study on family allowances in Canada. Letellier asked the committee to make a report on the respective jurisdiction of both federal and provincial parliaments in the matter. J.S. Woodsworth, the leader of the Ginger Group and member for Winnipeg North Centre, seconded the motion, claiming that children were treated as a liability in Canada's industrial state, and that some provision had to be made for families with children. Several years earlier, in December 1926, he had told the Commons that family allowances would help redistribute the nation's wealth and finally allow fathers to earn a family wage to provide for their families. Woodsworth also noted that the wage system failed to account for workers with family responsibilities and paid them on the same basis as single men and those without families.

When he spoke briefly in support of his motion, Letellier praised the Liberal government of Prime Minister William Lyon Mackenzie King for its commitment to social policy. The Honourable Peter Heenan, King's minister of labour, told the House that the government agreed that the Standing Committee should consider the matter, and that it would support the motion.[1] Prime Minister King had created the Standing Committee on Industrial and International Relations to consider such matters as Canada changed from an agricultural to an increasingly urban and industrial society, and he had often reminded the House that the very existence of the committee was a testament to his government's concern with social issues. After all, the Liberals had passed the Old Age Pension Act two years earlier.[2] Not surprisingly, Letellier's motion was carried, and the debate on family allowances began among Canada's policy makers.

The investigation into family allowances came at a time when Canadians and their governments remained wary of the state providing too much in the way of social welfare. The federal government continued to insist, somewhat feebly, that the Constitution Act, 1867, had assigned exclusive responsibility for health and social welfare to the provinces. The provinces themselves were proceeding only slowly into the social security arena, but by the late 1920s most of them had adopted some form of workers' compensation and mother's allowance. Scholars have argued that these initiatives defined the nature of early welfare programs. Workers' compensation programs were to ensure the economic independence of male workers, but through mother's allowance the state essentially recognized women's role as mothers. As James Struthers has argued, mother's allowance shows "that the reproductive work of women merited some degree of social entitlement."[3] Still, many Canadians, including the major political leaders of the time, believed the state should play a limited role in the provision of social welfare. The committee immediately turned its attention to Letellier's resolution, although it was clearly understood from the outset that the system of family allowances then under investigation was a contributory social insurance scheme supported by employers. Several decades after family allowances had been introduced in many European countries, Parliament invited Canadians to offer their views on the granting of some system of allowances to families across the country, but it did not envisage a family allowance system funded solely by either level of government.

Over the next three months, several witnesses weighed into the debate and presented evidence before the parliamentary committee. Jesuit Father A. Léon Lebel, S.J., a philosophy teacher at in Montreal and one of the earliest proponents of family allowances in Canada, was the first to appear. He had coincidently met with Prime Minister King several months before Letellier had tabled his motion in the Commons, to press his case for Canada's adoption of a family allowance scheme to deal with the inadequacy of the average industrial wages and as a means of stemming the flow of people from Quebec to the United States.[4] Mackenzie King had listened politely to Father Lebel at their meeting in May 1928, but he had made no commitment beyond a promise to further explore the issue. He fulfilled his commitment by supporting Letellier's motion. Surely Liberal MPs, including those sitting in the Cabinet, would not have voted for an investigation into family allowances without the prime minister's consent, especially given that the Liberals were in a minority situation.[5] If nothing else, the parliamentary review would serve to reassure voters once again that Mackenzie King was indeed committed to the progressive program of social insurance he had first articulated at the Liberal Convention in 1919 when he was chosen as party leader.

Father Lebel told the committee that a progressive state like Canada had to recognize the family as its fundamental social unit, and it was incumbent on the government to provide for a family's well-being. Moreover, his view was clearly a pro-natalist one that encouraged an increase in the birth rate; he maintained that nations required a large and growing population: without large families of four or more children a nation would cease to exist. Using what he considered scientific economic analysis, Father Lebel warned the committee that new countries like Canada, with vast resources to exploit and burdened with a heavy debt, had to encourage large families and at the same time stem the flow of emigrants to the United States, often reputed to be the land of milk and honey. He reminded the committee that wages alone were not sufficient in Canada to provide for the needs of most families. At the same time, he insisted that family allowances must not be considered a form of wages, a conundrum that would plague the proponents of family allowances for the next two decades; rather, family allowances should be paid to families as recognition of the special services they rendered to society simply by raising a family.[6] Father Lebel also argued that family allowances were the most effective means by which the state could help families struggling with insufficient incomes. Support for Lebel's recommendation came from an unlikely source in Joseph Daoust, a Montreal businessman and owner of the Daoust and Lalonde Shoe Manufacturer. After questioning from the committee, he admitted that the wages then paid to workers indeed made it impossible for them to adequately maintain a family of four children. He joined with Lebel and urged the committee to seriously consider some form of family allowances. Clearly, not all in the business community were opposed to social programs.

There was little support from other witnesses for Lebel's recommendation that Parliament immediately consider some form of family allowance. Perhaps surprisingly, social workers were opposed to family allowances. Charlotte Whitton, the director of the Canadian Council on Social Welfare and one of the leading social workers in the country, vehemently opposed the introduction of family allowances. She was worried – like so many of her time – about the perils of too much state intervention. In her testimony, she maintained that the proponents of family allowances had exaggerated how poorly workers in Canada were paid: "The general standard of life of the working man in Canada," she asserted, "would compare favourably with that of the middle class bourgeois in France." And it was the obligation of the father, as head of the household, to support his family.[7] Whitton maintained that family allowances infringed on the rights of the individual. Any sort of state initiative to enact such a misguided scheme as family allowances, she cautioned, would impugn dangerously on the sanctity of marriage, and reduce it to one of "economic relations, capable of financial exploitation." Such state interference might "relegate women to mere slaves and employees of the state, and ultimately result in limiting and even undermining the position and privileges which women enjoyed in Canada."[8] Whitton argued that the introduction of family allowances would subvert the basis of family responsibility and ruin the country.

FIGURE 1   Charlotte Whitton founded the Canadian Welfare Council and was mayor of Ottawa when this picture was taken in 1951, but she was a social conservative, and her opposition to more liberal spending on social welfare increasingly placed her on the margins of Canada's social work profession.
Library and Archives Canada, Capital Press/Charlotte Elizabeth Whitton fonds, PA-121981, reprinted with permission

Her rhetoric was too much for aging socialist J.S. Woodsworth, who asked Whitton, "If motherhood is noble and so important, how would it depress the ideal by allowing it to be adequately supported?" Woodsworth saw family allowances as supporting traditional gender roles, but Whitton feared that such a program might undermine the role of the family breadwinner. She shot back at the Labour MP – echoing the sentiments widely held among the middle class – that the state must stay out of the lives of ordinary workers, and strive only to ensure that the nation's wealth is evenly distributed and that the condition of labour and housing was such that parents could discharge their legal obligations to their children.[9]

Whitton also claimed that if governments adopted social welfare schemes like family allowances, they were admitting their failure to govern and provide decent wages that would allow workers to afford a comfortable livelihood for their families. She said that she could not accept that that was the case with Canada: "I do not think that it is necessary for Canadians today to proclaim to the world, that a decent living at a decent minimum standard of life is such an impossibility for any proportion of her people that the state must intervene to pay allowances whereby life can be sustained at a decent level."[10]

Whitton also rejected Lebel's argument that Canada needed more people. "Canada," she reminded the committee, "is a land of wholesome, healthy, moral, self-disciplined people. There is wealth in her land, sufficient for all: there is vision, strength, and energy to develop it. Courage and statesmanship will be required to assure that equity and justice prevail in its distribution." This is a nation, she said, that enjoys one of the best standards of living of any people in the world. She warned the committee that it must not "seek to administer the stimulants, that old and slacked appetites required." To do so would "destroy the virility of youth by the physics of age," she maintained, once again bringing to light the classic middle-class values of her generation. "Have faith in the young strength of Canada," she implored the parliamentarians, "to develop her life here, in fullness and plenty, her future safe, because she had proved her past."[11]

Not only did other social workers support Whitton's conservative middle-class ideology, but some of them also reminded the committee about encouraging the "undesirable." Family allowances would encourage not only idleness but also the proliferation of undesirables in Canadian society; this was another argument that proponents of family allowances would have to counter for more than three decades. Robert R. Mills, the director of the Toronto Children's Aid Society and president of the Social Workers' Club of that city, told the committee that a general meeting of the Social Service Council of Canada in Toronto had passed a motion opposing family allowance. Such a scheme, he said, represented an unwarranted interference with individual liberty and initiative.[12] Likewise, Mildred Kensit, the director of the Children's Bureau of Montreal, who appeared at the committee hearings with Whitton, said that as a social worker she knew only too well the type of people who earned low wages and had failed to provide the necessary support for their families. They were frequently the physically unfit, those of limited intelligence, and those with a "mental defect." Certainly, she said, the state should not encourage such a class of people to have larger families to "bring more unfit children into the community already heavily burdened in caring for this class of dependent child."[13]

The range of arguments presented to the Standing Committee on Industrial and International Relations surely left it perplexed. Social workers were opposed, but so too were some of the major labour unions, which represented the workers who would potentially benefit from the payment of family allowances. At its 1929 convention, the conservative Trades and Labour Congress of Canada declared its opposition to the introduction of family allowances for fear that such initiatives would depress wages.[14] Only the fledging All-Canadian Congress of Labour supported family allowances. Its president, Arthur Mosher, told the delegates gathered for its annual convention in Winnipeg that the Congress advocated change to improve the welfare of all Canadian workers, since it worked to free the Canadian labour movement from the influence of American-controlled unions. The Congress believed that family allowances were an important mechanism for a more equitable redistribution of the nation's wealth; they were also a means to reform the inherently unjust economic system. Mosher reminded the gathering that family allowances would increase consumption of staple commodities and, hence, improve the employment situation for all workers. Moreover, family allowances would encourage children to remain longer in school and keep them out of the workforce. Even though these arguments would be used by supporters of family allowances a decade or so later, the Congress's support for family allowances in 1929 had little impact on the Standing Committee on Industrial and International Relations since the major Canadian trade unions opposed family allowances. Given such opposition, Prime Minister King saw little reason to seriously consider the matter.[15]

Cameron McIntosh, chair of the committee, reported to the House of Commons on 31 May 1929. The Standing Committee on Industrial and International Relations steered a safe course and remained clearly noncommittal in its recommendations. Because family allowances were new for Canada, they required further study, and the report suggested that the government proceed cautiously. In the meantime, however, it recommended that the government consider before the next session of Parliament the whole jurisdictional question surrounding family allowances, a perpetual challenge to social policy development in Canada for generations. The Commons unanimously adopted the committee report on 6 June. Immediately, Peter Heenan, who had earlier supported the review, requested his counterpart in the Department of Justice, Ernest Lapointe, to prepare a legal opinion on the jurisdiction of family allowances. That task ultimately fell to Deputy Minister of Justice W. Stuart Edwards, who considered three categories of family allowances: 1) industry-based schemes established either by employers alone or by negotiations between workers and employers, 2) voluntary state schemes under which the state paid allowances and bore the whole cost from its ordinary revenues, and 3) compulsory schemes established by law. Edwards suggested that those programs initiated by industry, regardless of the form they might take, did not require legislative action and there was no question of jurisdiction between the federal and provincial governments. He considered that a compulsory system of family allowances established by law, even though funded by contributions from employers, impinged directly on the civil rights of employees and employers. The legislative jurisdiction for such a scheme was vested in the provincial legislatures under section 92 of the Constitution Act, 1867, under subsection 13 (Property and Civil Rights in the province) and/or subsection 16 (generally all matters of a merely local or private nature in the province), except where the Parliament of Canada wished to provide family allowances for the benefit of its employees. Edwards believed that the voluntary state scheme, though made possible only through legislation, did not raise the question of jurisdiction since the allowances paid through this mechanism were voluntary. Although he did not explain what he meant by "voluntary," officials in the federal Department of Health and Welfare later interpreted the word to mean "something like proceeding from the choice of the State." If indeed "voluntary" meant non-contributory, Edwards believed that family allowances were within the jurisdiction of Parliament because the federal government could raise money to spend as it wished.[16] However, his interpretation remained merely that of the department's legal counsel and not a court decision. Still, King apparently shared the view that family allowances were within the federal prerogative, at least while he was in Opposition. Shortly after his defeat in the 1930 election, King declared in the House of Commons that it would be in the best interest of the country if all forms of social insurance, as social welfare was then frequently called, were national in scope.[17] In 1929, however, when King was still prime minister, the parliamentary investigation into family allowances clearly showed not only that various interest groups and professionals, notably labour and social workers, were opposed to the initiative but also that King and the Liberal Party, in spite of their interest in facilitating the parliamentary investigation, were not yet committed to a program of social security for Canada that included family allowances.

Within a year of Ottawa's report, the Quebec government began its own study into family allowances, as part of the mandate of its Social Insurance Commission that was appointed to investigate a variety of social issues.[18] The commission, under the leadership of l'Université de Montréal economist Edouard Montpetit, considered family allowances in its third report, released in 1932. After studying the general problem of child welfare and investigating social insurance systems in various European countries, the commission concluded that there was no equity and social justice in the salary paid to the workers who had larger families in Quebec. After hearing from many of the same witnesses – in particular, Charlotte Whitton and Father Lebel – that had appeared before the Commons Standing Committee on Industrial and International Relations, the commission unanimously recommended that "for the moment there is no opportunity of taking legal measures instituting officially family allowances in this province." The commission considered family allowances a European solution to low wages there, even though it recognized that wages were similarly low in many Canadian industries. However, it feared that a system of family allowances would only ensure that wage rates would not increase and, at the same time, disadvantage Quebec industries if they had to fund a family allowance program for the province. Moreover, like Charlotte Whitton and other social workers of the period, the Montpetit commission feared that it was not only impossible but also dangerous for the state to assume a prominent role in the family, which might then become little more than an agency of the state. The commission concluded that any initiative on a family allowances scheme would be virtually impossible given the economic difficulties in the midst of the Great Depression. And even if the government had the political will and the financial resources to move ahead with family allowances, such a scheme might accelerate the migration from the rural to the urban areas of the province, something that few in Quebec wanted during the early 1930s. Clearly then, the Montpetit commission saw no greater need for family allowances at the provincial level than the King government had seen at the federal level.[19]

However, the belief in a limited role for the state in social welfare legislation changed considerably within a decade. The Great Depression discredited many of the traditional ideas of rugged individualism and made it patently obvious, as many writers have shown elsewhere, that the "old system" was bankrupt of ideas. The foundations of the democratic political system were everywhere under siege, and even Mackenzie King remarked after his 1930 electoral thrashing at the hands of R.B. Bennett and the Conservative Party that "the old capitalistic system is certain to give way to something more along communist lines."[20] That did not happen in Canada, of course, but the decade witnessed a profound change in the attitude of governments and in Canada's two major political parties, largely because of the growing influence of a group of intellectuals and progressive reformers who believed that Canada's social and economic policies had to be reformed to deal with the chaotic world in which they found themselves. In fact, historian Doug Owram argues in his study on the role of intellectuals and the Canadian state that the "elite saw the reform of economic and social policies as imperative if order were to be brought into a chaotic world." Many of those reform-minded people dismissed 19th-century classic liberalism and the notion of the state as an organic expression of society; rather, they came to see the state as a mechanism to be used as necessary for the promotion of social well-being. To them, social well-being was defined in terms of material standards of living, not in spiritual or moral terms, as an earlier generation of intellectuals had seen it.[21] The intellectual community that found influence in all of Canada's political parties by the mid-1930s believed that there had to be an evolutionary method of social reconstruction. At the beginning of the Great Depression, their views generated debate in universities and other intellectual circles, but through the 1930s, many of the intellectuals became engaged in political activities, so that by the 1940s many of their ideas were widely accepted both inside and outside of government. Concrete policy developments would consequently emerge, albeit piecemeal, over the coming decades.[22] Christie and Gauvreau have argued that the Protestant churches have also played an important role in the development of modern social policy in Canada: they provided the funding, personnel, and organizational structure for social reform accomplished in the decades following the First World War. The expertise of university-trained social scientists didn't begin to have much of an impact on federal legislation until the mid-1930s. Still, as these two scholars acknowledge, the outlines of social welfare legislation emerged from the liberal collectivist ideals of social evangelism, not from the influence of Protestant churches on the democratic socialism of the Co-operative Commonwealth Federation (CCF).[23]

The connection between the intellectual elites led by thinkers such as Frank Underhill, Eugene Forsey, and several others in the League for Social Reconstruction, and the CCF that had been created in 1932-33 is widely acknowledged.[24] However, the intellectuals also played a role in the more established political parties too; Owram suggests that "in some ways [Prime Minister R.B.] Bennett and his party were almost as advanced as the CCF in forming contacts with various interested intellectuals."[25] The Conservatives brought together various experts in scholarly conferences to talk with the politicians about social and economic problems. The first of these political summer schools was held in Newmarket, Ontario, in 1932, when a number of intellectuals presented formal papers and engaged the Conservatives in discussion over current social problems and possible remedies. Prime Minister Bennett himself never developed close ties with the intellectual community, even though he was responsible for the expansion of state activities such as the Canadian Broadcasting Company and the Bank of Canada, and for considering more systematic planning at the end of his mandate that so many of these intellectuals had advocated.[26]

FIGURE 2   William Lyon Mackenzie King was prime minister during the debate on family allowances.

National Archives of Canada, C-027645

With the Liberals and the CCF the intellectuals had greater influence, although Mackenzie King, the Liberal leader, himself with a doctorate in economics, was uncomfortable with the suggestion of rapid change; he remained extremely cautious with all matters of party policy. Still, King had strong contacts with the intellectual community, particularly through O.D. Skelton, who had been his deputy minister of external affairs and one of his senior advisers, and with Norman Rogers, his private secretary. But it was the wealthy patrician Vincent Massey who, as party president after 1932 and as one of the leading proponents of the "New Liberalism," was committed to reforming Liberalism with innovative ideas that were resonating within the intellectual community. He arranged a weekend meeting at his family estate in Port Hope in the fall of 1932 that brought a number of the intellectuals together with King and other Liberal MPs for a far-ranging discussion on social security and economic planning. Although King did not immediately embrace the new ideas as official Liberal policy, Massey had succeeded in bringing the Liberal Party establishment together with those from outside the party to discuss the important social and economic issues of the day. In September 1933, Massey also launched the first Liberal summer school or policy conference with politicians and experts at Trinity College School in Port Hope, as the Conservatives had done in Newmarket a year or so earlier. Mackenzie King was uncomfortable with the whole process and with many of the ideas bantered about at the gathering, but Massey acknowledged progress, noting that the summer school marked the beginning of a transformation of the Liberal Party from the "laissez-faire traditions of the party to a new, more technocratic and interventionist view of government." Even as King repeatedly criticized Massey for not understanding the realities of politics, the party, as Owram has shown, changed its traditional position that "government intervention was dangerous to civil liberty and [moved] towards a vision of the party more in accord with what [Norman] Rodgers [another of the reformers] termed 'the left wing of Liberalism.'"[27] The new orientation of the Liberal Party was revealed in the Port Hope summer school, and in the public musings of young Liberals such as Ian Mackenzie of British Columbia and Paul Martin of Ontario. Even if he did not accept all he heard from reform-minded Liberals, King also came under the spell of their rhetoric; in his victory speech following the triumphant return of his Liberal Party to power on 14 October 1935, he championed the dawn of a new era where "poverty and adversity, want and misery are the enemies which Liberalism will seek to banish from the land."[28]

Not only were the intellectuals finding influence with the country's major political parties, but they were also moving in large numbers to the civil service in Ottawa. The intellectual reformers were already a force in Ottawa when King was returned as prime minister, and they had started to consider in broad outlines the reforms they thought were essential in a modern Canada. In the Department of Finance, W.C. Clark, the former Queen's University economics professor who had become the deputy minister in October 1932, had pushed the federal government to support initiatives to deal with social housing. He also supported the major recommendations of the National Employment

Commission, which called for an increased role for the state in ameliorating unemployment during the Great Depression. Moreover, the 1939 federal budget seemed to suggest that the hold of classical economics on Canadian fiscal policy was starting to loosen. The outbreak of the Second World War in the same year accelerated the movement toward a more planned economy. By the end of hostilities in 1945, university professors and other members of the Ottawa-based intelligentsia – as Prime Minister King liked to call them – had access to the levers of powers.[29]

These individuals rose to positions of power as Prime Minister King and other world leaders became extremely concerned about stability and social order in the postwar period. Even though King belittled their political sense, the intelligentsia played an important role in moving King to support a more activist role for government.[30] Also, the memories of the turmoil and uncertainty in the aftermath of the First World War were fresh in all their minds, and there was general agreement that the instability that followed the Great War had to be avoided after the end of the Second World War. Similarly, they simply could not risk a prolonged economic crisis like that of the 1930s if they were to maintain order and stability in the peaceable kingdom. And the political realities in Canada were never far from King's mind.

It has been noted elsewhere that Mackenzie King was noteworthy more for the ideas he borrowed from others than for what he himself generated.[31] This was certainly the case with King and social security. Mackenzie King was not alone in recognizing the need for greater social security as part of the new world order he often spoke of during the Second World War. In fact, he might have been merely echoing the chorus resonating throughout the Allied nations. "It [social security] is on the tip of every man's tongue," opined a contributor to *Saturday Night*, and "all the United Nations' war leaders have declared it as a leading social objective of this war."[32] President Franklin D. Roosevelt, who had established himself as a leading reformer with his New Deal legislation at the height of the Great Depression, advocated greater social security for the postwar world. In January 1941, he told the US Congress that international security rested on four essential human freedoms. One of these was freedom from want. Only when each nation could provide an acceptable standard of living for its people would there truly be freedom. Anthony Eden, the British foreign secretary, had similarly told his compatriots on 29 May 1941 that the postwar aims of the British government were to establish "social security abroad as well as at home, through coordinated efforts of Britain, the Dominions, the United States and South America to stabilize currencies, feed starving peoples, avert fluctuations of employment, prices and markets."[33]

Roosevelt and British Prime Minister Winston Churchill reiterated some of these principles when they met in Newfoundland on 14 August 1941 to sign the Atlantic Charter: "[We] desire to bring about the fullest collaboration between all nations in the economic field with the object of securing, for all, improved labour standards, economic adjustment and social security." In fact, many of the Allied nations felt a certain irony and embarrassment that they had to call on their citizens to fight and die for their country, which had previously shown little interest in their welfare. That irony was not lost on Sir Alan Herbert, the well-known British cynic, whose doggerel for *Punch* would have found its way into the hands of many policy makers:

Oh, won't it be wonderful after the war –
There won't be no war, and there won't be no pore.
There won't be no sick, and there won't be no sore,
And we shan't have to work, if we find it a bore ...
Now there's only one question I'd like to explore;
Why didn't we have the old war before?[34]

There was a growing realization then, as early as 1941, that social security was rapidly becoming a prominent and necessary feature of the postwar period. Moreover, by this time, the ideas of social security had entered the international mindset and were influencing public debate in most Allied nations. As Edward Phelan of the International Labour Office wrote in an article that appeared in the October 1942 edition of *Canadian Welfare*, "We are constantly being reminded that the main objectives of the present war are social rather than political or even economic." At a conference on social security in Chile in September 1942, more than twenty countries from North and South America agreed that they would adopt policies promoting greater social security. The conference coordinator, Nelson Rockefeller, captured the thinking of the participants when he stated, "This is a war about social security; it is a war for social security."[35] Particularly in Canada, the debate was also informed by growing support in Britain for social security, and family allowances in particular, which had been first introduced in Grenoble, France, during the Great War. Since then, Australia and New Zealand as well as several other European countries had established family allowances.[36]

King's thinking on this subject reflected the growing international consensus that the transition from war to peace had to be made without a return to the problems of unemployment and want that had characterized the pre-war period. On 4 September 1941, when King addressed the Lord Mayor's Luncheon at

Guildhall in London, England – that same luncheon at which Winston Churchill praised Canada as the linchpin of the English-speaking world – he proclaimed that the promises of the importance of a new world order would be merely empty rhetoric if governments waited until the end of the war to build a new society.[37] "When the war is won, there will be an immense task to repair the great physical destruction caused by the war," King later told the American Federation of Labour at its 1942 convention in Toronto. "These tasks alone will provide work for millions of men and women for many years. But the work of repairing and restoring the ravages of war will not be enough." Governments everywhere had to work to eliminate the fear of unemployment and the sense of insecurity workers faced when their capacity to meet the needs of their family was threatened. "Until these fears have been eliminated," he told Canada's labour leaders, "the war for freedom will not be won. The era of freedom will be achieved only as social security and human welfare become the main concern of men and nations." The specifics of social welfare, he admitted, would have to be spelled out in due course, but the new order he envisioned for Canada would include, as a national minimum, adequate nutrition and housing, health insurance, social security, and of course full employment. "Men who have fought in this war, and others who have borne its privations and sufferings, will never be satisfied with a return to the conditions which prevailed before 1939," King acknowledged. "The broader and deeper conception of victory will be found only in a new world order."[38] The war gave King the opportunity to achieve some of the social objectives he had advocated in various ways for more than a generation, and on which an international consensus had emerged. King would not lose sight of that fact in the months ahead.

Postwar reconstruction planning in Canada was a major concern almost from the onset of hostilities. Many Canadians, including Ian Mackenzie, himself a veteran of the Great War and in 1939 the new minister of Pensions and Health, knew only too well that the government had not handled the transition from war to peace very effectively following the end of the Great War in 1918. Shortly after Canada declared war on Germany, Mackenzie was shuffled out of the National Defence portfolio he had held since 1935 and into Pensions and Health, where he immediately became an advocate for various social security measures.[39] His move to Pensions and Health was clearly a demotion for the long-serving British Columbia MP, but Mackenzie emerged as a champion of social security in Canada. Given his close friendship with Prime Minister King, and his effective oratorical skill, he became a driving force within government to push the Liberal government toward early reconstruction planning.[40] When most people were thinking only of mobilization for war, on 20 October 1939 Mackenzie wrote the prime minister that the government should immediately direct its attention to the questions and problems that would arise after the cessation of hostilities. He suggested the government create a committee to gather information on the matter, to which King immediately agreed.[41]

By 8 December 1939, the Cabinet had formed the Committee on Demobilization and Re-establishment, made up of the government's most powerful ministers; Ian Mackenzie was the chair.[42] He later noted in the debate in the House of Commons, "Our men are fighting for Canada ... and we must realize and recognize that the remaking of Canada will constitute the major post-war reconstruction into which all our rehabilitation plans must be shaped and functioned." And as if to show how progressive he was in his thinking, Mackenzie quoted from the influential Harold Laski at the London School of Economics, who warned the world, "Our choice is between the dark age of privilege and the dawn of an equal fellowship among men."[43] Initially, the committee was only interested in the demobilization and reintegration of the Armed Forces into civilian society, but in February 1941, Mackenzie again convinced the Cabinet to expand the mandate of the committee "to examine and discuss the general question of post-war reconstruction, and to make recommendations as to what Government facilities should be established to deal with this question."[44] To investigate the general issue of reconstruction, Mackenzie turned first to some of the nation's intellectuals. He recruited an impressive group, including Dr. Cyril James, principal of McGill University, as chair, Queen's University principal R.C. Wallace, businessman J.S. McLean, labour leader Tom Moore, and Edouard Montpetit, the leading Quebec economist who had chaired the Social Insurance Commission for the Quebec government a decade earlier. Leonard Marsh, director of the School of Research at McGill University and member of the League for Social Reconstruction, was appointed research director. Marsh had worked with the British reformer Sir William Beveridge at the London School of Economics before coming to Canada. In September 1941, the Cabinet formally recognized Mackenzie's group as the Advisory Committee on Reconstruction with a mandate to report to the General Advisory Committee on Demobilization and Rehabiliation, which was a committee of civil servants. It was to report on the economic and social implications of the transition from war to peace.[45]

Mackenzie was interested in social reform, though there is no evidence to suggest that he had established any personal links with the intellectual community with whom he shared many of the same goals. What this shows, however, is that the ideas being bantered around in the university corridors and in intellectual circles were also finding resonance with the Canadian public and with politicians. Ian Mackenzie himself reflected the fear of possible postwar instability felt by many Canadians when he told the Canadian Club in Quebec City in June 1941 that "if old dogmas and old doctrines – old philosophies of government – cannot solve that problem – then we must look to newer remedies and new faiths and newer solutions." He reassured his audience that their national government would act. They were now considering, he said, how best to develop a great national scheme of social security through which Canadians would be protected from those fears spawned by insecurity, poverty and want, and ill health.[46] Speaking later, in September 1942, he said, "I want the working man in the factory, the soldier on the battle front, the young mother caring for her overseas husband's little children to know that the Government in whom they have reposed their confidence not only shares their aspirations for a brighter tomorrow, but is, in a direct and positive way, planning to that end."[47] Mackenzie wanted Canada to be a part of the new world order.

Still, it appears that Mackenzie's interest in social security was not reflected in the work of the James committee. Even though Dr. S.K. Jaffary, a professor of social work at the University of Toronto, and Dr. George Davidson, the executive director of the Canadian Welfare Council, had been asked earlier in May 1942 to prepare a study for the committee on various social issues, Jaffary told a meeting of the Committee on Canada in the War and Post-War Reconstruction Period created by the Canadian Association of Social Workers later in November of that year that the James committee was primarily interested in economic issues and how to promote full employment after the war.[48] Marsh even commented years later that social security was not a priority of the James committee, since its members believed that economic prosperity – not greater social security – was the best way to ensure the preservation of democratic institutions.[49] And the James committee's preoccupation with economics and its lack of interest in social security were obvious in the first memorandum it prepared for Mackenzie. The committee suggested that the major aim of reconstruction policies was to have adequate employment opportunities for veterans and displaced workers who had been engaged in war production: "If, for any reason, reconstruction should not proceed smoothly during the postwar recession the country would inevitably be confronted by rapidly mounting unemployment and widespread dissatisfaction." The memorandum went further: "Even though, as individuals, we may regret the passing of the older order of free trade, competition and capitalism, the democratic-capitalist order of society suggests that the attainment of reasonable economic security for the average individual will demand a large measure of coordination and governmental control."[50] When James appeared before the Special Committee of the House of Commons on Reconstruction and Re-establishment on 14-15 May

1942, he noted that full employment in Canada was critical, and he made it clear that his committee saw it as the only way to preserve the Canadian system, which was based on free enterprise and personal initiative in both the political and economic life of the nation.[51] Later, when the James committee produced a series of recommendations calling for, among other things, a minister of economic planning to administer the planning for the postwar period with advice from a committee such as his, it raised the ire of the powerful bureaucrats in the Economic Advisory Council (EAC), a group of senior officials in Ottawa managing the war effort and reporting directly to Mackenzie King. They saw James and his committee as a nuisance. W.C. Clark, the EAC chair, penned a lengthy and ultimately persuasive memorandum for the prime minister on the recommendations regarding ministerial responsibility for reconstruction planning that were contained in the Report of the Reconstruction Committee.[52]

Clark pointed out that the James committee was correct in its recognition of the importance of coordinated planning to smooth the transition from war to peace, but he insisted that it was simply impractical for a single ministry to handle that file. He claimed it would require the new department to assume responsibility for probably half the functions of government. He reminded the Cabinet that it had rejected an earlier recommendation from the EAC to co-ordinate the formulation and administration of wartime economic policy since the task was simply too large for a single department. Then Clark turned to what he considered the limitations of the existing apparatus for postwar planning in Ottawa. He noted that the James committee had been established to provide insight and recommendations to the Cabinet. Although James and his group had performed their task admirably, it was unreasonable to assume that a committee of private citizens serving part-time in Ottawa could be expected to make an important contribution to the government's postwar planning process. Such a committee, Clark noted, would be removed from the day-to-day contact with the workings of government that was both necessary and fundamental if the committee were to make effective policy recommendations. Because so much of the work of government was confidential, he did not consider it appropriate that that information might be made available to a committee that operated at arm's-length from the government. Moreover, such groups would not be able to provide the necessary coordination that was needed, and many postwar problems involved relations with other governments, a matter for government officials responsible for international negotiations. Clark further noted that in both the United States and the United Kingdom, planning for the postwar period was primarily the task of officials in various departments of government who were familiar with policy development and in constant touch with the day-to-day workings and decisions of government. Hence, Clark recommended that responsibility for postwar planning remain within government, and that the government place primary responsibility for such planning on the officials in the existing departments and agencies.[53]

Still, Clark acknowledged that the government required an advisory interdepartmental committee to arrange for investigations into various issues, to allocate particular issues to various departments, to coordinate the flow of information, and to prepare material for the Cabinet. Because the EAC was performing a similar function for the war effort, Clark suggested that it would be particularly well suited to perform a similar role in planning for the postwar period. This would not mean the dismantling of the James committee; rather, the committee could act as a representative group of private citizens bringing in a non-governmental view to assist the government in reaching decisions for the postwar period. Perhaps more importantly, Clark said, the committee would be useful in preparing the public mind for the policies that might have to be followed and the programs that might have to be implemented during the postwar period. It might stimulate and guide public discussion of postwar problems. These could all be best achieved, Clark suggested, if the Committee on Reconstruction, like the EAC, reported directly to the prime minister through the Privy Council Office. Common responsibility to the same minister would make it easy to establish the necessary liaison and cooperation between the two committees working on reconstruction problems and to avoid undesirable duplication and conflict of effort.[54] It also meant that Clark's committee would lose none of its influence once the war ended.

Clark's report went directly to King, and it was very clear that Clark believed he and his colleagues should control postwar planning. His memorandum had the support of A.D.P. Heeney, the clerk of the Privy Council, who shared Clark's belief that postwar planning should take place within the regular civil service.[55] The Cabinet agreed with its senior bureaucrats; at its meetings on 23 December 1942, it decided that the primary responsibility for postwar planning should rest with the government and its officials, not with intellectuals outside the bureaucracy. In January 1943, the James committee subsequently became a subcommittee of the EAC to supplement the work already completed within the government bureaucracy; it was renamed the Advisory Committee on Reconstruction. Meanwhile, as Clark had hoped, the EAC had its mandate broadened, giving it authority to deal with postwar economic policy.[56] The decision to have the James Committee's recommendations overseen by Clark's group has been interpreted as a failure of the committee and an attempt by the government to weaken the committee's recommendations on social policy.[57] Too much should not be read into this bureaucratic wrangling, however, as no one should have expected the government's senior bureaucrats to have willingly surrendered their authority over postwar planning to a committee of outsiders. What is clear – and what Clark's machinations demonstrated – is that there was considerable interest in and pressure for increased social security as part of the postwar reconstruction process, both inside and outside of government, and that the bureaucracy was determined not to permit outsiders to establish the agenda, no matter how well intentioned the private citizens might be.[58]

Social security was nothing new to Prime Minister King. He considered it an important aspect of the new world order he envisioned for the postwar world, and he spoke of the great need for it early in the war. When he joined Roosevelt at the White House for dinner on 5 December 1942, the president raised the British report on reconstruction, "Social Insurance and Allied Services" – popularly known as the Beveridge Report after its author, Sir William Beveridge – that had been released a few days earlier in London. King was impressed when Roosevelt suggested they work together on social reform for both their countries. Of course, King pointed out that much of the program Beveridge had recommended could be found in his *Industry and Humanity: A Study in the Principle Underlying Industrial Reconstruction,* which King had written in 1918.[59] Still, he was relieved that he and Roosevelt could now turn to matters other than the war, and he thought it was time for him to think more about a policy of reconstruction for Canada since the war seemed to be turning in the Allies' favour. "I would have something to say in that matter," he told his diary the next day.[60] It is unlikely at the time, however, that King realized the impact the Beveridge Report would have in Canada. The report arose out of the work of the British Departmental Committee on Social Insurance and Allied Services, appointed in June 1941 by Arthur Greenwood, the UK minister of reconstruction. When the report was released, it had an immediate impact. It was praised as marking a revolution not only for its practical recommendations for social security measures but also for its articulation of the philosophy underpinning the need for social security. King shared with Beveridge the view that the war was not fought for dominion or revenge but for peace; moreover, they both agreed that peace and security could be best achieved by ensuring that their citizens enjoyed freedom from want and despair.

In the weeks following his conversation with Roosevelt, King continued to contemplate the issue of social security, and there prodding him every step of the way was Ian Mackenzie, by this time the greatest advocate within the government for new social welfare initiatives. When Cyril James presented him with a draft memorandum from the Committee on Reconstruction earlier in December 1942, Mackenzie had let James know that he was disappointed there was no specific mention of social security. That more than anything else, Mackenzie reminded James, occupied the attention of the peoples of the world.[61]

Others, such as the various social agencies in Canada, complained that the committee's interest lay primarily with economic issues,[62] and they feared that social security would not be a high priority in the postwar period. George Davidson wrote Harry Cassidy, who was then teaching social work at the University of California in Berkeley, that the James committee had been "quietly retired from the scene in favour of Dr. Clark's Advisory Committee on Economic Policy. These are pretty obviously the boys who are going to write the post-war ticket," he lamented, and he did not hold much hope for any great social security measures with that group: "once again we have an imposing line-up of money economists with hardly a drop of humanitarian blood in the lot of them." He thought they would pay little attention to Leonard Marsh, the committee's research director. Davidson also believed that King would simply "play for time" and do nothing, hoping that the interest in social security that the Beveridge Report in the United Kingdom had stirred up would disappear as Canadians increasingly turned their attention to the final stages of the war in Europe.[63] Yet, as Ian Mackenzie later told the Special Committee of the House of Commons on Reconstruction and Re-establishment that had been appointed in 1942, the revised mandate of the EAC merely reflected the growing sense of urgency with regard to postwar planning. He added that the government wanted action on the social policy file and only a department of government could organize and act quickly.[64] Davidson's expectation of King was subsequently proven wrong, of course, when King and the Liberal government went further with social security in the early 1940s than many had expected they would, even if what was eventually implemented by the Liberals was far less than what many had demanded.

Immediately following the release of the Beveridge Report, Mackenzie asked his deputy minister to arrange for a Social Security Committee within his department to prepare a social security program for Canada. The minister suggested several members for the committee, which he made clear would be kept entirely separate from the reconstruction committee and entirely confidential. The committee was directed to study the social security system of New Zealand and the Beveridge Report as well as incorporate the work already done on social security within the department.[65] The next day, on 3 December, Mackenzie telegraphed Vincent Massey, the High Commissioner in London, asking him to airmail copies of the Beveridge Report.

Within two weeks, W.S. Woods, the associate deputy minister in the Department of Pensions and Health, had prepared for Mackenzie an overview of social security legislation in other countries. In his thirteen-page report, Woods paid particular attention to the British experiment but he also reviewed the social legislation of thirty-eight other countries. He concluded that there was a general trend toward social security in all the nations he examined, with the most far-reaching proposals coming from the United Kingdom, New Zealand, and the United States. In fact, the Eliot bill that was to expand social security in the United States had been introduced in Congress on 9 September 1941. Woods considered the proposed American legislation "far-reaching, novel and unique," and remarked to his minister that "so far as Canada is concerned, our national social legislation had not advanced to a degree that most other countries have achieved." He also reminded the minister that world leaders who were united in the defence of freedom had named social security their first objective of postwar planning.[66] This comment must have rankled King; he had earlier told Roosevelt that Canada already had much of what Beveridge was recommending for the United Kingdom, but Woods evidently saw little to support King's claim. However, Mackenzie would push King hard on the issue of social security in the weeks that followed.

The first opportunity to do so arose when Mackenzie accompanied King to Brockville, Ontario, on 5 January 1943, where they had gone to bury Senator George P. Graham, a former Cabinet colleague. By that point, however, King knew full well that social security issues had become important in Canada and, indeed, throughout the Allied nations. Even so, Mackenzie took the opportunity to further press on him the need for a public declaration of the government's commitment to social security, and insisted they promise a postwar program for it. King later wrote in his diary, "I agreed with him that nothing could more completely please me if I had the physical strength and endurance."[67] In the meantime, as he began to consider policy for the coming session, King asked Mackenzie for more information on social security. The minister was prepared, his arsenal well supplied and ready for immediate action. He promised King that he would have a memorandum on social security the following day, and he did. On 6 January 1943, Mackenzie delivered a lengthy and comprehensive document on social society compiled from the materials his department had been working on for some time. The memorandum included Woods' report on the international commitment to social security, various reports on health services, the Conservative Party's resolution at their recent convention in Winnipeg, and a memorandum on the work of the general advisory and reconstruction committees. In the weeks that followed, Mackenzie sent King additional materials on social security, including reports by Leonard Marsh and George F. Davidson. He also included a summary of the Beveridge Report.[68]

Later in the month, King received a lengthy memorandum from Vincent Massey. Massey, who had earlier tried to steer the Liberal Party toward accepting a more enhanced role for the state, provided King with his analysis of the Beveridge Report as well as a speech that Beveridge had made after the release of the document. Massey pointed out that although the report was the first of its kind for which a press agent was appointed and which followed a carefully scripted publicity campaign, the reception it had received clearly showed the "vitality of the British in the midst of so stern a struggle." He told the prime minister that it would be difficult to exaggerate the interest the Beveridge Report had generated in Great Britain since it was the subject of universal discussion, and that it might in fact become one of the most important documents in the social history of the British people. In addition, he reminded King, Beveridge had warned all of Britain in a radio interview that many people might reject democracy if it failed to provide citizens with a fair measure of social security. As a former Liberal Party president, Massey reminded King that the support for the Beveridge Report did not follow strict party lines. Although it had been welcomed by the Left, Massey correctly noted that many Conservatives embraced it as well, largely because they saw it as a bulwark against social unrest after the war. The report also enjoyed considerable support within the civil service. Appealing to King's sense of social justice, Massey also noted that Beveridge credited Prime Ministers Lloyd George and Churchill for their creative social security measures earlier in their careers and saw his report as an important continuation of their efforts. King was surely impressed, and he was not to be outdone, of course: he confided to his diary, "I should be happy indeed if I could round out my career with legislation in the nature of social security."[69] In December and early January, following the release of the Beveridge Report, King had received many letters from individuals and institutions across Canada praising the report and urging him to provide additional social security for Canada.[70]

King acted immediately. At a meeting of the Cabinet on 12 January, he pointed out the need to discuss social security in the upcoming session. However, he found a number of his powerful Cabinet colleagues, including the minister of finance, J.L. Ilsley, the minister of munitions and supply, C.D. Howe, and the minister of mines and resources, T.A. Crerar, opposed to the idea of greater social security. Such resistance prompted King to write, "The mind of the Cabinet, at any rate, does not grasp the significance of [the] Beveridge Report."[71] He had encountered similar opposition in 1940 when he began discussions on the unemployment insurance bill,[72] but he pressed on to enact the legislation over the wishes of some of his most powerful ministers.[73] Again, despite the opposition of senior and influential ministers, King pushed ahead and outlined in the 1943 Speech from the Throne his government's objective to pursue a policy of social security for Canada.

Discussing plans for social security seemed to rejuvenate King, who was then approaching his seventieth year and his sixteenth as prime minister. With the aid of his *Industry and Humanity*, of course, King chose to personally write the section on social security for the Speech from the Throne. He discussed those sections with both the Cabinet and the caucus so there would be no misunderstanding the government's intentions later on.[74] In the Speech from the Throne on 28 January 1943, the governor general announced the government's commitment to social security and stated that a "comprehensive national scheme of social insurance should be worked out at once which will constitute a charter of social security for the whole of Canada." However, King did make it clear that the first and immediate objective of his government was to win the war. Only with victory in its grasp could the government fully concern itself with other matters. Moreover, he told the caucus, he would never allow an election on the matter of social security during the war, as this might be interpreted as a bribe from the public treasury. He said his government was committed first to a postwar policy of full employment, and "it was wrong to think of increased outlays on anything that could be avoided until victory was won. Important, however, to keep everything in readiness for peace."[75] Incidentally, D.R. Rodgers, the acting chair of the Wartime Information Board, had written to King a week earlier, informing him that a Wartime Information Board Survey on 16 January had revealed that a majority of Canadians regarded the postwar period with "something akin to dread." Rodgers suggested that both soldiers and civilians must "feel they are fighting for the positive goal of a better Canada" if morale was to be maintained in the country.[76] On 3 March 1943, King moved in the House of Commons for the appointment of a special committee on national social insurance to "examine and report on a national plan of social insurance which [would] constitute a charter of social security for the whole of Canada."

Clearly, then, by the midpoint of the Second World War, and with images of the upheaval and chaos of the Great Depression very much in mind, King had joined those who found the earlier approach to social security wanting. New and progressive thinking about the importance of social security became important ideas bantered about internationally during the Second World War, and they served to inform public policy debate in Canada during the period. Like King, many leaders in all the Allied nations embraced the *principle* of social security and promised important initiatives in the field as a means of maintaining world peace and preserving human dignity. Like national governments elsewhere, the Canadian government firmly believed that it was its own responsibility to make the postwar world a better place for all Canadians and create a new social order. Many individuals both in and outside government and nongovernmental organizations, as well as many in the business community, believed that what was at stake in the postwar world was the survival of the democratic, free-enterprise system; many believed social security, together with a greater role for government in the economy, was necessary to safeguard Canada as a liberal democratic state. King wanted Canada, and thus himself, to be seen – not just at home but internationally – as playing a lead role in implementing social security. He believed this would cement his claim as a reformer and pioneer in social welfare.[77] It would signify the dawning of a new era in Canadian social security.

2
Family Allowance Comes to Canada, 1943-45

WHEN PARLIAMENTARIANS GATHERED in the Red Chamber on Parliament Hill on 27 January 1944 to hear the governor general, the Earl of Athlone, read the Speech from the Throne to open the Fifth Session of the Nineteenth Parliament, there was an air of optimism sweeping the country. Much of the human suffering and deprivation that had resulted from the economic chaos of the Great Depression had disappeared in the wartime boom, and the European Campaign had finally turned in the Allies' favour. Canadians were starting to look beyond the war as the nation prepared for the return of peace. It had become clear through the five years of war what an activist state could accomplish, and many Canadians looked to their government to be equally proactive with the issues that might confront their nation in the postwar period. Many also hoped that the nation would accelerate its slow march toward the comprehensive social security state that had been the subject of much media attention in recent months.

The governor general had fuelled their optimism when he declared in the Speech from the Throne that social security and human welfare were to become the primary postwar objectives of Canada's domestic policy. The Earl of Athlone told those gathered in the Senate chambers on Parliament Hill in Ottawa that the government of Prime Minister Mackenzie King intended to establish "a national minimum of social security and human welfare ... as quickly as possible." And to give concrete evidence of its commitment to progressive social security legislation, the government announced its intention to begin a family allowance program, an initiative the venerable Canadian periodical *Saturday Night* had claimed in June 1941 was "becoming standard equipment in socially progressive countries." Family allowances had already become well established in Europe and elsewhere throughout the world where they were seen as a benefit to the whole community. By the end of the Second World War, Canada would join more than thirty other nations and implement its own family allowance program.[1]

The first modern family allowances originated in Grenoble, France, during the First World War as a means of supplementing wages of workers with large families. Since the coming of industrialization to France in the 19th century, employers had frequently provided employees with dependent children special grants to help families through periods of economic difficulty. By 1914, some thirty firms had adopted such rudimentary programs. In Grenoble, employers were growing increasingly concerned by the gap between what workers with large families earned and the income required for them to provide for their families. In 1916, a benevolent Catholic manager, E. Romanet, persuaded his heavy metal firm to pay six francs a month to its employees for each of their children. Other employers in the Grenoble metal industry subsequently followed suit and provided a similar allowance to their employees with dependent children. To ensure a reasonably even distribution of the financial burden among all firms and to avoid any single employer bearing exorbitant costs because their employees had a higher proportion of workers with dependent children, the employers agreed to contribute to an equalization fund on the basis of their wage bill. From this fund, the allowance was paid to those who qualified.

The initiative proved popular, and by the end of 1930, there were 230 equalization funds throughout France, distributing 380 million francs in allowances and covering nearly 2 million workers and 7 million children. This system worked informally until 1932, when the French government required all employers in industrial, commercial, and agricultural sectors, as well as the liberal professions, to join an equalization fund approved by the minister of labour that would pay allowances to workers with dependent children. The allowance was paid to children until they reached the school-leaving age of fourteen, or to seventeen if they remained at school.[2] By the late 1930s, there had been a tendency to either drop or diminish payment for the first child in a family. The allowance was paid monthly, usually to the mother to emphasize the distinction between the allowances and wages paid to workers. Labour groups supported family allowances in France, especially after 1932, when the government legislated universal payments and made them law.[3]

The Grenoble system was one of three ways family allowance schemes operated in various parts of the world. In addition to these private systems in France where employers collectively bore the cost of payments for their employees, in Italy, for instance, the beneficiaries contributed as well as the employers and the state. A third arrangement existed in New Zealand, where every child in the country was included in its system of family allowances, and the state financed the program out of its general revenues. The New Zealand experiment with family allowances began in 1926, when its Conservative government passed the Family Allowances Act, providing benefits to the mother for the maintenance of children of parents with limited income. By 1942, all children under the age of sixteen were covered, and the threshold level for the weekly family income was raised to £5 5s.[4]

By the time the Second World War began in 1939, family allowances had largely come to be regarded as a public policy that benefited national communities. In April 1940, *The International Labour Review* reported that the interest in family allowances had grown considerably in the 1930s, and that states were increasingly likely to bear the whole cost because such programs had become a right of citizenship in many nations. National governments were providing family allowances in Belgium, Hungry, Italy, the Netherlands, Spain, Chile, Japan, New Zealand, and New South Wales. Both Norway and Sweden had appointed special commissions to examine family allowances, and each subsequently recommended some form of aid to large families. Moreover, the twenty-one states gathered at the Pan-American Conference in Lima, Peru, in December 1938 adopted a resolution recommending the establishment of a family allowance scheme in each country. Subsequently, Argentina, Bolivia, Brazil, Chile, Paraguay, Peru, and Uruguay all introduced family allowances before the end of the Second World War. Incidentally, Argentina had a very limited family allowance program for municipal workers in Buenos Aires and for a small number of private enterprises much earlier, but in 1941, the National Congress introduced family allowances as part of a general scheme of social insurance. The program was supported by employers' contributions, and it paid to married wage earners and salaried employees an allowance of 5 pesos per child under eighteen and still at school. A similar system was implemented in Brazil in April 1943, and in Uruguay some seven months later. In 1942, both Portugal and Bulgaria introduced family allowance schemes that were financed by workers, employers, and the state.[5]

Australia was one of the few countries that had instituted a national system of family allowances for all families regardless of income. The Australian system had its beginnings in a program that provided allowances for children of workers in public service at the end of the Great War, though the government of New South Wales expanded its program widely through the Family Endowment Bill that was introduced in 1926. In 1941, the Conservative government in Australia, with the support of the Labour opposition, passed the Children Endowment Act, which paid five shillings per week to the mother for all children under the age of sixteen, beginning with the second child in each family. The allowances were paid from the government's general revenues and were partly supported by the discontinuance of income tax deductions for the second and all subsequent children in the family.

During the Second World War, there was also considerable interest in family allowances in Great Britain, a country that continued to exert significant influence on Canada throughout this period.[6] The United Kingdom had had a private scheme of family allowances for years, and by 1942 there were more than forty institutions and industrial firms paying family benefits. However, by the time of the Second World War, there was heightened interest in a national child endowment system as British religious leaders, Members of Parliament, industrialists, and other influential groups had joined with social agencies to demand a full discussion of a state-run family allowance system. On 16 June 1941, a deputation of members of the British House of Commons visited the Chancellor of the Exchequer, and asked him to investigate the possibility of introducing a family allowance program for the country. There was no immediate acceptance of the idea, but the chancellor presented a report on family allowances to Parliament a year later. On that occasion, he merely reviewed the practical considerations of a family allowance scheme, but his report nonetheless signalled that family allowances were very much on the minds of the British public and their elected representatives. In the meantime, the British Trades Union Congress reversed its long-standing opposition to family allowances, and agreed with the Labour Party on the need for a national scheme to be fully funded by the state.[7]

It was becoming clear by the Second World War, then, that consideration of family allowance programs could be separated from the issue of wage rates, which had caused such concern when both the federal government and the provincial government in Quebec investigated the matter in the late 1920s and early 1930s. Since then, such programs had largely become accepted as a form of state assistance to families to offset the cost of raising their families. Many states had also come to recognize, it seems, that the maintenance and well-being of children were an important matter for the whole nation. As D.C. Rowat, an official with the Department of Finance in Ottawa, had pointed out in his memorandum on international trends in family allowances prepared in late 1943 for W.A. Mackintosh, special assistant to the deputy minister of finance, states were increasingly participating in family allowance schemes because they were "becoming a new right based on the principle that national income should be distributed according to family requirements."[8] This view represented a fundamental change in Canada over what had been expressed in the family allowances debate more than a decade earlier. Yet even in Canada there had been some recognition that those who were caring for children should receive some special consideration. When the Income War Tax was introduced in 1917, for example, the state had recognized family responsibility and had provided an exemption for dependent children.[9]

With the outbreak of hostilities in 1939, Ottawa also provided dependent allowances for children of enlisted soldiers. Although it was not regarded as a form of family allowance, the government had decided at the beginning of the war that the state had a responsibility to provide an allowance for the children of enlisted soldiers to help the soldiers' families. Initially, the government provided an allowance of $12 per month for each of the first two children, but under pressure from soldiers' wives, who were finding it increasingly difficult to provide for their families given the increase in the cost of living during the war, Ottawa authorized monthly allowances for a third and fourth child at the rate of $9 and $6, respectively. Even that increase proved insufficient, however, and on 1 January 1943, allowances covered up to six dependent children on a decreasing scale: $12 each for the first two children, $10 for the third child, and $8 each for the fourth, fifth, and sixth children. Through these allowances, the government assumed some responsibility for the maintenance of families of members of the Armed Forces, eliminating the necessity of mothers' appeals to charities like the Canadian Patriotic Fund, which had been common in the First World War. Besides providing for the families of enlisted personnel, those wartime allowances also established a precedent for the government to provide allowances for dependent children, and as the King government liked to point out through the Dependents' Board of Trustees it created in 1942, the allowances were not charity, and they did not affect the regular pay of soldiers.[10]

Not surprisingly, there were several groups in Canada that wanted to see the government extend similar allowances to all families with dependent children. Social workers at the Montreal branch of the Canadian Association of Social Workers (CASW) were among the earliest to push for family allowances. Concerned with the rise in the cost of living in Montreal, they created a national committee to investigate the feasibility of family allowances for Canada. The CASW issued a report entitled *The Rising Cost of Living*, which unsurprisingly found that the cost of living had increased in the first years of the war, thereby placing severe strain on all families. While the national association stopped short of recommending the introduction of family allowances, it called for further study of the measure, noting that many in Britain saw the solution to similar problems there in the provision of family allowances.[11] In 1941, the National Social Security Association of Canada, a non-political and non-sectarian organization based in Calgary, called on King to implement a comprehensive program of social security for the people of Canada, including family allowances, based on the New Zealand model.[12]

It was Sir William Beveridge, however, who helped create a wide and receptive audience for improved social security measures in Canada. He had maintained in his path-breaking Beveridge Report in England that family allowances, health services, and the avoidance of unemployment were absolutely necessary for a satisfactory scheme of social security. Children's allowances were the most important element, since he believed that much of the poverty in England resulted from the fact that wage rates did not take into consideration the size of the family. Beveridge argued that family allowances were necessary because wage rates could not be varied according to the size of an employee's family; a family allowance program would allow the state to establish a national minimum by subsidizing the earnings of large families to cover the minimum maintenance needs of all. He proposed allowances for all children under the age of sixteen attending school beyond the first child when the head of the family was working, and for all children when the head of the family was in receipt of unemployment, disability, widow's or guardian benefits, or an industrial pension. He also suggested the cash grants be graduated to reflect the cost of raising a child, and that these allowances be "non-contributory, provided wholly out of taxation, and not to any extent out of insurance contributions." Beveridge maintained that the simplest plan was to make allowances universal,[13] and if there was concern that the state was subsidizing prosperous families, those funds could be reclaimed through the tax system.[14] The *Canadian Forum* praised the Beveridge Report in January 1943, suggesting that Beveridge's plan would be a vast improvement on anything then existing in Canada. George Davidson, executive director of the Canadian Welfare Council, noted in *Canadian Welfare* that the report had the best press coverage of any social document since the Rowell-Sirois Report and that "interest [in it] in official circles in Ottawa is deeply significant."[15]

Shortly after the release of the Beveridge Report, the Committee on Reconstruction had Leonard Marsh, its young research director and a disciple of William Beveridge with whom he had studied in London before coming to Canada, undertake a similar study for Canada. As we saw earlier, Ian Mackenzie also had his officials consider a similar plan for Canada. On 21 December 1942, he told Cyril James, the chair of the Committee on Reconstruction, that he wanted to present a "general Social Security plan to Parliament in February [1943]." Within two days, Marsh met with Mackenzie's secretary to discuss an outline of the proposed study. It was clear that Mackenzie wanted the study completed within a few weeks.[16] It is also clear that Prime Minister King, who was sent a draft copy of the report on 5 February, wanted it to appear as a preliminary report to the Advisory Committee on Reconstruction rather than as an official document from the Committee on Reconstruction; in official Ottawa, the document was seen as merely the view of the research director of the James committee, and it did not represent any evolving government policy. Moreover, King wanted the report presented to the parliamentary committee on reconstruction and social security as soon as the committee was set up.[17] Incidentally, the "Report on Social Security for Canada" bore Marsh's name, making it clear that the government was taking a wait-and-see attitude on how it would be received. Marsh maintained that he considered his report an "educational" document, and he later claimed he believed that employment, housing, urban planning, and the fate of the wartime controls were all more important than social security planning.[18] Even so, Marsh's "Report on Social Security for Canada," or the Marsh Report, has been described as "the most important single document in the history of the development of the welfare state in Canada."[19]

The Marsh Report was first presented to the Special Select Committee of the House of Commons on Social Security, as King had wanted. The House committee had been established on 8 March 1943 "to examine into and report to the House of Commons on a national plan of social insurance which will constitute a charter of social security for the whole of Canada, and ... to examine and study existing social insurance legislation of the Dominion and the provinces." Mackenzie and others believed that it was imperative for Canada to remain in step with other nations that had embarked on a greater social security agenda. In his statement to the Special Select Committee when he tabled the Marsh Report along with the Advisory Committee's "Report on Health Insurance" and a draft bill on health insurance, Mackenzie went to great lengths to show that both the Atlantic Charter, which had outlined the postwar goals of President Franklin Roosevelt and Prime Minister Winston Churchill on 14 August 1941, and the Beveridge Report had greatly influenced public thinking on social security in Canada, as they had throughout the world. Mackenzie pointed out that the Canadian government formally subscribed to the articles of the Atlantic Charter at the Declaration of the United Nations in Washington on 1 January 1942. He claimed that when the Progressive Conservatives declared their support at their 1942 national convention for social security as outlined in section 5 of the Atlantic Charter, it showed how closely aligned were the views of the two major political parties in this regard. Once again, Mackenzie praised the Beveridge Report as a "magnificent and admirable document. It is the work of a most enlightened and progressive authority on social science. Its motives and its reasoning are applicable to humanity everywhere," but its recommendations had reference only to the United Kingdom. Interestingly, Mackenzie just mentioned Marsh's report to the Special Select Committee but praised the report on health insurance, which had become a priority for him, as "the most comprehensive report ... ever compiled in this or any other country." He also paid personal tribute to the author of the health report, Dr. Heagerty, and his committee, "whose unflagging labours and incisive grasp of the problem are responsible for this magnificent achievement."[20] Mackenzie would be disappointed that the Marsh Report attracted so much attention and press coverage that it derailed his plans for public discussion of health insurance.[21]

The Marsh Report proposed a "comprehensive and integrated social security system for Canada, set out priorities for implementation of the different proposals, dealt with decisions respecting administration and constitutional jurisdiction, and with financial considerations."[22] Above all, the report demonstrated how the thinking about social welfare had changed in Canada since the Great Depression. Then, it was widely accepted that citizens who were not working or had not saved while they were gainfully employed should not expect support from the state. The basic premise underlying the Marsh Report was that it was in the interests of society that all of its citizens be provided with a minimum level of goods and services or purchasing power, even when ill health, unemployment, or other conditions, like age, made that impossible. "Social insurance," Marsh wrote, "is a floor to alleviate poverty and prevent people from becoming destitute. It is a remedy for the most painful feature of assistance at low income levels because it obviates altogether the need for a means test in every specific case." In addition to a public works program to prevent widespread unemployment immediately following the end of the war, Marsh recommended contributory social insurance schemes to protect citizens from the universal risks of sickness, invalidity, and old age. For him, social insurance fell into one of two categories of risk: the universal risks such as those associated with illness, disability, and old age, and employment risks that came from the loss of wages. Each citizen would contribute a single payment to cover the universal risks, but employment risks would be charged to the employer. The report paid particular attention to the needs of children. Marsh believed that children should have an important place in social security policy. Children's allowances were clearly a part of a national minimum and a way to deal with poverty created by insufficient wages. The report also proposed a system of survivors' pensions to replace mother's allowance to maintain family stability. In essence, the report was a plan for freedom from want for every Canadian from the cradle to the grave, and included maternity benefits, children's allowances, unemployment assistance, sickness benefits, free medical insurance and pensions for permanent disability and surviving widows, old age pensions, and funeral benefits.

In addition to the contingencies that these reflected – unemployment, sickness and health, disability and death – Marsh also believed that family size had a profound impact on whether or not families could adequately maintain themselves on the income they received. Yet he realized that the maintenance of children was not an unpredictable risk like some of the others he considered in his report; it was a continuous requirement, at least until children reached adolescence. Since wage levels were not always sufficient to provide for large families, family allowances were in his view a logical complement to any social insurance scheme that intended to establish a national minimum standard of living. Marsh dismissed the concern expressed by social workers nearly a generation earlier that cash grants to families would encourage the "wrong" parent to have larger numbers of children. "Quite irrespective of whether the right parents have the most children, children should have an unequivocal place in social security policy," he argued, borrowing an idea from Beveridge, who had argued that children's allowances were essential for a satisfactory scheme of social security.

In Canada, the state had already shown its concern for children by permitting deductions for them through the income tax system. A program of family allowances would benefit all children, even if their parents did not have sufficient incomes to pay income tax. An allowance paid on behalf of children would allow parents a measure of choice because they would decide how the payments could best be spent in the interests of the child. Moreover, the allowances would be universally available and would be paid even if the parent was unemployed. Marsh noted that children's aid societies throughout Canada had estimated that between $14 and $20 per month was necessary to maintain a child. With more than 3.5 million children in Canada, Marsh realized that allowances at those rates might be financially challenging for any government. He suggested instead that an allowance in the range of $8-$9 might be more sustainable, especially if the allowances were graduated according to age and the number of children in a family.[23] Still, the price tag would be about $200 million, or roughly one-half of the pre-war federal budget.

When he appeared before the Senate Special Committee on Economic Re-establishment and Social Security three months later, Marsh emphasized the connection between social security disbursements and consumer purchasing power. He told the senators, "One of the things we have to consider in the post-war period is ways and means of replacing the sums now being disbursed for war purposes." Once the munitions factories and other war-related industries ceased production and the economic activity returned to normal, there would inevitably be a period of dislocation, which would reduce the national income and create unemployment. Family allowances were one very effective way of maintaining purchasing power among Canadians, Marsh suggested. Such a cash disbursement would not require any equipment, nor would it be a works program, but it would flow into the market immediately: "If we want to use it, it is a means of helping out the problem of maintaining markets and it may be that children's allowances should be considered on that score alone."[24]

Not surprisingly, Marsh's "Report on Social Security for Canada" generated considerable excitement and newspaper and magazine copy in Canada. The Wartime Information Board noted that in the first week following the release of the report, more than 160 newspapers made it the subject of their editorials.

It was welcomed as Canada's Beveridge Report and endorsed by a large number of editorial writers and such organizations as the CASW.[25] The Montreal *Gazette* wrote that the Marsh Report and the Report of the National Resources Planning Board in the United States both came about as a result of the British social security plan outlined by Sir William Beveridge. The *Gazette* claimed that Ian Mackenzie requested that Marsh make his report after the minister talked with Beveridge in England, late in 1942. Moreover, it noted that "more significant than the probable monetary cost and the estimated domestic benefits of such a plan to any of the democracies are the international aspects of this widespread interest in and demand for greater social security. They are inseparably related to the aims expressed in the Atlantic Charter and that document is as essentially global as the war which produced it."[26] The Vancouver *Province* echoed similar sentiments when it noted that the Marsh Report would keep Canada in step with the worldwide trend toward greater social security.[27] The Toronto *Globe and Mail* considered it a "worthwhile document," noting that "there must be protection against the evil days that are bound to come to some in any system of free enterprise."[28] The Woodstock *Sentinel-Review* agreed that "the people want social security; they want to be assured that if they give their lives to the country, in working or in fighting, they shall not be in want." Many newspapers, including Ottawa's *Le Droit*, praised Marsh's recommendation for family allowances.[29] The board of directors for the CASW passed a resolution on 27 March 1943 giving its support to the Marsh Report.[30] In a subsequent brief to the Advisory Committee on Reconstruction, the association reiterated its support for the principles and recommendations enunciated by Marsh, noting that the government must make family allowances available to all families as an integral part of a national social security scheme.[31]

Not all of the press commentary was positive, however. The Ottawa *Morning Journal* expressed misgivings over the projected costs of Marsh's recommendations. It wondered if the Canadian economy could sustain the annual price tag of $200 million. The *Toronto Telegram* agreed, claiming that, if implemented, the Marsh Report would "bankrupt the country and precipitate chaos."

One of the most virulent and vocal critics of the Marsh Report was Charlotte Whitton, perhaps Canada's best-known social worker. She had opposed family allowances when they were first discussed for Canada in 1929. Within hours of the release of the Marsh Report, Progressive Conservative Leader John Bracken visited Whitton and asked her to complete an analysis of it. She agreed to do it for $10 per day and, as she told Bracken, "a service to something in which I believe."[32] On 1 June, Whitton provided Bracken with the first draft of her comments not only on the Marsh Report but also on the Beveridge Report and the report of the US Natural Resources Planning Board. The analysis was later published as *The Dawn of Ampler Life* by the Macmillan Company of Canada. Whitton even wrote Bracken's introduction to the book, and had him saying, "No instruction nor restriction was placed upon her [Whitton's] commission, other than the broad stipulation that her report should be of such a nature as to be of general use on a non-political basis, and that criticism of principles or proposals should carry the responsibility of alternative suggestions." Actually, given the subject matter and her earlier views on family allowances, her insistence on the "non-political" nature of her work was hardly credible. She was worried that H.H. Wolfenden, the actuary who assisted her with the financial analysis, might compromise her report for his avowed opposition to any form of social security. R.A. Bell, Conservative Party president, was also worried about Wolfenden's association with the report his party had commissioned, but Whitton assured him and Bracken that she would hold herself responsible for the actuarial work and keep Wolfenden's name out of her final report.[33]

Whitton began her criticism of the Marsh Report by claiming that it was a "markdown" of the Beveridge Report and thus a misguided document for Canada. It was naive for Marsh to prepare a blueprint for Canada along the lines of the Beveridge plan, she wrote, when Canada had emerged from a different social background than that of the United Kingdom. What Canada required, Whitton asserted – as she had in 1929 – was a distinctively Canadian approach to a unique Canadian problem: "This calls for knowledge and love of this land, inventive imagination and courage." She refuted Marsh's claim that "Canada [was] now definitely past the stage of being primarily an agricultural or rural country," and stated that because Marsh saw Canada in European terms, he emphasized social insurance and social assistance as mechanisms to maintain incomes. Canada needed social utilities, which Whitton described as those services necessary for citizens to enjoy good living standards, such as schools, hospitals, child care, and protection agencies, and a variety of resources available on a community basis, "affording educational, health and welfare services for all the people, under varying auspices and available on varying bases." The social utilities, Whitton stated, "are a direct social investment in the maintenance and development of human resources, with a claim upon the whole community, and therefore their cost is more justly borne when met from general taxation than when added to the cost of production as an element in wage fixing or assessed only against particular industrial or occupational groups." Moreover, she claimed that the Marsh Report – as well as the American and British reports – dealt simply with "income maintenance through welfare planning" and took a very limited view of social reconstruction.

Not surprisingly, Charlotte Whitton remained opposed to family allowances. Her views had not changed much in the fourteen years since she had appeared before the parliamentary committee that had first investigated family allowances. As in 1929, she continued to argue that Canada was a land of opportunity, and that it was a defeatist attitude for the government to impose a social minimum through income support. Rather, she argued, "it is contended that the first objective of social policy in Canada should be the organization of gainful occupation on such a basis as to offer to the conscientious and efficient worker valid hope of an income from his efforts, sufficient to maintain, in reasonable decency, the family obligations which he might normally be expected to acquire." She claimed that Marsh's recommendation of children's allowances of approximately $9 per month up to sixteen or seventeen years of age was unsuitable for Canada. In her view, these measures flew in the face of all the opportunities available in Canada. Such allowances, she maintained, transferred to the taxpayer the burden, as well as the problem, of adequate wages and prices from where it belonged.

Whitton also considered the issue of direct cash grants untenable, since there were no adequate assurances that the state's investment would be used as intended. In Canada, such grants "could not, of themselves[,] assure wiser or more nutritional provision for the urban child, nor affect greatly the plight of the rural child. They would bring neither health nor educational services to the remote or undeveloped districts where they are most needed and where their establishment involves problems that it is just not within the power of parents or small groups of parents to meet of their own initiative and planning." She claimed that the amounts required from the government to maintain the allowances would be exorbitant, exceeding the expenditure on all forms of education in Canada. The administrative costs of children's allowances would absorb an undue portion of the government's provision for the allowances. Moreover, cancelling the income tax exemption for dependent children, which had been implemented when the Income War Tax Act was passed in 1917, would destroy what she described as the fine psychological value in the state's recognition of the parents' job in the home, and she urged the government to increase the tax exemption. She also believed that children could be better served by the strengthening and enlarging of social utilities for children through health services, better schools, higher salaries for elementary and secondary teachers, and more widely developed child care facilities, and child protection and training facilities. Instead of children's allowances, funds were better directed toward low-cost housing with preference given to young and large families.

However, Whitton was not completely opposed to the social insurance schemes Marsh had suggested. She argued that they were fundamental in any state, and especially in Canada. However, she disagreed with Marsh that such social assistance programs as unemployment assistance and children's allowances belonged under the authority of Ottawa. She believed such initiatives should remain with the provinces and municipalities, as was intended by the makers of Canada in 1867. She also advocated a dominion assistance and utilities fund for the provinces, financed by the consolidated revenue fund of the Dominion government, to provide the necessary resources to allow the provinces to subsidize the various social welfare programs.

Even though she supported such initiatives, Whitton's report was widely interpreted as a throwback to an earlier era; in the early 1940s, all but the most ardent conservatives eagerly embraced social security and welcomed it as an integral part of the dawning of a new age. Leonard Marsh recalled later that the social workers with the Canadian Welfare Council, for instance, were unhappy with Whitton's opposition to family allowances,[34] but (perhaps strangely) Whitton's opposition helped focus even greater attention on the issue at the time.

Even before the Marsh Report was released, D.H. Stepler had helped generate considerable interest in family allowances with a brief essay for *Behind the Headlines*, a series of pamphlets on current issues published jointly by the Canadian Institute of International Affairs and the Canadian Association for Adult Education. Like others, Stepler saw some form of family allowances as an appropriate way to deal with the problems of poverty, disease, and undernourishment among children. As others had argued for more than a generation, she maintained that the case for family allowances rested on several anomalies in the wage system. Wage rates were based on the payment for work performed, and did not consider the size of a man's family. The expenses of keeping a family were greatest when the children were young and dependent, and disappeared when they became self-supporting. Stepler reasoned that it was therefore incumbent on the state to provide a suitable environment for children. She cited studies – primarily British – that showed a correlation between poverty and the existence of disease, physical disability, and premature death in children. One British study found that the equivalent of one Canadian dollar for each child per week would have raised over 70% of the families from below the poverty line to a decent standard of living. Moreover, Stepler tried to dispel fears held in some quarters that low-income families – often referred to as undesirables – would produce more children if a system of family allowances were introduced. She maintained that this was not so, as such parents already produced all the children they could without having an adequate income to provide properly for them. Rather, family allowances might encourage the middle class to have more children, as those parents delayed having children until they could assure themselves of a decent standard of living. Stepler concluded that family allowances were an important part of the "universal crusade against disease and undernourishment" and "if Canada lags behind, it will be at the peril of her national existence."[35]

H.M. Cassidy also made a case for family allowances in *Social Security and Reconstruction in Canada,* which also appeared shortly before the Marsh Report. Cassidy found that the typical Canadian family of four required an income three times as great as that of a single person for a comparable standard of living, and very large families needed four or five times as much income as a single person. Yet, family income was derived from the earnings of the adult head (usually the father), and fathers were paid no more than single men for the same kind of work. There was no relationship between family income and needs; income per family member declined with an increase in the size of the family unit.[36] George F. Davidson of the Canadian Welfare Council, a close friend and colleague of Cassidy's, said in 1942 that "the adjustment of family income to family responsibilities must be made ... through a system of family allowances, supplementing wages earned with an allowance *as a matter of right, and not of need,* for every child in the family unit."[37] Davidson suggested that family allowances were destined to come to the forefront as Canada turned its attention to planning for social security. He had argued at the Lake Couchiching Conference in August of that year that family allowances were the "foundation stone of the edifice of social security" for Canada, and maintained that family allowances might be the only way to adjust family income to family responsibilities.[38]

Many others accepted his view. Margaret McWilliams, the chair of the Sub-committee on Post-war Problems of Women, had written Davidson on 30 March 1943, claiming that every member of her committee was "sold on the subject of family allowances as soon as possible." Even Davidson, who earlier in March had told Cassidy that he was not hopeful of any major initiatives in social welfare, had changed his mind and told McWilliams in mid-April that family allowances "might very well be put on the number one priority list." Davidson suggested they would help sustain the purchasing power of Canadians who were either released from the military or lost their jobs in war industries.[39] Martin Cohn, president of the CASW, and Elisabeth Wallace, executive secretary, wrote in the April 1943 issue of *Canadian Forum* that "family allowances ... would seem to be a necessity, if children are to cease to be one of the greatest causes of poverty, and are to take their rightful place as the country's greatest asset."[40]

It seemed to many observers that the government was moving further on social security than expected; the *Canadian Forum* had suggested earlier in January that the "old parties" would try hard to obscure the clamour for social security by reluctantly embracing some elements of Beveridge's social insurance program. "The [Beveridge] report may well become the price that Liberalism is willing to pay in order to avoid socialism."[41] Clearly the public discussion was having an impact: when Ian Mackenzie appeared before the House of Commons Special Select Committee on Social Security on 16 March 1943 to discuss the government's health insurance plan, he talked briefly about the importance of family allowances.[42] The Special Committee had been appointed by King on 8 March 1943, and Cyrus Macmillan, who had served on the 1929 Parliament committee investigating family allowances, was appointed the chair.

Even though the Marsh Report was merely a position paper by the James committee on reconstruction, and not official government policy, it had become clear early in 1943 to most inside and outside Ottawa that the King government was committed to a policy of social security. For instance, when R.B. Bryce, secretary of the Economic Advisory Council (EAC), produced a memorandum for W.C. Clark, the deputy minister of finance, suggesting what items should be included in a statement of postwar economic policy, he reminded him, "The government will endeavour to develop and broaden the social security system of Canada."[43] Young Bryce, who had studied with John Maynard Keynes at Cambridge University, was influential in disseminating Keynes' ideas of demand management in North America in the 1930s and early 1940s. Bryce knew that the Department of Finance would be receptive to a program of family allowances as a stimulus to the economy after the war, and he had already observed much earlier that the Canadian government would pursue a new social and economic philosophy after the war. On 27 January 1943, he had suggested to Dr. W.A. Mackintosh, Clark's special assistant, "It begins to look already as though we are in for some type of Beveridge plan."[44] Alex Skelton at the research branch of the Bank of Canada also realized the pressing demand for social security measures across Canada. However, like his colleagues in the Department of Finance and on the EAC, he believed that the best hope for economic security lay with full employment opportunities following the war. In an important policy statement that went through several stages of revisions by senior bureaucrats before it went to the Cabinet, Skelton outlined how economic security might be achieved. To him and others, it was clear that a part of the postwar period needed to include improvements in health and social security, which he believed would "be pressed forward as rapidly as conditions permit. The government will endeavour to develop and broaden the social security system in Canada."[45]

Yet King seems to have paid little attention to the Marsh Report, although he was fully aware of the excitement it had created. Certainly, some of King's ministers – and perhaps King as well – thought Marsh was closely aligned with the Co-operative Commonwealth Federation (CCF), but Ian Mackenzie tried to allay their fears. Mackenzie suggested that Marsh's cooperation with J.S. Woodsworth and others in the League for Social Reconstruction that had produced *Social Planning for Canada* in 1935 was the nature of work to which "any young man with idealistic leanings could easily be attracted." In the end, Mackenzie prevailed and Marsh was kept in Ottawa for a short time after completing his work for the James committee.[46] Still, King might have simply believed he really had no need for Marsh; after all, he himself was the expert on social security, and he maintained that he had seen years earlier the need for much of what Marsh and Beveridge were only now recommending. Even so, King continued to consider the issues as framed by Marsh.

At the same time that the nation was abuzz over the Marsh Report and family allowances, the King Cabinet was also wrestling with developing a new labour policy to deal with the increasing discontent among disgruntled workers throughout the summer of 1943, and struggling to maintain the government's wage stabilization policy that had been implemented early in the war as a means to control inflation. Senior civil servants picked up the transnational idea of family allowances and began to discuss the possibility of having the government introduce the program not simply as a social security measure but also as an alternative to wage increases for the growing number of disaffected workers whose wage rates were controlled by government agencies. The civil servants agreed that wage rates had to increase or some alternative had to be found to achieve the same ends. On 8 June 1943, Norman Robertson, the undersecretary of state for external affairs, wrote to Prime Minister King about the matter. Robertson indicated that he had attended a small meeting with Judge C.P. McTague of the National War Labour Board (NWLB), who was investigating labour conditions in Canada, and together they thought family allowances might meet the needs of workers who were demanding higher wages. It is noteworthy indeed that Robertson, who was among the most informed officials in Ottawa on contemporary debates on the international scene, would make this suggestion to King; it was further evidence that family allowances had become an important subject in international discourse. Robertson told King that family allowances were inevitable in the long run, and they would go a long way to meeting the current demand – both in Canada and internationally – for social justice. Even so, Robertson suggested that family allowances would not be sufficient to appease labour. The trade union representatives, he suggested, wanted collective bargaining for low-paid workers in the expectation that such a concession would enhance union organization in the industries where such people are employed. Still, he advised King, if the government put forward a balanced labour policy that combined family allowances with the new labour charter defining the rights and status of workers and their organizations, it would bring labour on board, and make possible the "establishment of national minimum standards of working conditions in Canada."[47] The NWLB later recommended the immediate introduction of family allowances as a means of maintaining the government's wage control legislation.

Senior government bureaucrats were fully aware that King had committed his government to fundamental social and economic change after the war, and they hoped they would be able to solve the crisis with labour by linking it with payments through social security.[48] From his vantage point as the governor of the Bank of Canada, Graham F. Towers was also able to monitor the machinations of senior mandarins as well as the workings of the King government with which he worked closely. In a June 1943 memorandum to W.C. Clark – a copy of which he also sent to the Honourable J.L. Ilsley, the minister of finance – he also suggested that children's allowances be introduced to allow the government to maintain its wage stabilization policy as an anti-inflationary measure. Towers feared that if the NWLB endorsed the proposal before it to remove the ceiling on wage rates and allow free collective bargaining on rates of up to 50 cents an hour, the board could not possibly prevent similar increases in the wages of those already receiving more than the 50 cents minimum; labour groups would argue that the existing differential in wages between skilled and unskilled had to be maintained. If wages were permitted to rise, then the whole price and wage stabilization program to control inflation would come unravelled. Moreover, according to Towers, unrestricted wage bargaining would result in increased unionization and considerable industrial strife that would negatively impact essential war industries. "Children's allowances are the most direct and economic method of meeting the current strong demand for relaxation of wage control in respect of the lower wage rates," Towers suggested. He reminded Clark that the government was determined to introduce a "reasonable minimum of [social] security after the war," and while he would have preferred to see family allowances introduced then, he realized that this particular social security measure would meet the "legitimate needs" of labour by placing more money in the hands of workers while allowing the government to keep the rate of inflation under control. Towers, quoting extensively from the Beveridge Report, further maintained that children's allowances were an indispensable part of any large-scale social security program.[49]

Towers later told the Annual Meeting of the Canadian Manufacturers Association that the government's most important objective for the postwar period was to ensure reasonable living standards for everyone. He hoped that private business would do the job, but if not then government would have to accept responsibility.[50] The principle of children's allowances, he pointed out, was not new or revolutionary; the government was already paying an allowance of $108 for each child in the form of an income tax credit to wage earners. Those who earned more than $1,200 per year received the credit; those who earned less than that threshold, and desperately needed the assistance, did not get it. Family allowances, he added, deserved a higher priority than old age pensions because "children are even more helpless than old people, and money spent to ensure children's minimum health and education needs are more likely to be a productive national investment." Like Robertson, Towers also suggested that the introduction of family allowances would enhance Canada's prestige internationally as well as safeguard its economy at home. Moreover, he saw a further advantage to be gained by Canada's adoption of family allowances: Canadian wartime controls had become an example to those in the United States who wanted to control inflation, he told Clark, and children's allowances "would be striking proof that Canada intended to push ahead with progressive policies after the war." It could have "appreciable influence in strengthening the hand of like-minded administrations in other countries."[51]

In the meantime, senior officials in the Department of Finance prepared a series of memoranda on family allowances. One of the first was prepared on 21 June. After reviewing the case for family allowances as an anti-inflation device, and examining the various reports that had recommended family allowances, the lengthy memorandum turned to some of the administrative and political problems the government might encounter if such a program were implemented. First, it warned that even though the federal government could implement family allowances as a wartime measure, there might be constitutional problems in the postwar period over the allocation of responsibility for the social security measure. A more pressing and immediate problem was one of obtaining reliable and efficient administrative staff to oversee the program during the war. The memorandum suggested that staff at the Dependents' Allowances Board, which administered the affairs of dependants of members of the Canadian Armed Forces, might be used. Another option suggested the establishment of a new federal department responsible for social insurance and family allowances. This department would then rely on local welfare departments to determine eligibility and investigate reported abuses of the program.[52]

The memorandum noted that the government could also expect family allowances to create controversies of the worst sort: those of region and race. It warned that there was a strong possibility of cleavage based on regional and racial jealousies, and that English Canada might object to family allowances because it would appear to favour French Canada, where large families were more common. There was a fear among English Canadians that French Canada, with its high birth rate, threatened future domination of the country, a threat

that could spawn an "emotional reaction" given Quebec's opposition to conscription for overseas military service. Quebec had nearly 33% of the nation's
children, but only 29% of the total population. The ethnic argument might be
exacerbated, the memorandum noted, by the fact that in the rural areas of
western Canada, particularly in Saskatchewan, the birth rate of Canadians of
non-Anglo-Saxon extraction (particularly Ukrainians) exceeded that of English
Canadians. Still, the departmental memorandum noted that most authorities
maintained that there was no reason to believe that allowances would encourage a higher birth rate in Quebec where it was very high already. Rather, allowances were more likely to encourage earlier marriages and more births among
the English-speaking population, which had accepted family limitations when
there was insufficient income for the rearing of children.[53] Perhaps the memorandum's author did not realize the racist overtones of such comments, but
this line of reasoning was often attributed to Lord Beveridge, who claimed in
his report (as well as in many public utterances) that there were many parents
who wanted to have more than one or two children but chose not to out of
"fear of damaging the prospects of their children already born." Beveridge believed that children's allowances would make it easier for those parents to have
additional children.[54]

The discussion of family allowances also created considerable interest and
debate in other official circles in Ottawa during June and July 1943, as demonstrated by the memorandum from H.R. Kemp to Donald Gordon. Then at the
Wartime Prices and Trade Board (WPTB), Kemp was a former economics
professor at McMaster University who had served as a researcher with Clark
and a consultant to former Prime Minister R.B. Bennett. He later joined Gordon
at the WPTB, and wrote a lengthy memorandum that emphasized the need for
adequate preparation before the government committed itself to providing
family allowances. Gordon sent Kemp's memo to Towers, who had R.B. Beattie,
an economist at the Bank of Canada, prepare a response. Towers sent both
Kemp's memo and the response to Clark. Kemp pointed out that the government needed to consider a number of political, economic, and administrative
aspects of the scheme before it committed itself to the principle of universal
family allowances. He also wondered what impact a state-funded monthly cash
payment for family support would have and how the other political parties
would react to such a government initiative. Moreover, how would the state
decide on the appropriate allowance for each child and at what income level
should the taxpayer receive from the state more than he pays in taxes? Also, who
was entitled to receive the allowance, the mother or the father? Finally, Kemp
warned that organized labour, while interested in the economic conditions of
the low-paid workers, would regard family allowances as an act of paternalism,

and such a measure would do little to satisfy its demand for collective bargaining.[55] An earlier memorandum had warned that trade unions would likely oppose any form of family allowance unless it was paid in kind because they believed it would hinder negotiations for wage increases. Still, in Australia and New Zealand minimum wages had continued to rise since the introduction of family allowances.[56]

Beattie responded to each point Kemp raised, offering an impassioned defence of family allowances. Canadians would not see family allowances as a political bribe, he claimed, since it was unlikely any political party or politician would publicly oppose the measure. All children would have to be covered since the first child often presents the greatest expense to the family and the allowances would be paid to mothers because they had primary responsibility for the children in Canadian society. He agreed that unions might be opposed because family allowances would detract from the force of their arguments for better wages, but the government must be concerned not with assisting union organization but with improving the "interests of the most defenceless groups in the community."[57]

The mandarins in the powerful EAC were convinced of the efficacy of family allowances as a way to reconcile the wage stabilization program with the growing demands of labour. R.B. Bryce, who penned the EAC memorandum on the thorny issue of labour, claimed that the price and wage stabilization policies had to be changed to address the difficulties confronting labour while maintaining the effectiveness of the government's policy. If labour were permitted to bargain for and obtain wage increases of up to 50 cents an hour, it would precipitate an increase in the prices of civilian goods, which would then lead to an increase in the cost of living bonus and subsequently to further increases in costs and prices. After reviewing several options, Bryce concluded that "no possible reconciliation can be found between maintaining the price ceiling and permitting general increases in wages below any specified figure that would be tolerable to labour." However, there was a suitable alternative that would be popular with the general populace and with farmers and labour and, at the same time, it would be an important and well-timed step forward in social security. Hence, in a draft memorandum first circulated on 7 July 1943, the EAC proposed that Canada *immediately* create a nationwide system of family allowances *to come into effect in January 1944*. Bryce noted that children's allowances were "widely recognized as an important element in modern systems of social security; they [were] in effect already in Australia and New Zealand and they [had] been recommended for Britain." In his memorandum to the prime minister, who he knew was sympathetic to family allowances, Bryce noted that the introduction of such a policy as a wartime measure "would be the most convincing possible evidence of the government's intention to proceed with progressive measures. This in itself would gain much support for the policy from labour." However, some EAC members argued that family allowances should be introduced only as a part of a postwar social security program. Still, the EAC saw family allowances as only one part of the solution. It also urged the government to consider compulsory collective bargaining, to promote the use of an incentive wage system, to more effectively use the existing cost of living bonuses, to change the rules to allow the Regional War Labour Boards to handle regional labour issues, and to undertake a campaign to educate the public regarding the government's wage and price stabilization policies.[58] Even so, W.A. Mackintosh, the vice-chair of the EAC, wrote later in November as part of his committee's review of the recommendations of the Report on Reconstruction that the EAC had "not undertaken any work towards the formulation of concrete measures" since it had not received "any direction" from the government despite its earlier reports in June and July.[59]

When the NWLB completed its public enquiry and on 19 August 1943 issued the majority report known as the McTague Report, after the board chair, it agreed that labour did not "understand or fully appreciate" government policy on price control and wage stabilization. McTague laid much of the blame on the government itself for its failure to dispel the notion that the "sacrifice imposed upon [labour] is disproportionate," and recommended that the government remove wage controls and allow wages to rise so wage earners could provide for their families. As had been anticipated by senior officials in government, the McTague Report rather tentatively suggested that Ottawa might implement a system of family allowances for heads of family with children below the age of sixteen years to deal with the demands for wage increases. However, a careful reading of the report shows that McTague was at best lukewarm toward using family allowances as part of a wage control policy. He clearly and unequivocally stated, "We prefer that workers earning less than 50¢ per hour or less should be left free to bargain without controls." However, he wrote – perhaps as a sop to senior government officials such as Clark – "if such a recommendation would, in the opinion of the government's financial advisers, place too great a burden on the price ceiling, we recommend in the alternative a system of family allowances."[60]

It did not take long for the press to learn of the family allowances discussion in government. While there was much praise for the measure, there was almost universal condemnation for any attempt by the government to link family allowances with the wage stabilization policy. Of course, much of the labour movement continued to voice its opposition to the measure, but the Confédération des travailleurs catholiques du Canada unanimously passed a resolution in support of family allowances at its annual convention in September 1943. However, at its annual meeting in September 1943, the Canadian Congress of Labour passed a resolution instructing the incoming executive committee "to protest vigorously against this proposal [for family allowances], and to take whatever action is necessary to prevent its adoption."[61] Organized labour's representative on the NWLB, J.L. Cohen, had issued a minority report into the cause of labour unrest and argued against the use of family allowances to support wages. He warned the government that labour would never accept such an arrangement. J.W. Buckley, the vice-president of the Trades and Labour Congress, wrote the *Toronto Daily Star* that his union opposed family allowances, and that it had never asked for them. "We are not looking for dole to supplement wages," he wrote, but merely for a decent wage that would allow workers to support their families in decency. The *Toronto Daily Star* agreed and wrote in a lead editorial that same day that "family allowances should not be a substitute for wage increases where they are justified." Still, it supported the notion of family allowances as a social security measure to maintain a "minimum of subsistence."[62]

The discussion in King's Cabinet revolved around how best to develop a new labour policy that would appease workers and allow the government to control wage rates and the cost of living. Some of the senior bureaucrats assumed that the principle of family allowances had been accepted by the government,[63] but in the Cabinet there was considerable debate among the ministers on whether wage controls could be maintained by paying allowances to families, thus avoiding the need to raise wages. The Cabinet considered the Memorandum on the War Labour Reports that Clark had submitted from the EAC. In its memo, the EAC said that "family allowances ought not to be specifically related to wage control," even though it realized that a system of family allowances as an instalment of a general social security program would have great merit and some particular advantages in the circumstances of war. Still, Clark reported to Cabinet the division over the issue within the EAC: some members of the EAC wanted to link family allowances to the wage stabilization policy, but others, particularly those with the Department of Labour, insisted that children's allowances must not be considered in light of the wage control problems.[64] Clark said that the matter was one for the Cabinet to decide, "[since] the conclusion reached depends on judgment as to popular response to such a policy which the Government is more skilled in exercising than are officials."[65] King listened to the arguments, but he took every opportunity in the debate to cast family allowances as a social security matter, separate from wage rates. He later confided to his diary, "I found the sentiment of Cabinet swinging towards that course [subsidies to large families], on which I think a real policy may be founded for dealing with social security measures."[66] Later, Thomas Crerar, the minister of mines and resources, wrote King that it would be a mistake for the government to mix up the issue of family allowances with the matter of wages since the "principle of paying family allowances ... should come under the heading of social security measures."[67] Bryce had written in a 17 September memorandum that a "family allowance plan [was] desirable in itself as a permanent, important social security measure."[68]

Some Canadian academics have argued that there was a direct link between the introduction of family allowances and the government's desire to retain wage controls.[69] However, that connection has been overstated despite the discussion going on within the various government departments. It is also worth pointing out that there was a debate within the government at the same time over how it might best achieve its promise to Canadians to provide a better system of social security for the postwar period. It is true as the *Financial Post* and other newspapers had reported in late September 1943 that the civil servants in the federal government had contemplated the introduction of family allowances as an anti-inflationary measure based on the recommendations of the McTague Report. However, much of the editorial comment welcomed family allowances, but all of it warned the government that the program must not be linked to the issue of wages. The view of the *Toronto Star* on 22 September 1943 illustrates that held by many editorial writers across Canada: "It [family allowance] is a form of state aid for the maintenance of dependent children and as such has no relation to the source of income or the condition under which it is obtained." In a remarkably accurate story a day later, the Montreal *Gazette* reported that despite the earlier discussion in King's Cabinet about introducing family allowances as part of the wage stabilization program, it was leaning toward making family allowances an "essential and indeed fundamental" part of the social security program it had promised in the 1943 Speech from the Throne. Many of the same newspapers, including the *Financial Post*, reported on 9 October that "the possibility of any immediate payment of family allowances has apparently been vetoed by the Cabinet as administratively impractical and politically unwise at the present time." The *Post* suggested that the whole question of family allowances should be considered by a royal commission with a mandate to examine postwar social security possibilities. M.J. Coldwell, the leader of the CCF, was clearly disappointed with the delay. He issued a statement on 14 October criticizing the Liberals for abandoning family allowances, although he insisted that the movement toward any such program must not be linked to wages.[70]

When King announced in a radio broadcast on 4 December 1943 the government's new labour policy to deal with worker unrest in Canada, the implementation of family allowances was still a full nineteen months away. Yet virtually all of the Canadian social scientists who have mentioned family allowances in their studies of social policy have made a direct connection between the government's new labour policy and the introduction of family allowances. One of the most quoted essays that makes such a connection is Brigitte Kitchen's, which points out that King did not mention family allowances in his December address to the nation: "To have acted differently," she contends, "would have left Mackenzie King and his Cabinet open to attack that family allowances had been deliberately chosen as a device for the protection of the government's wage and price stabilization policy. It would also have meant that family allowances would have inevitably and possibly forever been associated with low wage levels."[71] As I noted above, McTague and some civil servants in the government had connected the payment of family allowance to the maintenance of the government's wage stabilization plan, and there had been considerable discussion of the two issues within the government, but King had insisted throughout the discussion that family allowances were a part of his social security pledge. The reason he did not mention family allowances in his December speech was simply because the Cabinet had not made a decision about the program and would not do so until early 1944. Kitchen's contention is mere speculation; she did not provide any archival evidence to support her assertion. Even so, it has been repeated in many articles. Indeed, the Cabinet had not even begun its discussion on family allowances when the labour policy was adopted; they turned to the subject only at the beginning of January 1944, nearly a month after King announced his new labour policy.

Further, a promise to labour in December 1943 to enact family allowances sometime after July 1945 – nearly two years hence – would do little in the short term to make wage controls more palatable to workers who were becoming increasingly angry with King. It also seems somewhat naive to think that the government would respond to what everyone realized was a short-term problem with labour by committing itself to annually spending between $180 million and $200 million dollars – the anticipated costs of family allowances – when it could offer workers other forms of direct payment such as the cost of living bonuses and wage incentives the McTague Report had indeed suggested. King wrote in his diary that in the Cabinet discussion on the wage stabilization process, "McTague was most emphatic about not allowing any discussion of family allowances to become a part of the labour policy." We must remember as well that the King government did not accept deficit financing and Keynesian macro-economic management until after the war in 1945, and the conservative King had told the Cabinet during the discussion on the price and wage stabilization policy that "to tell the country that everyone was to get a family allowance was sheer folly; it would occasion resent everywhere. Great care has to be taken in any monies given out from the Treasury as distinguished from exempting portions of income already earned."[72] We must not forget that Keynes himself noted in *The General Theory of Employment, Interest, and Money* that government spending could certainly be used to stimulate the economy, but if prices became too inflationary, the government had to limit its expenditure and cut back on its economic stimulus. Being a skilled political leader, King must certainly have realized that eliminating such an economic stimulus as family allowance benefits once they had been introduced would be suicide for his party, even if many Canadians were still wary of such government spending. When the Canadian Institute of Public Opinion ran its survey on 21 October 1943 and asked respondents their view on the government paying an allowance of $9 for all children from all income groups (the proposal most often reported in the newspapers), 49% said it was a good idea, 42% a poor idea, and 9% were undecided.[73]

Still, labour had legitimate grievances to be addressed. Throughout the fall of 1943, the Cabinet wrestled with how best to do that. In the end, to appease labour and to stand firm against the threat of inflation, the government decided to amend the wage control policy, implement a new code of labour relations, and establish a price floor for major farm commodities. The cost of living bonuses that had been implemented earlier in the war for war industries were incorporated into the basic wage rates, which in effect resulted in an overall wage increase. The government also promised that if the cost of living rose above 3% for two consecutive months, it would review the whole program of price and wage control and take appropriate action to deal with the problem. Moreover, the NWLB was instructed to remove gross inequalities in wages when it examined applications for wage increases. The most important gain for labour was to restrict the power and authority of management and legitimatize the role of labour. King did this not by promising family allowances but by promising a new order that recognized labour unions and made compulsory collective bargaining legally binding in all collective agreements. King also promised that unfair labour practices would be routed out and remedies provided.[74] This was a new code of labour relations for war industries, King told the nation in his radio broadcast billed as "The Fight against Inflation." King believed that the new cost of living bonus meant a "permanent rise in the standard of labour for a time to come." And he saw the radio broadcast as an opportunity to reassure Canadians that his government was developing new policies. In the postwar period these would assure farmers of a floor for farm prices and establish a national minimum standard of living for all Canadians through postwar social security and human welfare policies. After the broadcast, King wrote in his diary that he "went a long way in stating government policy without further consultation with the Cabinet." Such policies, he hoped, "[would] also improve the lot of hundreds of thousands of farmers and working people from one end of Canada to the other. [They] dealt [a] strong blow for the living standards of the masses of people from coast to coast." Always with an eye to the party's political fortunes, King also wrote, "I think I have cut out the ground in large part from under the CCF and Tories alike and certainly have given the Liberal Party a place of new beginning, if we will only follow up with effective organization."[75] George Davidson, the respected executive director of the Canadian Welfare Council, had told the Honourable Cyrus MacMillan, the chair of the parliamentary Social Security Committee, that even if minimum wage levels rose, they would be hardly high enough to meet the needs of every family unit; hence, family allowances would still be necessary to assist many families.[76] King believed that, too.

In the meantime, though, Bryce, Mackintosh, and a few other officials in the Department of Finance had already begun to prepare a series of memoranda on family allowances. Clark had asked Mackintosh on 30 November 1943 to examine various plans and the anticipated cost of each. At this point, department officials assumed that the principle of family allowances had been accepted, and over the ensuing few weeks they produced an incredible volume of paper for consideration. They made it clear that a state-run, non-contributory scheme was preferable since it was administratively easiest and would be the most effective in getting money into the hands of all Canadians. Organized labour would be less likely to oppose this approach and such a scheme "would be more likely to strike the public imagination as a bold act of social justice, as some counter-weight to the hardships of war privations, and as a signal of the national interest in children, than would any other." Moreover, the payments would be in cash rather than in-kind since the former was quick and efficient. Also, the officials recommended that if the objective of the program was to provide a national minimum of subsistence for all children, then payment should be made for all children, regardless of income levels and whether or not parents were wage earners.[77]

However, the Department of Finance made it clear that the actual cash payments for family allowances had to be calculated on the basis of what the nation as a whole could, or thought it could, afford rather than on what was necessary for parents to maintain their children. There were many alternative arrangements for paying benefits, and the department was of the view that there was no single model it could look to in determining the size of payment. There was considerable discussion over whether or not the first child should receive a family allowance or whether benefits should be given only after the birth of a second child. If $213 million were set aside for the program, it would support a payment of $5 to each child, but $8 if the first child were excluded. The Department of Finance recommended that all children be included, but noted that if the government wished to reduce its expenditure on family allowances, the first child should be excluded rather than the whole scale of allowances reduced. Likewise, the officials considered the implications of graduating the payment upward, according to the age of the children, and recommended that higher allowances be paid for older children because of the higher costs for their maintenance. The department was clear, however, when it came to the age limit: family allowances should be available to children only until they reached the school-leaving age, which was sixteen in most provinces. The department realized that this stipulation would give incentive to parents to keep their children in school and encourage all the provinces to raise their school-leaving age to sixteen. It suggested the following allowances:

For ages 0 to 5 years	$5 per month
For ages 6 to 9 years	$6 per month
For ages 10 to 12 years	$7 per month
For ages 13 to 15 years	$8 per month

The Department of Finance also suggested that the basic rates be reduced by $1 for the fifth and each subsequent child in the family. And, of course, the department recommended that the income tax exemption for children be eliminated when family allowances were introduced; this would save the Treasury about $75 million. Still, the net cost to the government would be about $200 million.[78] All this information was passed to Clark on 6-7 January 1943.

Meanwhile, Mackenzie King and the Liberal Party were growing worried about the increasing popularity of the opposition parties, both of which seemed to be attracting considerable popular support and threatening to outflank the Liberals with their emphasis on social security. Much ink has been consumed over the years by historians and others who have claimed that it was only when the CCF slipped past the Liberals in a 1943 public opinion poll and won four federal by-elections in Western Canada in 1942 and 1943 did the King Liberals rush to embrace new policies such as family allowances and other social security measures. The analysis above does not bear this out. The Liberals and the Conservatives (who had become the Progressive Conservatives in 1942 to reflect their new and progressive policies) embraced new ideas and adopted new policies not because the CCF in Canada had done so[79] but because new ideas and policies had been pushed to the forefront by the growing national and international interest in the ideas of social security and other policies during the Second World War. Even if the CCF was the first political party in Canada to adopt social security as part of its platform, other parties soon followed. The proposal for family allowances was not necessarily connected with socialism; in countries that had enacted a program of family allowances, the governments had varied from conservative (as in New Zealand and Australia) to totalitarian (as in Japan, Italy, and Germany). In addition, the ideas of family allowances and social security did not emerge from within the CCF. Both Mackenzie King and John Bracken, the Progressive Conservative leader, were well aware of the discussions within Canada and internationally, and had come to realize that it was in the interests of society that all citizens be provided with a minimum standard of living. That the CCF or its gain in public support should be credited with providing the impetus for family allowances ignores the fact that Canada often followed the lead of the United States and Britain, the world's two great democracies, in completing major reports on social security in late 1942 and early 1943. All three nations (as well as others) seemed to be moving forward together in considering greater social security measures.[80]

The Liberals were worried about the political successes of the CCF in the early 1940s, but clearly the extent of the threat has been exaggerated by scholars. Walter Young and Reginald Whitaker, for instance, have argued that because there was a massive shift of public opinion from the left, the CCF was a credible challenger for national power.[81] The CCF had won less than 9% of the popular vote in each of the two previous national elections and only seven and eight seats, respectively, in 1935 and 1940. When the Ontario Liberals were defeated by George Drew's Conservatives on a progressive platform in August 1943, the CCF became the official opposition; the Liberals placed third. Subsequently, the Liberals lost four federal by-elections, two to the CCF, one to the Bloc populaire canadien, and one to the Communists. "In my heart," King said, "I am not sorry to see the mass of people coming a little more into their own but I do regret that it is not the Liberal Party that is winning the position for them. It should be and still can be that our people will learn their lesson in time."[82] For King, the setbacks came from the lack of party organization, not government policy. Yet not even he could ignore the fact that both the CCF and the Conservatives had included social security as part of their platform. The *CCF Program for Reconstruction*, which was announced in July 1942, promised a program of "adequate" social security "not only to increase the health and efficiency of the population, but also to distribute income to low earning groups."

Included in the policy statement was a commitment to provide children's allowances.[83] It is important to note, however, that children's allowances were not the party's primary proposal in order to achieve social justice and promote social security; rather, it called first for the establishment of decent minimum wage levels.

Similarly, the Progressive Conservatives also embraced social security as one of their main aims for the postwar period. In its policy statement adopted at the national convention in Winnipeg in December 1942, the party embraced the idea of "Freedom from Want" that had become a popular issue among the Allied nations. "Freedom will be a reality when social security and human welfare become a fundamental objective of the nation," the policy statement promised. "Freedom from want and freedom from fear are essential to a happy and normal family life. Want and fear must be banished and security brought within reach of all Canadians." While the Conservatives did not promise family allowances specifically, they embraced a program that would assure Canadians of a "reasonable standard of social and economic security."[84] Within the Conservative Party, there was considerable pressure for policy reform. J.M. Macdonnell, the vice-president of National Trust, and other prominent Conservatives arranged to have the party's policy discussed at Port Hope in September 1942. They hoped to move the "progressive" elements of the party to accept the "concepts of state intervention and planning that were common to both the CCF and, increasingly, the Liberal government in Ottawa." The Port Hope conference pushed for improved labour relations, housing programs, and other social security measures, which were adopted at the Conservative convention a few months later.[85] It was the Progressive Conservatives the Liberals feared more than the CCF, and in the 1945 election, the Tories cut into King's majority government by winning 66 seats. The CCF captured 28 seats, but 18 of them came from Saskatchewan where Tommy Douglas has led the party to victory in 1944.

To reassert the progressive nature of King liberalism and to garner lost support, the National Liberal Federation convened in late September 1943 and outlined its platform for the postwar period. Whitaker sees this as simply another instance of King co-opting and absorbing ideas from the political left.[86] However, Whitaker fails to recognize that both the Liberals and the Progressive Conservatives rode the wage of social reform in the latter years of the war. Also, these ideas were not confined to Canada; they had captivated much of the Western world. When Liberals from across Canada met in 1943, they agreed on the necessity of a program of social security, noting that social security and national prosperity were indivisible, and recommended children's allowances as one of the major planks in its social security program because they would contribute to a healthy nation with good family life and adequate support of raising children.[87] This was a program that would not radically alter Canada and the prevailing capitalist system.

Brooke Claxton, one of the rising stars in the Liberal caucus and King's parliamentary assistant, complained to the prime minister that the Liberal government was not doing enough to promote its accomplishments and new policies.[88] In June 1943, he had crafted a memorandum for King strongly urging him to set out the government's intentions for a new national policy based on ideas coming out of the James and Mackintosh committees as well as the several parliamentary committees. He also attached a memo prepared in April 1943 that showed that 45% of the respondents surveyed by the War Information Board said they wanted to know more about the government's plans for the postwar period. The board noted in its memo that of the hundreds of Canadians interviewed, "almost all [were] concerned with social security, the abolition of unemployment and equality of opportunity for all."[89] In a separate note to the prime minister, A.D.P. Heeney, the clerk of the Privy Council, supported Claxton's argument, and told King, "Claxton's report illustrates very clearly the need of early action."[90] A short time later, when Leonard Marsh appeared before the Senate Special Committee on Economic Re-establishment and Social Security, he reminded senators that social security must be considered – and was being considered – in the midst of the war because such policies boosted the morale of both soldiers and civilians, and they would help win the war. "People on the home front, and certainly people in uniform," he said, "are very much concerned about the way things go when the war is actually over."[91] Cyril James also told King, when he submitted the Final Report of the Advisory Committee on Reconstruction to the government on 24 September 1943, that he should give immediate consideration to social security if the government intended to adopt a realistic approach to postwar reconstruction. While James offered his unequivocal support for a system of family allowances, he reminded King that it would be partial and inadequate planning to institute children's allowances without considering other programs for children such as medical care, educational facilities, and nutritional services.[92]

When the National Liberal Federation met in convention in Ottawa later in September 1943, it was apparent to King that the party had to make social security one of its primary concerns, though not, of course, because his party was not already committed to social security; in King's mind, clearly it was committed, as indicated by the 1943 Speech from the Throne and a variety of earlier Liberal policies, ranging from old-age pensions to unemployment insurance. Still, Canadians needed to be reminded again of the "task of Liberalism." When King spoke at the convention, he told delegates, "The task of Liberalism will not

FIGURE 3   Brooke Claxton (1898-1960), a veteran of the First World
War, was appointed the first federal minister of health and welfare.
*Library and Archives Canada, E. Brooke Claxton fonds, C-071165, reprinted
with permission*

be finished when the war is won. That great moment will but mark a place of
new beginning. The future of the Liberal party will not be found in defending
the privileges of the few or in arousing the prejudices of the many ... In meeting
the problems of the post-war period, the task of Liberalism will remain the
preservation and extension of freedom."[93] The party reaffirmed its commitment
to social security, and recommended that the government consider a program
of children's allowances to provide adequate support to the upbringing of children and for the maintenance of family life. The party claimed that it "recognized
that the family and the home are the basis of national life, and [it would] seek

to promote conditions to [sic] which the family will be secure and have a decent home." To that end, it promised a national scheme of social insurance that would offer protection against the social problems resulting from unemployment, accident, ill-health, old age, and blindness.[94] Liberals left the convention confident that their political agenda – just like that of the CCF and the Progressive Conservatives – finally included social security measures. King felt confident that both the party and the government "had the right principles and policies and the best of records on which to win [the next election]," but he continued to be disturbed about the poor state of the party's organization.[95]

King saw family allowances as one of the most important items on the legislative agenda as his Cabinet prepared for the 1944 parliamentary session.[96] He was committed to a program of social security, and continued to believe that family allowances for larger families went "to the very root of social security in relation to the new order of things which places a responsibility on the State for conditions which the State itself is responsible for creating."[97] And of course King was aware that the latest statistics showed the terrible plight of children in Canada: far too many of them died before reaching their first birthday. In 1941, sixty out of every one thousand babies born alive died before the age of one.[98] Statistics also suggested that nearly one-third of Canadian children were born into families in which the family income was insufficient to adequately clothe and nourish them. A 1943 government report found that Canada had more than half a million undernourished children.[99] Dr. George Weir of the Department of Pensions and Health prepared a report on the connection between social security and liberalism for Ian Mackenzie, who passed it to the prime minister. In his wide-ranging treatise, Dr. Weir stressed the importance of the family and the home in safeguarding the social order and attaining higher moral and economic levels in Canada. "The stability of the family," he argued, "is an indispensable condition to the stability and general welfare of our civilization." And social security, especially family allowances, he told Mackenzie, will "buttress the stability of the home."[100]

King also saw family allowances as a way to emphasize the centrality of the family and family life, which had been terribly disrupted during the war.[101] Although King feared that the debate on family allowances would create great diversity within the Cabinet, he saw the issue as one on which he could leave his distinctive stamp. After all, when he visited Canada in 1943, Sir William Beveridge had told King that family allowances were the most revolutionary item in his entire report.[102] Despite his usually cautious nature, King continued to see himself as a progressive reformer, and he believed the time was right to demonstrate his reform and progressive tendencies.

The recent literature that offers a gendered analysis of Canada's social welfare does not see much progress in King's family allowance program; rather, it finds that the program perpetuated the traditional place of women in Canadian society,[103] and argues that gender is crucial to understanding the origins and development of social welfare in Canada. Many earlier scholars failed to find a role for gender since the various archival records of government departments dealing with such programs as unemployment insurance and family allowances did not include any lengthy consideration of gender. As Ruth Roach Pierson points out in an essay on unemployment insurance, just because the discussion around the origins of social programs within government in the early 1940s did not discuss women, it does not mean that gender was not an important fact contributing to how particular programs were designed. It is worth quoting Pierson at length:

> But if we understand gender to be a fundamental social category, we are justified in asking where and how concern for women fit into the Depression-era discussion of unemployment insurance. And if we further understand gender to be relational, to be a category comprising all that which shapes social relations between the sexes, then we are justified in examining the gender implication for women of the silences regarding them; that is, of the measures that made no mention of them, of the concepts into which they were invisibly enfolded, and of the assumptions through which masculine priority was inscribed.[104]

Clearly, King and his government saw the Canadian family as one with a male breadwinner and a stay-at-home mother, and it is that particular model of the family the government was to strengthen. Some scholars have also argued that one of the government's primary reasons for the payment of family allowances to mothers was to ease and encourage the transition of women back into the home after several years in the workplace.[105] However, as Nancy Christie has noted, there was no campaign among men during the Second World War to relegate women back to the domestic sphere.[106] The available evidence from wartime employment statistics suggested that most married women engaged in wartime economy planned to return home with the arrival of peace, and many of the female commentators continued to support the traditional view of the family with its male breadwinner supporting his dependent children and his spouse.[107] Of the many memoranda and discussion papers considered for this book, particularly within the Department of Finance, this issue appears to be one on which the officials were silent; however, as Pierson reminds us, silence cannot necessarily be taken to mean that they did not see a particular role for women in the postwar period even if the role of women was not discussed. Women's groups did support family allowances, since they believed that there should be state support for raising children and some recognition of the work women did for their families.[108] One of the few references to the connection between women and family allowances is found in the Final Report of the Subcommittee on the Post-war Problems of Women of the Advisory Committee on Reconstruction. When the report was released on 30 November 1943, Mrs. R.F. McWilliams, the chair of the subcommittee, noted that they supported family allowances as a social security measure, but suggested as well that there was a "psychological factor" that added "value" to the implementation of family allowances in the postwar period: "As we have already pointed out, a considerable proportion of the women who have been doing war work plan to return to the life of homemaker. They have been earning their own money, much of which has been spent on their homes and their children. The addition to the family income from children' allowances paid to the mother and spent by her for the welfare of her children may well be an alleviating factor in the mental attitude which may result from the surrender of the double income."[109] Which parent received the benefits became an issue for the officials and politicians. They certainly knew that in France, for instance, payments were made to women to distinguish family allowances from wage rates and in the belief that women were more likely than men to spend the benefits for the family.

Throughout the early 1940s, Canadians expressed a strong demand for progressive government, one that was less inclined to leave the fate of their country to the mercies of the unregulated free enterprise system after the war. This view was evident in the commentary and reporting in the major newspapers and magazines of the period; Martin Cohn and Elisabeth Wallace noted this trend in an opinion piece for the April 1943 issue of *Canadian Forum:* "Social Security is, with just cause, a popular slogan ... and good propaganda. A constructive welfare program is of cardinal importance to any party interested in the fundamentals of good government, and not least to a socialist party." The political parties also competed with each other to present progressive measures for the postwar period in the fields of social security and rehabilitation of service personnel, and in promising full employment. These ideas had now clearly become mainstream in Canada, and the Canadian government also seems to have embraced the ideas about social security as the other Allied countries had. This acceptance was further reflected in the attitudes and ideas expressed by many of King's ministers; Ian Mackenzie was the best example, but there were others who shared similar views. In November 1943, King asked his Cabinet for their suggestions on policies for postwar reconstruction, and canvassed them directly on family allowances.[110] Of those that responded, all but C.D. Howe suggested that the government pursue family allowances. Louis St. Laurent, rapidly becoming one of King's favourites, told the prime minister that family allowances were the most important of all social security measures contemplated. Finance Minister J.L. Ilsley did not reply to the prime minister until 4 January 1944, but he suggested that Canada establish a minimum of social security legislation and urged that Cabinet approve the principle of family allowances; it was on Ilsley's recommendation that King decided to bring the matter of family allowances to Cabinet.[111] Only C.D. Howe wrote that he opposed family allowances, claiming they would "encourage idleness and thus defeat our objective of maintaining production at its present level."[112]

The Cabinet turned to family allowances on 6 January 1944 as part of its larger discussion on postwar social security, what King described as "help to those who are unable to help themselves."[113] Within a few days, the Cabinet had agreed to establish three new government departments – Veterans Affairs, Reconstruction, and National Health and Welfare – but family allowances remained a controversial issue. A week later, King decided he wanted the matter settled. Of the Cabinet meeting on 13 January, King later declared, "[It was] one of the most impressive and significant of any I have attended ... I had let it be understood we would settle the Government's policy on Family Allowances which goes to the very root of social security in relation to the new order of things which places a responsibility on the state for conditions which the state itself is responsible for creating."[114] Ilsley, who had to leave for Toronto before the discussion got underway, had asked that W.C. Clark, the deputy minister of finance, present the case for family allowance.

When the seventeen ministers present on 13 January had taken their seats, King asked Clark to explain why the Department of Finance had come to hold the view it had on family allowances. In his presentation for Ilsley, Clark asserted the social claim for family allowances that had been made by proponents of the scheme since it was first raised in the late 1920s: that the wage system took no account of the size of the family and many workers were therefore unable to provide sufficiently for their families. Family allowances, he told the Cabinet, represented by far the simplest, wisest, and cheapest way of recognizing the fact that families with children had additional needs and that the state needed to provide supplementary income to those families. As Prime Minister King pointed out later during the parliamentary debate on family allowances, 84% of Canadian children under the age of sixteen were dependent on only 19% of the gainfully employed.[115] Ian Mackenzie had said as much when he told the House of Commons' Special Select Committee on Social Security on 16 March 1943 that the ideal behind the granting of family allowances was to relieve parents of some of the cost of rearing large families. Clark also reminded the Cabinet that if family allowances were immediately implemented they would not only deal with the inadequacy of the family incomes of wage earners but would also help the government maintain its wage stabilization and price-ceiling policies. Even as King continued to discuss family allowances as a social security measure and had divorced family allowances from the wage-stabilization plan, the senior officials in the Department of Finance hoped that family allowances would be introduced early in 1944 to ensure support among the general population for the government's economic policy.[116]

King agreed with Clark that family allowances would serve an economic purpose, but he argued strenuously in the Cabinet meeting that family allowances were an important social security measure that would create greater opportunity for all Canadian children as well as develop the future human resources of Canada. Clark noted that family allowances would remove the discriminatory feature of the income tax system against families in the lowest income groups.[117] Married persons whose annual income exceeded $1,200 were permitted to claim an allowance of $108 for each dependent child, but the state did not offer similar support for children whose parents were in a lower income bracket. Likewise, soldiers had been paid a dependants' allowance during the war, and Clark suggested that there would be considerable pressure after the war to continue the allowance. Moreover, family allowances might help alleviate the problem many families were having with housing, and also improve the level of education in Canada.[118]

Clark reminded the Cabinet, "Today the Dominion is a remote and intangible entity and in the public mind is more apt to be considered as a harsh tax collector and a stern controller rather than as a beneficent and useful agency. This cannot be conducive to sound, democratic government."[119] A program such as family allowances, he suggested, would bring the government of Canada closer to the people, help children live healthier and more productive lives, and might "allow even one Canadian Milton, Pasteur or Edison to realize possibilities that might otherwise have been frustrated by the accident of his father's income." Although family allowances might be radical for Canada, he reminded the Cabinet they had been tried in more than thirty-five countries around the world.[120] King agreed that family allowances would help Canadians feel a greater affinity with their government and, hence, help build a greater sense of community among the various regions of Canada. Moreover, he had realized for some time that social legislation had been linked to the notion of citizenship and rights. He had discussed this earlier with President Roosevelt and had immediately seen the importance of providing social programs as a means of meeting the objectives of economic advancement and social security as outlined in the Atlantic Charter. Coming out of the Second World War, King also realized the need for a new definition of citizenship in Canada, and saw universal programs like family allowance benefits not only as a means of creating unity. The notions of citizenship had become linked to the state assuming greater responsibility for its citizens, and during the period when his government considered social security – and family allowances in particular – King often referred to the program as part of his "charter" for a new Canada. The expansion of social rights for all citizens became important for postwar nation building in Canada.[121]

Clark also outlined some of the criticisms that might be levied against family allowances. He warned that there could be groups in the country, particularly extremists in English-speaking Canada, that would try to argue that the government was trying to buy the votes of Quebec and "foreign" or "new Canadian" elements of the population in western Canada, where families were traditionally larger and the benefits of family allowances afforded greater advantage than the Anglo-Saxon communities. He suggested that these arguments might be countered if the government clearly and forcefully explained the benefits of the scheme to all Canadians. This criticism could also be diminished if the program limited the number of children in the family eligible for allowances, and decreased payments as the number of children increased. Clark suggested that the government have a scale of allowances graduated in accordance with not only the age of the children but also the number of children. And of course Clark reminded the Cabinet that some critics would argue that there would be some parents who would simply waste any allowance they received for their children. Even so, he thought this should be a minor issue since this consideration was "based on a defeatist view of human nature." Historically, he claimed, rising incomes had produced a higher standard of living and created a demand for a still higher one; once achieved, it had resulted in lower birth rates rather than the reverse.[122]

Clark knew that the cost for a program of family allowances could be a major concern for the government. Some critics, he pointed out, would argue that a universal system of family allowances was excessive, and that it would wreck the country. He did not deny the potential costs – as much as $200 million per year – but he said that a system of family allowances would be worth far more than it would cost; "indeed," he told the Cabinet, "it may save the state all or substantially all its cost by enabling it to avoid being driven into unsound and costly *expedients* designed to *alleviate* some of the conditions for which children's allowances should provide a sound and constructive solution."[123] Still, the amount was staggering, about half the pre-war budget. King noted, "That was a pretty big item for Ministers to face, let alone swallow."[124]

Clark also reminded the Cabinet that organized labour might continue to oppose family allowances. Historically, labour believed that family allowances depressed wage rates, but Clark said that the argument had little support. In March 1942, the British Trade Union Congress had reversed its long-standing opposition to family allowances, and supported the Labour Party's call for a national scheme of state-funded child endowment. In Australia, it was the Labour government that improved that country's system of children's allowances; in Canada, the trade union support for the CCF had not been severed even though family allowances was a part of that party's political program. Still, as recently as September 1943, Percy R. Bengough, the president of the Trades and Labour Congress of Canada, wrote Norman Senior, secretary to Ian Mackenzie, that his organization remained opposed to the idea of family allowances. At its annual convention in 1940, the Trades and Labour Congress had unanimously voted against a resolution from the Toronto and District Labour Council that called for the introduction of family allowances, claiming that such a program would keep wages low.[125] Yet labour leaders could hardly sustain any criticism of a program that provided direct benefits to its members.[126] Clark suggested that any criticism on the part of labour leaders might be muted by support in other quarters if family allowances were introduced as an essential and permanent part of the government's social security program and applied not only to labour but to all Canadians.[127] Clark had sent Ilsley the October edition of *Labour News,* the newsletter of the Workers Education Association of Toronto, which argued that because the Canadian family allowance scheme would be state controlled and financed out of general revenues, there "should be no possibility of using the family allowance as an alternative to increasing basic wages or cutting it off during an industrial dispute."[128]

King later noted in his diary that Clark made a "very fine presentation." The Department of Finance stressed the importance of introducing family allowances immediately, but King refused to do so; victory in the war effort remained his most pressing concern. The Cabinet considered all of Clark's remarks, but by five o'clock, the Cabinet had not made a decision. Colonel J.L. Ralston, the minister of defence, suggested a five-minute recession. When they reconvened shortly past five, King asked each minister whether he was prepared to support the principle on the measure. Ilsley had left by this point, but his support for the measure was anything but enthusiastic even though he had earlier recommended that the government introduce family allowances. King had asked him at the beginning of the meeting if he supported the measure; on the topic, the prime minister wrote later, "[Ilsley] hesitated considerably and then said: I suppose I should; indeed, I do – or words to that effect." King also confided in his diary that he had first asked those he knew would support family allowances.

FIGURE 4   The debate in Mackenzie King's Cabinet was long and difficult. *Back row, left to right:* Hon. Dr. J.J. McCann, Hon. Paul Martin, Hon. Joseph Jean, Hon. J.A. Glen, Hon. Brooke Claxton, Hon. Alphonse Fournier, Hon. Ernest Bertrand, Hon. Gen. A.G.L. McNaughton, Hon. Lionel Chevrier, Hon. D.C. Abbott, and Hon. D.L. MacLaren. *Front row, left to right:* Rt. Hon. Louis St. Laurent, Hon. J.A. MacKinnon, Rt. Hon. C.D. Howe, Rt. Hon. Ian Mackenzie, Rt. Hon. W.L.M. King, Rt. Hon. J.L. Ilsley, Rt. Hon. James Gardiner, Hon. C.W.G. Gibson, and Hon. Humphrey Mitchell. This photograph is from Mackenzie King's personal collection.
Library and Archives Canada, William Lyon Mackenzie King Collection, 1964-087, C-026988, photographer: Paul Horsdal

He began with J.A. MacKinnon, the minister of trade and commerce, and later recorded the response of each minister:

Mackinnon thought it would be good politics but had not much to say apart from this. Power did not think it would be good politics but thought it was desirable from the point of view of social security. Angus Macdonald, to my surprise, said he would favour the principle but thought that great care would have to be taken in the provisions of the Bill ... He had previously expressed himself strongly against the measure but I think the emphasis that was placed on the maintenance of the family, etc. helped to influence his judgment. Michaud was favourable, Bertrand favourable. Howe, strongly against. He thought it meant taxing people of medium incomes to support others who were in many cases not deserving of support. He thought it was the worst thing the govt. could do. St. Laurent was strongly for. Fournier was for. Ralston, to my surprise, indicated he was favourable his grounds being that Canada needed a large population and that if this was going to help in that direction, he was favourable to it. McLarty, who previously had been quite strongly against, said that if the Finance Department favoured the proposal, he would favour it. Gardiner who had spoken strongly against it said he would be favourable in the light of the discussion that had taken place but advised doing away with all exemptions on account of children in income taxes and giving this amount to all. LaFleche was for. Gibson also was for but thought care should be taken about what would be involved in relation to the total programme of health measures. Mackenzie was strongly for.[129]

"When all had concluded," King later wrote, "I said I would give Council my own views and then spoke strongly along the lines that I have in *Industry and Humanity*." King told the Cabinet that modern society had changed dramatically and that "the present war was all a part of the struggle of the masses to get a chance to live their own lives." He reminded the Cabinet that it had already agreed to press forward with social security; "I said quite frankly that I thought the Creator intended that all persons born should have equal opportunities. Equal opportunity started in days of infancy and the first thing, at least, was to see that the children got the essentials of life." Finally, King read a statement that J.W. Pickersgill had prepared for him and presented it, he recounted later, "as a summary of the convictions which [he] held." In it, he reiterated much of what Clark had said at the beginning of the debate, but he emphasized yet again that family allowances were a social security issue. As he read Pickersgill's memo, he left no doubt with the Cabinet where he stood on the issue with phrases such as "equality of opportunity," "a minimum of welfare for all children," and "children's allowances as a natural policy for the Liberal party." He also pointed out those social security measures, like family allowances, might be necessary to save liberal democracies like Canada, and at the end of the debate he was blunt: "There is no better way for the government to show it really means business in the field of social security."[130]

King's long defence of family allowances was, of course, largely unnecessary since Cabinet support was nearly unanimous, a point that King himself realized and even acknowledged in the meeting. King was somewhat embarrassed by his own forcefulness, but later justified his impassioned defence of family allowance by noting, "I felt it was desirable I should speak my mind very strongly and let them see what I feel." Later that evening, while alone at Laurier House, King reflected on the Cabinet's deliberations and thought he might have been too aggressive at the end of the discussion in emphasizing the need for family allowances as a measure to create the new social and economic order, and he called Clark to apologize. Clark reassured him, "[In] dealing with this measure we had given real evidence of our zeal for social security and there could be no questioning of motives or sincerity of the government in its endeavour to do something practical in this way." King was pleased and ended the day with a sense of great accomplishment that his government was going to make a difference with family allowances: "I went to bed tonight feeling that a good day's work had been done and that my life has fulfilled part of its purpose."[131]

Despite the opposition of some of his most influential ministers, King and the Cabinet agreed to push ahead with family allowances. A few days later, King complained to journalist Grant Dexter, "[I] was the only radical in the Cabinet. Some of [my] colleagues still think they can go out and shoot a deer or bison for breakfast," he told the Liberal newspaper editor.[132] Later, in Toronto, Joseph Atkinson of the *Star* reassured King that family allowances were a "very absolutely necessary and right measure."[133] Even the life insurance industry in Canada had announced in 1942 its "hearty support to well-prepared and practicable social security plans for the maintenance of a minimum subsistence level for all classes."[134] The Canadian Medical Association also approved the adoption of the principle of health insurance in January 1943.[135] Despite what King thought in his own mind, an improved social security by early 1944 was widely accepted in Canada. An August 1944 public opinion poll found that 62% of youth and 71% of adults wanted to see "many changes or reforms in Canada" after the war.[136]

King's commitment to family allowance and social welfare legislation at the beginning of 1944 is perhaps best demonstrated by his unusual involvement in personally drafting the section on these policies for the Speech from the Throne, although he had also done so for the section promising increased social security in the 1943 Throne Speech. As he had a year earlier, he struggled to find the right words with which to introduce family allowances. Not surprisingly, he found some of them in his *Industry and Humanity*. (King must have fondly remembered that when he gave Sir William Beveridge a copy of his book on the latter's visit to Canada in May 1943, Beveridge praised him as "a pioneer in social insurance.")[137] Later, when King read a copy of the Throne Speech to the Cabinet, he was discouraged that several of his ministers, particularly Crerar, Gardiner, and Howe, persisted in their opposition to family allowances. King would have none of it, however, and promptly reminded them that the Cabinet had already agreed on family allowances;[138] the matter was no longer open for debate. Later, as the governor general read the Speech from the Throne, King was pleased that he had selected the phrase "the equality of opportunity in the battle of life" as the rationale for the introduction of family allowances, words he had written in 1918. Prime Minister King (and the other national political leaders, too) were well aware that it was in the interest of society that all its citizens be provided with a minimum standard of living.

The reaction to the Throne Speech pleased King immensely. *Saturday Night* showered him with praise, claiming that the Liberal's legislative agenda made Roosevelt's New Deal appear "amateurish, unorganized, [and] timid." The columnist continued, "It creates a model of national and social economy that will focus the attention of most of the United Nations on Canada, for none of them, not even Great Britain or the United States, has made an approach to anything like it ... It introduces the benefits of socialism but preserves and even bolsters and protects capitalism. It assures to the people enjoyment of the gifts of the liberty and democracy for which they are fighting and sacrificing."[139] A number of other editorials across Canada were making similar arguments. In a *Saturday Night* section known as the "Business Angle," P.M. Richards noted that people would not accept again the conditions of the 1930s and many business leaders fully recognized that the "upholders" of private enterprise had to embrace social security against the hazards of unemployment, ill-health, and old age.[140] Of course, King wanted to prove clearly that his role, and that of the Liberal Party, was merely a continuation of the process they had begun years earlier. To that end, King had J.W. Pickersgill prepare a brief outline of the main social legislation the party had introduced and the role he himself had played.[141]

As the legislation for family allowances was debated in Parliament, it was King who took the lead role.[142] When he stood in the House of Commons in June 1944 to introduce the legislation for family allowances, he repeated much of the rationale for their introduction. He emphasized that while the "primary justification" for family allowances was on humanitarian and social grounds, it was also a great economic measure to stimulate the economy by increasing the purchasing power of the public; in other words, family allowances were a wonderful reflection of Liberal ingenuity that would benefit all the people of Canada.[143] But more than that, King participated eagerly in the debate and gave, according to reports, one of his most rousing speeches in years.[144] With the unanimous passage of the legislation in the House of Commons a few weeks later providing for family allowances to begin in July 1945, Prime Minister King was pleased that his government, which had earlier introduced old-age pensions and unemployment insurance, had once again demonstrated to Canadians that it was the champion of social security, even if King and his government were embracing an idea whose time had finally come.

3

The 1944 Family Allowance Debate and the Politics of It All

PRIME MINISTER WILLIAM Lyon Mackenzie King was not alone, of course, in recognizing the need for greater social security. He could be regarded as merely echoing the chorus that was resonating among the Allied nations and major political parties in Canada. Yet King and his government were to make good on their promise of social security, even though their efforts would fall far short of what was needed to provide a decent standard of living for all Canadians. In the 1943 Speech from the Throne, King promised a "comprehensive national scheme of social insurance ... [and] a charter of social security for the whole of Canada."[1] A year later, King went even further, announcing his plans for a new department of national health and welfare and for family allowances for all children, initiatives that the Co-operative Commonwealth Federation (CCF) and the Progressive Conservatives also supported.[2] Throughout 1944, the King government implemented several new pieces of legislation as part of its social security agenda. As planned, in June it established the three new departments of Veterans Affairs, Reconstruction, and National Health and Welfare. On 27 June 1944, King reminded Parliament these measures were enough evidence that his administration was aware of the social problems that would confront the country once the war was over, and that they were "not waiting for the end of the war before providing the means needed properly to effect their solution." In introducing the legislation to create the Department of National Health and Welfare that would be responsible for administering most new social policy initiatives, King had said that the federal government had to take the leadership if the country wanted anything in the nature of a national social security scheme.[3]

In all this, though, there had been little obvious political advantage for the Liberals, since the Conservatives and CCF supported all of the Liberal initiatives in social policy. Public opinion polling throughout May and June 1944 showed that the CCF, which had led both the Liberals and Conservatives in the late summer of 1943, remained popular, while the Liberals struggled to win back the support of voters. Moreover, on 15 June 1944, T.C. Douglas routed the Liberals in Saskatchewan to establish the first CCF government in Canada.[4] In the debate on the bill creating the Department of National Health and Welfare,

Gordon Graydon, the Conservative House leader, left little doubt that the Conservatives would support the government in its efforts to improve the welfare of all Canadians. He told the House, "I want to range myself and this party in support of the advancement of human welfare in our politics, our economy and our society." Graydon even chided King for his tardiness and timidity in social welfare, telling him that the whole problem of social welfare had to be attacked much more vigorously than the Liberals were planning, and adding that a Conservative government intended to be much more aggressive in the area.[5] Even as the Conservatives voted with the government on these new initiatives, they warned King that Ottawa must be careful not to infringe on the constitutional powers of the provincial governments, which had exclusive jurisdiction over social welfare.

By early summer 1944, King was ready to introduce the legislation to create the family allowance program, clearly one of the most ambitious Liberal initiatives designed for the postwar period. On 15 June, after the Cabinet reviewed its strategy for the coming debate, King told his ministers that the measure would not come into force until 1 July 1945. There were several reasons for the delay, even though there was pressure from within the Cabinet, from some government departments, including the Department of Finance, and from a variety of groups throughout the country to begin payments as soon as the legislation was in place. First, King maintained that it was politically unwise to spend public money just before an election; he had promised an election before 1 July 1945. Second, King believed that the electorate would be more likely to support the Liberals if an election took place after the act was passed but before the program was implemented; he feared that if the government rushed the program, there might be delays and disappointment if families had not received their payments or the amount they had expected before they cast their vote. Third, the newly created Department of National Health and Welfare that would administer family allowances required several months to prepare the administrative machinery and register the children.[6]

A few pockets of resistance also persisted in the Liberal Party. During the Cabinet discussion, Angus L. Macdonald, Thomas Crerar, and J.L. Ilsley expressed their skepticism about the proposed legislation, but the Cabinet nonetheless approved the provisions of the family allowance bill that had been drafted.[7] Although the Liberal caucus had given its approval on family allowances before the government announced the measure in the Throne Speech, a few members of the party remained opposed to the measure. George Fulford, the MP for Leeds in southeastern Ontario and a long-time friend of the prime minister, told the 29 June caucus meeting that there was considerable opposition to family allowances in his riding; many of his constituents saw the measure as a way to help French Canadians at the expense of all others. King was clearly annoyed, and as he later commented to his dairy, "I let myself go very strongly in Caucus [and] it was on the family allowances matter than I let out strongly." He told the Liberals that this was an issue that went to the root of their beliefs. "My Liberalism," he said, "was based on getting for men equality of opportunity." He had set out his beliefs in *Industry and Humanity,* and they could find in his book "the doctrine of a national minimum of living, and that everything that had been done since by Government, family allowances, too, were set out therein, evidencing my belief as to what was needed." King was committed to social security and improving "the lot of all people." He told them he "would gladly get out of public life tomorrow as far as [his] personal wishes were concerned except for what there was still to be done in the way of social reform." He also reminded the Liberal members, particularly Fulford, that "if equality of opportunity meant anything, it meant that every man, every child, should have his chance." Characteristically, King promised to give his "entire strength" to the battle for social reform in the coming months. Later, he wrote in his diary, "[They] gave me a great ovation when I finished."[8] He was clearly committed to family allowances, seeing the program as one of his lasting legacies, and he was indignant that anyone should question the efficacy of such a program or impugn his motives for pursuing such a policy. He was also annoyed that Cabinet colleagues and some of his caucus did not share his enthusiasm.

When King rose in the House of Commons on 25 July 1944 to move second reading of Bill 161 to provide for family allowances, he launched into a long and impassioned speech that was repeatedly interrupted by the loud and uproarious pounding of desks. The pounding served not only to silence the critics within his own party but also to embarrass Bracken and the Conservatives.[9] King repeated many of the same arguments that had been used in the Cabinet debate. As he had written in the Speech from the Throne, he said that "the family and the home are the foundations of national life," and that family allowances were intended "to aid in ensuring a minimum of well-being to the children of the nation and to help gain for them a closer approach to equality of opportunity in the battle of life." The principle behind the family allowances was not new: it had been recognized in Canada's income tax legislation since 1917, in dependants' allowances for servicemen, and in pensions for veterans and veterans' widows. He reminded Parliament that the state had an obligation to provide dependants' allowances for enlisted men when the Second World War began. Even the pre-war unemployment relief paid by municipalities and the provinces recognized the need for dependants' allowances.

King reminded the House that the state currently provided an allowance for children of high-income earners. Taxpayers with children were allowed to deduct from their income tax $108 per child, and family allowances would extend a similar benefit to those whose incomes were so low they received less than the full income tax allowances, and to those whose incomes were below $1,200 a year. The prime minister viewed the adoption of family allowances as extending the recognition of state support to the children of wealthier parents to children whose parents were in less fortunate circumstances. There were approximately 3.5 million children in Canada under the age of sixteen in approximately 1.5 million families, and the government estimated that one-third of these families received the full income tax allowances for children, one-third received partial allowances, and one-third – those with the greatest need – did not receive any. Moreover, according to the 1941 census, 84% of the children under sixteen were dependent upon only 19% of the gainfully employed. "In other words," the prime minister clarified, "the major burden of raising the next generation and perpetuating the Canadian nation falls on less than one-fifth of our working population." King praised the family man and said that, next to the soldiers defending the nation, "this one-fifth of our working population are performing the greatest of all national services by ensuring the survival of the nation. It is only fair that the financial burden of this national service should be shared by all."[10] Family allowances also provided additional security to ex-servicemen and their families. As King pointed out, with family allowances, the discharged servicemen would continue to receive for their children an allowance to which they had grown accustomed, even though the amounts paid might be lower than those paid while they were on active service.[11]

Of course, King saw the legislation for family allowances as just one more example of the Liberal Party's commitment to improving life for all Canadians. It was clear, he noted, that "equality of opportunity in the battle of life" did not exist for all the working people of Canada, especially those with large families. Canadians had too often accepted things the way they were; with an ominous warning for the future, King told a packed House of Commons that "the new order of things is going to take very little for granted; it is going to look into the heart of the existing situations and discover where the fault lies." There would be little patience after the war for an uncaring government that accepted the conditions that existed in the 1930s, and he asked Parliament to join with him as he removed the fear of want from the minds of all Canadians. He reminded the House that all three major political parties had promised to work to build a new social order in the postwar period. It was part of the business of the state to help all families and provide better opportunity for everyone, and that was what family allowances would deliver. The prime minister stated, "This measure proceeds on the assumption that children are an asset to the state and that, in considering the resources of the state, human resources are of much more importance than material resources. It is only recently that the world seems to have wakened up to the realization that, of all resources, human resources are the most important, and that, if scientific research, conservation and development are justified in these other branches of the national economy, so, too, they are in relation to human life."[12] The importance of a healthy, strong, and vigorous population had been demonstrated by the war. In King's view, the rejection rates for those volunteering for general service and those called up by the National Resources Mobilization Act (NRMA) were staggering: from April to September 1942, 27.6% of those summoned to serve were rejected as unfit for military service. From January to June 1944, more than 52% were rejected. King claimed that such rejection rates stemmed from a lack of nourishment, care, and development in too many Canadian families, all of which were things family allowances would help alleviate. In the Throne Speech announcing the program, the governor general had pointed out that the army's doctors were shocked by the number of young Canadians medically unfit for military service, especially in poor and working class families, but King promised that family allowances would remove some of the social inequalities experienced by children in poor families.

King also reminded Parliament that in Canada, as in countries that had also introduced family allowances, the wage system took no account of the family status of the wage earner. It was unfortunate, he noted, that throughout Canadian industry the wages being paid were not sufficient to provide workers with children an income that could keep their families in health and decency according to any reasonable standard. The family income had to be supplemented. The alternative would be that a substantial portion of the population would be condemned to extreme poverty and its inevitable consequences of disease, crime, illiteracy, and other forms of social degeneration. Allowances for all children, he said, would "afford the simplest, wisest and cheapest way of providing the supplementary family income." The government chose the term "family allowances" rather than "children's allowances" to stress the importance of "improving the whole family environment in the interests of the children." He reassured labour leaders that family allowances had never been intended as a substitute for higher wages. Rather, because family allowances would create a demand for commodities of all kinds, they would help create employment and opportunities for Canadians.

Family allowances also offered more than social and humanitarian benefits. King reminded the House that they were an important part of the government's postwar economic policy. It was hoped that the monthly family allowance cheques would provide an economic stimulus to the economy and help prevent widespread unemployment in the postwar period. The money distributed through the family allowance program would be spent each month, creating a demand for goods and services that would maintain production. Hence, family allowances should help prevent anything like the depressions that had followed in previous periods in the wake of war. In the notes prepared for King before the parliamentary debate, J.W. Pickersgill, King's secretary, had written, "In their economic aspect, family allowances are one form of 'anti-depression insurance' and a definite step in the direction of maintaining full employment after the war."[13]

Later, when Brooke Claxton, King's parliamentary secretary, joined the debate, he elaborated on the important economic benefits of the program: "Family allowances can be regarded as a means of increasing and stabilizing employment and form a substantial part of any adequate or well-balanced programme for maintaining adequate employment after the war." Claxton compared family allowances to government expenditure on public works, noting that like such measures, "family allowances increase the buying power of those groups who not only need that money but who are most certain to use it immediately. Just as with public works, there will be an increased demand for goods and services ... In the short run, therefore, family allowances represent a method of creating employment which is just as effective as public investment expenditure." At the same time, he noted, family allowances would raise the "quality of our people."[14]

The *Financial Post* reported that the government bureaucrats who held "the confidence of business" were enthusiastic about family allowances because they were an excellent device for stimulating purchasing power and providing postwar full employment. The newspaper quoted an unnamed official in the Bank of Canada as saying that "social security payments would provide more total man-hours of employment than the same amount of expenditure on public investment ... social security would appear to be more consistent with the maintenance of a predominantly private enterprise economy than public investment on a very large scale [and] social security would provide more total employment per unit of financial cost [than large-scale public investment]."[15]

King told the House that family allowances would be financed by the Consolidated Revenue Fund, and they would begin the first day of July 1945. The program would cost about $250 million per year, but the government hoped to recover between $50 million and $60 million of the existing income tax allowance for children, reducing the cost of family allowances to approximately $200 million. It was hoped that a large proportion of the cost would be recovered in the buoyant economy that family allowances would help foster. The plan was to be a universal one, King said, putting an end to the degrading form of relief that was means tested. Payment would be made to a parent of each child resident in Canada according to the following scale:

1 a child less than six years of age, five dollars per month;
2 a child six or more years of age but less than ten years of age, six dollars per month;
3 a child ten or more years of age but less than thirteen years of age, seven dollars per month;
4 a child thirteen or more years of age but less than sixteen years of age, eight dollars per month.

An allowance for all children avoided discrimination and social stigma and could be administered cheaply and simply.[16] King explained that the government had opted for a sliding scale according to age and the number of children because the cost of maintaining a child increases as the child grows. This was true for all costs from food and clothing to housing and schooling. However, the government promised to reduce the allowance by one dollar for the fifth child maintained by a parent, two dollars for the sixth and seventh children, and three dollars for the eighth and subsequent children. The government believed that as a family increased in number, there were many overhead costs, such as furniture and schoolbooks, that did not increase with each child.[17] In early discussions on family allowances in the Department of Finance, it was suggested that some scaling down for larger families might be necessary "to meet the social difficulties likely to be encountered in suddenly increasing very greatly the cash income of large families in rural areas." And of course such a reduction would meet the charge that family allowances favoured the "areas, groups and types of persons in Canada having large families."[18] Moreover, it was important not to raise income from allowances to a point at which it could provide families with enough resources to "eke out a bare existence and thereby tend to encourage idleness or thriftless parents."[19]

More specifically, the bill was to provide an allowance to all children under sixteen years of age who had resided in Canada since birth, and those who had lived in the country for at least three years prior to the date of registration. As well, all children born outside Canada to Armed Forces personnel were to be treated as being born in Canada. To receive the allowance, the child had to attend school or receive some equivalent form of education. However, if a female child married before her sixteenth birthday, she became ineligible, since her husband and not her parents would then become responsible for her support. Moreover, the allowance had to be spent exclusively toward the maintenance, care, training, education, and advancement of the child. If that were proven not to be the case, the allowance could be discontinued or made to some other person or agency, though a claimant could appeal any disallowance to a tribunal created under the regulations accompanying the Family Allowances Act. The allowance was paid to the parent – father or mother – who maintained or had custody of the child, but no allowance was paid to institutions that maintained children. Louis St. Laurent, the minister of justice, said in the debate that such institutions were maintained and financed by the provinces, and family allowances were not intended to relieve them of the cost of maintaining the children.

Brooke Claxton announced that family allowances were also to be paid to "Indians and Eskimaux [Inuit]" if they qualified as parents under the bill and maintained a child. However, duplication was to be avoided, and if Indians received other allowances they might not be eligible for family allowances. Still, for Indians on reserves, the allowances might be paid to the Indian agent rather than to the parent directly, depending on individual circumstances. The government made it clear that it would immediately move to amend the Income War Tax Act so that parents could not have both the benefit of the deduction for their children and the family allowance.[20]

In addition, family allowances would help rural parts of Canada. Too often, social services had been limited to urban areas. Children had become a financial liability, and "expenditure under family allowances [would] be used by the people in the rural areas to help to improve the health and the education of their children, help to gain for them more comfortable and sanitary homes and many opportunities that they otherwise would not have." Combined with a floor for farm product prices, family allowances would give real social security to rural Canada for the first time, King maintained.[21]

Prime Minister King spoke at length and with obvious pride that he could, once again, present himself as a pioneer in social security. He could not, of course, let the moment pass without responding to John Bracken, the leader of the Progressive Conservatives, who had earlier, before the debate began in the House, charged that family allowances were a political bribe designed to benefit the Liberal Party. Angered by the accusation, King now looked at the Speaker and said that he wished Bracken, who had not yet sought a seat in the House since becoming leader in December 1942, was present. When a Progressive Conservative member shouted across the floor of the Chamber, "There are others here to answer for him," King pounced: "Such an accusation [the charge of bribery] is an insult to the intelligence of the electorate. It reflects more upon the integrity of Canadian citizens. When it is suggested that the people of Canada will be governed in their appreciation of the laws of this country by bribes offered to them, a pretty serious charge is being made and one I believe that will be deeply resented by the people of Canada."

Certainly, King resented the charge, and his defence was predictable. He told the House he had chosen postgraduate studies of social problems rather than law because he was interested in the conditions of the people, and hoped to be able to serve by an understanding of the problems. He had not been seeking to bribe people when he turned his back on academic studies to join the Department of Labour, where he worked to improve the conditions for the people of Canada. He had contested a Conservative riding to "get into Parliament in order that my voice might be heard in parliament in regard to social problems and conditions of the people." Even after he had been defeated in 1911, he had once again turned to investigating the conditions of people, and had put many of his views in *Industry and Humanity,* which was "written in the hope that there might be found within its pages a statement of the principles which, if applied after the war, might help to remove the causes of wars and be a means of improving the conditions of the people." King went on to say, "The principles which Parliament has been applying in this very session, and in preceding sessions is the social legislation that has been brought down are all in accord with what is set out in that volume. If honourable members would read a chapter entitled 'Principles Underlying Health,' they would find the advocacy of a national minimum standard of life, the advocacy of a social security, the advocacy of the very measure we are introducing in Parliament at this time." Of course, he pointed out that his government had earlier introduced old-age pensions and unemployment insurance. And in a final defence of himself, he stated:

> Having given the greater part of my life to an honest endeavour to improve the lot of my fellow men in Canada, I do not propose now that I am in [my] seventieth year to begin a career of bribery to further this end. I have fought for measures of social security and national well-being in season and out of season, in Parliament and out of Parliament, in this country and in other countries. I have fought for them wherever the opportunity presented itself, and win or lose in the future, I intend to fight for them to the end of my days. When that moment comes there will not be any thought of bribery associated with my name in this country, if I can leave nothing else to my fellow men, I will at least leave to my party and to my country an honourable name.[22]

When King finally took his seat, there was a great ovation for him, "one of the most continuous I have received in Parliament," he later boasted in his diary. Still, he was not pleased with his performance, and commented later that his throat had given him trouble, and he was overcome with fatigue: "What distresses and depresses me is that this whole subject is so completely my own and I understand it so well but find myself at the time of greatest need of exposition, completely tired out and unable to deal with the different criticisms as they arise and to expound the merits of the measure as they should be expounded." He was disappointed that Hansard might not capture him at his best, but he said he felt too tired to attempt another speech to close the debate.[23] That would all change after the opposition parties had their say on the proposed family allowances legislation.

The parliamentary debate on family allowances, which lasted only nine days in all, proved to be one of the first tests for the "new" Progressive Conservatives.[24] Would the party be able to criticize the family allowances legislation – as was expected of Her Majesty's Loyal Opposition – without undermining its commitment to progressive social legislation, and be able to present itself to the electorate as credibly embracing many of the new ideas circulating within the country on social security? This would prove to be a difficult balancing act, and one that the party managed fairly well in the House of Commons. However, the success the party had achieved in the parliamentary debate was undone by Conservatives outside of the House. Although the party officially embraced social welfare as part of its new and progressive platform, the opposition to family allowances from several party members, notably Charlotte Whitton, the prominent Canadian social worker, and Premier George Drew of Ontario, would undermine much that was accomplished during the parliamentary debate. This afforded the Liberals the opportunity to cast the Conservative Party as pretty much the same old reactionary party it had always been. Despite the best efforts of many within the party, many Canadians did not see much progress in the Conservatives' approach to social legislation in the 1940s. This could only work to the political advantage of King and his Liberals in the next election.

John Bracken had retained Charlotte Whitton as an adviser on social welfare policy. This was hardly a progressive move, given that many social workers and public commentators considered her rivals, such as Leonard Marsh and Harry Cassidy, as progressive and modern while they considered her a conservative embarrassment and a relic of any earlier era. Their advocacy of greater centralization and increased state intervention in the field of social policy was celebrated in the 1940s, while Whitton's insistence on community responsibility was simply dismissed.[25] The doctrine of "subsidiarity" underpinned much of Whitton's thinking on social welfare issues, but it garnered scant support from the social work community at the time. Whitton believed that nothing should be done by larger organizations (like the federal state) that could be accomplished by smaller and competent organizations. As her biographers have pointed out, Whitton believed that when "the State steps in other support steps aside; that an overdependence of State subsidization diminishes individual effort to help one's neighbour, and that the vacuum would be filled by an impersonal bureaucratic machinery that dehumanized services and reduced the common person to a mere cipher."[26] Moreover, a centralized state would not be able to differentiate between individual and community needs. For Whitton, the needs of the Maritimes were quite different from those of Ontario, and those of rural Canada were different from those of urban areas, and a universal program of family allowances could not respond to such differences. In raising these issues, Whitton stressed her subsidiarist principles. As noted earlier, she had claimed in a report prepared for Bracken that the Marsh Report was a "markdown" of the Beveridge Report. Canada required a system of "social utilities," which she described as institutions such as schools, hospitals, child care, and protection agencies, and a variety of resources that would be available on a community basis, "affording educational, health and welfare services for all the people, under varying auspices and available on varying bases" to improve the lot of children. Instead of children's allowances, the funds should be directed toward low-cost housing for young families. If Canada embarked on a system of social security (which she did not dismiss totally), such programs as children's allowances should be placed under the authority of the provinces and municipalities in keeping with the British North America Act. As she argued in 1929, Canada was a land of opportunity, and the government imposing a social minimum through income support was a defeatist attitude. Whitton contended that the first objective of any social policy in Canada should be full employment that allowed "the conscientious and efficient worker valid hope of an income from his efforts, sufficient to maintain, in reasonable decency, the family obligations which he might normally be expected to acquire." Moreover, she feared that there were no adequate assurances that the state's investment through direct cash grants would be used as intended.[27]

To outline several fundamental principles to guide the party's approach to social security, Whitton wrote "Progressive Conservatism and the Public Welfare" for Bracken. The principles were 1) the provinces must retain the sole constitutional prerogative to deal with social welfare matters; 2) municipal governments had to have a role in dispensing social welfare; 3) Ottawa had to change taxing powers to give the provinces the resources needed to fulfil their constitutional obligations with regard to social welfare; 4) Ottawa had to work with the provinces to ensure social protection through social utilities; and 5) Ottawa had to ensure that wages were sufficient to allow every adult male to support his spouse and two or three children. After reading her report, respected Conservative MP H.H. Stevens wrote Gordon Graydon, the Conservative House Leader, that Whitton's document failed miserably as party policy because it did not reflect any of the current thinking about social security. Further, it was a philosophy that no political organization could accept as part of its general policy. He reminded Graydon that Whitton's suggestion that social welfare policy was a provincial matter and that Ottawa should pursue new policies only if it had the cooperation of the provinces was remarkably similar to King's view during the Great Depression, and it was surely a "retrograde step" for the postwar period. Stevens advised Graydon to ignore Whitton's suggestions.[28] However, it was Stevens' advice that Graydon and the Conservatives leadership largely ignored.

Dispensing further advice, Whitton told the Tory caucus that Bracken should take a strong stand against family allowances. A day later, on 24 June 1944, Bracken issued a statement charging that family allowances were a political bribe and compared the program to the dole of the 1930s. This was not exactly the "hard-hitting smash" Whitton had recommended, but it was enough to create considerable damage to the party's postwar hopes, as Stevens had warned might happen if Bracken listened to Whitton. Bracken told the press that any program that promised voters $200 million annually months before an expected election, must be seen as "an election bait to gain the support of the electors, or to fool them, or both." Instead, the government should have been lifting the ceiling on low wages and ensuring that employers paid a decent wage to their workers so they could provide for their families.[29] Still, Bracken's statement was enough to encourage the Liberals, who thought that with a few ill-considered words, like comparing family allowances to the dole, Bracken had undone much of what the progressive elements within the Conservative Party had achieved in reorienting the party to the new realities of the post-depression era in which social security promised to play a prominent role.[30] The Liberal Party, which had not seen its fortunes rise in the public opinion polls after its promise of family allowances, still hoped that its commitment to social security could become a huge political advantage, especially if the Conservatives could be portrayed as opposing family allowances. Yet much rested on what the Conservatives did in the parliamentary debate on family allowances.

When Gordon Graydon stood to speak on the proposed family allowances legislation on 27 June 1944, he took every opportunity to demonstrate that the Conservatives were as progressive as the Liberals when it came to social security. The Conservatives wholeheartedly supported the purpose and object of the family allowance bill. They too agreed with the government's policy to support the cost of raising a family, especially among low-income groups, and all initiatives that promised to strengthen the Canadian family. Graydon came very close to praising King and his government for the initiatives they had put before the House during the session, noting, "What was considered heretical thinking

FIGURE 5 During the debate on the family allowance legislation in the House of Commons, many of the newspapers that supported the Progressive Conservatives ran political cartoons portraying family allowances as a Liberal election tactic (*Globe and Mail*, 23 June 1944).
Reprinted with permission of the Globe and Mail

during the last generation has become almost orthodox in this generation."[31] This statement shows how thinking about social security had changed since the Great Depression. Still, he admonished the prime minister for presenting himself as a representative of the poor, telling him that the proposed legislation did not go far enough. The Conservatives wanted more. They saw family allowances as simply one piece in a comprehensive welfare and social security plan to strengthen the home and family by providing more for Canada's children. Graydon warned King that universal family allowances must not be allowed to become an obstacle to a more comprehensive social program for those most in need.[32] He also said that the proposed legislation denied the basic principle of social justice, because social justice "does not call for the mass treatment of all people in the same way; rather it must treat citizens as individuals, and recognize that the needs of families are different." The Conservatives maintained that a family in Ontario, for instance, had different needs than a family in Cape Breton. Graydon's argument was that a universal demogrant, paid to all Canadian families, was not the most effective use of government funds, as Whitton had noted. Although he could not have foreseen it, this criticism significantly contributed to the demise of family allowances fifty years later.

Despite his party's general support for family allowances, Graydon told the House that the Conservatives had some concerns about Bill 161, aside from its timing and its potential political benefits for the Liberal campaign in the next election. First, it would prevent the establishment of adequate minimum wage standards, as family allowances might become a substitute for higher wage. When the Cabinet discussed family allowances, it was worried that organized labour might oppose the legislation for this very reason.[33] The Canadian Congress of Labour insisted that family allowances were a subsidy for low wages, and that taxpayers should not be required to support industries that refused to pay a decent wage. It maintained, like the Conservative Party, that family allowances should be adopted only as part of a comprehensive social security system and then for families in which the number of children exceeded the national average.[34]

Second, Graydon said that family allowances placed a severe strain on national unity. With that argument, Graydon introduced into the debate what we might today term an anti-Quebec sentiment, though others within the party would seize on this issue much more vigorously than he did. Graydon's attack in the House was quite mild, and raised few eyebrows. He simply noted that Quebec had maintained a high birth rate and large families, which had been so characteristic of Canada's pioneers. Yet, at the same time, Quebec's contribution to the aggregate national revenue was much lower than what it would receive from Ottawa in family allowances. For Graydon, this meant that the other provinces would be unfairly subsidizing family allowances in Quebec, and such an arrangement was surely detrimental to national unity. He also accused the Liberal government of building a giant peace-time bureaucracy for family allowances with its inevitable controls, offices, inspectors, and machinery when the people wanted a return to smaller government. Moreover, Graydon warned that Bill 161 placed too much power in the hands of the minister, who alone would have the discretion to appoint a system of committees, boards, tribunals, and agents with undefined powers to deal with all of the regulations under the act, and hold within his office denial of appeal under unspecified heads and with prosecutions for infringement of the act.

However, the Conservatives' main criticism of the proposed legislation was that it was unconstitutional: it invaded the jurisdiction of the provinces. Even constitutional experts, such as F.R. Scott, had earlier warned that Canadians should expect "no well-rounded system of social security ... in Canada under the pre-war Constitution."[35] Graydon saw nothing extraordinary in telling the House that family allowances were "a direct thrust at the rights and responsibilities of the provinces, who doubtless will oppose such an illegal encroachment upon their recognized field of social welfare services."[36] After all, the 1935 Dominion-Provincial Conference, which had met in part to consider provincial and federal responsibility on economic and social matters, had failed to reach any consensus on the jurisdictional divide between the two orders of government.[37] Moreover, when the Royal Commission on Dominion-Provincial Relations reported in 1940, it recommended that welfare responsibilities be transferred from the provinces to Ottawa only in the areas of unemployment and contributory old-age pensions; all other areas of social security fell to the provinces. Still, the commission argued for a national standard in social programs as one way of equalizing the fiscal capacity of the provinces.[38] In addition, André Laurendeau, editor of the nationalist journal *L'Action nationale,* had called for a strong provincial government in Quebec to oppose the centralist government in Ottawa. He even advised Quebec to reject social reforms coming from Ottawa.[39] Graydon thought he was standing on firm constitutional principles when he moved an amendment to send the bill to a special committee on social security with instructions that it be studied and redrafted after consultation with the provinces. He said he hoped the government would follow his advice to prevent "such an unconstitutional and unworkable piece of legislation from being tossed into an election campaign where there might be a temptation to make three and a half million political footballs out of Canada's children. At all costs they must not be made pawns in a political game. The public are bound to regard a bill so patently unconstitutional and unworkable, brought in at the dying days of a dying parliament by a dying government, as a last straw to which this drowning administration clutches to save itself in the churning sea of political unpopularity."

Louis St. Laurent answered Graydon's charge that the bill was unconstitutional, claiming that when the Privy Council ruled on the Employment and Insurance Act of 1936-37, it concluded that Parliament had the authority to make direct grants out of general revenues to individuals in any of the provinces for any purposes for which Parliament considered desirable. In any case, the Speaker ruled Graydon's amendment out of order because Standing Order 75 stated that every bill had to be read twice in the House before any changes were allowed.[40]

The Conservatives did not commit any egregious mistakes in the first days of the debate, perhaps because significant elements within the party supported family allowances. W.K. Esling, the member for Kootney West, warned Graydon that it would be politically foolish to oppose family allowances: "I feel that opposition to it might jeopardize the position of Progressive-Conservative candidates' in the next election," he told Graydon, even though he agreed with others in the party that the constitutionality of the bill was questionable. He asked Graydon to use his good judgement in dealing with the matter.[41] John Diefenbaker and others suggested that the government ask the Supreme Court to rule on the constitutionality of the measure before the next election so that Canadians would not be deluded by false hope. Still, Diefenbaker told the House, "I believe that no more tremendous or important issue can come before this parliament for the post-war period than the one we are now discussing." He promised to "support the principle of this Bill and get behind the carrying into effect of any bill, brought in by any party in this House, which I believe is of the welfare of the people." The Conservatives who supported the bill fully realized that such programs had become commonplace in other countries, and that it was politically inept to be seen to be on the wrong side of such issues. "I care not what others do," Diefenbaker said in debate, "because I believe we are living in a changing world."[42] Howard Green, the Progressive Conservative member for Vancouver South, told Parliament that he intended to support the measure: "I do so in the hope that it will benefit Canadian children and Canadian parents, thereby benefiting the Canadian nation as a whole."[43]

Nevertheless, there was some real opposition within the Conservative ranks, even if the party officially supported the legislation.[44] One was former Conservative leader Arthur Meighen, who had advised Graydon on 20 July 1944 (after the two had discussed family allowances in Toronto) that the party should oppose what Meighen called the "baby bonus" on constitutional grounds. He also warned Graydon, "I think it would be very serious and later very, very embarrassing if you did not take an attitude of definite opposition."[45] Herbert

FIGURE 6   John Diefenbaker was one of many in the Progressive Conservative Party that supported major social policy initiatives such as family allowances and had made it clear that they would back the legislation making such programs available to Canadians.

The Diefenbaker Centre, JGD4908, reprinted with permission

A. Bruce was perhaps the most vocal and public critic, yet his opposition was clearly at odds with much of his social activism. Throughout his career as a distinguished Toronto surgeon, as the lieutenant governor of Ontario from 1932 to 1937, and even as the Member of Parliament for Parkdale, he had embraced similar social causes and had even lobbied hard for the appointment of a special committee to investigate slum clearance and housing in Toronto. In Ottawa, he had been an active member of the advisory committee on health insurance. However, Bruce believed that the most effective social security was based on services and not financial grants. While he realized that grants had a role to play in some cases, he was clearly opposed to the government giving grants indiscriminately.[46] It was on this basis that he told Parliament that the plan for family allowances was misguided. It disregarded family need and the type of family that would receive the payment. In his view, hardworking Canadians would be taxed to subsidize the lazy and shiftless. The Liberals leaped on Bruce's charge, reminding him that many parents in the lower income brackets too often went without food or medical attention, even endangering their own health, to provide for their children. They reminded Bruce that poor parents were no less "devoted to the well-being of their children than parents in more fortunate circumstances."[47]

But that was only Bruce's opening salvo. As he continued to criticize the proposed legislation, he turned his fury directly to Quebec, chastising the Liberals for introducing programs to benefit a province when it had failed to contribute its full share to the war effort. As a veteran of the 1914 campaign, Bruce (like others in the Conservative ranks) condemned what he saw as Quebec's feeble contributions to the Second World War. As he told the House, "I am afraid that if these cash payments are to be made on the basis [proposed] they will not fulfill their objective, for the money will not go to the provinces which did most of the fighting and suffered most of the casualties." Moreover, Bruce felt that family allowances would only encourage large families, and he advised King, "If we are to encourage large families, then I think care should be taken that they are eugenically of the kind that will be most likely to improve our race. This bill will result in many cases of bonusing families who have been unwilling to defend their country. May I venture to suggest that our object should be quality rather than quantity?" He also said that because 63% of families of ten or more were in Quebec, the rest of the country would subsidize that province: "When eight provinces realize that they are being taxed for the benefit of one province, will it not accentuate the disunity which has shaken Canada from coast to coast because the government chose to listen to the powerful voice of this same province which refused to share equally with others fighting the common enemy?" And returning to the earlier charge of political bribery Bracken had levied, Bruce also accused the government of rushing the legislation through Parliament to help the Liberal Party in the upcoming provincial election in Quebec.

It is doubtful that either Graydon or Bracken could have prevented Bruce from participating in the debate, but they should not have been surprised with what he said. Earlier, when Graydon solicited the views of the Conservative MPs prior to the family allowances debate, Bruce had made it very clear that he considered the bill "a flagrant attempt to bribe Quebec at the expense of taxpayers in other provinces – chiefly in Ontario." Yet Bruce saw such grandstanding as leading to political advantage for the Conservatives in the coming federal campaign: "I think the sooner we realize that we will get no support from Quebec, the better," he wrote Graydon, "and we should, therefore, say that we are opposed to baby bonus for large families in Quebec, at the expense of taxpayers in other provinces."[48]

There was considerable condemnation of Bruce's comments. The Liberals rebuked Bruce and the Conservative Party for attempting to capture votes in English Canada by emphasizing the divisions between Quebec and the rest of Canada over Quebec's contribution to the national war effort after 1939. King added, "I myself think it is fortunate we have the honourable member for Parkdale in this House because he does belong so obviously to a past era ... There is no greater disservice that any member of parliament can render Canada than to seek to raise in this country any form of prejudice, whether it be racial prejudice, religious prejudice, or prejudice against classes or regions. Everyone knows that Canada is a difficult country to govern. Everyone knows that, at a time of war, we should, above all else, be as united as we possibly can." Likewise, Hughes Cleaver, the Liberal member for Halton, Ontario, told Parliament, "I am not going to sit by and allow any member to sew [sic] discord and disunity in Canada. One party leader [Bracken] outside this House is doing a lot of that today and the infection is spreading to this party's members in the House of Commons." The Labour-Progressive member from Montreal, Fred Rose, joined with the Liberals in condemning Bruce, noting that it was unfortunate that members criticized family allowances because they considered it a subsidy to Quebec. "It is not to subsidize Quebec," he said, "but to help all Canadians."[49] Even the conservative *Financial Times* chastised Bruce for his comment that "only eugenically right people" be encouraged to have large families. "It is a supreme pity," the editor proclaimed on 4 August 1944, "that the serious arguments advanced against the baby bonus and similar schemes, are weakened by the inane comments of men with pet ideas: it is a greater pity still if these ideas happen to be quite foreign to every Canadian concept and if they smack too much of that very spirit of regulating lives that abounds abroad and against which so many of the eugenically wrong people today are pitting their bodies and their souls."[50] However, a number of newspapers across the country noted that Bruce's charge of political bribery was not without substance. After all, the legislation had been introduced in the middle of the Quebec election campaign and few could deny that the federal Liberals would campaign on family allowances in the upcoming federal election.[51]

The CCF, on the other hand, welcomed the introduction of family allowances. They demanded, however, that the Liberals promise that family allowances would be merely a part of a more comprehensive social security program that the government would introduce over the coming months. CCF leader M.J. Coldwell said he regretted that the Conservatives had raised the constitutional matter, and noted that they had done so in an attempt to scuttle the legislation. Even so, Coldwell also had criticism of the proposed legislation. It was inappropriate, he said, to have a deduction for each family with more than four children. This amounted to a form of discrimination against large families. Coldwell also wanted the age limit raised to eighteen years from sixteen to keep children in school longer and to encourage more to seek some form of higher education. It would also keep young people out of the job market and, hence, reduce the pressure for jobs as soldiers returned after the war.[52] Coldwell also chastised King for not introducing family allowances earlier in his political career.

In his response, King shed considerable light on his own political instincts. He had, after all, been prime minister of Canada for all but five years since 1921, and he had not embraced social welfare initiatives until near the end of the war nearly twenty years later. "The use of power without having public opinion with you," he told Coldwell, "is to adopt the Nazi method of proceeding which is contrary to the spirit of Liberalism ... Part of the art of government lies in knowing when it is best to do things and when it is best to leave them alone." King went on to remind the CCF leader that before the war, the country would not have accepted such measures as family allowances, nor would the people have wanted such a measure in the early years of the war. By mid-1944, however, the country saw the need for great change and finally understood the importance of social welfare. "This is the opportune moment," King said, "to bring down this measure and we are seizing opportunity by the hand ... Fortunately, I think, they [the people] are now in a mood to support this measure." Of course, King also dismissed Coldwell's claim that the CCF's stand on social security had prompted him to act; he spent considerable time explaining to the House how he and the Liberal Party had been concerned with human issues since 1911.[53] After his speech, a sympathetic *Toronto Star* characterized King as a "leftist," if – it said in a lead editorial – that term was used to describe one committed to social service reform.[54]

For historians, the timing of particular initiatives like the provision of family allowances is, of course, important. Attempting to explain why a political leader like King did not act sooner on a particular issue is not easy, nor is King's delay unusual. In Saskatchewan, for instance, Premier Tommy Douglas was in office for nearly two decades before he introduced the legislation to create Canada's first provincial medicare system, the achievement that recently won him the title of "Greatest Canadian" in a CBC television series. King clearly believed in his own mind that Canada was a difficult country to govern; most countries are, but in exaggerating to himself the internal difficulties inherent within the Canadian polity, King might have used his concern over such important issues as federal-provincial disharmony, English-French discord, urban-rural and regional cleavages, and the fear of class conflict as a way to justify his own inaction. On the other hand, when the international community, and many Canadians, too, embraced social welfare as an important issue for the postwar period, King seized the moment and pushed aside – momentarily, at least – most of the items that had caused him such worry earlier in his career. As King told Coldwell, he knew when to seize the moment, and that might indeed help explain King's longevity in Canadian politics.

When Brooke Claxton, King's parliamentary secretary and Liberal Party strategist, rose to debate the motion for second reading on 26 July 1944, he attempted to take full political advantage of some of the Conservative comments, particularly those from Bruce. Claxton repeatedly suggested that the Progressive Conservatives were the only party opposed to family allowances. In a speech that was later widely circulated, he said the Tory opposition, particularly as demonstrated by Graydon's and Bruce's speeches, showed the clear difference between Liberals and Conservatives. Over Graydon's shouts that the Liberals had no monopoly on social issues, Claxton told Parliament that the Conservative opposition was "important only for the reason that they showed to all the people of Canada how fundamental [was] the difference in outlook towards the social and the humanitarian questions with which the people of Canada are concerned as between those hon. gentlemen [Graydon and Bruce] and the Liberal party and the government." Later, Paul Martin, the young and ambitious Liberal from Windsor, Ontario, pointed out that Graydon and the Conservatives had failed to fall into step not only with progressive thought throughout Canada but also with progressive thought throughout the world.[55] Martin failed to note that even C.P. McTague, the national chair of the Conservative Party and a candidate in the 1945 federal election, supported family allowances while chair of the National War Labour Board. McTague had even told the annual meeting of the Canadian Chamber of Commerce on 29 October 1943 that there was "no use glibly talking about family allowances being a substitute for wages. No one suggests it is. It represents a measure of social security to people whose status really requires it."[56] Martin told the House that Bracken and Graydon clearly represented the Conservative Party, and they were obviously opposed to such innovative legislation as family allowances. Martin knew otherwise, but the Liberals had much to gain by presenting the Conservatives as being opposed to family allowances.

The vote on the second reading of the family allowance bill was unanimous, the first unanimous vote since 1939, when the House voted to investigate the Bren gun contracts. However, only 139 members actually voted to approve family allowances. More than 71 Liberals and 17 Conservatives abstained from the vote, or were absent from the House when the question was called. Before the vote, Graydon reiterated his party's support for family allowances, telling the Liberals that if they considered family allowances such an important measure, then they should implement them immediately. "Our opposition to this bill is not that it goes too far, or not that it is too comprehensive," Graydon had written in his speaking notes, "but rather that it does not go far enough, and is too limited and restricted in its proposals, and fails to fit in with a general scheme of effective and adequate social security plan in this Dominion." Not surprisingly, the Liberals cheered loudly when Graydon rose to vote for the bill.[57] Always the political operative, Claxton wrote King the next day: "Never before has a major party changed its position in consequences of a debate."[58] The Conservatives had spoken against aspects of the bill in debate, but on the whole it was a piece of legislation they supported. Later, when the family allowance bill was being debated in committee, Diefenbaker remarked that he believed the Liberals were disappointed the Conservatives had supported the legislation. If the Tories had voted against the bill during the upcoming election campaign, the Liberals would have cast the Conservatives as a party opposed to social change. Diefenbaker said, "We believe in social legislation. We believe in ensuring relief for all individuals as against poverty, invalidism, and security. We believe in freedom from fear and freedom from want. No political party has a monopoly in that direction. But we do say that as we make advances, let us advance with legislation that is constitutional."[59] The *Toronto Telegram*, which continued to express its opposition to family allowances, noted that the baby bonus, as the family allowance came to be called, had "sapped the moral courage" of some parliamentarians. The Toronto newspaper noted that those few MPs in Parliament who were opposed to the legislation refused to speak their minds. The *Globe and Mail* similarly asked, "Is it to be assumed that they [the Conservatives] voted as they did for fear of losing support in their individual ridings, because they doubted their own ability to sell their own constructive program to the people?" Both papers noted that even those who opposed the family allowance legislation for different reasons remained silent and voted in favour of the measure because it was the only sensible political course to follow.[60] It was not politically advantageous for any of the political parties in the 1940s to oppose social welfare legislation. Both the Liberals and the Conservatives had been able to silence those within their parties who were opposed to family allowances.

When King reflected on the vote in his diary, he was clearly pleased and also aware of the political advantage the Liberals had gained: "I think I laid a good foundation for the campaign itself. Indeed the campaign of 1944-45 is already upon us. This debate had been the opening round. It is a campaign that will be long remembered in Canadian history." The following day, King noted his personal satisfaction with family allowances:

Though very tired, I feel a great peace at heart and an assurance that I am carrying out the purpose of my life in the social reforms in which we have at last entered ... It will be part of a memorable period of the life of the Dominion. How far reaching it all may be, God alone knows. I am sure that the 100 percent of the House of Commons in support of the Family Allowances Bill will have an enormous effect in other parts of the world, particularly in Britain. The whole campaign that follows will arouse the peoples in all countries to the new conception of industry being in the nature of social services and the right of all the people to their share of the transformed natural resources which God has given the people as a whole and not to individuals for their use. It is truly a conception that will help to bring in a new order, and which will help to give to the lives of the humble the world over something of the dignity which God has meant those who have been made in His image, to possess ... I should not forget ... the beautiful teachings of Christ ... "Suffer the little children to come unto Me."[61]

Before the bill passed third and final reading, the government had to decide which parent would receive the family allowance benefit. King said that the act provided for payment to a parent, but he would decide on the mother or father after discussions with the provinces and with those officials who would be involved with child welfare in the provinces. King said that there might be no nationwide policy; instead there might be an effort to have the payment made according to provincial preference. Incidentally, the first draft of the bill stated that the allowances would be paid to mothers. It was changed after St. Laurent informed Ilsley that designating the mother as the recipient might cause legal and political complications in Quebec because of the nature of the civil law.[62] However, when the matter was discussed in caucus, a number of members wanted mothers designated as the recipient across the country. Claxton urged King to reconsider, and wrote him that when he met to prepare several Liberal members for the discussion in Parliament, they felt strongly that paying benefits to mothers would have a greater political appeal than payment to fathers.[63] The principle of designating mothers as the recipients of the benefits for children had been clearly established in various provincial mother's allowance programs created in the 1920s. As James Struthers has argued, such arrangements created a unique moral relationship between mothers and the state, even if benefits were provided to mothers as incentive for them to be proper stewards of the state's resources, to ensure the well-being of families and children.[64]

Cora J. Casselman, the Liberal member for Edmonton East, was most insistent that mothers be designated as the recipients of family allowance benefits, though she, like many others, did so because she believed that women would spend the money wisely on their children. She reminded King that mothers had more control over buying items for their children, and had a greater knowledge of their needs than fathers: "I think the money would be spent to better advantage if it could be placed directly in the hands of the mother."[65] CCF member Stanley Knowles agreed, and moved an amendment that the payment be made to the mother. He and others, including Coldwell, argued that as the primary caregiver, the mother had to provide food and look after clothing the children. Knowles and the others also argued that the bill was "a children's bill and it should be considered primarily from the point of view of the child." As such, the CCF and many Liberals believed that preference for payment to mothers should be inserted into the legislation, except where provinces desired that it should be made to the other parent. The CCF amendment was defeated, even though King said that he would prefer to see payments made to the mother. Still, he realized that some provinces, particularly Quebec, might object to having payment made to the mother, and King argued that it would be best to let each province decide.[66] A final decision on who would receive the benefits would be worked out later.

The bill came to Parliament for third and final reading on 1 August 1944. It passed without opposition. The following day, Ian Mackenzie accused Harry Bruce of being conveniently absent for the vote. Bruce took the bait and told the minister that had he been present, he would have voted against the measure. He told the House, "I regarded this measure at the beginning as a bribe and I still regard it as a bribe. I have said so and I will not retract that statement, Mr. Chairman." The statement to which he referred was, specifically: "I now declare the measure is a bribe of the most brazen character, made chiefly to one province and paid for by the taxes of the rest." He refused to withdraw the remark, and after an uproar he was suspended from the House for the remainder of that day's sitting. The *Vancouver Daily Province* opined that the spectacle of the entire Liberal side rising to oust Bruce was "one to make angels weep."[67]

The Liberals tried desperately to seize on Bruce's comments. Within days, several Liberal members took to the airwaves to praise the family allowance legislation. In a radio broadcast on 7 August, Mackenzie, one of the earliest proponents of social security and an individual who had been largely marginalized during the family allowance debate, said that the family allowance program was one of the pillars of a great national structure of social security and social justice that King had promised during the darkest period of the war in 1941.[68] Casselman, the only female Liberal member in Parliament, also outlined the rationale for family allowances in a national radio broadcast on 19 July 1944. It was no coincidence, of course, that Casselman was chosen to deliver the broadcast. In it, she briefly described the program but reminded listeners that the grants were not large: a child's expenses would always be greater than the grants. Interestingly, the address was without any reference to the Liberal Party or the Liberal government.[69] While the radio broadcasts from Mackenzie and Casselman steered away from partisan politics, Brooke Claxton's suppertime broadcast on family allowances over Montreal radio station CFCF was clear in its political intent. He told his listeners that the family allowance bill was part of the progressive Liberal agenda to deal with the social problems during postwar reconstruction, and that such measures distinguished the Liberals from the Conservatives who, he reminded his audience, were opposed to such legislation.[70]

The Conservatives might have escaped from the family allowance issue relatively unscathed had it not been for Charlotte Whitton and George Drew, who continued their tirades against family allowances even after the Conservatives in Parliament had endorsed the legislation and the party had adopted similar progressive social measures as part of its new policy platform. Whitton's views remained more or less unchanged from the 1920s, and, as a long-time Tory, her opposition became linked with that of the Progressive Conservative Party, particularly as she used the party apparatus to push for her social policy objectives. Moreover, there were persistent rumours that she was the Tory choice for the minister of social welfare position if the Conservatives won the upcoming election, and, of course, she had been Bracken's policy adviser on the Marsh Report.[71]

Just a few days after King announced in the Throne Speech that he would be proceeding with family allowances, Whitton told a joint meeting of the PC Business Women's Club and the PC Women's Association of Ottawa that the federal expenditure for family allowances was misguided. There would be little control over how the direct cash payments would be used, she said. She argued that more modest investment, through cooperation with the provinces, in child care and protection agencies, custodial care, family welfare services, housing, nursing care and hospital expansion, improved education facilities, and food subsidies would produce far better results.[72]

Whitton later argued that the debate about family allowances went to basic questions about immigration policy, economic variations among the provinces, and the nation's fundamental social philosophies. In a lengthy speech to the Ontario Public School Trustees' and Ratepayers' Association in April 1944, she warned that the family allowance proposal went against some of the basic principles on which Canadian life had developed. Family allowances, she stated boldly, would undermine both self-reliance and family responsibility. Moreover, they would encourage the "newer stocks," the non-British, who then made up 20% of the population, and would defeat the whole basis of Canada's selective immigration policy.[73] The *Ottawa Citizen* went to great pains to show its readers that Whitton had compiled statistics showing that the fertility rate of non-British women was much higher than that of women of British descent in Canada: the rate per 1,000 women of British descent was a paltry 128.63 compared to 242.15 for French, 163.06 for German, and 162.20 for Ukrainian.[74] George F. Davidson later wrote in *Public Welfare* in response to Whitton that if the "Anglo-Saxon strains" ceased to be predominant in Canada's population it would not be because of family allowances but because Anglo-Saxons "have not seen fit to assume their proper responsibility in the matter of reproducing themselves." Moreover, Davidson said the French-Canadian birth rate, while proportionally higher than the Canadian average, had also been declining since the 1920s.[75]

Charlotte Whitton was the only prominent social worker opposed to family allowances. The *Canadian Forum* noted this and commented that her opposition stemmed from the fact that she did not trust working-class parents to spend their income with any sense of responsibility.[76] The Canadian Association of Social Workers (CASW) clearly supported the program, and in a 1944 brief to the federal government it said that family allowances were an absolute necessity. Moreover, a survey of the heads of social agencies in Toronto and Montreal revealed that they were nearly unanimous in their support. The Canadian Welfare Council also gave its approval; the board of governors discussed the issue of family allowances when Bill 161 was before Parliament and a clear majority gave it the nod. On 31 July 1944, the council authorized its president and executive director to publicly declare its support.[77]

When Whitton prepared three editorials attacking family allowances for the *Ottawa Citizen* from 3 to 5 July 1944, the CASW immediately distanced itself from her. At a special board of directors meeting following Whitton's editorials, the CASW decided that it had "a very definite responsibility, as a national professional organization, for giving active support to a comprehensive federal social security programme for Canada, particularly in view of the opposition that had been mobilized against such a project."[78] In a letter to the *Citizen*, Elisabeth Wallace, the executive secretary of the CASW, said that the majority of social workers supported family allowances and were shocked that Whitton would present her views as representing them. She went on to say that in the editorials, Whitton had made a number of ridiculous claims such as the exorbitant administrative costs associated with delivering family allowances, the difficulties involved in administering such a vast program, the problems for taxpayers who would see their deductions reduced. Wallace said family allowances would benefit large numbers of Canadians, and social workers believed that they were necessary if Canada was to provide any real measure of social security for its citizens.[79] Despite all this, it was Whitton's comments criticizing family allowances that attracted the attention of the press.

Premier George Drew of Ontario, also opposed to family allowances, was committed to provincial rights, and he believed that family allowances were an invasion into provincial jurisdiction. His view on Quebec's position during the war also influenced his stand on a number of issues, including family allowances. Drew was fully aware of public ambivalence regarding family allowances in Ontario, and he saw his position as good politics in his province. After all, public opinion surveys had shown only lukewarm support for family allowances. A Gallup Poll by the Canadian Institute of Public Opinion asked two groups of people two separate questions. In early October 1943, Canadians were asked if they considered $9 per month for each child in the low-income group a good or bad idea. Forty-nine percent of respondents considered it good, while 42% thought it bad. Nine percent were undecided. A second group was asked their opinion on the payments possibly costing the government $180 million annually. The response was very similar: 45% believed the idea was bad, 43% considered it good, and 12% were undecided. The Wartime Information Board noted in its survey of press comments for the last two weeks of June 1944 that the family allowance bill had not found overwhelming support among newspapers editors, especially those in English Canada.[80] Public opinion surveys showed overwhelming support of 88% for family allowances in Quebec in late July 1944 compared to only 57% support in the rest of Canada. Incidentally, women demonstrated a greater support than men for the measure.[81] A survey done in October 1944 found that when respondents were asked if they considered family allowances a political bribe or a necessary law, 34% of respondents nationally considered it a necessary law, while 29% considered it a political bribe; 16% considered it both. In Quebec, 49% saw it as a necessary law and only 13% as a political bribe. In Ontario, on the other hand, 39% saw it as a political bribe and 26% considered it a necessary law.[82] Perhaps Drew believed he was expressing the view of the Ontario electorate.

Although he had been elected on a program of progressive reform in 1943, Premier Drew considered family allowances unconstitutional and saw the program as another instance of Ottawa attempting to introduce a permanent program on the basis of taxation revenue the provinces had given to Ottawa for the prosecution of the war. Social welfare, he claimed, was a provincial responsibility.[83] On 2 August, the day after the family allowances bill passed third reading, Drew told a Progressive Conservative rally in Richmond Hill, Ontario, "Never in Canadian history has there been such an insolent disregard for the rights of the Canadian people of Ontario as Mr. King has shown in his adoption of the $200,000,000 baby bonus." Drew said that it was unfair that Ontario taxpayers were footing the cost of family allowances for the country. If the provincial government could keep the amount that went to Ottawa, Ontario could pay more generous family allowances, he said, as well as contribute more to education, expand health and hospital services, improve the transportation system, and reduce the provincial debt considerably. He promised to protect Ontario's interest against an increasingly ambitious Ottawa that, in his view, was intent on unilateral action in policy areas where the provinces had a clear authority. For Drew, the King government wanted to control the direction for the postwar period, and its plan for family allowances was simply another attempt to move into areas like social policy that were traditionally within provincial jurisdiction. The Ontario premier also lashed out at Quebec, charging – as Bracken had done earlier – that the bill was a political bribe directed at Quebec. Even Premier A. Godbout of Quebec himself had claimed that the measure was the result of his collaboration with the prime minister. Such political favouritism by King, Drew charged, will result in domestic chaos.[84]

Not surprisingly, Drew's comments about Quebec ignited a firestorm across the country. The national reaction prompted the premier to explain himself to all of Ontario, and when he did, in a radio broadcast on 9 August, he launched a vicious attack on family allowances. Calling it the "most alarming constitutional crisis" since Confederation, Drew lashed out at Ottawa. He claimed that Ontario had handed over taxing power to wage total war against the Axis Powers, not so that the federal government could invade the fields of provincial jurisdiction without even a word to the provinces. Again, he reiterated his opinion that the family alliance program was a bribe directed at Quebec. However, he would act decisively, he promised, to prevent millions of dollars from being taken from the pockets of Ontario taxpayers to reward the people of Quebec: "I assure you that the Government of Ontario intends to do everything within its power to make sure that this iniquitous bill does not go into effect." And in a single comment that the Liberals later shamelessly exploited, Drew said, "It is not this bill alone but the whole principle involved which we intend to resist." Later, Drew retracted his statement and insisted that he was not opposed to family allowances.[85] His clarification had little impact; he had provided the Liberal Party with far more ammunition than it had obtained in the House of Commons debates to attack the Conservative Party on its social welfare platform.

A long-time vocal critic of what he considered Quebec's limited contribution of men to Canada's war effort, Drew was infuriated that Maurice Duplessis was returned to power as premier on 8 August on a pledge to reduce Quebec's participation in the war. The time had come, Drew told Ontario, "for the people of this and every other province in Canada to say that Quebec is not going to receive preferred treatment while it refuses to bear its full share of the burden of war ... Are we going to let one isolationist province dominate the destiny of a divided Canada?" Drew also claimed that there could be no national unity in Canada "while one province claim[ed] every advantage and denie[d] an equal obligation to share in the protection of their country in its hour of peril." He likened the treatment of Quebec to appeasement abroad, and warned that Canadians could no longer remain silent about what was happening in the country. "The path to unity is clear," he declared, and Canadians of all ethnic origins must give "full loyalty to the same Crown and march forward shoulder to shoulder as brothers in a great cause."[86]

The Progressive Conservative Party attempted to minimize the damage done by Drew and Whitton when C.P. McTague entered the fray. As chair of the National War Labour Board, he had recommended family allowances as one possible alternative to low wages in mid-1943. He subsequently resigned from the board, and was appointed the national campaign chair of the Conservative Party and the Tory candidate for South Wellington. Even though the Tory leadership in the House of Commons had supported family allowances, McTague wanted to reassert Conservative support for the measure. He attempted to do this (perhaps strategically) in Montreal on 12 October 1944 at a Progressive Conservative Association meeting after Premier Drew had very publicly opposed the program. Conservatives favoured family allowances, McTague insisted, and all Canadian children were "entitled to the same treatment whether they reside[d] in the province of Ontario or whether they reside[d] in the province of Quebec or any other province." However, in his opinion, family allowances should only have been introduced as part of a general social security program.[87]

There were others in the Conservative Party who were worried about Drew's and Whitton's antics as well. Dan Lamont, a prominent Toronto Tory, warned Richard Bell, whom Bracken had appointed as national director of the party in April 1943, that Drew's opposition to family allowances was potentially damaging to Conservative chances in the upcoming federal election. He reminded Bell, who circulated Lamont's memorandum to others in the party, that Drew's opposition had done immeasurable harm to the party, especially among those who saw family allowances as progressive and beneficial. Likewise, he observed that the criticism of Quebec had done little to benefit the party.[88]

The Liberal newspapers took full advantage of Drew's and Whitton's opposition to family allowances, even as Drew moved to do damage control and

claimed that there was "a well-organized attempt ... to misinterpret" his statement.[89] On 17 October 1944, the *Windsor Daily Star* noted, "Ever succeeding
Progressive Conservative reference to family allowances tends to confuse public
opinion more deeply." The paper indicated that the elected members in the
House supported the measure, or at least gave the appearance of doing do.
According to the newspaper, Bracken, on Whitton's recommendation, opposed
the measure like Drew, though the Ontario premier had clearly linked family
allowances to ethnic arguments. The paper also said that McTague wanted
family allowances only as part of a general social security scheme, and concluded
that the Conservatives seemed united only when calling the scheme a political
bribe.

The *Winnipeg Free Press* talked of factions within the Conservative Party,
noting the disagreement between Graydon and Bracken. It also claimed that
the Toronto clique led by Drew simply despised family allowances and were
working to oust Bracken from the party's leadership. Apparently, the Toronto
group represented the "old guard" Tories, a "reactionary, ultra-imperialist fac-
tion that held to obsolete policies that had been repeatedly repudiated by the
Canadian public and were professedly abandoned by the Conservatives convention which elected Bracken to the leadership." The *Toronto Star* suggested that
Drew's opposition to family allowances stemmed from "die-hard financial interests which have consistently opposed progressive social and financial legislation and have been traditionally powerful within the Conservative party."[90] Even
the usually sympathetic *Globe and Mail* considered Drew's outburst unfortunate
and noted the ambiguity of the party's policies on such issues as family allowances. However, it agreed with the premier's stand on Quebec. "We have less
unity now after almost five years of Mr. King's war administration than we ever
had before," it opined on 11 August 1944, "and that is thanks to the policy of
appeasement and sectional politics of the Government."[91]

The *Winnipeg Free Press* returned to Drew's antics on several occasions, once
suggesting his tirade against family allowances was an effort to camouflage his
position as a provincial autonomist. The paper argued that historically the
economically stronger provinces had always opposed the centralization of power
in Ottawa, and Drew was merely following in the footsteps of Mitch Hepburn
who, in 1941, had argued that the recommendations of the Rowell-Sirois Report
on federal-provincial relations was merely a federal initiative to rob Ontario.
Ontario premiers wanted Ontario's money to stay at home or, at least, not to
be used without Ontario's consent, the *Free Press* noted. A few weeks later, the
paper wrote that Drew's attack was really aimed at the financially weaker provinces in the west and in the Maritimes, but was designed to "attract the violent

anti-Quebec minority in Ontario – that minority whose mouthpieces are the Toronto *Globe and Mail* and *Telegram*." As Stuart Garson, premier of Manitoba and later minister of justice in the federal Liberal government, had done, the *Free Press* pointed out that Ontario's wealth was derived in large part from throughout the country and not solely from within the borders of the province.[92] Ontario's wealth was Canada's wealth.

Garson had also expressed reservations about family allowances, noting that social welfare was a provincial matter. He hoped that family allowances would not interfere with a wider plan for social security, which should have been first discussed at a dominion-provincial conference. On this point, Garson proved to be quite prescient: the federal government did not develop a comprehensive social security system; the cost to the federal government of family allowances and a variety of programs for veterans was a factor contributing to the failure to develop a greater range of social security initiatives.[93] In a statement on the family allowances legislation published in the Montreal *Gazette*, Garson wrote, "I do unhesitatingly favour family allowances generally but before I commit myself to the support of this particular scheme as applied to the Canadian picture I want a much greater assurance than has so far been forthcoming that it will not mean that Canadians have to do without something that we may regard as much more important than family allowances, an adequate health insurance program, for example." He also told the newspaper that Ottawa's decision to implement family allowances was a federal intrusion on a provincial field of jurisdiction.[94]

Garson's concerns prompted the *Globe and Mail* to write that there was "More Agreement Than Difference" between Drew and Garson on family allowances.[95] Clearly, the *Globe and Mail* hoped to show that all political parties had reservations about family allowances even if they agreed on the principle of the program, as both Drew and Garson had. However, the comparison with Drew infuriated Garson. He protested to the newspaper, citing four major differences between himself and Drew: first, Garson disagreed with Drew's claim that Ontario provided half of Canada's tax revenue; second, he believed that family allowances were as much an economic measure as a social security one; third, Garson insisted on dealing with the public finances of the country without linking them to any particular national issues; and, fourth, Garson was not obsessed with Quebec.[96] Garson's statement prompted Drew to lash out at the Liberals, particularly King, and what he called the Sifton newspapers over charges that he was anti-Quebec and refused to share Ontario's wealth with the less fortunate provinces. He said at another PC rally that he was ready to march "shoulder-to-shoulder" with Quebec when that province worked with the others to support great Canadian causes, but not when the Quebec legislature opposed conscription to send desperately needed reinforcements for the war in Europe.[97] The *Ottawa Journal* agreed with Drew. The paper had alerted its readers when Ottawa first introduced the family allowances legislation that the measure might become a threat to national unity, and Drew's comments had clearly shown that Canadians would not stand idly by when Quebec benefited so disproportionately from the program.[98]

Edward B. Jolliffe, the provincial CCF leader and leader of Opposition in Ontario, told the province in a radio broadcast on 13 September 1944 that Premier Drew was misguided to wage war on Ottawa and Quebec over family allowances. Reading from a report prepared by his party's national research staff in Ottawa, Jolliffe said that Drew's statements were wild and extravagant, and Drew could do nothing to prevent the act from taking effect. He said that the family allowance measure would be beneficial to large numbers of parents in Ontario. Moreover, he pointed out that the bill had passed unanimously in the House of Commons with the support of thirty-nine Conservatives, twenty-four of whom were from Ontario. Every Conservative in the House voted for it, even their House leader, Gordon Graydon, who claimed to be acting with the approval of John Bracken himself. Jolliffe suggested that Drew was standing opposite his own national party and his own leader in Ottawa to divert attention away from the issues facing his government in Ontario.[99]

In Quebec, support for family allowances was high. In its canvas of editorial comment in Quebec, the Wartime Information Board found widespread support among the French media. When the notion of family allowances was first floated in Ottawa, then Premier Adélard Godbout wrote King that his government favoured family allowances but he considered them part of a program of social security and, hence, under provincial and not federal jurisdiction. Edgar Rochette, Quebec's minister of labour, had created a contributory family allowance plan in 1943, but none of the province's employers had interest in the initiative and it quickly passed into oblivion. There has been some suggestion that King consulted Godbout before he introduced family allowances.[100] There was also some criticism in Quebec of the government's plan to reduce payments for the fifth and subsequent children; this was seen as a form of birth control.[101] The Quebec Board of Trade, for instance, telegraphed King on 1 August 1944, "We appreciate stand taken by your Government, re: family allowances. Would favour uniform rates however and share opinion editorialized by *Saturday Night* and *Action Catholique.*" Those opinions suggested that even if family allowances were constitutional, the provinces should have been consulted because social welfare is a provincial responsibility.[102] After Duplessis was re-elected as premier of Quebec on 8 August, he said that his government would investigate the constitutionality of family allowances. The *Ottawa Journal* praised him for showing restraint in the discussion over family allowances, given Drew's outburst against Quebec.[103]

The Conservative press continued to express several reservations about the program, however. The *Ottawa Journal* asked first of all why the Liberal government needed to rush the bill through Parliament in July 1944, when the date for implementation was more than a year away. Was it for political advantage? The *Globe and Mail* agreed that it was for political gain, noting that family allowances, while important as part of a broad scheme of social security, were being adopted by the Liberal government for "political expediency." The Montreal *Gazette* also considered the legislation for family allowances rushed and believed that the people should have been given ample time to carefully examine the family allowance proposals. The Winnipeg *Tribune* said it could be for no other reason than to win friends and influence parents. The Vancouver *Daily Province* agreed, but it also suggested that given King's record on social security, one could not suggest that he was not sincere in his desire to improve the lot of Canada's children.

The Liberal newspapers, notably the *Toronto Daily Star* and the *Winnipeg Free Press,* provided extensive coverage of family allowances, noting, of course, that the program came from the Liberal Party in Ottawa. The sympathetic *Toronto Daily Star,* over which King's friend and supporter Joseph Atkinson ruled supreme, wrote that when enacted, family allowances would place Canada among the modern nations of the world that had used their resources to provide some measure of basic security for the nation's people. It reported that family allowances were among the most popular pieces of legislation where it had been introduced. The paper even quoted from a recent article in the *British Medical Journal,* pointing out that family allowances and other social security legislation were important for the survival of the nation because they removed an element of fear of deprivation from the minds of the citizens and at the same time increased human efficiency on which the wealth of the nation depends. It also quoted Dr. George Davidson, the executive director of the Canadian Welfare Council, who had told a National Welfare Conference in Winnipeg that family allowances were a particularly outstanding development in the children's field. The *Toronto Daily Star* went on to note that most social workers and social agencies favoured family allowances. When debate continued long after the passage of the bill, the *Toronto Daily Star* continued to voice its support, expressing its opinion on one occasion that the annual injection of $200 million into the national economy would be of definite benefit to Canada.[104]

One of the most thorough and supportive analyses of family allowances came from Grant Dexter, the associate editor of the *Winnipeg Free Press*. During the summer of 1944, Dexter wrote eight editorials on family allowances that were later published in pamphlet form by the newspaper. Dexter pointed out that the projected expenditure for family allowances was extraordinary given that the expenditure on all social welfare initiatives, including relief, in 1937 was only $250 million. He reviewed the opposition to family allowances and noted that the critics, from various newspapers to the Conservatives to Charlotte Whitton, missed the major reason for the program. Family allowances were not introduced for political reasons. The federal Cabinet had known all along that the political advantages were extremely doubtful. The idea for the program emerged not with the politicians, Dexter suggested, but with the senior civil servants – or what he referred to as a "brain trust" – who believed that social legislation like family allowances were important to safeguard the national economy by preserving the free enterprise system. The aim of such legislation, he concluded, was to improve social conditions for families without seriously harming the economy. In other words, the best way to maintain full employment after the war was to increase the incomes of those who earned the least. If purchasing power were increased, employment would be sustained and the economy would not contract after the war.

At the same time, Dexter noted, there was a steady growth in public sentiment in favour of a greater measure of social security. Yet it was the "brain trust" in Ottawa that picked up on the notion of family allowances. Family allowances proved attractive because they could be paid relatively simply to all parents, rural and urban, and because they were universal; that is, they came without any social stigma. Moreover, family allowances avoided the constitutional constraints that engulfed some of the earlier attempts in social legislation. In Dexter's view, for the first time, the federal government had chosen to recognize need, regardless of area, and Canadian rather than provincial citizenship.

Regarding the criticisms related to ethnicity, Dexter dismissed them as "inconsequential." Quite simply, if Canada was a nation, children could not be distinguished on racial lines. Dexter also maintained that there were two main arguments against family allowances: first, Canada was a self-reliant country that valued individual initiative and enterprise and family allowances threatened these values; second, the vast sums spent on family allowances would be more effectively spent on schools, hospitals, children's aid, and health and welfare generally. He rejected both criticisms.[105]

The Liberals, anxious to take the credit for family allowances, did not wish to leave the friendly press to make their case alone. In December 1943, Brooke Claxton had complained to Prime Minister King about the lack of publicity about the government's postwar plans.[106] Just before the debate on family allowances began in the summer of 1944, Claxton again fired off a long memorandum to the prime minister on the lack of political organization within the Liberal Party. The party had done little to get its message to the public, and public support for the Liberals was such that the best they could hope for was a minority government in the next election. "The present situation," he wrote, "is due to our failure to define and make plain the issues."[107] However, King may have been part of the problem since he was anxious to avoid the appearance of straight political propaganda. As a result, plans for a national publicity campaign were only slowly put in place, even though the National Liberal Federation had started to lay the groundwork for such a campaign after its convention in September 1943.[108]

The party did realize that there were benefits to publicizing family allowances. At the insistence of Charles Gavan "Chubby" Power, a senior minister from Quebec, a leaflet on family allowances was prepared in French along with a condensed version of King's speech in Parliament. These were distributed in Quebec prior to the provincial election on 8 August 1944. The party also prepared several thousand copies of a pamphlet entitled "Family Allowances for Canada" for use by Liberals around the country.[109] By September 1944, the National Liberal Federation had ordered 178,000 copies of the pamphlet for national distribution, including 58,000 for Ontario, 10,000 for British Columbia, 13,000 for Manitoba, 14,000 for Nova Scotia, 25,000 for Alberta, 30,000 for Saskatchewan, 15,000 for New Brunswick, and 8,000 for Prince Edward Island.[110] And to reach women within the party, Mrs S.C. Tweed, one of the National Liberal Federation vice-presidents, penned an article outlining the benefits of family allowances to send to all the women on the party's mailing list.[111]

By the time the House adjourned for the summer of 1944, there was widespread and growing support for family allowances in Canada, even within the labour movement. The Canadian Congress of Labour had insisted that family allowances were a subsidy for low wages, and taxpayers should not be required to support industries that refused to pay a decent wage. It maintained that family allowances should be adopted only as part of a comprehensive social security system and then for families where the number of children exceeded the national average.[112] Yet the national organization had become increasingly isolated as a growing majority of workers supported the program. The Oshawa and District Labour Council, for instance, wrote King that it approved of his legislation, though it expressed its hope that the government would soon move toward creating a national minimum wage.[113] The Canadian and Catholic Confederation of Labour continued to object to family allowances because of the reduced scale for large families.[114] The Vancouver Aeronautical Mechanics Lodge No. 756

passed a unanimous motion commending the government for passing the family allowances legislation. "We believe that this is a real step forward in social legislation and one which will have an important effect upon the people of Canada, particularly the coming generation," the secretary wrote King.[115] By the fall of 1944, the Canadian Congress of Labour, the Trades and Labour Congress of Canada, and the Canadian and Catholic Confederation of Labour had all changed their position and come out in support of family allowances.[116] All seemed to be going well for the Liberal Party.

There were other reasons why the Progressive Conservatives did not enjoy greater electoral success in the postwar period,[117] but the opposition to family allowances led by several key individuals associated with the party allowed the Liberals to present the Progressive Conservatives as a backward, reactionary party that continued to oppose the progressive legislation voters wanted in the postwar period. The Conservatives had failed one of their first tests to demonstrate that they were a progressive party. On the other hand, Prime Minister King was exuberant, confiding to his diary on 30 July 1944, just as the parliamentary debate on the family allowances bill was drawing to a close, "[The measure] was a far more reaching reform that has, thus far, been possible ... [and] I felt a great peace of heart and mind as though something has been fulfilled for which I have been striving throughout my whole life."[118] Of course, King also hoped that family allowances would serve his party well in the election he would call in the following few months.

4

Sharing the Wealth: The Registration for Family Allowances Begins, 1945

"CANADIAN PARENTS WILL receive two hundred million dollars a year in family allowances," Brooke Claxton told the Progressive Club of Halifax at the Lord Nelson Hotel on 20 February 1945.[1] Claxton was the minister of national health and welfare and one of a growing number of ministers in the government of Prime Minister King who favoured incurring deficits to spur consumer spending in the hope of averting a postwar economic collapse. "Can you imagine what a difference this amount will make to the health and welfare of the children of our country?" Claxton asked. However, before Canadian parents and children could share in the wealth their nation was offering through Canada's first universal social program, Claxton and the newly created department over which he presided had a monumental task before them: not only did they have to oversee the establishment of the new department, but they also had to register an estimated 3 million children for the family allowance program and ensure that 1.5 million families across Canada received their family allowance cheques in July 1945 and regularly each month thereafter.

The administrative challenge was tremendous and it exceeded any previous peacetime administrative organization in both size and scope. Application forms had to be prepared and sent to every household in Canada, national and provincial offices had to be established and personnel trained, office equipment had to be obtained, the ages of all Canadian children who were registered had to be verified, and addresses had to be available to send the cheques to parents. All of this had to be accomplished during a period of desperate wartime labour and equipment shortages, and with little infrastructure in place to facilitate such a task. However, the whole process went exceedingly well, largely because the government was able to call on the federal machinery that had been assembled during the war, and on the large pool of female volunteers who had been extremely active during the war. By the end of July 1945, nearly all parents with children under sixteen years of age had received their first family allowance cheques from the government.

Since family allowances were a federal initiative, Ottawa had to provide the administrative framework for the registration process. However, Ottawa had no control over vital statistics, information that was essential to the registration process. Because the constitutional division of powers gave jurisdiction for the recording of vital statistics to the provinces, the federal authorities needed provincial cooperation to access the data to effectively verify the birth date and death of children under the age of sixteen. Just after the government introduced legislation to implement family allowances in the summer of 1944, the Department of Finance realized the enormous difficulty that would face administrative officials as they had to verify more than 3.5 million births by 1 July 1945, as well the deaths of all children since 1928.[2] They knew the matter was complicated – as so many things are in Canada – by the constitutional division of power. The 1941 census had found that between 96% and 97% of all births in Canada were registered with the provincial authorities.

Working with the Dominion Bureau of Statistics during the fall of 1944, the Department of Finance considered three different scenarios in which it might effectively and quickly verify the birth of all Canadian children. It considered – and dismissed – the proposal that parents submit birth certificates with their applications for family allowances. Such a process would be easiest for federal government officials but would place too great a burden on provincial authorities who would be bombarded with requests for certificates. Moreover, parents would have to pay for the birth certificates from their provincial governments, and even when the official records were received with the application forms, the federal officials would not know if the child was still alive. Ottawa also realized that the existing arrangement with the provinces that required them to provide the Dominion Bureau of Statistics with typewritten copies of vital statistics was too cumbersome; the bureau had destroyed the materials that pre-dated 1940 because it did not have sufficient space to handle all the records. The department decided instead that the best method was to have the provinces supply the information needed for registration on microfilm to allow Ottawa to create a central registry of vital statistics for the express purpose of implementing the family allowance program.[3]

The task of creating a central registry of vital statistics fell to officials in the Department of Trade and Commerce and the Department of Finance. On 28 September 1944, officials from the Dominion Bureau of Statistics, the Dominion Treasury, the Dominion Council of Health, and the provincial vital statistics offices met in Ottawa to discuss how to create a national system of verification for births, stillbirths, marriages, and deaths. They agreed that the provinces would supply to the Dominion Bureau of Statistics microfilm forms of all vital statistics after 1 July 1945. The federal government agreed to provide each province with the equipment necessary to film the records, and to have the National Register of Vital Records in place for the family allowances registration process. As part of the arrangement, the provinces agreed that all births registered with the provinces from 1 January 1925 to 30 June 1945 would be photographed immediately and forwarded to the Dominion Bureau of Statistics.[4] Still, the federal authorities feared that there might be a problem with the information from Quebec, especially for older children, because there was no recognized central registration authority in that province. Quebec was divided into judicial districts, each with a records office under the care of the prothonotary of the superior court. The priests were the registers, and they were supposed to submit their registries at the end of each year. They were also required to provide a record of baptisms, marriages, and burials to the provincial Bureau of Health, but federal officials worried that these records did not have any legal status akin to the registrations completed in the other provinces. In the end, the federal officials had to proceed without having the necessary records from Quebec.[5]

With the machinery in place to provide for the verification of birth records, Ottawa then turned to establishing the administrative bureaucracy to undertake the registration process and provide for the smooth operation of the program thereafter. It considered two alternatives on how best to deliver the program to Canadians: it could either centralize the bureaucracy in Ottawa or create regional or provincial offices to perform the tasks. It chose the latter, and established provincial offices (though called regional offices) in each of the nine capitals, claiming that decentralization would produce a more efficient system and allow officials to respond more quickly to local concerns and problems. Yet two other factors clearly influenced Ottawa's decision. First, it continued to worry about accusations, particularly from Premier George Drew of Ontario (though others such as premiers Stuart Garson of Manitoba, Maurice Duplessis of Quebec, and social worker Charlotte Whitton voiced similar concerns) that Ottawa was usurping the constitutional power of the provinces over social welfare through its national family allowance program. Duplessis had written King that the legislation with respect to allowances was ultra vires because the federal government had infringed on the exclusive provincial jurisdiction over family life, education, and civil rights. King wrote Duplessis that his charge was erroneous since the act did not attempt to legislate in respect of family life, education, or civil laws. Rather, family allowances upheld the family and the home as the foundation of national life, including those in the province of Quebec.[6] The Quebec legislature passed its own Family Allowances Act on 21 February 1945, giving the provincial government the authority to negotiate with Ottawa for the "establishment of family allowances in conformity with the interests and the constitutional rights of the Province," though the effort was essentially symbolic.[7] Also, King and others had said several times during the debate on family allowances that such a program would bring the federal government closer to the people. When it established an office in each of the provincial capitals to administer family allowances, the government did, in part, bring itself closer to the people.[8] And the decision to decentralize the administration of family allowances was seen in the provinces as a positive development. Premier J. Walter Jones of Prince Edward Island praised Claxton for making family allowances a general community enterprise, one in which a provincial office was established and staffed by local people.[9] Still, once the program began, Ottawa would have monthly contact with virtually all of the families in Canada.

However, recruitment for the senior positions in the Department of National Health and Welfare to administer the family allowance program did not go smoothly. There was quite a negative reaction when on 15 December 1944 the Civil Service Commission advertised in Canadian newspapers for a director of family allowances in Ottawa and for nine regional directors. While the advertisements asked that the successful applicants hold a university degree and considerable administrative experience and training, what instead caused trouble was that the competition was restricted to males. Several women's organizations, including the Canadian Federation of Business and Professional Women's Clubs, the Canadian Federation of University Women, the Canadian Association of Social Workers (CASW), and the Canadian Association of Scientific Workers, were outraged that women were not permitted to apply for the positions. All of these organizations complained to Prime Minister King and Minister Claxton. CASW president Joy A. Maines wrote to Claxton, "Limiting applications to men is discriminatory and undemocratic." The CASW also reminded the minister that there were many more women than men qualified for social welfare administration in Canada, and that the nature of the clientele served by the program made it important that women be included in administrative positions.

The government realized it had erred and quickly relented. Claxton informed Maines and others who had protested that the Civil Service Commission had made a mistake; the competition would be open to both men and women.[10] It was a shallow victory for women's groups, however, since R.B. Cury, a former wing commander with the Royal Canadian Air Force and an educator in Nova Scotia, was hired as the national director of family allowances in the Department of National Health and Welfare in Ottawa. All of the regional directors were also male, most of them officers returning from the war. Even though there were more than forty-two thousand women enlisted in the Canadian military, the government was clearly in no hurry to appointment them to administrative and executive positions within the federal government. Muriel McQueen Fergusson, a graduate of Mount Allison and Dalhousie Universities who had also fought the discriminatory practices against women, became the first female regional director of family allowances in 1947 when she was appointed regional

FIGURE 7   Muriel McQueen Fergusson, shown here as the Speaker of the Canadian Senate, had her application for regional director of the family allowance program turned down because only males were being considered. She became the first director of a regional office when she was appointed director of the New Brunswick family allowance office in 1947.
Library and Archives Canada, John Evans/Alan Aylesworth MacNaughton fonds, PA-185700, reprinted with permission

director for New Brunswick, though her application had been rejected in 1945 because she was a woman.[11]

Women's groups were pleased, however, that the family allowance cheques would be made payable to mothers. There had never been much doubt that this would be the case in all of the English-speaking provinces, but Louis St. Laurent, the minister of justice and King's Quebec lieutenant, had worried during the parliamentary debate in the summer of 1944 that designating mothers as the recipients in Quebec might create additional problems for the provincial Liberal government as it headed into an August 1944 election. There was already considerable disenchantment in Quebec with the Liberals over the issue of conscription, and St. Laurent did not wish to further aggravate the political situation. Under the Civil Code in Quebec, all property belonging to a woman at the time of her marriage, as well as that of her husband, was held in what was called a Community of Property. The husband, as head of the family council, controlled this unless the woman had specifically contracted otherwise. King had said during the parliamentary debate on the family allowances bill that while his government would have preferred to have mothers receive the family allowance cheques, it would designate a parent only after consultation with the provinces. However, after the Quebec election (which the Liberals lost), and with the federal election won, St. Laurent told the Cabinet on 19 June 1945 that he was now indifferent on the matter and was quite agreeable to having cheques payable to mothers, though there might be some question of interference with the law of Quebec that would have to be worked out. Even so, King believed that the government should be consistent, and if family allowances were paid to mothers in all the other provinces, then it should be so in Quebec. "Now is the time to take a definite stand," King told his Cabinet, and it was subsequently arranged that cheques would be printed in the name of the mother instead of the father. King had insisted during the debate in the House of Commons that family allowances would strengthen the family unit, and he had long maintained that the mother was central to family stability.[12]

Not surprisingly, his decision did not raise any opposition; it was met with approval and praise. There had been considerable pressure on King to have the cheques paid to mothers across Canada.[13] Thérèse Casgrain, a popular feminist from Quebec, wrote King, after she had lobbied Claxton, to warn him that if family allowance cheques were not sent to mothers in Quebec as they were in the rest of Canada, this would be seen as discriminating against Quebec women. Such humiliation could hardly help Canadian unity, a matter to which King was firmly committed. She also reminded King that St. Laurent's insistence that payment to mothers might interfere with the Civil Code was simply misinformed, since family allowances were a federal matter on which provincial law had no impact.[14] Even the Quebec legislature passed a resolution urging that cheques be sent to mothers. The Canadian Federation of Business and Professional Women's Clubs also wanted the cheques paid to mothers across the country.[15] Similarly, a Gallup Poll found that 77% of Canadians surveyed wanted mothers to receive family allowance cheques; even in Quebec where many commentators had suggested there would be opposition to designating mothers as the recipients, the survey found that only 25% of those polled wanted fathers to receive family allowances.[16] The National Council of Women, convening in Sackville, New Brunswick, for its 52nd annual meeting, expressed its pleasure to King for issuing the cheques to mothers in all provinces. Canada must not be allowed to return to its pre-war discriminatory policies toward women, given their contribution to the country during the war, the council told King.[17] King clearly agreed. Although it is not considered here, it would be revealing to know how fathers reacted to the government's decision to pay family allowances to mothers. Did the decision cause a crisis in masculinity, and did it undermine in any way the traditional notion of the male as the head of the household and the provider for his family? A related question that needs to be considered is the impact of the regular family allowance benefits on empowering mothers in the postwar period. Clearly, when the government made an attempt to terminate the program in the early 1970s for some Canadians, many middle-income women protested vehemently, claiming they stood to lose the only source of income they received independent of their husband's.

To provide training for the national registration as well as to serve as a trial run, Ottawa asked Prince Edward Island Premier J. Walter Jones if it could run the process in his province for several months to gain some valuable experience before the national registration began on 15 March. Jones agreed.[18] On 1 February, registration forms were mailed to all the homes in Canada's smallest province, which then had a population of less than 96,000. By the time the regional office was established in Charlottetown, a few days later on 6 February, Claxton told the press that more than 40% of the families in the province had been registered. Given the response to the registration process from the parents, he said it was clear that everyone in Prince Edward Island was in favour of family allowances,[19] though it was unlikely that many Canadian parents – in Prince Edward Island or elsewhere – would chose to forgo the benefits for their child whether or not they agreed with family allowances in principle. As it would in each province, the Department of National Health and Welfare appointed a regional director for Prince Edward Island. Allan Nicholson, a former school principal at Montague and a discharged army veteran, was selected for the post. His task of overseeing the registration process was made considerably easier because Claxton and his officials had enlisted the support of the Liberal government in PEI, recruited a group of volunteers through various women's voluntary services to handle the large volume of mail, and arranged for officials (including Claxton himself) to speak to community groups, especially the local service clubs, about family allowances. They also blanketed the province with print and radio advertisements covering all aspects of the program.[20] Claxton told the Canadian Club in Vancouver just three days before the national registration began that if they received the same kind of cooperation on the part of the other

FIGURE 8   The Family Allowance office in Charlottetown, PEI, the city where the plan was introduced.
Library and Archives Canada, National Film Board, neg. no. C45315

provinces, municipalities, and voluntary agencies as they had in Prince Edward Island, they would be able to handle the national registration very quickly and efficiently.[21]

Claxton and his department strived to keep Canadians informed about the family allowance registration. Before the national registration began, Claxton wrote all Members of Parliament, explaining how his department proposed to handle the registration of children and the payment of the first cheques for July 1945. He briefly reviewed the success they had with the PEI registration, and tried to reassure parliamentarians that he intended to work closely with the provinces. Moreover, he said, all appointments in the department to oversee family allowances were being made by the Civil Service Commission and without any political interference. He also included with his report a draft booklet on family allowances that his department had prepared to mail with the registration forms to parents. The booklet was printed in mid-March as "Family Allowances: A Children's Charter." The title was obviously selected to reflect Canada's commitment to fulfilling the Declaration of the Rights of Children, or the Children's Charter, as it was called, that had been adopted at Geneva and endorsed by the League of Nations some years earlier. Signatories to the charter promised to provide for the normal development of the child, both materially and spiritually; the charter also called for children to be fed when hungry, nursed when sick, guarded against exploitation, and cared for when orphaned.[22] The booklet, designed for editorial writers, teachers, clergymen, and health care workers, asked and answered forty-five questions about all facets of the family allowance program. One section of the booklet compared the total federal tax collected and the anticipated family allowances payments by regions and provinces (see Table 2).[23]

On 15 March 1945, the Dominion Post Office delivered to every household in Canada – with the exception of Prince Edward Island – a registration form, a sheet of directions on how to complete the forms, and a postage-paid, return envelope addressed to the regional director of family allowances in each province. Parents were asked to complete the seven questions on the form and return it to the regional director. Because the Dominion Bureau of Statistics was working with the provinces to compile a national registry of births and deaths, parents were not asked to provide documentation verifying the birth of their children. Even though only less than 4% of the applications returned in Prince Edward Island required additional information from the parents, the Department of

Table 2

Redistributive nature of family allowances

Region	Total federal tax		Estimated family allowances	
	($)	(%)	($)	(%)
Maritimes	109,000,000	4	28,000,000	11
Quebec	905,000,000	34	84,000,000	33
Ontario	1,235,000,000	47	75,000,000	29
Prairies	186,000,000	7	54,000,000	21
British Columbia	206,000,000	8	15,000,000	6

National Health and Welfare had made minor changes to the form for the national registration.[24]

The registration forms asked parents to list the full names of all their children as well as their places and dates of birth. Both parents were asked to provide their names and mailing addresses, and when both signatures were not available, applicants had to explain why one was missing. The application also asked parents if all children over the age of six regularly attended school, and if not, to provide the reason for their absence. It wanted to know if all the applicants' children were living with them, and if they had been living continuously in Canada for the past three years. Finally, parents were asked if either the father or the mother had been a member of the military at any time since 1939. Accompanying the application form was a sheet of illustrations designed by the National Film Board to assist parents in completing the registration form for their children. The informational guides were directed at mothers, whom the Department of National Health and Welfare wanted to complete the application form.[25]

At the same time that the registration forms were mailed to households, the department began an advertising blitz targeting movie houses, radio stations, and newspapers and magazines. In all, the advertisements appeared in 947 publications, including 715 weekly newspapers and 47 foreign language publications, with a combined circulation of 9.3 million. Information bulletins were broadcast over eighty-three radio stations. The first of advertisements ran in early March, alerting parents to the fact that the registration forms were to be mailed shortly. It also briefly explained that the allowances were to aid parents in rearing their children and would be paid monthly, beginning in July 1945. The second advertisement, about a week later, announced that the registration forms were mailed to every household on 15 March and parents had to register to receive the family allowances. It also reminded parents that they were helping their children when they registered for family allowances. The third and fourth advertisements included a picture of the registration form and coached parents on how to complete the form. The next ad in the sequence featured an unhappy child asking, "Hey Mom! Why haven't you sent in that form?" The final ad in the series was also a reminder that the registration process was well underway and that all children should be registered immediately. This advertisement showed a mother completing the registration form with her three children looking on with approval. Only mothers and children were captured in all seven advertisements, and the department asked mothers to sign the applications with their given names and their married name, for example, Mary Ann Jones rather than Mrs. William John Jones. Each of the seven advertisements also included two maple leafs and the words "For a Greater Canada," which served as a constant reminder that the allowances were coming from the Government of Canada,[26] and to capitalize on the government's objective of making Canadians aware of the new features of their Canadian citizenship.

Brooke Claxton was very much involved in the publicity campaign. On 21 March 1945, he explained the registration process in a national radio broadcast. He reiterated much of what was contained in the newspaper and media advertisements, and he also provided information on the connection between family allowances and income tax. This was an issue that worried some Canadians, and Claxton assured them that family allowances were not taxable. He reminded those who had been receiving tax deductions for their children that they would not be able to continue to claim the deduction and receive the family allowances at the same time. Even so, those taxpayers were eligible to apply for family allowances, but their income tax deductions were to be reduced by the amount of the family allowances they received.[27] The relationship between family allowances and income tax deductions proved particularly difficult to explain to Canadians. When Parliament passed the Family Allowances Act, it agreed that there would be no duplication of benefits between family allowances and income tax credits for the same child. However, Claxton admitted, there was some confusion stemming from the adjustment between the income tax and family allowances. He attempted to explain the matter in a subsequent radio address, using the information that Finance Minister J.L. Ilsley had released on 18 April 1945. Since 1917, when the income tax was first introduced, married workers with incomes above $2,000 were permitted to claim a deduction for each dependent child. Family allowances were designed to improve opportunities for children of parents with low incomes, and the government attempted to argue that family allowances were essentially an extension of the existing system of income tax credits to families not receiving the full benefit of the $108 tax credit for dependent children. King had said on a number of occasions during the debate on family allowances that the program would extend a benefit to those whose incomes were so low they received less than the full income tax allowance. Until the Income War Tax Act could be amended to take account of family allowances, the government made a temporary arrangement to cover the last six months of 1945 to avoid duplication of benefits under the tax system and the family allowance program. Not surprisingly, since family allowances were designed to help equalize and improve the opportunities for children of parents with low incomes, that group – those with annual incomes of less than $1,200 – was to receive the maximum benefit from family allowances. Those with incomes greater than $1,200 and less than $3,000 retained the full value of their income tax credit for their dependent children as well as a percentage of their family allowance payments. However, those with a taxable income in excess of

Table 3

Family allowances and income tax deductions

Income for year		Percentage of family allowances retained
< $1,200		100
> $1,200 but not over $1,400		90
$1,400	$1,600	80
$1,600	$1,800	70
$1,800	$2,000	60
$2,000	$2,200	50
$2,200	$2,400	40
$2,400	$2,600	30
$2,600	$2,800	20
$2,800	$3,000	10

$3,000 were not permitted to benefit from family allowances, and their tax credits were reduced by the full amount of any family allowances they received. The Department of Finance produced the table that appears above as an interim arrangement, showing Canadians the percentage of family allowances they could retain in addition to any deduction claimed under the income tax rules (see Table 3).[28]

The concern over the relationship between family allowances and taxation was only one of Claxton's worries. While the minister had received a number of letters from individuals seeking information on the impact family allowances would have on their income tax,[29] the government became extremely worried over reports that large numbers of Canadians were not registering for benefits. The Wartime Information Board reported to the Cabinet that there was some reluctance among many Canadians to register their children for family allowances. A.D. Dunton, the general manager of the board, noted in his report on 26 March that some were uncertain whether to register or not, though he suggested that the government's advertisements were proving helpful. Many Canadians were fearful, Dunton told the Cabinet, that the government would investigate their earnings and increase the taxes they owed the state.[30] The Canadian correspondent for the *New York Times* reported on 29 April 1945 that Canadians were reacting slowly to family allowances because there was considerable uncertainty as to what the family allowance program would do to their incomes and what the government would do with the personal information it gathered on the registration forms.[31]

The government could not afford any delays, however, and Claxton took to the airwaves once more to explain the goals of the family allowance program and registration process. Family allowances were designed to give Canadian children greater opportunities for health, food, education, clothing, and shelter, irrespective of the size of the father's earnings, the size of the family, and the place of birth. He told Canadians that the government was not seeking any private information from its citizens, and asked them to trust their government, since it was interested only in the information necessary to show the children for whom an allowance should be paid and how much should be paid to each family. He told them that the registration process was going smoothly and assured them that thousands of Canadians had already registered their children. He also asked for patience, stating that the registration was a new and major undertaking; in such a circumstance, difficulties and mistakes are inevitable, he admitted, without alluding to the complaint that in some cases English forms had been sent to French-speaking homes and French forms to English-speaking ones. Some homes had not received any forms, and in several cases there were not enough forms for everyone in a given community. All problems were being addressed immediately, he reassured his audience. Claxton concluded his radio remarks by telling people that family allowances were extremely popular, and encouraging them, regardless of their income, to help themselves and the government by filling out their registration forms if they wanted the family allowance.

The government subsequently approved a further $32,500 publicity campaign to help remove the confusion that appeared to exist in the public mind regarding the relationship between family allowance benefits and the income tax system. A series of advertisements in both French and English were prepared by Cockfield Brown and Company Limited and Canadian Advertising Limited, two advertising agencies closely connected to the Liberal Party.[32] The Liberal Party itself did not stay in the background. In a decidedly political speech that several times attributed family allowances to the Liberals rather than to the government, Mrs. S.C. Tweed, one of the National Liberal Federation vice-presidents, encouraged parents to register their children. She reassured them that they would not lose any of their income as a result of the program, even if family allowance benefits increased the amount of money coming into their homes: "After all, the Liberals planned family allowances to help the children in the homes where there is not enough money for their needs. They want these children to have a better life. They certainly are not going to give them [family allowance benefits] with one hand and take them away with the other."[33]

At the end of May, by the time the government had hoped many Canadians would have registered their children for family allowances, a Gallup public opinion poll uncovered another problem. The survey found that many Canadians believed that parents would misuse the estimated $200 million paid in family allowances. The Gallup Poll asked Canadians who had heard of family allowances, "In your opinion, are a large number of Canadians likely to use this money for purposes [other than food, clothing, and education for children], or are only a few likely to use it improperly?" Thirty percent of respondents said they believed that many families would use the monthly payments improperly, while 56% said only a few would use it improperly. However, the survey also found that 50% and 58% of those surveyed in Ontario and Quebec, respectively, believed parents would use their family allowances properly.[34] Still, the government was clearly concerned that more than one-third of Canadians believed that the financial resources committed to family allowances would be wasted by many who received the benefits.

Of course, this view that allowances would be wasted did not surprise King and Claxton. Shortly after the government had indicated that it was going to implement family allowances for all Canadians, critics of the initiative had warned that parents could not be trusted to use the money as it was intended. Charlotte Whitton had been vociferous in this regard, and Claxton had tried in every public pronouncement on family allowances to dismiss such attitudes as those of cynics and reactionaries. In one radio address he had said, "If you look at everything with a cynical attitude of mind you can never assure yourself that any good will not be abused." He reminded Canadians that the Dependents' Allowances Board made six hundred thousand payments a month to the wives and dependants of service men, and the board had determined, through careful scrutiny, that the great majority of parents used that assistance wisely. Even so, as the family allowance registration process moved into high gear, Claxton was not content to rely solely on parents doing the right thing with their family allowance benefits, though he hoped that making the cheques payable to mothers increased the likelihood of the money being spent wisely.

In one radio address just before the cheques were mailed, Claxton praised the virtue of mothers: "No one knows better than the mother of a family where the shoe pinches, and we know the great majority of mothers will spend the allowances in the best interests of the children."[35] He reassured Canadians that arrangements were being made by his department with various social agencies and the provincial governments to monitor the use of family allowances to ensure that the benefits were directed toward the well-being of children. If parents misused the money, the regulations accompanying the act allowed the department to suspend payments and/or divert the allowance to some other person who would ensure that it was spent properly for the benefit and advancement of the child. And in the case of school attendance, family allowances would help immensely. No child over six years of age would receive family allowances unless she attended school regularly, which Claxton said would assist the provinces in enforcing their school attendance law without interfering with education in the provinces.[36]

To address the specific concerns raised in the Gallup survey, Claxton turned once again to another advertising campaign. This series of graphic illustration and posters was directed at mothers to encourage them to spend their family allowance cheques as the government intended, and to reassure Canadians that their government would not tolerate misuse of the family allowance benefits. The first advertisement told mothers, "It's Up to You to Spend your Family Allowances Cheque Wisely." In a series of illustrations, it suggested spending the benefits on necessities such as food and clothing for the children, and on items that made for better living conditions for children. Then it told mothers, "Make your spending plans fit the size of your cheque" and "for your children's benefit get full value from your family allowance cheque." The second advertisement was titled "Ask yourself these Questions" and encouraged mothers to ask themselves four questions each month when they received their benefits cheque: Are you giving your children proper food? Are your children receiving the medical and dental attention they need? Are your children properly clothed for school and play? Have your children the things they need to make their home a pleasant place to live in? To encourage proper use of the federal monies, the advertisements encouraged mothers, "Make certain your children are receiving the care they need during their growing years to make them happy and useful citizens."[37]

Making better Canadians was precisely one of the purposes of the program. Echoing what Prime Minister King had said in the Cabinet and in the parliamentary debate on family allowances, Claxton frequently reminded Canadians that the Canadian family had been strained during the war years, and his government wanted to strengthen family life. In one radio address, Claxton stated, "We want to create for the family the most congenial environment in which its members can grow and develop into useful citizens – into good Canadians. In Family Allowances we have an act which goes far towards providing this environment." In a later speech, he returned to the government's most general objective in family allowances: "Let us regard it [family allowances] as a corner-stone on which to build a greater, stronger Canada."[38] The federal government saw all aspects of social security as being of paramount importance in strengthening national unity, which had been severely threatened during the five years of war. When the government prepared its proposals for the Dominion-Provincial Conference in August 1945, for instance, it said that a nationwide social security program would strengthen Canadian unity. Social security was designed to provide a network of protection for all Canadians and to stimulate the national economy. The government's proposals also noted that social security measures might be "less tangible perhaps, but in some ways most important of all" if they made "a vital contribution to the development of our concept of Canadian citizenship and to the forging of lasting bonds of Canadian unity."[39]

Of course, in 1945 the benefits and privileges of Canadian citizenship were not distributed evenly to all Canadians. This was surely the case with Aboriginal Canadians, who, as mentioned earlier, were at the time commonly referred to as Indians and Eskimaux (Inuit).[40] When the family allowances regulations were approved by an order-in-council on 3 August 1945, they included two separate sections for the registration of Aboriginal Canadians. One dealt with Indians, the other with Eskimos (Inuit) and nomads. The first accepted the definition of an Indian as described by the Indian Act and made it clear that the regulations applied only to those Indians who lived in an organized territory and resided permanently on a reserve. The Indian agent was given considerable authority when Aboriginal children were being registered. Since the registration form was normally completed under the supervision of the Indian agent and/or passed through his office, the Department of National Health and Welfare accepted his advice on such matters as whether or not the applicant was the parent of the child, cared for the child, and whether or not a child had been legally adopted. A separate section covered Eskimos and nomads. Applicants were designated as Inuit if they appeared on the roll or records of the Bureau of the Northwest Territories and Yukon Affairs of the Department of Mines and Resources, the federal department then responsible for Aboriginal affairs. Inuit were to mail their completed registration forms to the registrar of vital statistics of the district of the province or territory where they resided. The registrar would attempt to verify the information and send the application to the regional director of family allowances. A nomad was defined as a person of mixed Indian or Inuit blood, residing in the Northwest Territories or the Yukon Territory, who was neither an Inuit nor Indian, but who followed the Indian or Inuit mode of living.[41]

By the time the registration process had been finalized, the government had decided that the registration of Indians and Inuit would be made through Indian agents and the Northwest Territories offices of the Department of Mines and Resources. It was also decided that family allowance benefits for Inuit and Indians could be in either cash or kind, whichever the Indian agent considered most advisable.[42] Even so, the regulations stated that the allowance would be payable to the mother if an application had been made jointly by both parents. Notwithstanding this clause, the director of family allowances could, on the advice of the Indian Affairs branch of the Department of Mines and Resources

FIGURE 9   Martin Donnan, RCMP Constable, registering Nalvana's new baby for family allowance, Coppermine, NWT, 1949-50.
Library and Archives Canada, Richard Harrington/Richard Harrington fonds/PA-147231, reprinted with permission

and if he deemed it in the best interest of the child, direct the benefits to the Indian Agency Trust Account of the agency where the parents resided. There it was to be administered for the children by the Indian agent according to the guidelines provided by the Indian Affairs Branch. In the case of Inuit and nomads, however, the regulations did not specify that payments had to be made to the mother. Rather, it stated that payments were to be paid to the Bureau of Northwest Territories and Yukon Affairs, to be distributed by the bureau on behalf of the child for whom the allowance was paid, in accordance with the provisions of agreements from time to time made between the director of family allowances and the bureau.[43] Inuit families were required to use a portion of their benefits for such items as dried milk and dried eggs, pablum and other children's foods, regardless of the supply of their traditional foods. These practices clearly illustrated Ottawa's distrust of Inuit parents to make wise and sensible choices for their children, and there was considerable concern in official Ottawa that the income security program would create a sense of dependency

FIGURE 10   The federal government mandated that a portion of the family allowance to Inuit families had to be spent on what it considered essentials, such as powdered milk. Here, storekeepers Mr. and Mrs. Sigvaldasson are seen issuing Family Allowance to an Inuit woman in the form of powdered milk, Cape Smith, NWT [Nunavut], 1948. *Library and Archives Canada, S.J. Bailey, PA-167637*

among the people of the North. Because of the difficulty of communications in the North and the absence of a comprehensive census of Inuit people, most families did not receive benefits until 1947, and it was 1950 before all families were registered. Inuit families living in the Mackenzie Delta were paid by cheque beginning in 1953, and by 1961, this practice was adopted for all families.[44]

One of the issues that had to be settled for Aboriginal peoples was the requirement that beneficiaries of family allowances be in regular attendance at school. Given the settlement patterns of many Aboriginal parents, school attendance was not always possible. Yet the regulations presented an opportunity for the federal government to improve the level of education among Aboriginal children. The director of the Indians Affairs branch in the Department of Mines and Resources wrote in a 1945 memorandum to all those involved with Aboriginal peoples that where Indian day schools had been established on the reserve and were readily accessible, attendance of Indian pupils needed to be rigidly enforced. He recommended that the refusal of an Indian parent to send his child to school, or the refusal of the child to attend school, result in the immediate cancellation of the allowances. However, the director realized that where no school facilities existed or when attendance at non-native schools was simply impossible, the allowances should be paid. Still, he noted that the legislation on school attendance presented an excellent opportunity to substantially raise educational levels among Canada's indigenous peoples, and for that reason alone, the law needed to be strictly enforced.[45]

R.B. Curry, the national director of family allowances, was more accommodating. He wrote all regional directors that "the interpretation of the school question need not follow the same pattern as it does for whites [non-Aboriginals]. Indians, in most cases, live a different type of life from white people and we should be able to regard Indian children as receiving equivalent training when they are trapping or working at home." He advised a liberal interpretation of the Family Allowances Act, and told the officials in the provinces and territories that the only Indian child for which he would not make a payment was the one living in a residential school, hospital, or some other institution maintained by a religious organization or the government. There was no similar regulation governing the children of Inuit and nomads. For them, the government decided that where there were no schools provided, the parents would continue to receive family allowances as long as the Bureau of the Northwest Territories and Yukon Affairs was satisfied that the child was receiving training by his parents according to the prevailing Inuit or nomad customs.[46]

The impact of such federal programs on the Inuit requires further investigation and study, but it is important to acknowledge here that "The Report of the Mackenzie Valley Pipeline Inquiry" (the Berger Report) noted that family allowances had a pervasive influence on people living in the North. Despite what Curry might have written to regional directors, Justice Thomas Berger claims that many Inuit and Indians came to understand that they would not receive their benefits if their children did not attend school regularly. As a result, many of them left the barrens to settle in communities and attend schools where the curriculum bore no relation to their parents' way of life or to the traditions of their people.[47]

In the middle of the registration process, Prime Minister King announced a campaign of a different sort. On 13 April 1945, he told Parliament that Canadians would go to the polls on 11 June to vote in the much anticipated federal election.[48] Throughout the campaign, the Liberals stressed their ability to govern during difficult times. King repeatedly told the electorate that the Liberals had successfully brought the country through the war with sound leadership and good management, and asked voters for a third straight mandate to govern Canada in the uncertain times ahead. In one radio address, he said that Canadians would have to decide either to allow the national affairs and international relations of the nation to be carried out by his experienced and trusted administration or turned over to unknown and untried hands.[49]

In addition to leadership and experience, the Liberals emphasized their commitment to postwar planning and reconstruction. Much of the Liberal campaign advertising focused on the party's plan for the future rather than on its management of the wartime economy and its contribution to winning the Second World War. King told Canadians, "My life interests, I need not tell you, have been with the cause of peace and with the promotion of human welfare and social reform."[50] In addition, King and the Liberals reminded voters that they did not wait until the war was over to begin what was necessary to meet the challenges that lay ahead. They had already placed on the statutes of Canada law after law to deal with the situations that would have to be met through the coming years: "We come now with a series of measures which ... will help to make our country more prosperous than it has ever been before."[51]

Not surprisingly, family allowances – an important part of the Liberal social agenda – played a role in the campaign, though it is difficult to determine precisely how influential they really were. The Liberals tried to use the opposition to family allowances from some high-profile Conservatives, principally Premier George Drew of Ontario and Charlotte Whitton, to convince voters that the Conservative Party was against all the progressive social security measures that the Liberals favoured and that the government had started to implement. However, the Conservatives fully realized their vulnerability on social welfare issues and worked diligently to convince voters that they were as progressive as the Liberals in their plans for family allowances and social security in general.

The Conservatives' stand on family allowances was one of the major issues as their candidates gathered in Ottawa on 10 April 1945, just three days before King called the election. Bracken presented several considerations to guide the candidates in the upcoming campaign. First, he reminded them that family allowances had become the law of the land in part because the principle of family allowances had enjoyed the unanimous support of all parties in the House of Commons. Second, the Conservatives were committed to family allowances and, if elected, they would not eliminate the program, as the Liberals had charged. Third, he admitted that there had been considerable confusion in the media regarding the party's position on family allowances over the preceding months, but candidates had to tell voters that the party had endorsed the program and continued to do so. Bracken reminded the candidates that his characterization of family allowances as a "political bribe" did not mean that the measure was a bad one or that he did not support it; rather, it meant that he believed the Liberals had rushed the act through Parliament for their own political gain. Bracken also defended George Drew to the candidates. The Ontario premier had been an outspoken critic of the Liberal's handling of the measure, even though he, like Bracken himself, favoured the principle of family allowances. Fourth, Bracken repeated to candidates what he had said for months: family allowances represented an invasion of provincial rights and they should have been implemented only after consultation with the provinces. Finally, he advised candidates not to criticize family allowances too strongly, because it would aid the Liberal propaganda machine in labelling them as "Tory reactionaries who are against this measure of social reform."[52] However, Bracken and Conservative candidates must surely have known that it would be extremely difficult to undo the political damage that had already been done to the party.

Not surprisingly, the Liberals took every opportunity during the campaign to tell the electorate that the Conservatives opposed family allowances. The Liberal *Toronto Star* ridiculed the Conservatives' assertion that they supported family allowances in principle but were opposed to the manner in which the Liberals had enacted the legislation creating the program. The newspaper described the Conservative social welfare policies as reactionary, as Bracken had predicted the Liberal press would. In one of its editorials, the *Star* asked voters if they wanted a government whose social philosophy feared that family allowance benefits would raise the birth rate of the "chronic dependents" and the French-speaking citizens, and lead to a deterioration of the nation.[53]

This type of argument was not restricted to the Liberal press. Brooke Claxton, who seemed to be speaking almost nightly to Canadians over the radio from March to July either in connection with the election campaign or the family allowances registration process, made the same point in his political broadcasts. To be fair, Claxton's radio addresses dealing with registration for family allowances never mentioned the Liberal Party or the election, even though many Canadians could not have distinguished between Claxton, minister of the crown, and Claxton, Liberal politician. His campaign speeches made numerous references to family allowances. In one radio speech over CKPR in Fort William, he called the record of the Conservative Party on family allowances a despicable chapter in Canadian political history. He reminded his listeners that the Conservatives had attacked family allowances when the legislation was introduced in Parliament, and not even their vote for the Family Allowances Act could hide their contempt for such social welfare innovation. He told Canadians not to be fooled by Bracken's conversion, and dismissed it as a desperate ploy to win votes. The Liberals, Claxton reassured his audience, had always been committed to social security, and Prime Minister King had introduced every social measure on the statute books on the Dominion Parliament.[54]

The National Liberal Federation used family allowances extensively throughout the campaign. It prepared a series of flashy well-crafted advertisements and leaflets on the program, as well as materials for use by candidates in their ridings. One of the most effective booklets was entitled *Building a New Social Order for Canada: Liberal Family Allowances*. The front of the four-page leaflet featured a smiling, happy family of five, walking confidently into the future. Inside, family allowances were described as "the BIGGEST step forward in our march to POST WAR PROSPERITY!" In addition to presenting family allowances as the means to provide greater social justice and equality of opportunity for all Canadian children, the campaign brochure described family allowances as a means of providing "more jobs [and] steady jobs for Canadians ... as it will keep thousands of workers in all ranks of life permanently busy supplying the things which they can now afford to buy." The Liberals also tried to respond to Co-operative Commonwealth Federation (CCF) criticism for not introducing family allowances earlier in their parliamentary mandate. It quoted King's explanation (noted above) to M.J. Coldwell, the leader of the CCF, as to why the Liberals had not acted sooner on family allowances: "to use power without having public opinion with you is to adopt the Nazi method of proceeding, which is contrary to the spirit of Liberalism. Part of the art of government ... lies in knowing when it is best to do things and when it is wiser to leave them alone." The booklet noted King's observation that once the mood of the country changed, the Liberals seized the family allowance opportunity. Of course, the brochure also reminded voters that parents would receive a cheque every month for children under sixteen years of age.[55]

A four-page leaflet appeared later in the campaign under a similar title, *Building a New Social Order in Canada*, which had been selected as the theme for the Liberal campaign. This document took direct aim at the Tories and presented them as the party opposed to family allowances. The pamphlet asked voters in bold print "Shall Family Allowances Be Victim of Typical Tory Tactics?" In this brochure, the Liberals played very loosely with the truth. It claimed, "Liberals Believe Family Allowances are Simple Justice to Children ... a corner-stone in the New Social Order for full post-war employment and social security ... and one of the Four Freedoms for which we have been fighting ... Freedom from Want." It also claimed that the Liberals pressed the family allowances bill through Parliament in the face of Tory opposition. Then it asked, "Are you going to allow the Tories to prevent your children from achieving equality of opportunity in the future development of Canada?" It insinuated that Canadian children would not enjoy the benefits of health care, education opportunities, and even nourishment unless the Liberals were returned to power. It also made the issue very simple for voters: "Shall all Canadian Children Have an Equal Chance? It's up to You on Election Day!"[56] In other literature prepared for the campaign, family allowances were presented as one of the twelve practical steps the Liberal government had taken to make Canada a better place in which to work and bring up children.[57] Matthew MacLean, a Liberal member from Nova Scotia, wrote King, "I think the information [I have circulated] will have quite an influence in deciding the vote in this constituency."[58]

Among the materials prepared for Liberal candidates was a thirty-page document discussing all aspects of family allowances, including an explanation of the sliding scale of benefits, the connection to social security, and the rate of payment for all children. It even included a list of criticisms likely to be made against the program, together with responses.[59] Candidates were also sent a fourteen-minute radio talk on family allowances suggesting what they were to say to Canadians. Making particular reference to family allowances being an important part of the new social order the Liberals were building, the radio talk told candidates to espouse the virtues of the program. Family allowances, the Liberals candidates were to say, were the best investments we could make in our national future in providing healthier and better-educated children: "Because they will be stronger and wiser adults than we are, they will be able to speed the progress of Canada faster than our generation had."[60] Perhaps the most effective tool of all was a breakdown, by constituencies, of the estimated monthly payments of family allowances.[61]

Many of the bulletins to candidates and speakers emanating from the national office dealt directly with family allowances. One of the bulletins discussed the immediate implications of the program, such as reductions in infant death rates, improvements in the nutritional standards of Canadians, in the educational opportunities of young children, the fight against child labour, and provision for the security of children. Moreover, family allowances were presented as a democratic and unifying initiative that would treat all Canadian children the same regardless of their ethnicity, colour, creed, nationality, or place of residence, and would allow parents their democratic right to exercise their freedom to select and buy what their children needed. Another of the bulletins described the differences between the Liberals and Conservatives in their trust in parents to do the right thing and spend family allowance cheques properly.[62]

Claxton also dispatched a letter to all Liberal candidates explaining the principles behind the family allowance program, suggesting materials that could be used in their own campaigns, and reminding them that family allowances were one of the most important features of the Liberal record.[63] The National Liberal Federation also distributed a number of quotable quotes to candidates for use in their campaigns; at the top of the list was a comment from the partisan *Toronto Star*, which read, "The return of the King Government to power will ensure the continuance of family allowances. The humanity of the state will be confirmed."[64] When used by Liberal candidates, the implications of such a quote were clear: the election of their Tory opponents would threaten family allowances.

Bracken found it very difficult to defend his party against Liberal allegations. At a rally in Kenora, Ontario, midway through the campaign, he lashed out at Paul Martin, the Liberal MP from Windsor and secretary of state in King's government, for continuing to mislead the voters over the Conservative position on family allowances. According to the *Windsor Daily Star*, Martin had challenged Bracken to "say whether he intended to live up to his assertion that he would remove from the statute books the federal Family Allowances Act." Martin had told voters in his riding that Bracken had called the Family Allowances Act a political bribe, and promised "to erase it from the books were it passed." Bracken accused Martin of lying, although he continued to insist that the timing of the legislation clearly had political advantages for the Liberals. The Tory leader had said there was ample evidence to suggest that the Liberals acted quickly for pure political gain. The Liberals, he said, had hoped family allowances would turn attention from the government's mishandling of conscription. Moreover, family allowances were an issue that appealed to Quebec, where Liberal support had declined sharply as a result of the conscription issue. The massive advertising campaign for family allowances was further evidence, Bracken said, of how the Liberals were using family allowances as "political bait," and how they were perpetuating the lie that the Conservatives opposed family allowances. Moreover, Bracken accused Claxton and the Liberals of "using the taxes [Canadians] pay not only to pay Family Allowances but to pay for the political propaganda of the Party he [Claxton] supports." Bracken reminded the electorate that the Conservatives' policy was "to secure the highest measure of social security the State can afford, short of a measure of taxation and a degree of benefits which discourage enterprise and initiative."[65] He promised to put family allowances on a uniform basis,[66] regardless of the number of children in a family, because his party saw social security as a social obligation and national responsibility.[67]

On 11 June, the Liberals were returned to power with 127 seats, a slim majority of 9 in the 245-seat House of Commons. The result was a stinging rebuke for Prime Minister King and the Liberal Party from the Canadians who had rewarded them with 181 seats just five years earlier. King even lost his own seat in Prince Albert. The Conservatives made major gains, climbing from 40 seats to 67, although they won 23 new seats in Ontario, where 48 Conservatives were elected. Quebec had stood solidly behind the Liberals, giving them 50.8% of the popular vote, and 53 seats to 2 for the Conservatives. The CCF, despite its relatively strong showing in national public opinion surveys throughout 1943 and 1944, remained a minor force in national politics with 28 seats. Still, the Liberals were far ahead in the popular vote with 41.3% compared with 28.5% for the Conservatives and 14.7% for the CCF.

What role did family allowances play in the election outcome? By the end of the campaign, the vast majority of Canadians were familiar with family allowances: a survey conducted by the Canadian Institute of Public Opinion at the end of May 1945 found that 95% of those interviewed had heard of family allowances, and most of them favoured the measure.[68] There was no doubt that family allowances were a central part of the Liberal campaign, and one can only wonder if it saved the Liberals from a stunning political defeat. However, it is likely that the Liberal victory, slim as it was, resulted from a number of factors; parents who voted Liberal in 1945 had not been the victims of state (and Liberal) manipulations. One cannot deny that family allowances certainly enjoyed considerable support among a vast majority of Canadians, many of whom likely associated the program with the Liberal Party. Yet after more than six years of war, during which the state assumed such a pervasive role in the lives of virtually all Canadians, many voters would have come to regard family allowances as the acknowledgement of the state of its financial obligation for all Canadian children. Family allowance benefits came from the state regardless of what political party was in office. Still, many in the Conservative Party, especially Richard B. Hanson, the Conservative House leader, believed the Liberal adoption of family allowances contributed to the Tory party's poor showing.[69] After reviewing the Wartime Information Board's surveys and opinion polls, A.D. Dunton, the general manager of the board, told the Cabinet in a confidential memorandum on 18 June, "The Liberal success is attributed chiefly to the desire for stable government, to the wide appeal of its social legislation and to the 'solid accomplishments' of the administration."[70]

During the election campaign, Canadians completed the forms to register their children, and returned them to the regional office in each province. The Women's Voluntary Services organization in the provincial capitals[71] assisted by handling the envelopes, date-stamping the applications, and sorting the applications to facilitate the registration process and help the program's permanent administrative staff, who numbered about 500 across the country.[72] By 17 July, more than 1.25 million children had been registered, and Claxton once again addressed the nation through the radio service provided by the CBC: "Starting tomorrow morning, we begin mailing Family Allowances cheques to mothers right across Canada." He promised that as soon as the statistics on the first month's family allowance payments were compiled, they would be made available to the public.

Claxton subsequently announced in August a breakdown of what parents in each province had received in family allowances for July: $177,058 in Prince Edward Island, $921,333 in Nova Scotia, $849,136 in New Brunswick, $5.94 million in Quebec, $4.83 million in Ontario, $1.02 million in Manitoba, $1.39 million in Saskatchewan, $1.28 million in Alberta, and $1.11 million in British Columbia. The average allowance per family ranged from a high of $16.76 in Quebec to a low of $11.61 in British Columbia; the national average was $14.18, and the total disbursements from the federal government were $17.56 million for the first month alone, as had been predicted.[73] For the fiscal year 1945-46, the family allowance program contributed more than 2% of Canada's personal average income, which was slightly more than $9,000.[74]

Verifying the birthdates of children had gone smoothly in all of the provinces except Quebec. There it took until 1950 for the authorities to give Ottawa access to provincial birth certificates and vital statistics records. The delay was Duplessis' way to protest Ottawa's intrusion into provincial jurisdiction. The other eight provinces had worked with Ottawa to create a national registry of vital statistics. On 30 July 1945, George Davidson, now the deputy minister of welfare in Ottawa, wrote B.C. McIntyre, the comptroller of the Treasury at the Department of Finance, that Ottawa had not been refused access to the provincial records in Quebec, but that the negotiations were difficulty and lengthy. Davidson was optimistic and told Finance that he believed Premier Duplessis was merely stalling until the Dominion-Provincial Conference planned for August 1945. Claxton had written to Duplessis asking him to complete the arrangement as soon as possible and reminding him that the proposed Vital Statistics Agreement between the Dominion Bureau of Statistics and the province was merely an extension and modernization of an arrangement that had been in existence since 1926. Even so, Duplessis was in no hurry to expedite the arrangement. This meant, of course, that the federal government had to pay family allowances to those who registered in Quebec, without being able to verify the information presented on the registration forms.[75] The negotiations might not have been helped when Quebec learned that the family allowance cheques were printed in French and English only in Quebec; for the rest of country, the cheques were only in English. Several organizations, notably la Ligue des interets nationaux, la Ligue d'action nationale, and the Association d'éducation de canadiens français du Manitoba, protested, claiming that the sole use of English outside of Quebec denied the bilingual nature of Canada and went against the spirit of confederation.[76]

If the letters written by many Canadians to King, Claxton, and the Department of National Health and Welfare can be taken as an indication of the initial reaction to the receipt of the first monthly cheques, family allowances were an immediate success. After receiving her first family allowance cheque in late July 1945, Anna E. Wilson of Hudson Heights, Quebec, wrote King and praised him for personifying what Canadianism was: "You have attempted to find a way in which human beings can maintain the native dignity and self respect that is the right of all men and yet participate in the material benefits with which this country is so greatly blessed."[77] Many letters told of what parents were able to purchase for their children, notably clothing, footwear, and food, as well as other items that promised to improve the health of their children. Others welcomed family allowances because it allowed them to outfit their children and send them to school. One mother wrote: "This really has been the first year I have been able to send our kiddies off to school right on the first day school was open. Other years I had to wait until my husband could raise enough money to get their books, shoes, and clothing for them, and that would be about two weeks after school was open, so I think that we sure have something to be real thankful for." In many cases, the family allowance cheques seemed to strengthen the bonds between citizens and the national government, as was hoped and expected: one mother from Ontario wrote, "I thank Canada more than I could say for I will be the mother to tell my children what Canada had done for them in their young age."[78]

However, there were also a few letters expressing concern. One wrote to complain that the life insurance companies, like the North American Life Assurance Company, started advertising policies for children after the payment of family allowances began,[79] and Charlotte Whitton complained that parents were actually opening savings accounts for their children's family allowances. "Anything more fantastic in the fiscal policy of the state it is hard to imagine," she wrote. "Parents are taking the payment of children's cash grants, wrung from the taxpayer, not for need but to create their own savings and bank accounts."[80]

On 4 August 1945, the *Financial Post* reported its survey of 210 parents in Toronto. The survey supported what parents had written in their letters to the government: "There appears to be very little reason to fear that the baby bonus[,] once it has become accepted routine every month, will drive people either into the beer parlours or away from their own responsibilities." To ensure that this did not occur, Claxton announced in the fall of 1945 that his department would commence an education program for mothers in receipt of the family allowances. A good parental education program that helped mothers spend their family allowances wisely and that promoted good nutrition and child care practices, he said, would benefit the whole nation and, at the same time, remove the necessity of spending money on policing parents.[81]

The family allowance program was off to a good start. So efficient was the registration system that the federal government was able to find all the children born on the day of Queen Elizabeth's coronation in 1952 and present them with a silver spoon to mark the occasion.

5

The Impact of Family Allowances up to the 1960s

"THE PAYMENT OF FAMILY allowances was the best place to take the first step ... in building a social security program for Canada," Brooke Claxton told delegates gathered in Washington, DC, for the National Catholic Welfare Conference just eight months after the family allowance program began. For Claxton, minister of national health and welfare, and the Liberal government, family allowances represented the emergence in Canada and elsewhere of the notion of collective responsibility for children and the state's duty to provide a measure of equality among all children: a new charter of rights for children, perhaps, as part of the new social citizenship that emerged in Canada and other nation-states after the end of the Second World War.[1]

Claxton told his American audience that Canada's family allowance program had its critics in Canada who argued that there were more pressing needs (than those of children) to be addressed, but the government of Prime Minister William Lyon Mackenzie King believed that the payment of a monthly allowance for each child under the age of sixteen would make a significant difference to ordinary Canadians. Although Mackenzie King never fully embraced Keynesianism, family allowances were perhaps Canada's best example of the new economics. Social security initiatives emerged at an agonizingly slow pace in a federal system like Canada's, but the regular payment of even a small sum of money – the average monthly benefit per family of $14.27 at the time – was making an enormous difference. Such payments permitted parents to provide more food, better clothes, and greater medical attention to their children, as well as keep their children in regular school attendance.[2] While Claxton may have exaggerated his government's commitment to a comprehensive social security system for Canada,[3] his enthusiasm for family allowances was shared by thousands of Canadian parents. They would have agreed with his assessment that family allowances had raised the standard of living for many Canadian families. Indeed, all of the reports prepared by a variety of groups – from the federal government itself to the press, from social agencies to international observers – all agreed that family allowances were having a beneficial impact on Canadian families and Canadian society.[4]

The family allowance program was one of the most popular federal policies in the immediate postwar period. Both print and electronic media regularly reported on family allowances; various social, farm, church, and political groups discussed the program endlessly; and more than 75,000 Canadians, on average, took pen to paper each month in the first year of family allowances to correspond with their regional offices about some aspect of the program.[5] Yet despite the enthusiasm for and interest in family allowances across the country, R.B. Curry's first annual report as national director of the program was all very matter-of-fact; it did not reflect any of the excitement that many Canadians and, certainly, the government felt about the program. He simply surveyed the first year's activities in methodical fashion, providing information on such issues as staffing, office space, the registration process, birth verification, the payment of allowances, the special arrangements made for Aboriginal families, the investigation of the misuse of family allowance benefits, school attendance, and the high volume of letters received from recipients each month. In his view, the first year's activities had unfolded as they should have. If he was excited about anything in his report, it was that provincial governments had provided his office with useful information on school attendance; the news on that score was indeed good for a former educator like Curry.[6]

As mentioned earlier, compulsory school attendance was one of the few coercive features of the program. The Family Allowances Act had stipulated that parents would receive family allowances only if their children attended school in accordance with the regulations in the province in which the children resided. Most provinces had included similar clauses regarding school attendance in their mother's allowance programs for more than two decades.[7] Curry was determined that the regulation be enforced, and he worked with each province to ensure that it was. Yet he and his successors at the national headquarters fully realized that the provinces jealously guarded their prerogative in the field of education, and the family allowance officials acted only on the receipt of information from the proper educational authorities in each of the provinces.[8]

Curry's officials worked with each department of education but used different approaches across the nation. In British Columbia, school principals reported flagrant absenteeism to provincial inspectors, who then alerted the Department of Education, which in turn passed the name of the delinquents to the family allowance regional office in Victoria. During the first three months of 1946, 398 letters had been sent to parents in British Columbia regarding school attendance. In Alberta, on the other hand, the superintendents of each school division reported non-attendance directly to the regional office. There were 1,289 investigations in 1945-46, and 156 suspensions of family allowance payments in that province. A similar procedure was followed in Manitoba and New Brunswick; in the former, 6,200 letters were sent from the regional office to parents regarding poor attendance of their children at school and, in the latter, the monthly average of accounts placed in suspension due to unsatisfactory school attendance was 42.

In Ontario, the regional office established a school attendance unit, which then sent forms to school inspectors and secondary principals for reporting school absences. Curry reported that on average the regional office had received 60 reports each day, but warnings to parents, as well as suspension of payments in the most serious cases, brought a high proportion of the offending children back into the classrooms. In Nova Scotia, the regional office considered 6,419 cases of non-attendance, but Curry reported that the province noted a marked improvement in attendance over previous years. Prince Edward Island was the only province to appoint a school attendance officer, who received from each school a report of children not satisfactorily attending classes. The names of these children were then forwarded to the regional office and each case was investigated. Curry noted that such investigations had resulted in an increase of the average daily attendance by 1,274 in PEI; in percentage terms, attendance rose to 80.8% in 1945-46 compared to 74.6% a year earlier.

Only in Quebec had Curry not been able to make an arrangement with the Department of Public Instruction (the closest thing Quebec had to a department of education) that would have allowed them to monitor school attendance, but even there, total enrolment increased from 84.7% by the end of 1945 to 87.5% in 1950.[9] Duplessis refused to cooperate with the regional family allowances office and insisted that officials in the Department of Public Instruction not provide the federal authorities with the information they sought. Still, the department's senior officials saw family allowances as a great opportunity to enforce the Compulsory School Attendance Act that had been introduced in the province in 1943, and they worked with federal officials to ensure that all children attended school regularly. So too did the Federation of School Boards and the Catholic bishops.[10]

It was clear that school attendance had increased across the country, and school superintendents attributed the rise to the payment of family allowances: the percentage of average daily attendance in public and elementary schools rose from 84.2% in 1940 to 86.3% at the end of 1945, and continued to increase each year that followed, reaching 90% in 1950 and 93% in 1960.[11]

However, school officials were not alone is praising family allowances. When child welfare workers from across western Canada met in Regina in mid-March 1946 for their annual convention, they unanimously agreed that family allowance legislation had already proven beneficial. Norah Lea, assistant director of the Canadian Welfare Council, told the gathering that social welfare organizations and children's aid societies throughout the country indicated that family allowance cheques had been immediately put to constructive use: better dental and medical care, warmer clothing, and more sufficient diets, Lea said, had been provided to children because of family allowances. She told the Regina media that the program had meant the difference between existing and living for many families, saying that those who had claimed that the measure would lead to abuse had been wrong.[12] As Mackenzie King had hoped, the Canadian Welfare Council reported that the program had strengthened the family unit: social workers had noted a decrease in child protection cases. It seems family allowances had raised family incomes and allowed parents to give better care to their children.[13] The Ontario Farm Radio Forum, which held more than five hundred meetings throughout Saskatchewan during the winter of 1946, shared Lea's enthusiasm for family allowances. It found that nearly all of the 9,000 members who attended the forum meetings supported family allowances because it helped parents better provide for their children.[14]

Even some of the earlier critics of family allowances changed their mind once the impact of the benefits became apparent. One such person was Griffith Binning, the medical director of schools in Saskatoon. He had sent J.W. Estey at the Supreme Court of Canada a copy of an article he had written, asking him to see that it reached Prime Minister King. When the notion of paying a family allowance had first been raised, Binning had argued that there would be too much abuse of family allowance payments to make them worthwhile. Within a short time of the launch of the program, however, he had changed his mind. He attributed the success of family allowances to the fact that the cheques were issued to mothers. How could family allowances fail if mothers were responsible for the cheques? And as if to chastise the critics – and praise motherhood at the same time with more than a tinge of paternalism – Binning lamented that those who had criticized family allowances "forgot that our women-hood has spent more than eighty percent of the family income, and has spent it so wisely as to make our Canadian homes the envy of the world. [Mothers] buy wisely and economically and in such a manner that our standard of living is rising over the years instead of lowering ... even during the period of war." Continuing his paternalistic tribute to mothers, he concluded, "Family allowances already are showing their success amongst our lower income groups in the better physical conditions of their school children and in countless other ways."[15] Even the *Globe and Mail* reported that 95% of family allowance recipients in Toronto spent their cheques on necessities for children, while the other 5% somehow included their payments in the family budget.[16]

Like the *Globe and Mail*, other newspapers eagerly pronounced on the efficacy of family allowances. They usually covered reports from various social welfare agencies as well as had their own reporters investigate how family allowances were working. The *Toronto Evening Telegram* completed a three-part investigation of family allowances in February 1947. Allan Kent, the staff reporter on the story, wrote that the federal expenditures on family allowances meant that Canadians would never return to the low tax levels that existed in the pre-war period. Family allowances were a recognition that the whole nation and each taxpayer had a vital interest in the welfare and quality of life of children, and that the family was the nation's basic social unit. Moreover, while the benefit was paid to mothers, in actual fact it was paid to them as trustees for their children. And to determine how well mothers were handling their responsibility, Kent conducted an investigation of numerous families at various income levels throughout Toronto and, through the Department of Welfare, in all regions throughout Ontario.

Kent found that in the great majority of cases, the family allowance cheques were spent directly or indirectly on the children they were designed to help. In his view, mothers had shown a "fine sense of obligations as trustees of this income of their children." In low-income families, he discovered, the payments made an enormous difference to the children. Mrs. L., whom he described as the mother of two sons and whose spouse was a labourer in Toronto's west end, lived on $1,700 a year, and had told him, "The baby bonus is a godsend to me. It is still a struggle to make ends meet ... but we are all better off as a result of the extra money." Because of family allowances, he reported, her children had better clothes than the year before and had been able to eat better food in spite of higher food prices. With high-income families, Kent found that many families had opened savings accounts to pay for their children's university education.

Kent also concluded that the impact of family allowances was even greater in the rural areas, which tended to be poorer. A mother from northern Ontario said that although she and her husband had always tried to do the best for their children, family allowances permitted them to purchase items like fruit juice for the first time. Since the payment of family allowances, she reportedly told Kent, "the children are getting orange juice and have new shoes to go to school in." Kent noted that of the hundreds of letters written to the Department of Welfare each month, "the majority are authentic expressions of gratitude and gladness, telling with simplicity and humility just what the monthly cheques mean to the public in terms of wider horizons for the nation's children."[17]

Kent also noted there was quantitative evidence to support the general improvements brought on at least in part by family allowances. In the first year of family allowances, he found that school attendance reached its highest level ever in Ontario. Throughout Canada, milk consumption increased by 8%[18] and department store officials told him that the demand for children's clothing had risen considerably; they'd seen a marked increase both in quantity and in quality of clothing sold. Kent stated, "It seems safe to conclude that, on the whole, Ontario's 29 percent share of the $250,000,000 distributed in family allowances in Canada every year is being spent properly by the mothers in ways that bring real benefit to the children ... The Government's intention of giving assistance to persons who are trying to bring up families is being fulfilled."[19]

The *Canadian Home Journal* was no less enthusiastic in its praise of family allowances. It found that the program was having a major positive impact on families. Staff writer Margaret Ecker Francis left little doubt of her impression of family allowances. She began her article: "Little Jimmy in Northern Saskatchewan had his first snow suit last winter and so he was no longer a prisoner in his parents' farm house. Little Mary who lives in Prince Edward Island had been able to have her tonsils out at last and she's no longer the thin, sickly child she used to be. Young John in the interior of British Columbia hasn't missed a day at school this year because he now has sturdy, weather-proof boots to keep out the winter cold and the spring slush." She too talked to a large number of parents, and found that high-income families, who could usually provide everything their families needed, were sometimes critical of the program. On the other hand, not surprisingly, those families that struggled to provide for their children – the majority in Canada, she claimed – saw the program "not as a piece of paper but as warmer blankets for their babies' beds, oranges and cod liver oil."[20]

While there was much praise for family allowances, some of it was automatically suspect, like the interim report on the impact of family allowances in *Canada Welfare* in December 1946. The author, Mae Fleming, was also the chief supervisor of welfare services at the Department of National Health and Welfare; her report might be interpreted as government propaganda.[21] Less open to criticism, however, were the findings of the Gallup Poll from the Canadian Institute of Public Opinion. In July 1947, the poll found that nearly three in every four adult Canadians approved of family allowances. When the institute first asked Canadians about family allowances in October 1943, only 49% of those polled approved of the idea; by 1944, the number had risen to 57%, but two years after the program began, three-quarters of Canadians surveyed considered family allowances a good idea. By then, only 16% of the general population saw family allowances as a bad idea; disapproval was highest, at 29%, among Canada's business and professional men, including proprietors of small business. By 1948, the percentage supporting family allowances had reached 75%, and those who considered it unnecessary had fallen to 13%. Equally important, by 1948, 69% of those polled believed that family allowances were being spent properly, up from 56% in May

1945. During the same period, the percentage of those who thought family allowance cheques were spent improperly had dropped from 30% to 16%.

There was still occasional criticism in newspapers across the country, but the widely accepted view was more akin to that of Norah Lea, then executive secretary of the Protestant Children's Homes, who told the *Toronto Daily Star* in February 1949, "The *Family Allowances Act* was the most progressive and worthwhile piece of legislation ever enacted by a government. It has been a godsend to parents all over the country." Many Canadians agreed, and the Gallup Polls showed that the level of support for family allowances continued to grow, as illustrated by Table 4. By May 1950, 84% of those polled said that family allowances were a good idea; the number who considered the program a "bad idea" had dropped to 9%.[22] The next national poll on family allowances in 1953 showed that 90% considered the program a "good thing" compared with just 6% who were opposed to family allowances.[23]

When King and his Cabinet had first considered family allowances in the mid-1940s, they agreed that the payment of monthly benefits would make the Canadian state much more meaningful to Canadian families. This notion of social citizenship has now come to be regarded as an integral aspect of the expansion of the welfare state after the Second World War.[24] In a nation like Canada where ethnic, linguistic, and regional cleavages are particularly pronounced, social welfare policies provide citizens with a set of common programs to deal with similar social problems regardless of where they live. Thus, universal social programs strengthened the sense of community in Canada, and the redistributive function of family allowances in particular helped create social cohesion. Moreover, family allowances and other social programs that became a hallmark of Canadian citizenship were also particularly important in the territorial expansion of Canada when, in 1949, Newfoundland finally joined the Confederation. Although there were a number of factors that contributed to the union of Newfoundland and Canada, both the Confederate leaders in Newfoundland

Table 4

Growth in public favour of family allowances (%)

	1943	1947	1948	1950	1955
In favour of	49	74	75	84	90
Not in favour of	42	16	13	9	6
Undecided	9	10	12	7	4

Source: Gallup Poll of Canada, *Toronto Star*, 12 March 1955.

and politicians and officials in Ottawa emphasized the benefits that would flow from Canada's social programs, such as family allowances, old-age pensions, and unemployment insurance. As I argue in *Canadians At Last: Canada Integrates Newfoundland as a Province,* once Newfoundland narrowly voted for union, federal officials believed that the sooner Newfoundlanders enjoyed the social benefits of union, the sooner they would regard themselves as Canadians. Officials from Ottawa worked assiduously to register its newest citizens for Canada's social program, and the strategy worked: when the first benefits of Canada's social security system poured into Newfoundland and Labrador, "Canada's newest citizens in even the remotest reaches of the province received the first visible signs that they were now Canadians ... federal social programs were the most recognized feature of the union with Canada, and they gave the process instant credibility."[25]

Family allowances were of course popular outside of Newfoundland and Labrador as well. One of the most important investigations in the early years of family allowances came from an American social science researcher. Edward E. Schwartz of the Division of Statistical Research in the Children's Bureau within the Federal Security Agency in Washington, DC, began an investigation into family allowances in late 1946. His report was subsequently published in the influential *Social Services Review* at the University of Chicago Press later that year. Schwartz described family allowances as one of the outstanding social security achievements of recent decades, and praised Canada for its bold initiative. However, in his analysis, he cautioned that it was extremely difficult to attribute all improvements in the welfare of Canadian children solely to the family allowance program, when general economic gains in the postwar economy also played a role in improving the economic well-being of Canadian society. Still, with his expert viewpoint he left little doubt that the impact of family allowances was enormous.[26]

Schwartz considered social workers a valuable source of information for his analysis, even though they had already made many positive pronouncements on the benefits of family allowances. When the Canadian Conference on Social Work met in Halifax in June 1946 for its tenth biennial conference, it included a panel discussion on family allowances. Elinor Barnstead, supervisor of casework for the Family Welfare Association of Montreal, who had consulted more than a dozen large private family welfare agencies across Canada for her research, asked if (and how) family allowances had helped improve the standard of living of families in their communities. Schwartz's report quoted at great length from Barnstead's presentation. Barnstead had found that "middle and marginal income groups [had] noticed both a financial improvement and a lessening of tensions due to increased incomes. It [had] provided families with more sense of security." Moreover, Schwartz's own interviews with social workers at a variety of institutions in Montreal and Toronto confirmed Barnstead's findings. The consensus of social workers, he concluded, was that the family allowance program was socially beneficial; the allowances were helpful in improving the conditions of low-income families, and children in rural families benefited most.[27] His interpretation was further confirmed by Joy A. Maines, executive secretary of the Canadian Association of Social Workers (CASW). She reminded Schwartz that the CASW's national board had supported family allowances from the outset, and that it had not received any criticism about the program from its branches across the country.[28]

As others had done in their investigations, Schwartz also reported on the increase in school attendance, a fact already well publicized by the federal government but a welcomed endorsement nonetheless from what the Department of National Health and Welfare considered an impartial review. Schwartz's interviews with public health officials and others in the medical community also credited family allowances for allowing mothers to purchase special foods and medicines that improved the health of their infants and young children. Schwartz also noted that labour had dropped its opposition to family allowances, an indication, he concluded, of the benefits of the program. He wrote that one top official with the Trades and Labour Congress told him that the union movement had altered its position on family allowances for several reasons: the program assisted large low-income families, it did not require a means test, it put additional money into circulation, and it contributed to full employment. The Canadian Congress of Labour passed a resolution at its 1945 annual convention approving in principle the payment of family allowances. Schwartz claimed that a president of a provincial federation of labour had told him there had been no indication that family allowances had been used against labour in collective bargaining situations. Schwartz even discovered that employers' associations and organizations representing business interests generally favoured family allowances, even though they continued to resent the time they had to spend completing the complicated payroll deductions in the first year to prevent workers from claiming an income tax deduction for children while receiving family allowances. The conclusion of the report was that there was unanimous agreement among Canadians that family allowances had improved the immediate welfare prospects of children in low-income families. Schwartz also reminded his American readers that they should pay close attention to the Canadian experience with the program, since they could benefit from following Canada's lead.[29]

Along with his officials, Paul Martin, who replaced Claxton as minister of national health and welfare in 1946, clearly welcomed Schwartz's endorsement of family allowances;[30] after all, Schwartz's investigation applauded the Department of National Health and Welfare for its policy innovation, characterizing it as one that was "highly informed, progressive and [imbued with] socially-minded attitudes." As a result, Martin and Prime Minister King included parts of Schwartz's article, along with similar reports from Kent and Francis, in their own promotional literature on family allowances.

On the second anniversary of family allowances, Paul Martin praised the program as an economic stabilizer for maintaining incomes and purchasing power at high levels throughout the country, as well as for the direct benefits it provided to the nation's children.[31] Martin's officials also compiled a series of press releases (most of which came from the minister), various reports and speeches, newspaper articles (including Kent's from the *Toronto Evening Telegram*), and other materials that applauded the benefits of family allowances. These materials became a publicity package for the government to illustrate the effectiveness and efficacy of family allowances.[32]

In addition to the Canadian government, many groups and organizations took advantage of the tenth anniversary of family allowances to assess the impact of a decade of benefits. Two important reviews came from within the Department of National Health and Welfare in Ottawa. George Davidson, the deputy minister of the welfare section of the department, wrote a retrospective for *Children,* a publication of the Children's Bureau of the US Department of Health, Education and Welfare. R.H. Parkinson, who had joined the regional family allowance office in Saskatchewan in 1946 and eventually became supervisor of welfare services for the Department of National Health and Welfare in Ottawa, did a similar assessment for *Canadian Welfare.* The two essays were alike in their approach and the conclusions reached. They both began with the premise that family allowances had been introduced for two reasons: it was a social welfare measure designed to promote Canadian family life by assisting those who were raising a family, and it was an economic measure to stimulate the economy. Davidson asserted that although many in Canada claimed the program as their idea, the real founders of the family allowance program were among the most responsible and conservative elements in Ottawa: none other than the highly respected officers of the Bank of Canada and the Department of Finance.[33]

On the economic side, both Davidson and Parkinson agreed that the family allowance program had achieved its goal. In the decade since 1945, the federal government had paid more than $3.06 billion in family allowances. Family allowances had helped redistribute wealth within the country from those with

Table 5

Total federal tax collections and family allowance payments, 1953-54

Region	Total federal tax collected ($ millions)	(%)	Total family allowance payments ($ millions)	(%)
Atlantic	154.4	3.5	45.5	13.0
Quebec	1,299.2	30.0	111.5	31.9
Ontario	2,146.6	49.4	104.5	29.9
Prairies	416.7	9.6	62.2	17.8
British Columbia	323.9	7.5	25.9	7.4
Total	4,340.8	100.0	349.6	100.0

Source: Report of the Department of National Revenue for the fiscal year ended 31 March 1954.

the greatest to those with the least. Even a cursory examination of a comparison of the distribution of the federal taxes collected to family allowances paid by region for 1953-54, for instance, shows that to be the case, as illustrated by Table 5. In that fiscal year, the Atlantic region and the Prairies together contributed about 13% of all federal taxes collected. At the same time, they received about 30% of all family allowances. Ontario, on the other hand, contributed 50% of the tax revenue but received only 39% of the family allowance payments.[34] Clearly, the major beneficiaries of the program, relative to their contribution of federal tax revenue, were the Atlantic provinces and the Prairies, the most economically distressed regions of the country.

There were also a number of benefits on the welfare side, and both Parkinson and Davidson pointed out that many of these had been noted in numerous studies during the early years of the program: school attendance had improved across the country, the consumption of highly nutritious foods had increased, parents purchased better clothing and footwear for children, children enjoyed better health and dental care, and many children were able to participate in such extras as music lessons and summer camp. However, Parkinson noted that family allowances could not take sole credit for all these benefits; the general improvement in economic conditions had also been an important contributing factor.[35]

Both authors noted how quickly the opposition to family allowances had vanished in the ten years since 1945. Most of the labour leaders who had warned that family allowances would impede their ability to negotiate acceptable factory wage increases had been proven wrong. If anything, wages had steadily risen each year in which family allowances had been paid. Others had argued that family allowances would prevent other welfare legislation from being enacted.

Although the federal government had not made the progress on social security many had hoped it would in the postwar period, there were still some notable achievements at the federal level, including health grants, improved old-age pensions and old-age assistance, blind pensions, disability allowances, and improvements in unemployment insurance. The feared misuse of family allowances had not materialized, either. Parkinson pointed out that in 1955 there were only 337 accounts being administered by third parties because the families had misused their benefits, not a bad record given that 2 million cheques were mailed each month to families across Canada. Likewise, family allowances had not caused a more rapid rise in the birth rate than that in countries, like the United States, that had not adopted such programs. In fact, there had been a decline over the ten years in the number of families with five or more children. It is also interesting to note that the crude birth rate in the United States was greater than that in Canada. Parkinson noted that family allowances had become so popular that all of the national political parties liked to claim they were the originators of the idea; the Conservatives, he pointed out, went to great lengths to show they never opposed the concept.[36] Still, Davidson pointed out, family allowances retained a few critics, though the criticisms were measurably different from what they had been in 1944. By 1955, the critics of family allowances were beginning to note that the value of the monthly benefits was shrinking as the cost of living and annual wage rates both increased; thus, they wanted the amount paid to parents increased.[37] That criticism would grow louder as inflationary pressures throughout the 1960s further diminished the value of the monthly benefits.

In many respects, the family allowance program was a static one in that during the first ten years, there were few changes in either the legislation or the regulations covering the program. This stemmed in part from the popularity of the program across Canada, which made politicians reluctant to consider major changes to the program. There was also concern, particularly within the Department of Finance, about the extent of the government's postwar financial commitments. The cost of the family allowance program was already high, having reached $383 million in 1955, making it the third largest budgetary expenditure in Ottawa behind defence ($1,838 million) and the charge on the public debt ($514 million).[38] Therefore, calls for increases to the monthly payments were largely dismissed. In 1946, for instance, Brooke Claxton, then minister of national health and welfare, had recommended amending the Family Allowances Act so that an immigrant child who had been a resident in Canada for one year would be eligible for benefits rather than having to wait for the three years mandated by the act. The minister of finance, who was extremely anxious about the huge costs of social security and the difficulty of increasing taxes on persons of low and medium incomes in order to meet these costs, refused to relax the rules governing eligibility.[39]

However, the Department of National Health and Welfare achieved its objective regarding immigrants in 1949 when two amendments to the program were introduced. The requirement that children had to reside in Canada for three consecutive years prior to registering for family allowances was reduced to one year. The Interdepartmental Immigration Labour Committee, comprising the deputy ministers of labour, mines and resources, and national health and welfare as well as a representative from the Department of External Affairs, had argued that the three-year residency restriction represented a serious barrier to family immigration and to the successful settlement of immigrant families in Canada. They were able to convince the Cabinet that such a change would increase the number of immigrants coming to Canada. With all three major political parties supporting the amendment, it passed the House of Commons in a single day.

Ottawa also eliminated section 3 of the Family Allowances Act, which had reduced the total benefit for each family by one dollar for the fifth child, two dollars for the sixth and seventh children, and three dollars for the eighth and subsequent children. When the legislation was introduced in 1945, it was thought that the cost of raising younger children would be lower because parents could reuse the clothing, school books, etc., that had been purchased for the older children. However, family budget studies subsequently demonstrated that this was not the case, and there were other increases in family expenses for large families, like housing costs.[40]

Both these amendments were criticized by Charlotte Whitton, who argued that the government should be targeting other areas of society, like the indigent aged, rather than directing additional tax dollars to a program she claimed was misguided. Moreover, she charged that family allowances had already become, by 1949, a major vote winner for the government, and that fact alone was driving the program rather than social need.[41]

It was the question of how soon immigrants could avail themselves of family allowance benefits that would eventually prompt further changes in the program. Although the act had been amended in April 1949 to reduce the waiting period to one year, Walter Harris, the minister of citizenship and immigration, and the officials in his department wanted to extend family allowance benefits to all immigrants on their arrival to Canada. They believed that the one-year residency requirement made Canada less attractive to immigrants when countries, such as the United Kingdom and Australia and others in Europe, allowed immigrants immediate access to social programs. In early 1952, Harris subsequently proposed to his colleague in the Department of National Health and Welfare that the

Family Allowances Act be amended to bring Canada in line with practices in other countries for new arrivals. Paul Martin advised Harris that his department should not recommend such an amendment because it might be very unpopular among Canadians:

> We have given some consideration to the possibility of a provision which would make it possible to pay family allowances immediately to any family which was given a permanent land card by the Immigration authorities. I am a little doubtful, however, whether Canadians generally are yet ready to accept the suggestion that families who have never been in Canada and have never contributed to the economic development of the country should be able to step off the boat at Halifax and qualify for one of our most important social welfare benefits before they have put in a "probationary period" in which they have made some contribution to the economic life of the country and have paid something by way of indirect, if not direct, taxes.[42]

Even though he admitted the benefits would assist immigrant families in adjusting to their new life in Canada, Martin reminded Harris that family allowances were never conceived of as an aid to immigration or as assistance to new arrivals.[43] Moreover, Martin's deputy minister, George F. Davidson, warned that it would be administratively impossible to distinguish between tourists and immigrants.[44]

Still, the issue would not go away, and in the following two years, the Department of Citizenship and Immigration continued to insist that family allowances be made available to immigrants with children on their arrival in Canada. By 1955, there was a serious decline in the rate of immigration to Canada: the number of new arrivals dropped to 109,000 from 164,000 just five years earlier.[45] The federal government completed an intensive review of the selection and recruiting techniques, together with a study of the circumstances in Canada that might explain Canada's apparent lack of appeal among immigrants. Much to the strong approval of the Department of Citizenship and Immigration, the investigation concluded that one of the factors contributing to the drop in the level of immigration was the general exclusion of immigrants from social security benefits in Canada until they had fulfilled their residency requirements. The report stated that if Canada hoped to attract larger numbers of immigrants, it would have to change the practice, and one way of doing that was to assure prospective immigrants that they would share in Canada's social security benefits on their arrival.[46] At the same time, the Canadian Welfare Council and more than fifty other community and national organizations were lobbying the federal government to change the legislation, which they claimed discriminated against immigrant children admitted to Canada.[47]

After the investigation, J.W. Pickersgill, who had replaced Walter Harris as minister of citizenship and immigration, decided changes in the time frame for immigrants to access social security benefits were indeed necessary. When the issue had first been raised in the early 1950s, Pickersgill had agreed with Paul Martin that family allowances were never intended as an aid to immigration, and he did not protest vigorously in 1954 when Martin had vetoed the idea.[48] However, when the level of immigration dropped off considerably in the mid-1950s, the matter assumed greater urgency for Pickersgill (and the nation), and he wanted policy changes that would make Canada more attractive. To Pickersgill, it had become obvious that one way to attract greater numbers of immigrants was to provide additional financial assistance during the early period of their establishment in Canada. Pickersgill could make some changes in his department's programs, but other changes, like those to family allowances, would have to come from his colleagues. He went on the offensive, effectively lobbying Prime Minister Louis St. Laurent and Walter Harris, who had moved to the Department of Finance (and was obviously sympathetic to Pickersgill's request), as well as Paul Martin at the Department of National Health and Welfare to get Cabinet approval for the changes to family allowances.

In a series of letters to his colleagues in October 1955, Pickersgill made it clear that he had long agreed with Martin that family allowances were not conceived as an aid to immigration, but in light of recent immigration patterns, they should take another look at the matter: "The newcomer's need for assistance with respect to his family is certainly no less greater than [sic] that of many Canadians, and most newcomers do contribute to public funds during their first year here through the payment of direct and indirect taxes." To avoid changing the provisions of the Family Allowances Act, and perhaps to deal with any political backlash Martin had warned of earlier, Pickersgill suggested that after each immigrant had completed one year's residence in Canada, he would receive an amount equivalent to what he would have received had he been eligible for family allowances immediately on arrival. The plan would be administered by the family allowances branch of the Department of National Health and Welfare. Such an arrangement would associate the grant with the regular payment of family allowances but avoid possible criticism that immigrants were receiving payments native-born Canadians did not.[49]

The Cabinet first discussed the matter on 11 January 1956. It agreed that immigration numbers had to be maintained, and it was willing to use a program similar to family allowances to achieve that goal. However, it did not agree with the proposal Pickersgill had put forward, and it refused to use family allowances for purposes not originally intended.[50] The Cabinet discussion went on inter-mittently for nearly three months until a compromise was reached. As Pickersgill subsequently informed the House of Commons on 19 March 1956, the govern-ment had decided on two measures to maintain immigration levels. First, it would make assisted passage loans available for the wives and children of im-migrants. Second, it would provide assistance for family settlement, to be paid to each immigrant or settler at the rate of $60 annually for each child under sixteen years of age residing in Canada and supported by him during the first year, when family allowances were not paid for that child.[51] Instead of amending the Family Allowances Act, government would create a separate program, the Family Assistance Scheme (FAS), to be administered by the Department of Citizenship and Immigration to facilitate these provisions. When the plan went into effect on 1 April 1956, it paid immigrant families (in advance) a flat rate of $5 quarterly for each dependent child regardless of age. The program largely duplicated the machinery that already existed in the family allowances branch of the Department of National Health and Welfare, and the administrators of the FAS coordinated their procedures with the family allowances branch as much as possible to ensure that the transition of the immigrant children from family assistance to family allowances after their first year's residence in Canada was done without interruption of payments.

The officials at the Department of Citizenship and Immigration emphasized to immigrant parents that family assistance was only an interim measure, and gave them instructions on when, where, and how to apply for family allowances. Despite those efforts, there was much confusion among immigrants about the two programs. Frequently, immigrant parents failed to grasp the significance of the instructions and often did not register their children for family allowances until a lapse in FAS payments brought the matter to their attention. Because family allowance payments were not retroactive, the result was often a loss of several months' benefits until the child was registered for family allowances. This confusion only served to renew the demand that family allowances be made available to immigrant children from the date of their landing in Canada.[52]

It was not always clear that government officials were overly concerned with the issue. *Jedinsto,* a Croat-Serb-Slovene newspaper in Toronto, commented on this matter in early 1960, noting that many immigrant families often had to wait months before they became aware of the need to apply for family allowances. An official in the Canadian Citizens Branch of the Department of Citizenship and Immigration brought the article to the attention of the Department of National Health and Welfare, where it was given the title "Communist" when it was filed. Another official subsequently added a handwritten comment: "This looks as if the Communists are merely trying to stir up trouble. Nurses could easily help new mothers fill in the necessary forms."[53]

Even as the FAS was being implemented, the Canadian Welfare Council continued to lobby the government to have family allowances immediately available to immigrants. While it commended Pickersgill on the government's initiative, the council told him that it considered the FAS an intermediate step and urged him to include immigrant children in the family allowance program as soon as possible after their arrival. To do so would allow immigrants to gain from the higher benefits available from family allowances, and would have the advantage of making new arrivals feel more fully accepted as Canadians.

However, the changes were not made under the Liberal government, and the Canadian Welfare Council hoped for greater success with the new Conservative government. In June 1958, Richard E.G. Davis, the executive director of the Canadian Welfare Council, pursued the matter with the Honourable J. Waldo Monteith, minister of national health and welfare in Prime Minister John Diefenbaker's government.[54] But the Conservatives also moved slowly on the issue, and only agreed to bring the monthly rate of family assistance paid to immigrant children in line with the family allowance rate just weeks before Diefenbaker called a federal election in early 1962. By then, the level of immigration had dropped considerably: after peaking at more than 280,000 in 1957, the number dropped to its lowest level in a decade when only 71,000 new immigrants arrived.[55] In announcing the increase to the FAS, Minister of Citizenship and Immigration Ellen L. Fairclough stated that immigrant families should be entitled to the same social security benefits as other residents of Canada. Consequently, effective 1 April 1962, the monthly rate of family assistance for immigrant children would be $6 up to age ten and $8 for those aged ten to sixteen. The administration of the special allowance also passed from Citizenship and Immigration to the Department of National Health and Welfare.[56]

On the matter of increasing family allowance benefits, it would be twelve years after the initial family allowance legislation before the federal government would agree. Two Quebec labour organizations, the Confédération des travailleurs catholiques du Canada and the Fédération professionnelle des travailleurs du Québec, demanded that Ottawa index family allowances to inflation. Even Father Léon Lebel added his voice to the growing chorus, and between July 1954 and May 1955, unions, school boards, municipal councils, and various associations organized a provincial campaign in Quebec to demand increases to family allowances. Nearly 3,000 Canadians signed a petition presented to the federal minister of the Department of National Health and Welfare asking for an increase. Liberal MPs routinely raised the matter in Parliament, and many of them supported the opposition calls for increased benefits as well as extending the coverage to seventeen- and eighteen-year-olds. Even family allowance officials noticed the adverse effect of inflation on family allowances.[57]

Social welfare lost much of its urgency in the immediate postwar period as the federal government saw the return of a prosperous peacetime economy. Ottawa moved forward incrementally and slowly after 1945, providing a series of targeted programs such as national health grants in 1948, old-age security, old-age assistance, and blind persons pensions in 1951, disabled persons pensions and a new national initiative in 1954, and hospital insurance and diagnostic services in 1957. When the government opened its purse, it was to defend Canada from the Soviet threat rather than to provide its citizens with additional protection from the exigencies of life. During this period, the calls for increases to family allowance benefits had little impact. The national assistant director of family allowances, J.A. Blais, like most of his political masters, believed that Canadians wanted lower, not higher taxes. In 1954, after acknowledging that it would be desirable to increase the family allowance rates, Blais maintained, "We must never forget that those monies must come from the pocket of each Canadian and I am equally certain that public opinion would look poorly on any tax increases to this end."[58]

Only on 1 September 1957 did Ottawa raise the benefit rate for family allowances.[59] This increase, which had been announced before Prime Minister Louis St. Laurent dissolved Parliament and called an election for 10 June 1957, actually took effect after John Diefenbaker's Conservative government handed the Liberals a surprising defeat. The increase simplified family allowance benefits by creating two categories of pay rather than the initial four; with the change, children under ten received $6 per month and those aged ten to sixteen received $8. The Liberals had considered a flat rate for all children, but the cost of such an increase, over $70 million annually, was considered too great even if it significantly reduced the administrative costs of the program. Still, the changes created an increase of 10% in the average allowance per family, bringing the federal expenditure in 1957 to $397.5 million.[60] The increase had been made possible only after the Department of Finance insisted that the $10 planned increase to old-age pensions be reduced to $6 to pay for improved family allowance benefits. The strategy obviously backfired for the Liberals: Diefenbaker's Conservatives labelled Walter Harris, the minister of finance, "Six-Buck Harris" during the 1957 election campaign the Liberals lost.[61]

In 1958, Canada slipped into its first recession of the postwar period. The recession would last for nearly four years. By the time the economy recovered in 1962, fundamental questions were being asked about many of the nation's social security programs. In Canada, almost all of those involved with social security, including federal and provincial officials, as well as those in such non-profit agencies as the Canadian Welfare Council, were of the view that the social security net was not working as it should. They had expected the social welfare initiatives enacted since the Second World War to significantly reduce poverty among Canadians.[62] Yet Ottawa had allowed family allowances to atrophy over nearly two decades, and there was growing dissatisfaction with the universal, flat-rate type of programs that had marked the launching of the welfare state in Canada a generation earlier.

In 1964, David Weiss, the executive director of the Jewish Child Welfare Bureau in Montreal, reflected the view of many in his network when he wrote to Joseph Willard, the deputy minister of welfare in the Department of National Health and Welfare, that Ottawa should consider using family allowances more flexibly as an instrument of national social policy that would see the amount paid to families vary according to need.[63] The movement for reform in Canada was given added impetus when American President Lyndon B. Johnson declared war on poverty in 1964 to help the one-fifth of all American families that reportedly had insufficient income to meet their basic needs.[64]

Willard, who was also instrumental from 1964 to 1966 in creating the Canada Assistance Plan (CAP), a cost-shared federal-provincial program to consolidate and improve social assistance for all Canadians, would bring some of his ideas about the "working poor" to family allowances reform. He had insisted through the negotiations leading to the CAP that the plan had to recognize and protect the rights of the economically disadvantaged Canadians and that governments had to help those in greatest need. The CAP became an important instrument in moving Canadian social policy from a means-tested to an income-tested approach for social assistance, and Willard played a key role in redirecting thinking within the Department of National Health and Welfare away from universality toward selectivity during the 1960s and 1970s. It was this same thinking he brought to the family allowance program. Imbued with reformer's zeal, he asked the regional directors of family allowances and old-age security in each of the provinces to prepare a comprehensive review of both programs.[65]

The report from the regional directors made clear the impact of family allowances, but they clearly missed Willard's intent. As Willard's colleagues themselves acknowledged, from 1945 to about the mid-1960s, those officials and bureaucrats involved in the Department of National Health and Welfare were committed to social welfare advancement and reform, but their priority was the development of a comprehensive nationwide social security system.[66] It seems, then, that the regional directors saw the request from their deputy minister as an exercise in justifying the family allowance program rather than as a request for an honest assessment to determine if the program met its primary objectives. J.E. Green wrote from the regional office in Charlottetown that family allowances and old-age security combined to inject more than $10 million into the provincial economy, which was greater than the net income from PEI's principal industries, agriculture ($7.25 million), fishing ($9 million), and manufacturing ($8.25 million). Similarly, the regional director in Manitoba noted that family allowances were of greater economic importance in the less economically favoured provinces like his, where the program helped bring living standards somewhat closer to the national average. From British Columbia, the regional director reported that parents eagerly awaited the arrival of the family allowance cheques, and if for any reason they were delayed, the regional office was deluged with telephone calls from individuals requesting their cheques. Also, many merchants hired extra clerks on the 19th and 20th of each month to deal with the increase in customers. The regional directors acknowledged that the family allowance cheques were much more important to low-income families than they were to high-income ones.

J. Albert Blais, the director of family allowances and old-age security in Ottawa, prepared the summary report from the regional directors for Willard, but it too failed to confirm what Willard must have suspected when he asked for the review. Blais wrote in his report, "If the need for a program of this kind existed in 1945, and there are few who would argue that it did not, it appears that the same need exists today." He pointed out that family allowances served both a social need and an economic one; it was an income redistribution plan that put money into the hands of low-income families. While Blais noted that there had been few recent studies on the impact of family allowances in Canada, he claimed that there was no doubt in the minds of many that the family allowance program had had a considerable impact on various features of life in Canada. It was generally accepted that the presence of family allowances had contributed to an overall improvement in the welfare of Canadian children, particularly in health, nutrition, and education. Family allowances, Blais concluded, were generally considered "simply an integral part of the Canadian way of life."[67]

From his perch in Ottawa, and from his contacts with community groups across Canada, Willard realized that despite the widespread support for family allowances and how they had become a part of the Canadian identity, it was also clear by the early 1960s that the monthly family allowance cheques had lost much of the significance they had for so many families in the years after the program was implemented in 1945. They had witnessed a dramatic rise in the level of personal and family incomes, and the family allowance cheques no longer had the same economic value for many of the poorer families. He realized that under conditions of full employment, and with a range of social welfare benefits, many Canadians continued to live in poverty. Canadians had become complacent about family allowances, which, as mentioned earlier, had changed little for nearly two decades.

In 1968, Willard told a conference on social welfare that systems of universal payments were expensive and a nation like Canada would have to decide if it wished to abandon the universal approach in favour of some system in which payments were tied to income – in other words, selectivity or universality in social programs.[68] This would be one of the major issues to be addressed as Canadians policy makers and others became concerned about the persistence of poverty in Canada in the 1960s, and as provincial officials and politicians, particularly in Quebec, sought greater control over social policy. The major impetus for the reform of existing social programs came from the liberal-minded professionals, like Willard, who worked within the government.[69] In that period of upheaval and reform, family allowances would once again find a prominent place on the nation's public policy agenda.

6
Poverty, Politics, and Family Allowances, 1960-70

By THE 1960s, family allowances had become a fixture in Canadian social policy, but most Canadians and their government paid little attention to the program. Families were pleased to receive their monthly benefits, and as far as the government was concerned, the program was working well. Support for family allowances remained high; earlier critics had fallen silent. Yet family allowances would once again emerge later in the decade as an important public policy issue. They would be thrust to the forefront as some provinces attempted to reassert their authority following a period (beginning with the Second World War) that saw power centralized in Ottawa. This new era of province building was particularly led by successive nationalist governments in Quebec.

At the same time, there was a growing concern across Canada with the apparent ineffectiveness of public expenditure on social policy. Canadians were becoming aware of the persistence of poverty in their seemingly affluent nation, prompting many to call for a review of all social security programs so that they might more effectively deal with the persistent social ills. Yet as the events of the period were to show, Canadians had become accustomed to universality in family allowances, and most politicians were reluctant to tamper with a program many had come to regard as an integral right of their Canadian citizenship. It would take a political crisis generated by Quebec to persuade the Canadian government to begin a review of Canada's social policies in general and family allowances in particular.

Quebec's minister of family and social welfare, René Lévesque, who in 1961 had led the province's nationalization of the hydroelectric power companies, helped wake Ottawa from its lethargy over family allowances. In November 1965, he told a Quebec newspaper he wanted control of all the social security programs in his province, without any federal participation.[1] Quebec needed an integrated social security program – one designed to reduce the number of clients who were dependent on his department – that would create a provincial system of preventive social security.[2] The federally financed and managed family allowance program was no longer effective, and it required radical reform if it hoped to reduce the consequences of inadequate income for large families and serve as an effective anti-poverty measure. Lévesque's own plan for social security reform largely depended on getting control of the $180 million the family allowance program paid to families in Quebec. When he first announced his intention to reform social security, he stressed the importance of increasing family allowances in proportion to family size and age of the children, and tying benefits to the cost of living.

Following the method applied in France and elsewhere, the Quebec government wanted to eliminate family allowances for the first child in each family, even though Ottawa had insisted all children be covered. However, if allowances began with the second rather than the first child, the savings would permit higher benefits for the third and each additional child. Lévesque also suggested that Ottawa might double its expenditure on family allowances to provide a greater differential with respect to the age of the child.[3] He maintained that Quebec City knew better than Ottawa the particular needs of his province, a claim later reaffirmed in the 1963 "Rapport du Comité d'étude sur l'assistance publique" (Boucher Report) that recommended the federal withdrawal from joint social assistance programs and the compensation of increased Quebec expenses through extension of the taxation fields.[4]

Of course, the reforms Lévesque enunciated closely followed the masters-in-our-own-house rhetoric of a more autonomous Quebec. While the province had opted out of several federal-provincial programs throughout the 1960s, most notably the Canada Pension Plan and youth allowances,[5] the withdrawal from family allowances would mark the first separation of Quebec from the trio of long-standing national programs – the other two being old-age pensions and unemployment insurance – that Ottawa had established as purely federal initiatives to create a national social security program during and immediately following the end of the Second World War. If Quebec opted out of family allowances – a program considered by federal political leaders since the 1940s as an important aspect of Canadian citizenship – it would represent the strengthening of provincialism, particularly in Quebec, and an erosion of the strong central government that had emerged in postwar Canada.

The first reaction in Ottawa to Lévesque's comments was one of surprise, though Judy LaMarsh, the minister of national health and welfare, and some of her colleagues in Lester B. Pearson's minority government had become quite concerned over Quebec's propensity to "opt-out" of national programs and demand cash transfers to establish its own parallel programs. In LaMarsh's view, Lévesque was becoming increasingly and aggressively anti-Ottawa. She had Joseph Willard, the deputy minister of welfare, ascertain first if Lévesque really had the support of Premier Jean Lesage and the Quebec government or if he were merely speaking wishfully and for himself.[6] Once Willard determined that Lévesque did indeed enjoy the support of the provincial Cabinet, he advised LaMarsh that there would be "no point in making any comment [to the press]

FIGURE 11   Judy LaMarsh, photographed here with Prime Minister Lester B. Pearson, was one of the Cabinet ministers who were worried about Pearson's policy of attempting to accommodate the aspirations of Quebec.
Library and Archives Canada, Ron Roels/Duncan Cameron fonds, PA-117097, reprinted with permission

on [Lévesque's] statement ... as it would only mean getting drawn into a protracted discussion in the press about the matter." Willard reminded LaMarsh that if Quebec wished to discuss the control of family allowances with Ottawa, it should do so through the proper channels. Until a formal request came from Lévesque, Ottawa should do nothing, except perhaps remind the press that the

The wisdom of Solomon?

FIGURE 12   This editorial cartoon shows that the federal government was not able to give the provinces control over the family allowance programs. Here, Judy LaMarsh, the minister of national health and welfare, is ready to protect the family allowance program (often called the baby bonus) from provincial control (*Globe and Mail*, 13 December 1965).

Reprinted with permission of the Globe and Mail

family allowance program had been extremely well administered and that it had benefited many Canadian families since 1945.[7] When Pearson was asked about Lévesque's proposals, he too said he was surprised, though not about Quebec's proposals but by the fact that if Quebec were serious, it had failed to approach Ottawa to formally discuss the matter.[8]

LaMarsh contends in her autobiography that the government had decided it would take a firm position with Lévesque, and Quebec was to be told to keep its hands off family allowances. Yet she regretted that Pearson had "made a virtue of flexibility."[9] Pearson clearly believed social policy was a shared jurisdiction, and he obviously favoured collaboration with the provinces, as was demonstrated by the establishment of the Canada Pension Plan in 1966.[10] Like some of Pearson's detractors within the government, the *Toronto Telegram* suggested that the Liberals' approach was detrimental to the country. When the paper learned of Lévesque's proposal on family allowances, it reported that it was just one more example of the impact of Pearson's weak and vacillating position on Quebec. The article lamented that it was Pearson's policy to do everything in his power to accommodate the demands of Quebec that had encouraged Lé-vesque to demand even greater powers. It also accused Pearson of presiding over the erosion of the Canadian social fabric, hastening the descent toward the decentralization of power and contributing to the greater fragmentation of the country in the process. Most Canadians outside of Quebec were disturbed by the trend, the paper opined, though it fully expected Pearson to accommodate Quebec yet again on the grounds that such a gesture was necessary to save the Canadian Confederation.[11]

Meanwhile, Willard had his department prepare a more detailed memorandum on family allowances that LaMarsh passed along to Pearson. In it, Willard spelled out the initial rationale for family allowances and outlined his arguments against Quebec being given control over the program. The memo also clearly demonstrated how little the opinions on family allowances had changed in Ottawa over the previous two decades. Willard noted that family allowances should not be considered welfare payments but, rather, simply grants to aid parents in raising their children. Moreover, all Canadian children were entitled to the same benefit, regardless of family income. Also, Willard pointed out – either missing or choosing to ignore Lévesque's argument about the effectiveness of social security spending completely – family allowances were already decentralized, with a regional office in each provincial capital. Ottawa had to be concerned, he reminded the minister, about the fate of the 208 employees at the Quebec regional office if the province assumed control of family allowances. Quebec MPs would certainly oppose any measure of control by the provincial government of Quebec since they would undoubtedly prefer to continue in the position of receiving the credit for the provision of family allowances.[12] Willard gave no substantive consideration to the effectiveness of the family allowance program and how it worked in conjunction with other social security measures, either at the federal or provincial level. However, when Allan MacEachern replaced LaMarsh as minister of national health and welfare late in December 1965, Willard informed him that he had ordered a thorough review of family allowances that would include how the program might be reformed in the future.[13]

Ottawa did not have to wait long to be officially notified of Quebec's plan for family allowances. However, Lévesque had backed away, slightly, from the demands he had made in the press when he outlined his proposal for family allowances at the federal-provincial meeting of welfare ministers in Ottawa on 7-8 January 1966. He reminded his colleagues that poverty remained a persistent problem despite Canada's postwar prosperity. Quebec intended to address the issue of poverty by making its social welfare system more efficient and by co-ordinating the various programs, both provincial and federal, to deliver the greatest benefit. He described the existing social security initiatives, like family allowances, as passive and representing a sort of public extension of the outdated notion of private charity; those programs simply failed to help those in greatest need. Lévesque also pointed out that the Canadian Tax Foundation, an independent research organization established in 1945 to offer advice on an equitable tax system and promote economic growth, had recently argued that if the basis underlying family allowances was that family size created economic hardships, then larger families should be the primary beneficiaries. After all, the size of the family was an important contributory factor to poverty.[14]

There were several advantages to revising the family allowance program, Lévesque said. First, greater assistance to large families would help eliminate the spectre of dependency and allow needy families to enjoy better living conditions. Second, the state had to recognize that it had a responsibility to help the family, which remained one of the primary institutions in society but one increasingly under attack. Third, a revamped family allowance program that targeted those most in need would be an important weapon in the war on poverty. Fourth, because of the cultural differences between Quebec and the rest of Canada, it made greater sense for Quebec to administer its own social programs.

Lévesque made family allowances the centrepiece at the federal-provincial gathering. Although he made no formal request for provincial control of the program, he clearly set a trap for the federal government. He gave Ottawa the opportunity to introduce the reforms he considered necessary, but if they refused or failed to do so, he demanded that the program be transferred to the provinces. He suggested that the transfer could be justified on constitutional grounds; moreover, the provinces could more effectively manage the program with better social outcomes if it was integrated with a variety of existing provincial social welfare measures.[15] Lévesque insisted on using the word "repatriation" to describe the transfer of the family allowance program to the province, which suggests that, in his mind, Quebec would be merely taking responsibility for a program it once had. Several of the other provinces, including Manitoba, Ontario, and Newfoundland, expressed considerable interest in the Quebec proposal, but they stopped well short of Quebec's desire to assume responsibility for administering the program.[16] Ottawa indicated to Lévesque that it had no intention of surrendering its control over family allowances, and MacEachern reportedly commented, "We are in the family allowances field and we don't contemplate any withdrawal."[17] A few weeks later, during debate on the Throne Speech, Pearson reminded Quebec – and perhaps others, including the *Toronto Telegram* – that each level of government should keep strictly within its jurisdiction, and warned that Ottawa would "exercise great care in agreeing on joint programs with the provinces in which all provinces do not participate."[18]

Lévesque was undeterred. He kept the pressure on Ottawa. First, he wrote MacEachern, reiterating the position he had expressed at the Ottawa meetings: "I have not lost hope ... that one of these days in the not too distant future I will be able to convince you of the advisability of turning over to Quebec the whole program of family allowances. For reasons of good understanding, efficiency and culture, we are every day convinced that all these social measures – definitely in Quebec's case – should be taken in hand as soon as possible and coordinated at the provincial level."[19]

It soon became clear that the Quebec government was growing impatient with Ottawa's slow response to Lévesque's demands. During the debate on the Quebec Speech from the Throne in the National Assembly later that winter, Lévesque lashed out at the federal government. It was taking a "criminally long time," he said, for Ottawa to make a formal decision on the issue. He criticized the Ottawa "Establishment" for being so imbued with the "big brother approach or the senior government attitude" that it ignored the pressing social problems his province faced. The current system of family allowances was both obsolete and non-productive, and he wondered, "Why don't they [Ottawa] ask themselves if it is not time to meet the problem ... and accept solutions even if it comes from people, who on occasion, appear to them as so incompetent?"[20]

Tardiness may have been the least of Ottawa's problems. Lévesque's proposals had clearly taken Ottawa by surprise, and MacEachern and his officials had no response except that they thought the program was working rather well. Because the federal government had given such little attention to the family allowance program before Lévesque raised it as an important issue in federal-provincial relations, it had no rationale to guide its response, except that Ottawa had introduced the program and that the public seemed to like it very much. When MacEachern first asked his officials to comment on Lévesque's proposal at the welfare ministers' conference, they offered little more than quibbling over Lévesque's language and terminology. They also expressed concern about the implications for the tax exemption for the first child if the child were deemed ineligible for the benefit: Would it be the current level of $300 or would it be $550 as was provided for other children who were ineligible for family allowances?[21]

However, Willard hastily arranged a series of meetings in the Department of National Health and Welfare, and on 17 February, his officials produced several options: 1) maintain the present system but increase the benefits by 50% or 100%; 2) reorganize the program to pay a family benefit that would vary with the size of the family rather than a child's age; 3) retain both family allowances and youth allowances, but increase the rates for older children, including those eighteen years of age and attending school; 4) develop two new programs: one designed for children aged twelve and under, consisting of family benefits varying with the size of the family, and the other for children aged thirteen to eighteen, consisting of family benefits varying with the age of each child; and 5) eliminate the youth allowances by extending the coverage for family allowances to those currently covered under the youth allowance program and gradually increasing the benefits for all children over a five-year period. Each proposal involved a considerable increase in expenditure, ranging from a minimum of 28% for the fourth proposal to a 100% increase for the second.[22] This fact elicited a quick response from the Department of Finance. Deputy Minister R.B. Bryce immediately wrote Willard, "We simply must call a halt to further increases in expenditure on welfare and related programs for several years." He also noted, "Welfare has progressed a great deal in the past few years and I think you have had a reasonable turn." However, none of the proposals included any consideration for providing benefits related to both age and family size, as Lévesque had indicated was the clear objective of his government.

The pressure for an immediate response to Quebec dissipated, temporarily at least, when Daniel Johnson and the Union Nationale scored an upset victory over Jean Lesage's Liberals in the June 1966 election in Quebec. Even so, the Department of National Health and Welfare had been shaken from its lethargy over the family allowance program, and even the minister had to admit that the program had largely failed over time to maintain a payment bearing a reasonable relationship to its original purchasing power. Still, the department maintained that family allowances continued to provide a measure of additional income support to many Canadian families. Perhaps it was this general level of complacency with the existing family allowance arrangements and the removal of the determined Lévesque from the Quebec scene that together slowed to a snail's pace the general review of family allowances that had been initiated after Lévesque's demand that Quebec control the entire program. It took a plea for a formal review of family allowances in January 1967 from the National Council for Welfare, an advisory body of federal and provincial deputy welfare ministers, for the Department of National Health and Welfare to complete its investigation of family allowances.

However, the defeat of the Liberal government in Quebec had not halted the province's plans for new social security measures. Plans for a provincial family allowance scheme to complement the existing federal program were outlined in the budget speech on 16 March 1967. Quebec proposed paying an allowance twice yearly, beginning 1 July 1967, at the annual rate of $30 for the first child, $35 for the second child, $40 for the third child, $50 for the fourth child, $60 for the fifth child, and $70 for each additional child. In addition, there would be a supplemental annual allowance of $10, payable twice a year for all children between the ages of twelve and sixteen.

After encountering considerable difficulty in establishing and administering its schooling allowance in 1961, the government of Quebec asked the Department of National Health and Welfare for the information from the family allowance regional office that would be necessary for the province to have its first family allowance cheques paid on time. The federal Cabinet agreed that the family allowance division should cooperate with Quebec; however, Finance Minister Mitchell Sharp reportedly advised his deputy, R.B. Bryce, that at the same time, Canada should show "no uncertainty about its own position and intention to remain in this field."[23]

Following the first payment of Quebec's family allowances, Ottawa learned that little had changed in the attitude and aspirations of Quebec regarding the national program. Writing Allan MacEachern ostensibly to thank him for Ottawa's cooperation in helping launch Quebec's scheme and to tell him of the efficient manner in which the province had administered the family allowance program, Quebec Minister of Family and Social Welfare Jean-Paul Cloutier also offered to assume the administration of the federal family allowance program in Quebec on a contractual basis, to save the federal government the administrative costs of the Quebec regional office. Cloutier also suggested that the two governments would be able to absorb the federal employees displaced by the closing of the regional office in Quebec.[24]

Cloutier's request, though different from Lévesque's in that Cloutier did not ask that Ottawa transfer responsibility for family allowances, would have yielded the same practical result. If Ottawa conceded to the request, the Canadian government would have to continue to fund the family allowance program, but the cheques would arrive each month to families in Quebec from the province itself. This was totally unacceptable to Ottawa. First, Willard warned MacEachern that Cloutier's claims of an efficient and time-saving administrative system should be treated with considerable skepticism. Any efficiency Quebec might have achieved in its provincial program came largely as a result of Ottawa's help: Ottawa had provided records of the proof of age for all children in Quebec; without such information Quebec could not have got started for months, possibly years, because they would have had to verify the birth of each child registered.[25]

MacEachern responded to Cloutier in a carefully crafted letter reassuring him that his offer of distributing the federal program through Quebec provincial machinery had been thoroughly discussed in Cabinet. However, Ottawa saw no advantage in changing the present system since it was both as efficient and economical as could be achieved with the fundamental principle of ensuring good service to the public. Moreover, family allowances were a national program and would continue to be administered on that basis. However, the minister did not completely shut the door on Quebec. Ottawa was always looking for ways to improve the national system of family allowances, MacEachern wrote, and he invited Cloutier to make specific proposals to this end.[26]

Even so, Cloutier's proposal reminded the government yet again of the need for a re-examination of family allowances. In the Cabinet meeting of 21 November 1967, when the government decided to reject Cloutier's proposal that it turn over to Quebec the administration of the Canada family allowance program for the province, the Cabinet also agreed that it undertake a comprehensive review of family allowances and similar programs with a view to devising an overall program under which payments would be made more closely in accordance with the needs of recipients. In addition, a detailed study would be made of the cost implications of a guaranteed annual income program.[27] Shortly after, Pearson announced his decision to resign as party leader and prime minister, thereby pushing aside further discussion of the family allowances matter at the Cabinet for quite some time. Meanwhile, however, the research division in the Department of National Health and Welfare laboured away on the family allowance file.

Although the Department of National Health and Welfare and several of the provincial governments, notably Quebec, were already showing interest in making social programs selective rather than universal,[28] the election of Pierre Elliott Trudeau as Liberal leader and prime minister helped push the debate between the two options to the top of the agenda. On 4 April 1968 at the Liberal leadership convention, Trudeau stated, "In the field of social welfare programs it is my belief that we have enough of this free stuff ... We have to put a damper on this revolution of rising expectations ... We must not be afraid of this bogeyman, the means test. We must be more selective, to help those who live on uneconomic land or in city slums."[29] John Munro, who was appointed the minister of national health and welfare in Trudeau's first administration, shared his leader's sentiments. A briefing note that the department prepared for him in 1968 advised that family allowances should be modernized so as to provide greater income support to those children who really needed it.[30]

Munro subsequently told the *Globe and Mail* in May 1969 that he had considerable doubt about paying family allowance benefits to high-income families, but the government had not yet considered the issue. He admitted that the Cabinet Standing Committee on Social Policy had been studying a massive report Willard had prepared at the Cabinet's request to ensure that the federal welfare budget of $2.2 billion was being spent effectively on those in greatest

FIGURE 13   When Pierre Elliott Trudeau won the Liberal leadership convention in 1968 and became prime minister, he promised to reform social programs and target spending to those in greatest need.
Library and Archives Canada, Duncan Cameron/Duncan Cameron fonds, PA-111213

need.[31] For the first time since family allowances had been introduced, the prime minister and his minister of national health and welfare were keen to consider the universal nature of one of Canada's best-known social programs. They had come to realize that the redistributive function of the welfare state to move greater resources into the hands of low-income Canadians would be prohibitively expensive without bringing an end to universal social programs.

The concept of universality would remain entrenched in family allowances for another generation, although within government, support for universality had begun to diminish. Moreover, Canadians themselves were starting to change their views of universality in the family allowance program. A poll conducted by the Canadian Institute of Public Opinion in November 1969 found that 58% wanted benefits eliminated or reduced for the well-to-do, and of that group 80% reported that the rich did not need the money and it should go to the poor instead.[32] Still, when parents learned that the new prime minister might cancel the program, many of them wrote Trudeau to express their opposition to any attempt to eliminate benefits.[33]

Trudeau's election as leader of the Liberal Party and the new prime minister of Canada came at a time when Canada and many of the other liberal welfare states, including the United States and the United Kingdom, rediscovered poverty in their seemingly affluent nations. American President Lyndon Johnson had declared war on poverty when he introduced his Equal Opportunity Act in Congress in March 1964; the Pearson government had the same goal in mind when it announced in the 1965 Throne Speech intentions for the Canada Assistance Plan, a major cost-sharing agreement between Ottawa and the provinces for a variety of social welfare programs. Over the ensuing few years, there was a litany of reports and investigations that further highlighted the extent of poverty in Canada. Among the first was Senator David Croll's, which revealed the depth of poverty among Canada's elderly. The Economic Council of Canada's *Fifth Annual Review* (1968) declared that poverty in Canada was real, and noted that the number of poor were not in the thousands but, rather, millions. The council recommended that the eradication of poverty be a major national goal. This prompted the federal government to ask Croll to study poverty further, and he revealed in his 1971 report that Canada's $6 billion investment in its welfare programs still left one in five Canadians poor.[34] The *Report of the Royal Commission on the Status of Women in Canada* highlighted the poverty experienced by women, especially single mothers. Because the media extensively covered all of these reports, public awareness of poverty in Canada was high.[35] Perhaps such awareness contributed to the widespread support of Trudeau and his promise of a just society for Canadians in the federal election of 1968. Once again, the Quebec government began to insist that the federal government withdraw from family allowances and old-age security so that it could more effectively address poverty in the province.[36]

The growing concern over poverty amid Canada's rising expenditure on social programs[37] could not be ignored when the Department of National Health and Welfare began its extensive review of family allowances in 1967 and 1968. Willard presented a comprehensive set of income security proposals to Munro in 1969 that the minister took to the Cabinet. The reduction in poverty was the fundamental objective of the "Income Security Dimension of Social Policy," or the Green Book proposals, as the document became known in the department. The document had first taken shape when Willard had earlier undertaken his one-person review of the social security system. The Green Book represented a traditional liberal approach to social welfare, recognizing that the state had to help build earning capacity among the poor and reduce dependency by providing individuals with the opportunity and tools to lift themselves out of poverty.

At the same time, however, it recognized that the state had to offer protection against the risks of old age, death of the breadwinner, disability, sickness, family size, unemployment, and chronic low earning capacity. The Green Book argued for the continuation of some sort of family allowance, even as it recognized a growing disenchantment with universal programs as an instrument of social policy because of their high costs and their inability to meet the needs of the poor. It proposed that universal demogrants – non-contributory benefits given for whole sections of the population without a test of means or need – be abandoned or phased out in favour of more selective income redistribution initiatives designed to lift as many persons as possible above the poverty line.[38] Perhaps it was possible to raise benefits and introduce a special tax to recover all or part of the benefits paid to families with incomes above specified levels, a consideration that had been dismissed when family allowances were first introduced in 1945. Family allowances had not been subject to income taxation since their introduction, since such benefits were seen as state support to families for the raising of all children. Another possibility was the removal of the income tax exemption for dependent children (approximately $480 million) to fund a supplementary benefit paid either on a universal or income-tested basis.

For the first time, it seems, the Department of National Health and Welfare had raised the possibility of linking the income tax system with social security payments. The department was also considering an income security plan or a modest guaranteed income for families. This would provide $50 monthly for each adult in the family ($100 for both parents) and $25 per month for each additional person under eighteen. However, benefits were to be reduced once annual incomes reached $6,000. The proposals would lower the number of

'Be silent, unworthy one, and give me your ten thousand dollars that I might distribute them among the poor!'

FIGURE 14   When Trudeau's government announced its intention of changing the family allowance legislation to target spending to the poor, the *Globe and Mail* portrayed Trudeau as a heroic figure (*Globe and Mail*, 2 December 1970).
Reprinted with permission of the Globe and Mail

beneficiaries for family allowances from 13.5 million to 9.5 million, but would add an additional $180 million to the current expenditures for family allowances. One need not look hard to see that the Department of National Health and Welfare was committed to the income security plan when it recommended in its Green Book proposals that there was a clear need to modify family allowances so that they would become more effective as an anti-poverty measure. However, the department understood that any changes had to be achieved within the existing budgetary parameters. The proposals were referred to the Cabinet Standing Committee on Social Policy.[39]

Senior officials in the Department of National Health and Welfare realized that the Department of Finance would be opposed to any reforms to family allowances that would increase the costs of the program. As John E. Osborne, the director of research and statistics in National Health and Welfare, wrote to Willard, "It seems to us that Finance is more concerned with increasing revenues and showing a decrease in expenditures than they are with any of the effects of their proposals on the Family Allowances program." While the Department of Finance agreed with National Health and Welfare that programs like family allowances had to become more selective and that some of the family allowance benefits had to be recovered, it wanted reforms to the existing programs primarily to reduce government expenditure on social security. "Finance is not using the concept of 'selectivity' as our Department has used it," Osborne observed.

"We speak of re-arranging our programs to ensure that *better benefits* are provided to those who need them most, at the expense of those who need them less. By redistributing the total expenditures, we can pay *poor* families *more* and middle-income families less – this is our concept of selectivity. Finance proposes to pay poor families no more, and everyone else less." Moreover, Osborne noted, the Department of Finance did not understand that the whole purpose of family allowances was to equalize opportunities for children regardless of family size or income class: "[Their position] appears to be a retrograde step, [and] I would doubt that they would be acceptable to the general public, for they [Finance] seem to be increasing government revenue at the expense of families with young children."[40] Still, the two departments agreed on the need to recover some of the benefits paid to high-income families; they just disagreed on what should be done with any of the savings.

By late summer, when the Standing Committee on Social Policy turned its attention to the matter, the Department of National Health and Welfare had dropped the idea of an income security plan in favour of making family allowances a selective program targeted to low-income Canadians. The department continued to stress the importance of family allowances, noting that they had become a vehicle for redistributing income to meet the needs of families in poverty. Given continuing disparities in regional economies – a concern for Ottawa since the late 1950s – the department presented family allowances as a tool for redistributing income to the economically depressed areas of Canada where incomes remained below the national average. The department also considered the rate of benefits. Officials and politicians believed family allowance benefits to be woefully inadequate, and to maintain the purchasing power they had in 1945, the average family allowance benefit per child in 1966 should have been $11.01 rather than the $6.76 it was. Moreover, the bulk of family allowance benefits went to those in the middle-income group, not to those most in need. Yet the government, in adhering to its own rhetoric of a just society, had clearly stated its priority in assisting low-income families. However, any across-the-board increase in family allowances would substantially add to the cost of the program. For instance, each dollar added to the benefit paid would have necessitated additional annual expenditure of approximately $85 million, and marginal changes in the rates of one or two dollars would bring at best a negligible improvement in the impact of the program. Such increases were unlikely, given the economic situation, and Osborne and John Clark made it clear to their deputy that they understood the financial pressures on the government: "In the context of the present financial difficulties faced by the Federal Government and the many other urgent priorities over the next few years, it would seem unreasonable at this time to look for any improvement in [the] Family Allowances program by increases in the flat-rate universal payment. Therefore, if improvement in the program is to be achieved in the immediate future, the only practical approach would appear to be the adoption of some form of selectivity aimed at directing more of current outlays to low income families." Their memorandum pointed out that the basic issue with family allowances was really one of universality or selectivity.[41]

The department offered a series of recommendations in the interests of modernization and efficiency for the social policy committee to consider. First, it recommended that the school attendance provision be removed from the family allowance legislation. Because the school-leaving age had been raised in each province, it was no longer necessary for Ottawa to use family allowances as an incentive to keep children in school. Moreover, education was a provincial responsibility and the less the federal program intruded into the provincial field, the better. Second, it proposed the elimination of a pre-audit by the comptroller of the Treasury of each application for family allowance in favour of random checks. By doing so, 100-150 positions would be eliminated at a considerable savings in administrative costs. Third, and more important, the department presented three plans for restructuring the program.

The first plan suggested raising benefit rates for all children while imposing a special recovery tax that would recoup all or part of the benefit from families with incomes above a specified level. The levels would have to be determined by the Cabinet, but the cost of the increased benefits could be recovered through the tax system. The second plan would also not see any increase to the overall cost of the program. It proposed that the $300 personal income tax exemption permitted for dependent children be eliminated and that the revenue gained be used to pay a supplementary family benefit, either to all children or to those determined eligible, using some form of an income test. Finally, the third plan proposed changing the existing program from a universal to a selective one as part of a general tax reform policy that would make family allowances taxable for the first time, and tie exemptions for children to family income.

Perhaps as a final sop to the Department of Finance, Osborne and Clark wrote in their memo, "The steep upward trend in expenditure projections for the social development sector is of such proportions that the choice appears to be not one of increasing expenditure, but of either making the program selective to provide greater impact for low-income families, or providing a release of funds to finance other demands of greater priority." While they favoured a selective approach, they did not recommend the elimination of universality in family allowances; they warned against implementing any reforms that might attach any stigma to the recipients of family allowances.[42] Although Osborne and Clark considered various options, they remained wedded to universal benefits, although they believed that a portion – or even the total benefit paid – should be recovered through the tax system and any savings be used to increase payments for those most in need.[43] They were keenly aware that there was widespread support for reforms to family allowances: more than 58% of those polled by the Canadian Institute of Public Opinion in early November 1969 approved the idea of changing family allowances and either eliminating or reducing payments to the well-to-do.[44]

Of course, the debate on family allowances could not be separated from a wider discussion of other social issues. The Green Book proposals prepared by Joseph Willard and examined by the Cabinet Standing Committee on Social Policy during the summer of 1969 had identified several groups, notably pensioners, single families, and the working poor, that required additional assistance from the government. The Cabinet committee generally agreed that some federal funds were going to individuals or families who did not need them; the government had come to the conclusion that current social security programs like family allowances had to be distributed on the basis of need even if it meant there would be a reduction or elimination of allowances to middle- and upper-income groups. These discussions led to the decision to attempt to prepare a blueprint to meet the social needs of Canada and determine how the government might restructure the existing system to rationalize a patchwork of programs that had developed in the past generation. The result of the talks was the white paper on social security.[45]

On 28 November 1969, the plans for family allowances became part of the wider discussions in the proposed white paper on social security. As Trudeau wrote Allan MacEachern, chair of the Cabinet Standing Committee on Social Security, "As you know, I place the highest importance on the timely development of a coherent and effective social policy for the government." Trudeau and John Munro had discussed the government's evolving social policy agenda when the two were in Rome during the summer of 1969.[46] Trudeau made it clear that he wanted a review that allowed the government to assess each of its social security programs, consider the constitutional implications of each, and propose a series of initiatives and reforms that might lead to an integrated approach to social welfare along the lines that Quebec had been advocating. Munro told the Cabinet that a thorough review of social policy in a white paper would provide Ottawa with an opportunity to obtain the views of interested parties across the country and facilitate a dialogue with the public on the various options before the social policy committee. Once the federal government had gauged public reaction and ascertained the position of the provincial governments, it would be in a better position to proceed with the implementation of new legislation. Munro proposed a tight schedule for the white paper, suggesting that it be tabled in Parliament within six months.[47] The process turned out to be an agonizingly slow one, however; it would be more than a full year – 19 November 1970, to be exact – before the Cabinet agreed on what should be included in the white paper.

The preparation of the white paper was slowed by three imperatives endemic to most government initiatives: cost, politics, and bureaucratic infighting. Both the social policy committee and the Cabinet considered more than ten different options for restructuring family allowances, which clearly demonstrates the difficulties Ottawa was having with making a decision on the file. Although the government wanted to channel more of the money spent on family allowances into the hands of low-income families, any proposal – no matter how effective it might be – that exceeded the $560 million then allocated for the program would be rejected by both the Department of Finance and the Treasury Board. The Department of Finance insisted throughout the discussions that there were no new funds available for family allowances, a view largely supported by the Cabinet.[48] The Standing Committee on Social Policy had agreed on 28 July, for instance, that the government should abolish the existing family allowances ($560 million) and the $300 income tax exemption for dependent children under sixteen ($360 million) in favour of a more generous family income security program that would have raised the allowances by approximately $120 for many families. It would have more than doubled the amount paid to families living below the poverty line.

Moreover, the white paper proposal would have maintained the federal presence in every home with children through the payment of family allowance cheques, and it would have kept the concept of universality as it continued to pay a benefit to all mothers of dependent children under sixteen. However, it would have increased the tax burden of middle-income Canadians with incomes above $8,000 by eliminating the child tax exemption of $300, and eliminated benefits for 1.2 million or 39% of Canadian families. At the same time, 64% of one-child families with less than $8,000 income would have been much better off.

The Cabinet rejected this proposal. The Department of Finance also opposed any strategy that removed the income tax exemption for dependent children. If anything, the tax exemption effectively compensated families for the increase in the cost of raising their children and therefore should not be eliminated.[49] The Cabinet then directed Munro and the social policy committee to provide a plan in the white paper that included social welfare reforms through a realignment of the existing expenditures and without committing the government to any additional expenditures in the social security field.[50]

Even as it moved toward selectivity in benefits, the Cabinet worried that it would be politically dangerous to reduce benefits for middle-income Canadians. It did not want to create the impression among the middle class that it was being squeezed to get more money into the hands of the poor. Ministers realized that the Liberal Party had attracted significant support from the middle class and it could not afford to alienate that large group of Canadians. As Arthur Laing pointed out in the Cabinet, increasing the tax burden of the middle-income group would have negative political consequences for the Liberals. The Cabinet was also aware that the proposed changes to unemployment insurance rules would make members of the middle class such as teachers and civil servants pay premiums for the first time. Losing their family allowances on top of this would certainly create resentment toward the Liberals. Another concern was that if any mother lost her family allowance benefits, she too might exact her anger on the Liberals.[51]

Within the machinery of government, the Treasury Board, in addition to the Department of Finance, presented major hurdles for any proposals coming from Munro's department, though almost every member of the Cabinet realized that Munro could be counted on to plan a review that would place far more emphasis on what he considered necessary reforms than on the fact that there just weren't enough funds to pay for them.[52] However, the officials in the national health and welfare department clearly understood the position of the Department of Finance and learned to play by the simple rule that there was no new money for family allowances. The Treasury Board represented a problem of a different sort: the central agencies in government had begun to exert considerably more influence in directing overall government policy than they had in the past.[53] As Haddow has shown, the Treasury Board was among the most aggressive in pursuing the rationalist policy analysis that became popular when Trudeau became prime minister, and it looked beyond individual departments to address an issue.

At the same time, A.W. Johnson, a former civil servant in the government of Saskatchewan who had moved to Ottawa and would become one of Canada's most influential civil servants, was appointed deputy secretary of the Treasury Board.[54] He took an immediate interest in social policy. Johnson maintains that the Treasury Board developed and assessed proposals for the Cabinet on how to allocate resources based on the "priorities of the government and its policy decisions, the effectiveness of the programs in achieving the government's objectives, and the efficiency with which the programs [were] administered." Under his leadership, the Treasury Board was "unencumbered by departmental loyal-ties to particular clienteles," and this approach led it to look beyond tinkering with existing programs and, if necessary, beyond existing departmental bound-aries to ensure that all proposals were assessed by Treasury officials to check that they met the philosophy and goals of the government.[55] At the same time Munro was working on a general social security paper, Bryce Mackasey, his colleague in the Department of Labour, was preparing major reforms to the unemployment insurance program, and the Department of Finance was pre-paring a white paper on taxation.

Even before he moved to the Treasury Board, Johnson had prepared a lengthy – and apparently unsolicited – memorandum called "A Minimum Income for Canadians" that he sent to Prime Minister Trudeau. In it he noted that in the discussion of guaranteed annual income plans, he had been struck by the lack of a general philosophy or approach with respect to income security. He pro-posed that the government consider a minimum income plan for all Canadians that combined public sector support with an acceptable minimum wage level from the private sector. He told Trudeau that his thinking had been influenced by several considerations: 1) that it was desirable that the government of Canada develop some kind of general minimum income plan or a guaranteed annual income, since many of the opinion leaders across the industrialized world were moving in that direction; 2) that middle-income Canadians were opposed to any income security plan that might remove the incentive to work; 3) that Canadians were unhappy with current tax levels and would not tolerate any increase in taxation to finance public expenditure on welfare, especially if such universal programs as family allowance cut benefits for middle-income women; and 4) that the income security plans should be rationalized with more of the public payments being made directly by the federal government rather than provincial governments. Johnson said that working Canadians ought to be guaranteed an income large enough to support at least two people through the minimum wage laws. Where required, the state should be prepared to supple-ment minimum wages with universal family allowances.

Johnson's memorandum was sent to all the ministers; not surprisingly, it was greeted with considerable scorn in the Department of National Health and Welfare. "Al Johnson's treatise is simply another economic solution for poverty," J.I. Clark noted, reflecting the prevailing view in his department, adding "and [this] joins the long list of similar programs specifically designed with a selective income security approach." Moreover, Clark made it clear that the general dis-cussions in the department on the guaranteed annual income, and on income security in particular, did not lack a philosophy as Johnson had charged. The philosophy underlying income security was clear, Clark pointed out: "[It] is to provide money with a minimum of barriers to persons in need so that they may use this money to purchase their requirements in the market. The provision of money is not seen as a final solution, but it is recognized that it is a very important solution for many of the economic and social problems of poverty and low incomes."[56]

Johnson had another opportunity to push for a guaranteed annual income when the Cabinet asked him, M.A. Crowe (deputy secretary of the Cabinet), Simon Reisman (deputy minister of finance), and Willard to consider a draft of the white paper on income security. As far as the reform of family allowances was concerned, the Cabinet by then appeared to support Munro's much revised proposal for a major rationalization of the income security programs by redistributing the money already in the system as a way of preventing and alleviating poverty. Such a scheme would dismantle the existing family allowance program in favour of a family income security plan, which would direct most of the financial resources to the families in greatest need through a new extension of the guaranteed income concept based on income levels.

Still, this was not the guaranteed annual income Johnson had earlier advocated, and he noted that the overall problem with the proposal was that the government's underlying philosophy had to be more clearly and forcefully represented in the white paper.[57] Johnson insisted that the different approaches to income security be clearly identified so that the government's approach and its proposals could be examined in perspective. To him, there were two approaches: income protection and support, and guaranteed annual income. The former, he pointed out, assumed that people were able to work and provide for themselves and their families. The state would assure high levels of employment and require employers to pay a decent wage. However, Canadians who were unable to work for any reason would be provided with the necessary support to facilitate their participation in the workforce and the social assistance to maintain their families until that happened. A guaranteed annual income would provide everyone in the community with a decent standard of living. While Johnson favoured a guaranteed annual income, the committee liked the idea of addressing the difficulty that low-income families, especially those in large urban centres, were having in dealing with the pressure of rising prices, and it agreed that a reformed family allowance program was one of the few means the federal government had to get additional income directly to low-income people who faced the added financial burden of raising children.[58]

National Health and Welfare Minister John Munro tabled the "White Paper on Income Security for Canadians" in Parliament on 30 November, although the Cabinet had been disrupted from normal business – as had much of the country – when the *Front de Libération du Québec* (FLQ) kidnapped James

Cross and Pierre Laporte earlier in October.[59] The white paper proposed to re-structure the existing family allowances in favour of a family income security plan, and set out a preferred course of action that embodied four steps: 1) income tax exemptions for dependent children would be retained; 2) family allowances for families with incomes exceeding $10,000 would be terminated; 3) family allowances were to be taxable and considered a part of the income of the parent who claimed the exemption for any dependent children; and 4) the amounts earned from taxing family allowances and the savings from withholding pay-ments to high-income families were to be used to increase the benefits for children in families with up to $4,500 of family income, and to provide gradu-ated benefits to families with incomes between $4,500 and $10,000. The gradu-ated benefits were as follows: a) $16 a month for each child under sixteen in families with up to $4,500 incomes; and b) gradually reduced benefits in the $4,500 to $10,000 income range through a formula such as the reduction of the allowance by $1 monthly per child for each $500 of family income (or portion thereof) above $4,500.[60] The family income security plan was to begin in Sep-tember 1971.

Munro later wrote that an income ceiling of $10,000 was chosen as a reason-able level. Below that cut-off point, 70% of families continued to receive full or partial family allowance benefits. It was felt, Munro noted, that $72 a year in family allowances per child on an income of more than $10,000 was not a very significant degree of assistance for those families, but denying the allowances to such families would release $170 million for redistribution to low-income groups.[61] The minister pointed out that the changes were self-financing, since the benefits to the more well-to-do families were effectively eliminated by being taxable. He also noted that this was the first step toward developing a guaranteed income as a major anti-poverty policy. Yet Munro pointed out as well that the white paper defined "the challenge to arrive at a renewed affirmation of income security policy which will have the effect of assisting the people in greatest need, without detracting from programs designed to stimulate the economic develop-ment which operates at the basis of the entire system of well-being." After flirting with a guaranteed income, the Liberals pulled back, noting in the white paper that the "best approach for overcoming deficiencies in the existing system at this time does not lie in the direction of dismantling the system in favour of one overall guaranteed income programme. The best approach is to revise each of the four instruments of income security policy."[62] The government thus considered, but did not adopt an integrated approach to social security.

The response to the white paper was mixed. Ottawa realized, of course, that any new initiatives in the social security field would potentially raise problems with Quebec, which had insisted that it should control family allowances in its own province. It did not take long for the criticism from that direction to come.[63] The Canadian government had unilaterally announced its plans for the family income security plan, although Munro travelled to Quebec City as soon as the white paper was published to explain his proposals to Quebec's Social Affairs Minister Claude Castonguay and invite him to present his comments at the annual federal-provincial welfare ministers' conference scheduled for January 1971.[64]

Following that conference, Munro reported to the Cabinet that the greatest opposition could be expected from the provincial governments. Not surprisingly, Castonguay (like Johnson at the Treasury Board) criticized Ottawa's approach as "piecemeal." He insisted, Munro told his colleagues, that Quebec have primary responsibility in social policy, and Ottawa would have to recognize the province's exclusive jurisdictions in the field; in times of conflict between the federal and provincial governments, the provinces would prevail. Beyond that, Quebec and Manitoba had adopted the guaranteed income concept as a major policy objective, and the Quebec proposals in that area had gone much further than those put forward in the federal white paper. Quebec needed control of the social welfare field to allow it to implement its proposed guaranteed social allowance plan, an income security system that was to be integrated with its existing welfare and income insurance schemes.[65] Castonguay had insisted on clarifying the relative roles of the two governments before he would consider any proposed changes to the income security system. John Yaremko, Ontario's minister of social and family services, offered similar criticism. In a position paper prepared for the conference, he said the benefits had to take account of family size. Ontario wanted payments linked to the income tax system so those eligible would file a return to receive payments monthly. He did not want payment from a welfare department, noting that "if the existing tax system were used as a means of granting payments to the needy, the social stigma surrounding such payments would virtually disappear."[66]

The Atlantic provinces were generally pleased with the proposal, since each province stood to increased its percentage share of total family income security plan benefits as compared to the family allowance program from 10.5% to 14.1%.[67] In March 1971, a Gallup poll reported that 66% of Canadians supported the proposals, while only 25% were opposed.[68]

There were criticisms as well. While NDP leader Tommy Douglas welcomed the increased family allowance benefits to low-income Canadians, he criticized the plan for not taking account of family size. The North Bay and District Labour Council criticized Munro for eliminating universal payments and accused him of creating a program that stigmatized the recipients as low-income families; the NDP agreed with this assessment.[69] In addition, the Department of National

Health and Welfare received 893 letters from Canadians, fewer than they had anticipated. Robert Campbell, the director of information services, told Willard that 84% of the letters were critical of the family income security plan initiative. Only about 15% of the correspondence came from Quebec, despite the special efforts Ottawa made to attract comment from that province. The officials felt that the Quebec public was so oriented toward Quebec City in all government matters that it paid little attention to what the federal government did. Moreover, the editorial reaction in the press and panel discussions in the electronic media were relatively low-key. Many of the commentators divided along party political lines, but the white paper's recommendation of increasing benefits to the poor at the expense of high-income Canadians was very difficult to criticize. Campbell noted that even for lower-middle-income groups to attack this principle was something akin to attacking motherhood. Further, he thought it was very clever that the white paper suggested a guaranteed income was desirable but at that time too expensive. That comment, he suggested, allayed fears among the middle class that they might be taxed too heavily if the government moved too quickly or too far in the welfare field.[70]

The reforms to family allowances included in the white paper were intended as a trial balloon, and the Liberal government immediately realized that their proposals would require substantive revision if they were to find wide acceptance across the country. Munro knew that his proposals had angered the middle class; they would not support any plan to eliminate benefits for families with incomes above $10,000.[71] Munro even told a gathering in Toronto that to cut families off allowances at $10,000 was an "obvious injustice," and he subsequently told the Cabinet Standing Committee on Social Policy that he would reconsider his plans to eliminate benefits for families above the $10,000 threshold. Even though Munro and his department had quickly realized that there were serious problems with the reforms they had proposed in the white paper, they would not have the opportunity to respond to those criticisms as family allowances reform became inextricably linked to constitutional change in early 1971. With this change, Munro was shunted out of the national health and welfare portfolio, and responsibility for reforming the family allowance program moved to the prime minister's office.[72]

Family Allowances and Constitutional Change, 1968-72

THE QUESTION OF constitutional jurisdiction had been an issue since Ottawa had announced its plan in 1944 for family allowances.[1] At that time, both Quebec and Ontario, especially, had argued that Ottawa had exceeded its constitutional reach with the introduction of family allowances. However, with a strong central government clearly in the ascendancy, Prime Minister King dismissed those who challenged Ottawa's constitutional right to make payments to individual Canadians. The Exchequer Court later confirmed Ottawa's jurisdiction in the matter when it ruled in *Anger v. the Minister of National Revenue* in 1957 that the Family Allowances Act was within Parliament's general power to legislate for the peace, order, and good government of Canada, but that ruling did not settle the matter for long.[2]

By the 1960s, support for the centralizing tendencies of the immediate postwar period had waned as a new province-building era began.[3] Quebec demanded major changes in the operation of the federation as it challenged Ottawa's right and effectiveness in the delivery of many federal programs, especially those in the area of social policy. Not surprisingly, social programs, particularly family allowances, came to play an important role in the Canadian minefield of federal-provincial relations through this period, and the nation's political leaders proved quite willing to use Canada's best-known universal social program of family allowances as one way of maintaining national unity while appeasing the nationalist government in Quebec. When that happened, it effectively elevated much of the responsibility for social welfare policy from the realm of sectoral politics or "low politics" (from the domain of the minister of national health and welfare and his officials) to the realm of "high politics" (to the domain of the prime minister, the Office of the Prime Minister, and the Privy Council Office) as social policy became one means of reaching a new consensus with Quebec. Such developments also raise important questions about the validity of claims from scholars that "political ideology remains the decisive factor in explaining the development of social and economic programs."[4] During this period, social policy was about much more than creating social and economic programs that helped the less fortunate in Canadian society; the goals of policy making in the social policy file were subordinated to higher interests, namely, the constitution and intergovernmental relations.

At a federal-provincial constitutional conference in December 1969, Ottawa attempted to bring clarity to the question of jurisdiction in such matters as income security and social services when it presented a proposal to the provinces to engage in a discussion on the distribution of powers in those matters. Earlier attempts by Ottawa to introduce old-age pensions and unemployment insurance had proven difficult because of the constitutional uncertainties surrounding these matters. Many hoped that the greater clarity on question of jurisdiction in the social policy field could be established as the constitution was reformed. Most of the provinces accepted the principle that both Parliament and the provincial legislatures had and should continue to have powers to make general income support payments to individuals. Others agreed that it might be best if the federal government controlled basic income support payments and income security. Quebec stood alone in insisting that the provinces should have exclusive jurisdiction in the field of income support. The conference agreed that social services (such things as hospitals, for example) were the exclusive jurisdiction of the provinces.[5]

However, subsequent changes to family allowances were more a response to the political position taken by the government of Quebec than to any social policy review in Ottawa. Constitutionalists have long been aware of the key role social policy played in Quebec's ultimate rejection of the Victoria Charter, but they have ignored how federal negotiators attempted to use social policy to achieve their constitutional goals. Peter Russell and others, like Kenneth McRoberts, have argued that Quebec's social policy proposals did not fit with Prime Minister Trudeau's view of Canada because his government insisted on the importance of national programs across the country.[6] What this analysis ignores is that the Trudeau government used social policy, as had the Bourassa government, as a key strategy in the constitutional negotiations in the early 1970s. Clearly, social policies in Canada have lives long after they are implemented.

Ottawa realized that Quebec really wanted the best of both worlds when it came to income security. Quebec insisted that the provincial legislatures had paramountcy (or primary constitutional authority) to legislate in the field of social policy and income security, but that both levels of government shared the responsibility and the power to finance and operate programs within the policy objectives and priorities established by the provinces. However, Quebec maintained that if the province decided to move into an area where the federal government occupied the field, Ottawa would simply withdraw and turn over to the province the fiscal equivalent of all monies spent in that particular province. Clearly, the federal government was uncomfortable with such an approach, but it realized, too, that any confrontation with Quebec over the control of social policy would prevent it from patriating and amending the British North America

Act, a policy objective on which Ottawa had placed considerable importance and urgency. Moreover, any confrontation with Quebec would surely have serious implications for Canadian unity.

Such were the concerns over Quebec's stand on social policy that Mitchell Sharp, the secretary of state for external affairs, recommended to the Cabinet that the federal delegation avoid the subject of social policy in the constitutional conference scheduled for 8-9 February 1971.[7] That was quite unlikely, however, given that the Quebec government had clearly articulated its position on social security in the "Report of the Commission of Inquiry on Health and Social Welfare" (the Castonguay-Nepveu Commission) early in 1971, and Bourassa had made social security reform one of his government's major priorities. Essentially, the report made four points: 1) it accused the federal government of fragmenting social and income security policies; 2) it insisted that a policy approach geared to providing a guaranteed income commensurate with essential needs was the only means of alleviating the consequences of poverty; 3) it claimed that such a policy required a complete harmonization and coordination of federal and provincial programs in the field of social policy; and 4) an integrated approach was possible only if the provinces were given overriding responsibility for the social policy framework and objectives.[8] Moreover, many in Quebec approved of the clause in the 1970 manifesto from the Front de Libération du Québec that attacked the inequities of the capitalist system.[9] Castonguay, one of the most powerful members of Bourassa's Cabinet, had made it clear on numerous occasions that the existing constitutional division on social policy in Canada was unacceptable.

Meanwhile, the Quebec government was also preparing its position for the constitutional conference, which was generally referred to as the Third Working Session on the constitutional talks. R. Gordon Robertson, the clerk of the Privy Council and Cabinet secretary in Ottawa, regularly communicated by telephone with his counterpart in Quebec City, Julien Chouinard, whom Premier Robert Bourassa had appointed as secretary of the Cabinet. Four days before the conference, Robertson briefed Prime Minister Trudeau on what to expect from the Quebec delegation. He told Trudeau that Premier Bourassa had managed at the Cabinet meeting to get his ministers (especially Castonguay) to agree that the practical results, as outlined by the Castonguay-Nepveu Commission, should be their primary concern. Robertson told Trudeau, "[Bourassa] apparently persuaded the Cabinet that the constitutional aspect is secondary, and that the question whether constitutional change is necessary should depend on and emerge from discussions with Ottawa as to ways and means of achieving the practical results in terms of social policy toward which the Commission was looking." At the first ministers' meeting, the premier would be seeking agreement on two points: 1) the principle that assistance with regard to social security and income support should constitute "une politique globale intégrée" for which the fundamental basis of action should relate to "le manque de revenus," and 2) a commitment from Trudeau that the federal government would soon discuss the ways and means of realizing the first principle. It seems Bourassa had convinced his Cabinet to focus on the substance of action in respect to social policy and income support rather than pursue constitutional change. A sympathetic Robertson reminded the prime minister that Bourassa had had no easy time in getting his Cabinet to agree to such an approach, and "that he would have very great difficulty indeed if the federal government could not find the means to assist him along this line."[10]

Meanwhile, Robertson had R.B. Bryce, his predecessor at the Privy Council Office, convene a meeting of several government senior officials, including A.W. Johnson, Simon Reisman, and J.W. Willard, to further consider Bourassa's proposals based on their understanding of the government's policies and attitudes. While they agreed it might be possible to go some distance in endorsing the concept of an integrated approach to social policy, they preferred a coordinated approach instead of an integrated one because the latter was "more than the government would be prepared to implement." On the concept of a guaranteed income, they advised the prime minister not to agree, since it would involve higher expenditures than Ottawa could afford and it would create serious trouble with the other provinces.[11] Moreover, in late 1970, Ottawa had rejected a plan for a guaranteed income when it had discussed family allowances reform. The senior officials also suggested Trudeau postpone a decision on the family income security plan until after discussions with Quebec and the other provinces. In the meantime, they recommended that the prime minister reassure Bourassa that the federal government would endeavour to formulate and operate its social policies in a manner that would contribute to provincial social objectives and permit each province maximum flexibility in developing its own social policies. Even so, Bryce advised Trudeau, so that there was no misunderstanding later, the prime minister should be clear in private to the Quebec premier that Ottawa had no intention of surrendering its right to provide family allowances in Quebec. Nor should Bourassa expect a guaranteed income, since it would necessitate an unacceptable increase in the level of taxation. As Bryce wrote in his memorandum, "They [Bourassa and Castonguay] should not expect us to tax other provinces ... in order to provide them with the funds necessary to finance a more advanced social program than we are able and prepared to finance in other provinces."[12]

FIGURE 15   Social policy was an important item in federal-provincial relations during the 1970s. Here, Prime Minister Trudeau and Quebec Premier Robert Bourassa talk during a federal-provincial conference in the early 1970s.
Library and Archives Canada, Duncan Cameron/Duncan Cameron fonds, PA-206592, reprinted with permission

At the meeting, Bourassa stressed that social policy was a major issue for Quebec and it had to be included on the agenda for the upcoming conference on the constitution scheduled for Victoria in June 1971.[13] The communiqué from the meeting acknowledged the impasse between the federal and provincial governments: social policy was fundamental to any constitutional change for Quebec, but Ottawa offered only a coordinated approach that might lead to greater cooperation between the federal and provincial governments and allow the provinces to achieve their social policy priorities. It refused to transfer to the provinces the sums it expended on social policy.[14] New Brunswick Premier Richard Hatfield insisted that it was crucial that Ottawa maintain its spending power in social policy to protect the national interest, and Saskatchewan Premier Ross Thatcher made it clear that if Quebec secured greater powers it would mean the end of Ottawa's authority to deal with national problems. Thatcher was quite blunt in his assessment, noting, "If Quebec persists with the demands she is making today, perhaps she should become a separate nation."[15] Despite the gulf between Quebec and the other governments, social policy was on the agenda for the constitutional conference scheduled for June 1971.

It was clear by now that the Department of National Health and Welfare had lost any semblance of control over the proposed changes to family allowances and other social programs; such files became intrinsically linked with Trudeau's constitutional reform initiative and the pressing need to accommodate Quebec. A memorandum prepared for Trudeau on 16 February 1971 made the matter abundantly clear: the Cabinet did not want constitutional change in respect of social policy, but it realized "that unless Quebec [was] able to argue that it [had] obtained 'something of substance' in the field of social security there [might] not be agreement in Victoria on the constitutional proposals."[16] The Cabinet had decided some time earlier that it would continue to make direct payments to individuals. Yet Quebec had proposed an income security system that would see the existing programs, federal as well as provincial, folded into a unified structure, and it insisted that it had priority in the conception of income security policy if not primacy in matters of financing and administration. For the Trudeau Cabinet, then, the question became one of working out a mutually acceptable approach with Quebec as it kept in mind the interests of the other provinces.[17]

R.B. Bryce, by this time the economic adviser to the prime minister on the constitution, assumed control of the issue. One of his first moves was to establish and become chair of the Interdepartmental Committee on Federal-Provincial Social Policy Issues, which he did on 17 February 1971. The committee would consider the whole issue of social policy and its possible constitutional implications.

Bryce summarized Quebec's position for Cabinet on 1 March. Both Bourassa and Castonguay spoke of social policy broadly, seeing it as encompassing income security, social services, health services, vocational training, and manpower services. Those services had to be conceived and operated on a global, integrated basis, and the primary order of government responsible was the province, even though the administration and financing of elements might include the federal level. They insisted that if the existing distribution of legislative powers stood in the way of realizing their general goals, changes were necessary. Still, Bryce reminded the Cabinet, Quebec was dependent on federal financing for many of the programs for which it demanded primary responsibility, and that fact alone was perhaps enough to prevent the province from saying "that [its] approval of the present constitutional proposals is definitely contingent upon agreement on the constitution or other particular changes in this field." Yet Quebec had two objectives. One was ostensibly political: to stand up to the federal government and gain something of substance out of the constitutional discussions. The other was essentially one of policy: to make the most out of the resources available to the province to allow it to develop a program along the lines suggested in the Castonguay-Nepveu Commission to deal with the persistent problem of widespread poverty in the province. The federal government realized that the success achieved in these discussions would likely have an important bearing on Quebec's willingness to approve the proposals for constitutional revision Ottawa was preparing for the constitutional conference scheduled for June.[18]

In preparation for a meeting between Munro and Claude Castonguay on 29 March, at which the federal minister offered to make a number of changes in the family income security plan to conform to the principles underlying the family allowance recommendations in the Castonguay-Nepveu Report, Bryce spelled out the approach Munro should adopt. He prepared a lengthy memorandum divided into three sections: general objectives in discussions, suggested approach at first meeting, and points for more general discussion with Castonguay on social policy. In the first section, Bryce emphasized several general objectives, most of which had been already approved by the Cabinet. He told Munro to a) make concessions on the form of family allowances but insist on federal administration and identification; b) keep the cost of the program within the federal parameters already agreed to; c) discourage Castonguay from insisting on escalating family allowance benefits based on the consumer price index; and d) remind Quebec that it had all the powers needed to fulfill its objectives on social policy, but Ottawa was willing to discuss with the province a list of its priorities in the field. To allow Quebec to save face, Bryce said it may be necessary to consider some modest provision in the constitution relating to social measures that would not impair the powers of Parliament in making payments to individuals. In effect, Bryce told Munro what to say, and suggested that the minister first indicate sympathetic interest in Quebec's proposal to have the family allowance program address the requirements of large families, and then generally try and find out what Castonguay really desired with their income security policies.[19]

It was Bryce who reported to the Cabinet on the meeting between the minister and Castonguay; Munro had little influence left with the Cabinet. The atmosphere at the meeting, Bryce informed the Cabinet, was tense, even though Munro had said that he might consider modifying his proposals for family allowances in light of the Castonguay-Nepveu Report. This was not enough for the Quebec minister, though, who told Munro that he wanted family allowances to become completely a Quebec program, both in structure and administration. It was clear, too, that he expected Ottawa to transfer to Quebec the financial equivalent of the family allowance benefits it would pay directly in Quebec under a federal program. He dismissed Munro's concern over the cost of indexing of family allowances. There was no meeting of minds on the constitutional matter, either. Castonguay told his federal counterpart that his government had reached the conclusion that the constitution should give Parliament the power to legislate in a field of social policy only if Quebec did not; if Quebec chose to legislate in the field, its legislation would have precedence, and any subsequent federal initiative would not apply in Quebec, except to the extent permitted by Quebec law. In such an event, the federal government had to compensate Quebec for the amount that would have been spent in the province if the federal laws had been applicable. Castonguay then provided Munro with a preliminary draft text of a constitutional section that would satisfy Quebec. As an additional step, he insisted that the family allowance benefit be doubled immediately for the fourth and each subsequent child to accommodate Quebec's demand that the program help large families.[20] This was more than Ottawa was willing to concede.

By April 1971, just two months before the Victoria conference was to begin, Ottawa adopted a different approach: it decided to inject more money into the family allowance program. The Cabinet had realized that it would be extremely difficult and perhaps even impossible to reach an agreement with Quebec on family allowances if Ottawa continued to insist that the reforms had to be made within the existing expenditure for the program. The Cabinet authorized an additional $150 million for the family allowance program, bringing expenditure for the program to $800 million. It is most interesting that just several months earlier the Cabinet had steadfastly refused to allocate extra funds to increase benefits for families living in poverty. In fact, the $150 million then being earmarked for the family allowance program was the amount that the Cabinet Committee on Priorities and Planning had set as the ceiling that could be added to the 1971-72 budget for *all forms* of social security.[21] Now, all of it was being used to try and bring Quebec on side.

Although low-income families would still not be helped by the adjustments, the Cabinet was able to justify the new expenditure for family allowances on the grounds that it would go some way to meet the demands of Quebec and address some of the criticisms levied at the white paper on social security. It had been proposed in the white paper to eliminate benefits when family income reached the $10,000-income threshold. By implementing a more gradual threshold that also took account of family size – a long-standing priority of the Quebec government – the costs would rise by $50 million. Second, it would take another $100 million to drop the proposal in the white paper to make family allowances taxable.[22] On 16 April 1971, the Cabinet recommended that negotiations continue with Quebec along the lines outlined above, and recommended the allocation of $150 million to permit a major federal initiative in the field of family policy and to improve the bargaining position of the federal government vis-à-vis the new Quebec proposals.[23] However, the Cabinet insisted that Quebec would not be told about the additional funds until an appropriate or opportune time.

In many ways, the new Cabinet proposals were a clear win for Quebec. Federal representatives were told to continue negotiations with Quebec on family income security along the general features of a family income security plan that would meet Quebec's needs and also be acceptable to the other provinces. The Cabinet directed the negotiators to tell Quebec that in order to improve features of family income security along the lines as indicated, additional funds would be committed, but the officials were warned against indicating how much the additional amount would be. If Quebec were prepared to go along with the changes suggested to achieve a mutually acceptable plan, the federal government was prepared to supply additional resources. Even as the Cabinet sweetened its offer to Quebec on social policy, it maintained that a constitutional amendment to include family allowances in section 94A of the British North America Act was unnecessary, contrary to what Castonguay had insisted. Quebec was already in the provincial field and Ottawa was providing family allowances under its use of the federal spending power. If Ottawa agreed to Quebec's request for an amendment, it would be put in the impossible situation of implicitly agreeing that its long-standing use of the federal spending power to pay family allowances was constitutionally suspect. The best strategy, Ottawa thought, was to offer Quebec an administrative arrangement for coordinating family allowances in that province.[24]

However, on 4 May 1971, Minister of Justice John Turner warned the Cabinet that a deal with Quebec was unlikely without a constitutional amendment. His contacts in the Quebec government had told him and other federal ministers and officials that it could not possibly agree to the proposed constitutional charter to be presented in Victoria without a constitutional amendment regarding social policy if it hoped to secure the approval of any change in the Quebec Assembly. Turner reminded his colleagues that this was not what Bourassa had stated publicly, but the premier had to satisfy a variety of interests. Moreover, Bourassa had said at the constitutional conference in April that family allowances must be included in section 94A of the constitution so that it would read: "The Parliament of Canada may make laws in relation to old age pensions and supplementary benefits, including survivors' and disability benefits irrespective of age, *and in relation to family allowances*, but no such law shall affect the operation of any law present or future of a provincial legislature in relation to any such matters."[25]

Turner told his colleagues that they must decide what to do about Bourassa's proposal. The Department of Justice did not see any serious problem in accepting Bourassa's proposal from a legal perspective. However, Turner warned the Cabinet that there were risks to federal-provincial relations as well as political implications in doing so. The most serious, of course, was that Quebec might insist that the change was an important one, and it might eventually demand that Ottawa withdraw from the fields in which the province enacted legislation. Turner was worried that if Quebec exaggerated the meaning and implications of the amendment, some of the other provinces, particularly in Atlantic Canada and the west, might oppose any substantial weakening of the federal power in social policy. Acknowledging the position already adopted by the Cabinet, Ottawa could continue in the field of family allowance, and amend section 94A as Bourassa suggested, which would give Parliament full power to legislate with respect to family allowances in the same way it could with respect to matters enumerated in section 91. Turner recommended that the Cabinet accept Quebec's proposal to include family allowances in section 94A but only on the understanding that Bourassa and Castonguay fully recognize Ottawa's position. Even so, Turner reminded the Cabinet that they should inform Quebec of their decision only just before the ministerial meeting on the constitution on 31 May and 1 June, because if the issue were settled too early, Quebec might be encouraged to seek something else before June 14.[26]

Ottawa was much more hopeful that an accommodation could be reached with Quebec after Munro met with Castonguay for the second time on 9 May 1971. The federal proposals were put to the Quebec delegation in an *aide-mémoire*. Castonguay had reason to be pleased; the *aide-mémoire* began: "We [the federal government] are now prepared to modify our programs in a number of respects to fit into the Quebec structure and Quebec priorities." While Ottawa refused to accept Castonguay's request that tax exemptions for children be converted into family allowances of one kind or another, it promised to allocate funds from other sources to improve the family income security plan proposals if agreement were reached on an appropriate structure. Munro did not tell Castonguay that the Cabinet had already agreed to put an additional $150 million into the program. The federal government also accepted Quebec's proposal to exempt family allowance payments from the regular income tax even though Ottawa had proposed as much in the white paper. Instead, family allowances would be subject to a special tax or reduction based on income. On the issue of benefits, Quebec still wanted to vary the amount paid to families according to the number of children, while Ottawa wanted to pay $16 per child. It told Quebec it could not agree to anything less than the $16 per month recommended in the white paper, but it could agree to the introduction of a differential by age yielding an average payment of $16. Similarly, Munro informed Castonguay that Ottawa would accept Quebec's proposals of a basic income limit of between $4,500 and $5,000 and tying the upper-income limits (or cut-offs) to the number of children in the family. This could see the limit moving from $10,000 (Ottawa's white paper proposal) to $20,500. Ottawa also agreed to Quebec's demand that the plan cover children aged sixteen and seventeen rather than the previous plan of covering only those under sixteen years of age. Nonetheless, Munro made it clear that the federal proposals constituted a total package, and the whole thing was conditional on acceptance by Quebec. Later, Munro told the Cabinet that several times throughout the meeting Castonguay stressed that the federal proposals constituted a solid basis for discussions.[27]

The other provinces were not excluded from the discussions over family allowances, but they were not told the whole story, either. As Munro negotiated with Quebec, federal officials held consultations with the four Atlantic provinces and the four western provinces to discuss the federal income security proposals in preparation for the Conference of Welfare Ministers scheduled for 7-8 June. To facilitate the consultation process, Munro presented the provincial officials with an *aide-mémoire* that outlined Ottawa's new position on a number of issues. However, at no time did he intimate to those provinces that he had made these changes to satisfy the desires of Quebec.[28] The treatment of Ontario was not much different. After the Cabinet had approved the series of changes to satisfy Quebec's demands, Munro and his officials met with Thomas Wells, Allan Lawrence, and Darcy McKeough, ministers and officials from Queen's Park, to discuss the income security proposals.

As the federal government had done in similar meetings with other provinces, Munro laid out the most recent modifications to the family income security plan. Ontario continued to insist on using the income tax as a means for providing income security benefits. When Lawrence asked Munro about Quebec's reaction to new federal proposals, Munro was evasive, telling him that the federal proposals aimed to ensure greater flexibility to enable all provinces to apply their priorities in developing social programs. Moreover, the federal proposals were tied to the current discussions on the constitution and were aimed at being helpful in facilitating agreement on that question. Lawrence let Munro know that he was worried about the constitutional discussions under way and about Quebec's intention to run family allowances. Ian Macdonald, the deputy treasurer of Ontario, told Munro that Premier Bill Davis wanted the social policy issue settled before the constitutional conference: "If a province should change its view on social policy, this might change another province's view on some other aspect under the constitution, such as language rights." Munro agreed, though he hoped he already had a deal with Quebec.[29]

Jean Marchand, the minister of regional economic expansion and one of the leading Quebec ministers, Munro, and several federal officials met for the third time with Claude Castonguay on 19 May. A few days after Munro had presented Castonguay with the federal *aide-mémoire*, they had spoken on the telephone and agreed to have their officials discuss the outstanding issues. By the time the three ministers met, there were just two issues outstanding: the use of one basic income floor regardless of family size, and the lack of a substantial differential in benefits for children above and below the age of twelve. Castonguay was concerned that the federal proposal would reduce benefits for all families with incomes above $4,500, which would interfere with the operation of Quebec's general social allowance plan by creating a disincentive to work among families who might lose benefits through the income tests of both plans. Quebec proposed delaying the application of the family income security plan income test until general social allowance plan benefits had been reduced to zero; it suggested that the family income security plan reduction of benefits start at an income of $5,000 for a one-child family, $5,500 for a two-child family, and so on by intervals of $500 for each child. The federal officials agreed with this approach for the sake of integrating the two programs, but suggested that the income floor be set at $4,500 for a one-child family, rising by $500 intervals above the base for each extra child. Quebec wanted two levels of benefits with a substantial differential between each level rather than the three with a small deferential, as Ottawa had earlier proposed. To meet Quebec's concern, Ottawa proposed two age groups, birth to eleven and twelve to seventeen, with a difference of $5 between the monthly benefits provided. Castonguay agreed to this, but continued to insist that the constitutional division of powers in the social policy field remained a matter of concern.[30]

That was certainly evident when the federal-provincial constitution conference began in Victoria on 14 June. When he opened, Trudeau said repatriation and an amending formula had been the main objective of the conference but social policy had emerged as a major issue as well. He acknowledged that Quebec had proposed that the provincial legislatures be given the authority to limit the power of Parliament to make income security payments like family allowances in the provinces. However, if Canada acceded to the demands of Quebec to divert federal spending for social policy to the provincial treasuries to allow each province to determine how it spent the funds, it would not only lead to the erosion of the federal presence in such areas but might also undermine Ottawa's ability to collect taxes in the affluent provinces to support provincial programs in the have-not provinces.[31] Obviously, this would not be good for the country.

Although Trudeau and the federal government had high hopes for constitutional reform, they failed to appreciate that there were fundamental differences between Ottawa and the English-speaking provinces on the one hand and Quebec on the other. While Trudeau and the English-speaking premiers sought fairly modest changes that would protect linguistic and cultural rights and entrench a modest charter of human rights, they did not envision any fundamental change to the relationship between the two levels of governments. They wanted to modernize the British North America Act by removing certain articles that had fallen into disuse, and patriate the constitution with a new amending formula. As indicated above, Quebec had much more aggressive constitutional aspirations. It wanted to amend the constitution to clarify and enlarge the legislative and fiscal autonomy of the provinces with the goal of creating a "national" government in Quebec City. This was no more evident than in the area of social policy. The Castonguay-Nepveu Report, which had been released in January 1971, recommended a new and radical approach to social policy. It provided Quebec with the ammunition to insist that "legislative primacy" in the area of income security be enshrined in the constitution. This would allow Quebec the power to design its own social security programs so that it could proceed with its ambitious reforms to deal with poverty.[32] As mentioned earlier, the federal government was willing to go only partway to meet Quebec's demands.

For three days, the first ministers debated various constitutional proposals. Finally, the conference concluded at midnight on 16 June with a new Canadian constitutional charter. The Victoria Charter addressed a variety of issues, including political and language rights, the appointment of Supreme Court judges, and an amending formula. The crucial issue at the conference, of course, was that of jurisdiction over social policy, which, as one commentator noted, was a microcosm of the larger issue of the division of legislative and taxing powers.[33] Trudeau insisted that Ottawa would not surrender its power to make direct payments to individuals, but he agreed that federal legislation in social areas could "dovetail with their [Quebec] legislation in social areas and if there is a conflict, ours [federal legislation] will have to adjust to theirs."[34] The federal government agreed to amend section 94, but the proposed amendment did not fully satisfy Quebec. While it recognized provincial paramountcy in the fields of family allowances and other income security measures, it did not prohibit Ottawa from participating in income support programs or offer to provide financial compensation to the provinces if they chose not to participate in a new federal initiative.[35] The final communiqué from the conference, which promised that the premiers would meet shortly to discuss all aspects of the federal-provincial fiscal arrangements, did not give Quebec the decentralized federalism it sought.

Although Bourassa agreed to consider the Victoria Charter, he realized that there was little support for it in Quebec. Peter Meekison, who attended the conference as part of the Alberta delegation, contended that the Quebec representatives had decided before they left Victoria that they would not ratify the charter.[36] As Bourassa perhaps expected, the opposition in Quebec was fierce; Claude Ryan, editor of *Le Devoir,* wondered why Bourassa had accepted a document "qui tend à consolider la prépondérance du gouvernement central dans les affaires canadiennes et à ramener le Québec au rang de province comme les autres."[37] The Parti Québécois, the major opposition party in the province, saw Bourassa's acceptance of the charter as an act of treason against the people of Quebec.

The premiers had agreed that before 28 June they would indicate to Ottawa whether or not they would take the charter to their respective legislatures for ratification. Even as Bourassa considered the Victoria Charter with his Cabinet in Quebec City, Ottawa continued to search for ways to solve the impasse with Quebec over social policy. It was R.B. Bryce again who suggested a way forward. He recommended a solution that would "assist" Quebec without additional cost to the Treasury, without loss of ultimate control of future federal programs, and without creating the impression that Trudeau was doing anything special for Quebec. He proposed that Ottawa allow *all* provinces the option of determining how the federal benefit for each recipient would be made in their province. This was clearly in keeping with the Cabinet's insistence that "in developing the federal position on the substance of social policy it [was] important to bear in mind the need to avoid giving the appearance of a substantive concession to Quebec alone."[38] The federal government would continue to administer the family allowance program and send cheques directly to the parents, thus maintaining family allowances as a nation building tool that had been present since their inception. Bryce's plan would allow Quebec, for example, to determine how its envelope of funds was distributed in that province; it could decide the amount of the benefit paid to each child. It could increase benefits for the fourth and subsequent children in a family at the cost of some reduction in the scale of payments for other children. The added incentive for Ottawa, Bryce suggested, was that only Quebec was likely to be interested in such an option.[39] Bryce's plan clearly conformed to Trudeau's vision of federalism that was determined to reverse the trend toward special status for Quebec by allowing all provinces to make special arrangements with Ottawa in the delivery of social programs.[40]

The Cabinet liked the proposal. It clearly realized that it was making a concession to Quebec and any of the other provinces that might be interested in designing their own benefit scheme, but Bryce's proposal was calculated precisely to reinforce the nation building intent of the program since its inception in 1945. If Quebec accepted the proposal, then the linkages between the federal government and individual Canadian citizens in Quebec would not be severed. Even a reformed family allowance benefit that provided the province with a measure of control would remain a tool of nation building by the federal government, and it would continue to help foster a pan-Canadian citizenship and attachment to the federal government.

At a meeting on 18 June, the Cabinet asked the Privy Council Office and the Department of National Health and Welfare to prepare a document outlining possible new arrangements for family allowances under which the federal government would continue to make the payments and determine the total amount of entitlement in each province, while allowing each province to establish its own priorities and benefits scheme. However, the Cabinet insisted that Bourassa not be told about Ottawa's intentions until after the Quebec Cabinet had met on the evening of 21 June. Ottawa wanted to be prepared with additional incentives in case the Quebec Cabinet chose not to proceed on the constitutional proposal. The federal Cabinet did not think that Bourassa would make a decision on Victoria at that meeting, and it wanted to be prepared with additional incentives if the Quebec Cabinet wavered on the constitutional proposal. As the Record of Cabinet Decisions makes clear, "the possibilities for family allowance concessions could become an important factor and could be discussed with Quebec Ministers as an avenue which the federal government was willing to explore."[41]

A few days later, on 22 June, the federal Cabinet agreed that if there was a good chance Quebec would accept the charter, then the prime minister should inform Premier Bourassa of Ottawa's willingness to change the family income security plan to accord broadly with changes proposed by Quebec and *enrich* the plan by the allocation of an additional $150 million. Ottawa would also permit the provinces to tailor the program to their specific needs, provided that the cost was within the aggregate amount provided to each province by the federal government and that a national minimum was paid to all children in relatively poor families. However, any province that chose to alter the national scheme would have to make a contribution to the family allowance program through a provincial supplement amounting to 15% or 30% of the federal expenditure for the program in that province. This option was predicated on the assumption that Quebec wanted the right to plan, not administer, the family income security plan. The Cabinet knew the game it was playing with social policy, and the Record of Cabinet Decisions for 22 June noted that "it would be preferable to make no such offer unless it was essential to success on the Constitutional issue and it was clear that it would lead to Quebec's approval of the Charter."

The next day, Bourassa formally rejected the Victoria Charter, claiming that the limitations on the federal spending power in the field of income support programs were simply too modest. The social policy clause in the charter fell far short of what Quebec had demanded. Even though the charter had recognized provincial priority, it had also insisted on concurrent powers, and it made no mention of compensation. But Quebec wished to have transferred to the province a number of the large federal programs and all the money that was then expended through various federal social programs. The Quebec government maintained that these funds would permit it to implement the recommendations contained in the Castonguay-Nepveu Report. In addition, Trudeau's proposed amendment to the British North America Act "to guarantee prior consultation of the provinces before changing federal income security measures, and to protect provincial social allowance plans from interference by parallel federal programs" was unsatisfactory to Quebec.[42]

Ottawa had counted on Bourassa waiting until the deadline of 28 June before he rendered a final decision; his announcement caught the capital by surprise and clearly pre-empted the federal government's strategy. However, a statement from Bourassa's office gave a measure of hope encouraging enough for Ottawa to ensure that family allowances would remain at the top of the federal-provincial agenda. Bourassa also insisted, "Federalism constitutes for Quebecers the best way of attaining their economic, social and cultural objectives" and noted the failure of the constitutional reforms to deal adequately with social policy. "The texts dealing with income security," the statement noted, "leave an uncertainty that meshes badly with the objectives inherent in any idea of constitutional revision. If this uncertainty were eliminated, our conclusions could be different." He and Trudeau had decided to meet in a week or so, but Bourassa had made it clear to the prime minister that success was contingent on new powers for Quebec in the social security field. Trudeau also told the House of Commons on 25 June that further negotiations with Quebec were likely, and he pointed out that Bourassa had said that "ambiguities" in language were the source of difficulty with the Victoria Charter.[43] Ottawa certainly believed that an agreement with Quebec was possible, especially if a consensus on social policy could be reached. Not surprisingly, then, Bourassa's insistence on social policy reform continued to have a major impact on policy making in Ottawa.

On 25 June, the Cabinet decided to push ahead with the proposals for the family income security plan it had previously approved. Ottawa could not withdraw the $150 million it had committed to luring Quebec to sign the Victoria Charter: to do so would have caused a split in the Cabinet and, above all, shown how the Trudeau government had attempted to use social policy to manipulate the constitutional agenda. However, the federal government dropped its proposal to allow provinces to play a greater role in family allowances; it alone would determine the structure of the benefits, perhaps in retaliation for Quebec's rejection of the Victoria Charter.

The failure of the central agencies to deliver on the constitution allowed Health and Welfare Minister John Munro to regain a little of his influence in the Cabinet. He told the House on 29 June 1971 that he had revised the white paper to ensure that the federal plan would fit into provincial priorities and social policies. Munro insisted that the plan embrace the anti-poverty concept of selectivity by placing substantially large benefits in the hands of low-income mothers while preserving a measure of protection for middle-income families. Moreover, an improved family income security plan could be dovetailed with the proposed Quebec social allowance plan without interfering with its operations.[44] The new scheme was to begin in May 1972. Don Jamieson, the Newfoundland representative in the federal Cabinet, commented in his memoirs that many in the Cabinet believed that "what was at first a bargaining position involving give and take on both sides became a matter of Quebec taking while still uncommitted to give on the constitutional issue."[45]

Yet as the federal government prepared the necessary legislation and worked out the technical details to make payments under the family income security plan, the issue of Quebec continued to influence Ottawa. As Munro told the Cabinet on 22 July 1971, Quebec might attempt to frustrate Ottawa by introducing its own income security legislation in an attempt to "occupy" the field, leaving Ottawa to duplicate the program with its new legislation and forcing another confrontation with Quebec City. However, the main deterrent preventing Quebec from any policy innovation in the field was that it had to divert funds from other programs to pay for any new initiatives. Even so, Munro pointed out, Quebec might introduce a program with very low benefits and then claim that Ottawa was merely supplementing the Quebec plan with its new legislation. The Cabinet wanted to prevent Quebec from such manoeuvring and decided that it was best to explain Ottawa's new approach directly to the people of Quebec. Munro was subsequently authorized to undertake a publicity campaign in Quebec in advance of the reopening of Parliament to explain the federal position on income security and the constitution. However, he was instructed to provide a low-key and objective presentation and to avoid, at all costs, a confrontation with the Quebec government. To be sure that he did, the Cabinet told him to clear all aspects of his plan with both the Office of the Prime Minister and the Privy Council Office.[46] To that end, E. Gallant, deputy secretary to the Cabinet (federal-provincial affairs) in the Privy Council Office, wrote J.W. Willard, the deputy minister of national health and welfare, on 20 August 1971, asking his assistance in preparing a picture of federal activity for all regions of Canada, but especially for the province of Quebec.[47]

The Cabinet also agreed to proceed in early September with the legislation to replace family allowances with the family income security plan. Ottawa had realized that the bill might generate opposition, particularly in Quebec, but by tabling the legislation, it was sending a clear message, especially to Bourassa, that it was intent on moving forward on the reforms even if no agreement could be reached with the province.[48] Even so, the Cabinet also agreed that Trudeau should provide Premier Bourassa with a draft of the legislation, inviting him to propose changes to the federal plan; no evidence was found during the course of this study that the other premiers were given any such consideration or received notification of the impending legislation.[49]

The strategy forced Premier Bourassa to respond. On 2 September 1971, he wrote Trudeau that he hoped to find a way of "averting conflict" in the area of family allowances. Bourassa continued to insist that the province required supremacy in the design of social security programs to meet its own social policy priorities. He wanted the proposed federal legislation to reform family allowances to conform to any existing terms, conditions, and regulations of the family allowance legislation in Quebec. He also wanted the province to have control over designating the recipients, the nature and the amount of the allowances, the scale of benefits, and the total amount payable to the citizens in that province. Trudeau was optimistic that Bourassa had intimated that it was possible to find a legislative solution to the social policy question rather than a constitutional one, which had derailed the Victoria conference earlier that summer. When Bourassa referred to family allowances distributed by the government of Canada, Trudeau and his officials assumed that Bourassa had come to accept a federal role in the program. Trudeau suggested that federal and provincial representatives meet to discuss the Quebec proposal. However, as aforementioned, the government had already decided to table the new family income security plan, and when the legislation was introduced in Parliament on 13 September 1971, Trudeau told the House that a letter from Bourassa had arrived too late for the federal government to change the legislation it had already prepared.[50] Amendments would be introduced in due course.

The legislation for the family income security plan (Bill C-264) was to replace the family and youth allowance[51] programs then in force, which paid benefits to all families, irrespective of income, on the basis of the age of children. There was a growing chorus of support for selectivity across Canada. Under the new legislation, payments were to be made on the basis of family income, family size, and the age of the children. The revised family income security plan proposed to cover all dependent children under eighteen and provide benefits of $15 per month for children under twelve and $20 per month for children between the ages of twelve and seventeen. This continued to reflect a principle first established for family allowances in 1945 that recognized that children were more expensive as they became teenagers.[52] Munro told the House that the underlying purpose of the family income security plan was to make social security spending more effective by channelling more money into the hands of lower- and middle-income families, and to help the working poor, whose earnings were such that they did not qualify for provincial assistance.

When the government established a family income floor below which maximum benefits were paid and above which payments were reduced as income rose, it established the principle of selectivity. The government also eliminated the $10,000 ceiling or cut-off point for benefits to all families, as proposed in the white paper.[53] For a family with one child, the income floor for the family income security plan was set at $4,500; for a family with two children, the floor was set at $5,000; and in the case of families with more than two children, the floor was raised by $500 for each additional child. To avoid any disincentive to work, the legislation reduced the benefits per month in the very small amount of 33 cents for every $100 of income above the family income floor, rather than the $1 proposed in the white paper. If there were children aged twelve or over in a family, the income ceilings ranged from $10,560 for a one-child family to $15,060 for a ten-child family. If there were no children over twelve in the family, the income ceilings ranged from $9,045 for a one-child family to $13,545 for a ten-child family. The new benefits were not to be taxable.[54]

Munro also told Parliament that the family income security plan had been developed after extensive consultation with the provinces,[55] interested organizations, and individuals. Following the tabling of the "White Paper on Income Security for Canadians" on 30 November 1970, Munro and his officials had met with their provincial counterparts thirty times and convened two federal-provincial conferences of welfare ministers. This consultative process, he said, had led to a number of improvements in the plan, though it was clear that Ottawa would not be able to satisfy the demands of all the provinces. In the case of Ontario, for instance, Munro thought that they had gone quite a distance to meet its demands. The government of Ontario had argued for some time that family allowances should be made into a selective plan to get more of the benefits into the hands of the poor. Ontario also wanted family allowances to take more account of family size but did not want the benefits taxed. The Ontario Department of Social and Family Services had told the Senate Poverty Committee that family allowances should be a selective program in order to provide more meaningful benefits to those in greatest need. Several years earlier, in 1969, the government of Quebec had suggested in its "Guidelines for a New Quebec Family Allowance Program" that family allowances be based on family income and the number of children in the family. The Canadian Council on Social Development, although continuing to advocate universality in payment of the allowance, proposed selectivity for benefits since it thought the government should recover 100% of the benefits at certain income levels.[56]

The new legislation met all of these concerns; however, it did not address some of the more substantive demands Ontario had insisted were needed to make family allowances even more effective. Ontario wanted the family income security plan benefits integrated with the taxation system, noting that the federal approach to income redistribution was to overlay rather than integrate the various income support mechanisms. Munro said he had considered these issues but each of these programs, as well as the tax system, had different objectives. The family income security plan was essentially a welfare-oriented program to provide benefits to families according to specific criteria measured by income, age of child and number of children, whereas personal income tax was designed to collect taxes from people in accordance with the ability to pay. The tax system attempted to ensure vertical and horizontal equity in the distribution of the tax burden among the different kinds of taxpayers. Income tax, for instance, did not use the combined family income concept that the family income security plan did.[57] Yet the federal government recognized that social needs differed from one region to another, and through the family income security plan it gave the provinces the flexibility to implement and continue their own system of priorities in terms of supplementary schemes and family policies. Munro believed that the federal scheme, which increased benefits to many families, also provided the foundation on which the provinces could build the kind of family income support they preferred. All this, Munro held, was a clear indication of Ottawa's desire to cooperate with the provinces in helping them meet provincial priorities and to coordinate federal programs with provincial ones as long as basic national standards set by the federal government were maintained. In particular, the family income security plan could be coordinated with the various allowances Quebec had proposed.[58]

Munro also claimed that the family income security plan was a key element in the larger federal strategy to fight poverty among Canadians.[59] It was the third step in the government's action to improve the overall income security program in Canada. The first step had been taken in December 1970, when the combined old-age security-guaranteed income supplement was raised to $135 a month for single pensioners and $255 for married pensioners. The second step came in June 1971, when improvements to the unemployment insurance program extended the coverage to 96% of the employees in the labour force. Later, the weekly benefits were raised to two-thirds of average earnings, up to a ceiling of $100 a week, and the eligibility period was reduced to eight weeks of employment. Together with other programs, like the Canada Pension Plan, the government maintained that it had made considerable progress in protecting its citizens when their own resources were inadequate to meet their basic needs. However, the family income security plan was perhaps the most important anti-poverty measure, since it embraced the concept of selectivity and thereby concentrated resources on those with lowest incomes while preserving some measure of protection for middle-income families. It established the social policy principle of reducing benefits as income increased. Above all, the government continued to recognize that wages and most forms of income support, such as unemployment insurance, did not make any special provision for the children in a family. Accordingly, the family income security plan, much like the family allowances it was to replace, would give families with inadequate earnings the support necessary to help provide their children with the ordinary things needed in order to grow and mature into healthy, useful citizens.[60] Citizenship rights remained an important element in Canadian social policy.

Still, the piecemeal approach to poverty was criticized by the nation's editorial writers. The *Globe and Mail* wrote on 14 September 1971 that the legislation lacked a "coherent and cohesive plan based on a comprehensive philosophy" for the elimination of poverty. It went on to say, "The Government of Prime Minister Pierre Trudeau may be trying to glue the nation together with dollars, but it can't honestly claim to be fighting poverty."[61] Similarly, David E. Woodsworth, the director of the McGill University School of Social Work, told the annual meeting of the Canadian Council on Social Development that the legislation would do little to combat poverty; he added, "There are no new words or new thoughts [in the approach]."[62]

It is no surprise, of course, that the Liberal government, nearing the end of its mandate, saw social security reform as paying political dividends in the forthcoming election. To that end, John Munro had his department prepare a detailed package on the new family income security plan for all Members of Parliament. In a cover letter to the Members of the House, he claimed that the plan played an important role in the government's income security program for all Canadians. He reminded them how the initiative had been developed through extensive consultation and how the new program would be beneficial to all Canadians. Citing much of what he had said when the bill was introduced in Parliament, the minister wrote the MPs that there were compelling reasons for the federal government to be involved in this program, though social assistance was basically a provincial responsibility. He said that a national program like the family income security plan significantly contributed to the sense of a Canadian community. A federally administered family income security plan not only ensured portability and mobility from one province to another but also ensured that payments went directly to the targeted people rather than being diverted to the provincial treasuries where Ottawa would lose control of the funds.

The program was also a means of redistributing wealth between the richer and poorer areas of Canada. Moreover, with the program administered by Ottawa, the federal government was able to stabilize economic situations occurring on a national level. Much more than that, the family income security plan was a positive and intelligent program, especially given the "increasing rejection of a trend to more welfare programs." It placed an emphasis on the need for social insurance as *protection* rather than a universal or automatic right.

Accompanying Munro's letter was a package that included drafts for individual Members' press releases, fact sheets, drafts for speeches, and a variety of other materials, encouraging Members to tell their constituents about the plan and the positive advantages it would offer to all Canadians. The package also noted that when passed into law, the family income security plan would pour approximately $950 million in spending power into the hands of needy Canadian families. This represented a $150 million increase over the amount paid through the existing family allowance system.[63]

This Liberal initiative suggests that the process of reconsidering the principle of universality began with the Trudeau Liberals and not the Conservatives under Mulroney in the 1980s.[64] Yet with the family income security plan legislation, the government was merely following the advice of many of the bureaucrats in the Department of National Health and Welfare who were involved with family allowances and who had begun to question the efficacy of universality in the 1960s; they saw the new legislation as a way to address poverty rather than as an assault on the principle of universality.

Meanwhile, the Quebec government announced on 22 September its intention to establish its own family allowances. The program was essentially similar to the family income security plan, but differed in the recovery rate and in the provision of supplemental payments for the fourth and subsequent children in the family. The Quebec plan promised less generous benefits for smaller families and more generous benefits for large families than the family income security plan.[65] In Claude Castonguay's view, the federal approach to family allowances established a form of "parity in the standards of living affected by the existence of children," whereas the Quebec program dealt with the real economic situations of families. The Quebec program was also an important first step toward the global and integrated approach to income security that the Quebec government had adopted in wake of the Castonguay-Nepveu Commission. The Quebec plan, Castonguay said in a speech to the St. Laurent Richelieu Club on 7 February 1972, contributed to the vertical redistribution of income, while Ottawa's plan ensured only universal access to the minimum conditions for the development of the child.[66] There was concern in Ottawa that Quebec's desire to increase benefits for the fourth and subsequent children in the family might be interpreted by some as an attempt by Quebec to increase the birth rate in the province as well as ignore Ottawa's policy of family planning and population control.[67]

Officials from Quebec and Ottawa met on 30 September and again on 8 October to discuss the proposals in Premier Bourassa's earlier letter to the prime · minister. They quickly reached agreement on a variety of issues, including the basic standards to be included in the Family Income Security Plan Act, the recovery of excess expenditures and the adjustment of over-expenditures, and the definitions of income and family income. However, the two sides reached an impasse on the administration of the program. National Health and Welfare Minister Munro claimed that it became apparent in the meetings with Quebec that it had "a different position from that contained in the Quebec Premier's letter."[68] It appeared that Mr. Castonguay's position was clear: Quebec would have either provincial administration for the whole program or provincial administration of the income test through the provincial revenue department, leaving other administrative aspects to a joint Canada-Quebec board or commission. Quebec warned that if it could not reach agreement on either approach, it would have to abandon the objective of an integrated approach and administer its own allowances for sixteen- and seventeen-year-old youths as well as supplementary benefits for larger families. The federal Cabinet was told that it was clear from the meetings that the province was concerned not with the responsibility for planning and designing the family income security plan within the provincial social policy framework – as Premier Bourassa had implied – but with having full control or major control over the administration of the plan. As aforementioned, if this occurred, Ottawa's role would be limited to that of financing the plan, and it would mean the erosion of the federal view that it had the right to make direct payments to individuals. Munro recommended that the Cabinet authorize him to meet and discuss the matter with Castonguay, who had said at a press conference on 12 October that the issue could be resolved only at the political level. The Cabinet wanted to consider the Quebec position further before having Munro meet with Castonguay,[69] even though representatives of the federal and provincial governments had met several times in November and December to discuss the various arrangements that might be made for the operation of a modified family income security plan; Ottawa continued to insist that the basic benefit plan would be administered federally.[70]

With Ottawa struggling to meet Quebec's demands, there was no legislative action taken on Bill C-264 after it received first reading. The federal government had good reason to be patient because Premier Bourassa had told *Le Devoir* in late September that after Quebec had found a workable solution with Ottawa on family allowances it would begin new constitutional discussions. Although Quebec's ultimate goal was to obtain sole jurisdiction over all social policy, or legislative primacy, it appeared at times to be willing to contemplate something less. Quebec's preferred approach was to have a provincially designed basic plan for children under eighteen with a supplement for larger families included in a single plan. While it was agreeable to having the federal government issue the cheques, it wanted the province to play an important role that would include the following: having income statements verified by the province; identifying the province on the application forms, on all literature relating to the program and, most importantly, on the cheques issued to parents; and having the province determine final benefit amounts using the provincial definition of income.[71]

This was essentially a proposal Bryce had discussed with the Cabinet earlier in the year. Various federal departments, notably finance, supply and services, health and welfare, and the Privy Council Office, had discussed and considered Quebec's position through the fall of 1971. At the same time, Marc Lalonde, Trudeau's private secretary and constitutional adviser, was in constant communication with Bourassa and senior officials with the Quebec government, and he suggested on a number of occasions that the Canadian government was still interested in a constitutional solution to the problems social policy had created, but Julien Chouinard told him that Bourassa had no obvious enthusiasm for a particular constitutional solution. By December, the departments agreed that the Quebec plan obscured federal expenditure on the program while maximizing provincial identification. The proposal would inevitably lead to duplication, administrative inefficiency, and public confusion.[72] Even so, the officials realized that the proposal would meet Quebec's social policy objective by achieving the streamlined, integrated approach it had emphasized; any other option would be seen in that province as further frustration of its aspirations. Yet the federal authorities also wanted to ensure that it was not too easy for provinces to redesign the family income security plan; they thus insisted that each province that wanted to modify the federal plan contribute at least 20%

of federal expenditures to the redesigned program. Munro suggested that Ottawa proceed with Bill C-264 as it stood if the negotiations with Quebec failed.[73]

The *Globe and Mail* quoted a senior government official as saying that the only legislative item more urgent than family allowances was the federal-provincial tax-sharing agreement. That might explain why discussions with the provinces on the family income security plan continued through the latter part of 1971 and into the early months of 1972. Despite the seemingly endless delay, the Trudeau government remained committed to reforming the family allowance program, but the government allowed the legislation to lapse with the termination of the third session of the 28th Parliament on 16 February 1972. In the Speech from the Throne on 17 February 1972 that opened the fourth and final session of the 28th Parliament, the government announced its continued commitment to the family income security plan and its intention to reintroduce legislation covering the plan.

At the same time, the negotiations between Ottawa and Quebec on family allowance reform resumed, having stalled the previous November.[74] On 9 March 1972, in response to provincial demands for a redesigned, more flexible family income security plan that would allow them to meet their own provincial social policy objectives, Prime Minister Trudeau offered each province the right to redesign the plan for operation within the province, subject to certain minimum federal standards. This had been proposed in the period leading to the Victoria constitutional conference. In a letter to Premier Bourassa, Trudeau wrote, "Acceptance of a plan along these lines would represent, as you will appreciate, a very important change so far as the federal government is concerned." For the first time, a federally financed and administered program, legislated by Parliament, would be subject to modification by the provinces even though the amount of financial participation by the province would be small in comparison with that of the federal government. Provinces providing a supplement amounting to at least 15% of the total spent on their family allowances would be given the right to alter the monthly benefit rate, the reduction rate, and the income threshold for the family income security plan, given that total federal spending on plan did not exceed the amount that would have been spent had this right not been exercised. The benefits could not be set below 80% of the national benefit rate, the threshold could not be set below the income tax exemption level, and provincial definitions of residence could not be more restrictive than the federal definition.[75]

Moreover, Trudeau insisted that the federal definition of income would have to be used for the purpose of federal payments. Trudeau also said that the literature describing the program would clearly indicate that the plan in each province had been designed in accordance with provincial legislation, and there would be recognition of provincial financial participation.[76] Trudeau also told Bourassa and the other premiers that the federal government would proceed with the family income security plan legislation in the current session. However, the bill that would be presented to Parliament would not include the provision for the kind of flexibility he now suggested. He reassured Bourassa that Ottawa would amend the bill accordingly as soon as the provinces agreed to his proposal. What must have been encouraging, particularly for Bourassa, was Trudeau's suggestion that "the principles involved [with the plan] are clearly capable of extension to other income support programs" and might pave the way for constitutional change in matters relating to social security. Trudeau stated, "While the difficulties are considerable, the federal government would be prepared to consider this kind of extension of the principles I am proposing if a satisfactory constitutional basis can be found and if it solved the problem of social security which remained to be cleared up to permit further progress in the process of constitutional review."[77] Bourassa telexed the prime minister on 19 March, expressing his satisfaction with the proposal and telling Trudeau, "I have a conviction that we shall soon arrive at developing a successful formula for family allowances."[78] Constitutional reform was clearly on Trudeau's mind. In fact, when Trudeau met with Bourassa earlier in February, the prime minister had insisted that "les allocation familiales et la question constitutionnelle" be the first item on the agenda for the meeting.[79]

Trudeau's letter to the other premiers outlining the proposed changes had a different introduction from the one he sent to Bourassa. In his letter to the nine English-speaking premiers, Trudeau briefly reviewed the course of events following the Victoria constitutional conference, where Quebec had insisted on a provision in the constitution that allowed provinces to have some measure of control over federal programs, particularly family allowances, to suit the needs of each province. Trudeau pointed out that the conference had tried to meet the needs of Quebec by providing for an amendment to section 94A of the British North America Act, but that the government of Quebec had decided it could not accept the approach on income security included in the Victoria Charter. Trudeau noted, however, that in September 1971, Premier Bourassa had suggested to him that an administrative arrangement through the federal and provincial legislatures might achieve Quebec objectives in the area of income support if it was proving impossible to do so constitutionally. Since that time, Trudeau wrote, Quebec and federal officials had held discussions on the matter, but at all times Ottawa had insisted that any arrangements that might appear feasible would have to be the subject of a discussion with all provincial governments and to be equally available to all. The federal government was now prepared to modify the application of the federal family income security plan. He added, "While the difficulties are considerable, the federal government would be prepared to consider this kind of extension of the principles I am proposing if a satisfactory constitutional basis can be found and if it solved the problem of social security which remained to be cleared up to permit further progress of constitutional review."[80]

Many of the newspapers hailed these developments, which Trudeau made public in an interview on the Réseau TVA French station on 12 March, as a victory for Quebec. On 13 March, the *Ottawa Journal* claimed, "Quebec gets control over baby bonus" while *Le Devoir* saw it as "un triple gain pour le Québec." This triple victory, as reported by many newspapers, was that Ottawa agreed to 1) accept most of Quebec's proposals in the social security field, 2) consider a similar approach in other sectors of social welfare jurisdiction, and 3) consider family allowances as a separate issue from the other aspects of social welfare jurisdiction. The Toronto *Globe and Mail* saw Trudeau's offer of the jurisdiction Quebec demanded as a major policy shift in federal-provincial affairs. The *Windsor Star* went so far as to suggest that the "constitutional road [was] now open again." *La Presse*, too, hinted that the Victoria talks would soon continue, but some of the other newspapers in Quebec expressed considerable doubt on federal sincerity in allowing the provinces to take over family allowances: *Le Devoir* wrote, "Québec scrute la teneur de la réponse d'Ottawa."[81] Yet as *Le Droit* reported, "Bourassa se dit satisfait de la Proposition Trudeau."

In Trudeau's view, he had conceded little to Quebec. The federal government claimed that it did not recognize in the changes to the family income security plan any provincial supremacy, and it retained the undiluted right to make direct payments to individuals anywhere in Canada. Trudeau and his advisers had realized much earlier that there was considerable division within the Quebec Cabinet over social security policy. Nonetheless, Trudeau knew that Bourassa was his best chance for finding a solution within the current framework of Confederation. In his view, Trudeau's offer had simply allowed Bourassa to claim victory. The premier had described it as a "great step forward." As Trudeau said in his interview with TVA, there were many people in Quebec who did not want to see any agreements between the federal and provincial governments. Trudeau certainly must have realized that the agreement on family allowances would show that Confederation continued to work, and he certainly would have expected a more cooperative attitude from Premier Bourassa in the future on other important national issues.[82]

The Liberal government reintroduced Bill C-264 as Bill C-170 for first reading in the House of Commons on 15 March 1972. As Trudeau had acknowledged to Bourassa earlier, the bill did not yet include a provision to enable provinces to redesign the family income security plan within certain federal standards to meet provincial social policy objectives, though an amendment was intended. However, the legislation was criticized on a number of fronts. While there was considerable support for the shift from universality to selectivity, some of the newspaper editorials claimed that the family income security plan did not effectively address the problem of poverty in Canada. Moreover, there was criticism that the new program would for the first time attach a stigma to the receipt of family allowance payments. It was suggested that this could be avoided if the universal family allowance system were retained and benefits for some high-income groups recovered through the tax system. There was considerable concern that the planned changes to family allowances would hit the middle-income group – those with incomes above $8,000 – particularly hard.[83]

David Lewis, the leader of the New Democrats, criticized the legislation on this score, though with an eye to the coming election. The NDP research group reported to the caucus on 10 April that recent polls had indicated a significant increase in the number of undecided voters who had become dissatisfied with the Liberal government but were reluctant to turn to the Conservatives. A strong stand on a controversial issue consistent with NDP principles, the research group advised, would demonstrate that they were the real opposition in the House. Further, it was recommended that if the party strongly opposed Bill C-170 it could carry its opposition into the election campaign. Lewis obviously agreed.[84] He subsequently charged that the Liberal initiative would do nothing to alleviate poverty, and called for the continuation of universality in social programs and for changes to the income tax system so that the wealthy could return their allowances through the tax system.[85] The NDP could not accept the principle of taking family allowance cheques away from a million Canadian families, Lewis told the French-language Ottawa newspaper, *Le Droit*. The Liberals were beginning the first steps of phasing out family allowances and removing from the program everything but the welfare component. Family allowances, Lewis noted, were intended to assist in the raising of children – the nation's most important asset – and making payments selective would destroy that purpose. Bill Knight, an NDP Member of Parliament, told the House that family allowances must be treated as a basic social right in Canadian society, and for that reason the principle of universality must be maintained.[86] These sentiments were shared by organizations like the Alberta Anti-poverty Federation. Even Liberal members like Eugene Whelan complained to the minister.[87]

Interestingly, it was also suggested that the poverty of low-income mothers was being alleviated at the expense of mothers in high-income families. The family allowance benefits were often the sole source of discretionary income for women in better-off families; they should not have to bear the total burden of addressing the poverty of others. All taxpayers should bear the cost of increased benefits for poor mothers. Grace MacInnis, NDP member for Vancouver-Kingsway and the only woman elected in the 1968 federal election, warned Trudeau, "Hell hath no fury like a million mothers who have been scorned and whose social assistance has been cut off. This is not a war on poverty that the government is conducting. It is a war on women. It is a war against the family."[88]

The Conservatives, too, were worried about the large number of middle-class women who would be losing their family allowances. They pointed out what they considered flaws in the legislation, though they supported the bill because they favoured increased benefits to poorer families. The Conservatives warned that they would push for amendments when the bill reached committee stage.[89]

There was concern as well that the administration of the family income security plan was not sufficiently integrated with income tax administration and that it would duplicate the income-testing mechanism.[90] The family income security plan did nothing to eliminate or replace income tax exemptions for children; while the plan provided for reduced benefits as incomes rose, tax exemptions offset this by providing for increased benefits as incomes rose. It thus perpetuated the existing inequities in government support for children in rich and poor families, although to a lesser degree.

There was also deep concern about the federal-provincial jurisdictional aspects of the family income security plan, particularly in the Quebec government. As was frequently the case, many of the interest groups claimed they had had little opportunity for input into the policy on the family income security plan, even though business groups such as the Canadian Chamber of Commerce and the Canadian Manufacturers Association and poverty groups agreed on the principle of selectivity as a means of achieving increased support for the poor.[91] Even so, the Canadian Council on Social Development complained that middle and upper-income families with dependent children would bear an unfair portion of the cost of the proposed reforms because they would either lose their existing allowances or have them reduced. Moreover, the Council also claimed that FISP would create a 'stigma of inadequacy' among those receiving the benefits; it called for universal allowances and clawbacks, through the income tax system, of the money paid to higher-income families.

Following Trudeau's letter to the premiers on 9 March, federal and provincial officials met to make the arrangements necessary to give effect to the federal proposals. The first preparatory meeting took place on 27 March in Ottawa and resumed nine days later, at which time the officials created three committees to deal with publicity, policy and forms, and administrative and technical matters.

Great progress was being made, but Ottawa nearly scuppered the deal when on 8 May 1972 it announced in the federal budget significant improvements to the old-age security pensions and the guaranteed income supplement as well as the special income tax exemption for the aged, from $650 to $1,000. Although there had been considerable pressure on Ottawa to enrich support for seniors, Quebec denounced Ottawa's unilateral action on another income security program and it threatened to undo the deal on family allowances.[92]

Castonguay was livid. He unleashed a bitter attack on Ottawa, calling the proposal for the aged a "low blow" to Quebec's efforts to establish an integrated approach to all social benefit spending. Ottawa had acted without any prior consultation with or warning to the provinces. Trudeau's budget had demonstrated that Ottawa could not be trusted and any hope they had that the deal over family allowances marked the beginning of a new era that gave the provinces a measure of control over social policy was shattered. The *Toronto Star* reported Castonguay as saying that the administrative arrangements proposed by Trudeau and reluctantly agreed to by Bourassa could not work. Quebec needed full jurisdiction over all aspects of social security to implement an integrated social policy.[93] On 7 June, Castonguay told the annual conference of Canada's Learned Societies in Montreal, "It is pointless to expect sufficient consultation to ensure a unified conception of the programs concerning guaranteed income-social aid." He added that amiable, non-formal arrangements could not give sufficient guarantees, and that without constitutional change giving Quebec legislative primacy in social policy, the Canadian federation was threatened.[94]

Of course, Ottawa saw things quite differently. It blamed the government of Quebec for the delay as both Bourassa and Castonguay refused to precisely outline Quebec's position with regard to the family income security plan.[95] On 9 June 1972, Prime Minister Trudeau wrote yet again to Premier Bourassa. He reminded Bourassa that a great deal of progress had been made by the two sides over the past few months, and that the federal Cabinet had reviewed the various arrangements. Moreover, the federal government had conceded even more to the provinces, agreeing to fully fund benefits for children in the care and custody of social agencies and institutions (rather than funding half the benefits as Ottawa had preferred). Provinces with provincial family allowance programs would be able to modify the monthly benefit rate if provincial expenditure on allowances reached 15% of the federal expenditure on allowances, calculated as if the federal program had applied to all children under eighteen. This was instead of calculating the threshold based on 15% of the total spent on family allowances in that province,[96] as Trudeau had proposed in the March offer to the premiers. Ottawa further offered greater flexibility in the application of this provision by having the percentage based on a moving average over three years rather than based on each year.

Despite the posture taken publicly by Quebec, there remained the possibility of a bargain. Still, the two sides needed to resolve a few outstanding issues dealing with administration, but they had to move quickly. In a veiled threat, Trudeau reminded Bourassa of the tight time frame for the enactment of the legislation and told him that it was necessary for Quebec to decide quickly whether or not to proceed with the provincial option amendment to Bill C-170. The prime minister gave Bourassa a week to make his decision.[97]

Through the dialogue between senior officials from Ottawa and Quebec City, the Trudeau government learned that Bourassa would reply to the prime minister's latest letter by 20 June 1972.[98] Within Bourassa's Cabinet, Social Affairs Minister Claude Castonguay continued to argue that the only way for Quebec to control its social policy and implement an integrated policy on income security was through a constitutional process that addressed the division of powers in the field of social security. Castonguay also saw Ottawa as the barrier to Quebec introducing a coherent, integrated income security plan for the province. The Montreal *Gazette* reported that Castonguay threatened to resign after Ottawa unilaterally announced increases to the old-age security pension, but reluctantly decided to stay after Premier Bourassa assured him that Quebec would take a stronger stand with Ottawa. Castonguay made his quarrel with Ottawa public and asked Quebecers for massive public support for its tough stand in its bid for a better deal from the federal government.[99]

John Munro countered that without an agreement with Quebec concerning the federal family allowances plan, the allowances paid to the families of Quebec as increased benefits would not be available to the Quebec government for use in developing provincial income security initiatives. Still, Munro said he was pleased that Castonguay was "enormously disappointed" that the family income security plan was not granted third reading before the summer recess, because he had thought that Quebec was no longer interested in the progress of Bill C-170. Munro said that he and the prime minister had "every intention of completing the work of this bill at the first opportunity."[100]

Following Munro's statement, Claude Lemelin wrote in *Le Devoir* that Munro had simply failed to understand Quebec's ultimate goal of having a coherent and integrated social policy program,[101] a point made by Castonguay in a letter to Munro on 25 July 1972 after Munro had responded to Castonguay's news conference on 17 July in Quebec City. "Cette déclaration me permet de constater une fois de plus combien les objectifs poursuivis par le Québec dans le domaine de la sécurité du revenu et, de façon plus particulière dans celui des allocations familiales, semblent ne pas avoir été compris ou évalués dans leur perspective réelle par le gouvernement auquel vous appartenez," Castonguay wrote. He also challenged Munro to discuss the issue of social security on television.[102] However, even senior Liberals were admitting that it was unlikely that the legislation would be dealt with even if Trudeau recalled Parliament for the fall before an expected federal election.[103]

Bill C-170 died on 7 July 1972, the last day of the session, when it failed by one vote to receive the unanimous consent necessary for third reading before Parliament was adjourned until 28 September 1972. Paul Hellyer, a former Liberal minister but then sitting as an independent, stood alone against the bill, arguing that he was representing the view of many Liberals who saw it as a form of social humiliation because it based benefits on income and family size. In response to Hellyer's actions, a group in Winnipeg created the Citizens' Committee on F.I.S.P. As Jan Thompson, the chair of the group, wrote Trudeau, many low-income families were excited about the proposed legislation, but those opposed were relatively uninformed as to the nature of the proposal. Much of the opposition to the plan was "simply concern for the women who presently are using the family allowance as their personal pocket money and the fact that it is clouded with a lot of patronizing ideology." She wanted the issue to be an important one during the election campaign.[104]

The new program did not become an important issue in the campaigns of any party as some would have liked, but it was not totally absent from the campaign either. Both the NDP and the Conservatives promised a return to universality in family allowances. During the campaign, even the Liberals changed their mind, and Munro told a group in Winnipeg that they would consider the possibility of making the plan universal if they were re-elected. After all the time the government had devoted to reforming family allowances, the Liberals had, it seems, returned to where they began many months earlier, as their zeal for reform crashed on the shoals of universality, the social rights of Canadians, and an intergovernmental impasse. Any reform to the family allowance program that resulted in the loss of benefits to any significant group of beneficiaries in the middle class would be difficult.

8
Wrestling with Universality, 1972-83

ON 30 OCTOBER 1972, Canadians sent Prime Minister Pierre Trudeau and his governing Liberals a strong message that they were not impressed with their handling of affairs. The Liberals had adopted the slogan, "The Land Is Strong," and their main advertising showed tranquil images of the Canadian landscape. The Liberal campaign failed to acknowledge the growing level of unemployment and the general economic malaise that confronted Canada. The Conservatives, under new leader and former Nova Scotia premier Robert Stanfield, mounted an earnest, if troubled, campaign, and came close to defeating Trudeau, winning 107 seats to the Liberals' 109. The New Democrats elected 31 members, and held the balance of power in the new Parliament.

Social security had not emerged as a dominant issue in the campaigns as some had expected, but each of the three major parties had made it clear that changes were necessary in social policy. The Liberals had promised to introduce a series of programs to reduce unemployment and to reform the unemployment insurance program to curtail alleged abuses of the system; the Conservatives promised retraining programs for the unemployed and tied increases in old-age pensions to increases in the consumer price index; and the NDP promised increases for some old-age security recipients but to eliminate them for wealthy Canadians.

In the unsettled period following the election, Trudeau reorganized Liberal Party priorities to win support from the NDP by promising action on social policy and a program to increase the presence of the state in the national economy. These changes kept the Liberal government in office until 8 May 1974, but the compromises with the NDP effectively stymied any fundamental change to the family allowance program that would have targeted low-income families through selective measures contained in the family income security plan. Before the decade was over, however, the Liberal government would pursue a number of new initiatives in social policy, including the introduction of selective, or income-tested, benefits and the use of tax credits to deliver income support.

Following the election, the government took more careful notice of the opposition Bill C-170 had attracted. In Cabinet discussions following the election, it noted that the 30% of families who stood to lose their family allowances under the Liberal proposals evidently opposed the ending of universality. While the principle of selectivity might have helped low-income Canadians, it had clearly angered many middle-income voters. During the election, the New Democrats demanded a return to universality in family allowances.

On 27 November 1972, John Munro was replaced as minister of national health and welfare. He had told his colleagues immediately after the election that the government would only succeed in alienating the high-income groups if it continued to insist on diverting funds from them to low-income groups. It did not matter, he noted, that such strategies for social spending were endorsed by organizations like the Economic Council of Canada, because such anti-poverty measures were obviously not acceptable to the upper- and middle-income groups.[1]

However, opinion polls showed that broad support remained for changes similar to those proposed by Bill C-170. This came from a wide variety of groups such as a coalition of poverty groups in Winnipeg, which circulated a petition demanding the resurrection of the family income security program during the summer of 1972, and the Vancouver and District Public Housing Tenants Association, which had urged Trudeau to proceed with the reforms as quickly as possible.[2] Nonetheless, a minority – many of whom were women – clearly won the day. "There [had been] an incredible outpouring of letters from women [to the minister of national health and welfare] who would have lost their cheques," one commentator noted, "[and] their willingness to sit down and write letters of protest produced a steady erosion of political will."[3] Of the 726 Canadians who wrote the Department of National Health and Welfare about the family income security plan, 94% of them were opposed to the initiative; officials in the department later noted that the mail of the Cabinet ministers and other elected officials had been in similar proportions.[4] Even Liberal MPs had warned the prime minister before the election that "it would be a very grave political error if [they] were to proceed with the [changes to the family allowances] program prior to the election."[5] Trudeau's Cabinet had even considered the issue of timing when they discussed the proposed legislation in 1971 and realized that more than 1.6 million of the 3.4 million families (more than 57%) would be adversely affected by the proposed changes.[6]

Trudeau must have been appalled, though, that his important constitutional plans had foundered on social policy, and he handed the national health and welfare portfolio to Marc Lalonde, his former private secretary and constitutional adviser, to fix the social policy problem with Quebec. Leonard Shifrin, a former executive director of the National Council of Welfare and special assistant for policy development to John Munro, claimed that the prime minister "had a lack of interest in income security reform."[7] However, Trudeau made it clear to Lalonde that he wanted a major review of Canada's social security system, to integrate federal and provincial social security policies and reform the various programs based on a number of specific principles around which a national consensus of opinion might be formulated. This approach was to be designed to avoid the constitutional impasse that had derailed the earlier constitutional agreement in 1971.[8]

As the new minister, Lalonde was determined to be cautious in light of the poor Liberal showing at the polls, and he suggested to the Cabinet that over the coming months its position on the family income security plan should be simply to state that the plan was under further review. This would buy the government some valuable time.[9] He also said that the government would adopt changes to family allowances that represented the wishes of the electorate. He stated, "[It is clear] that Canadian housewives attach a lot of importance to that Family Allowance cheque, and there was a lot of resistance to the idea that ... about half of them would be losing that Allowance."[10] He vowed to listen to those Canadians.

It has long been maintained that universality in social programs is part of a political theory of state legitimization. Universality is generally acknowledged as a means of social integration and national unity in nations lacking other instruments of social cohesion. It fosters wide public support for the maintenance and expansion of social programs and helps build relations between various social groups and across the various classes that constitute any society. However, a Gallup report in March 1971 found that 66% of Canadians approved of the government's plan to reduce payment of family allowances to the well-to-do in order to increase payments to those with low incomes.[11] Throughout the 1980s and 1990s when there was much public debate on the principle of universality, public opinion surveys regularly found that 60% of the population supported the payment of government benefits like family allowances to those who had financial need, and many saw the ending of universality as an opportunity for meaningful social policy reform. Later, Ken Battle, one of Canada's leading social policy advocates, said, "With existing resources, it is simply not possible to increase substantially the benefits for low-income families and maintain the same level of benefits for middle and high-income families."[12] It would take until the early 1990s before the Canadian state would challenge the view of many middle- and high-income Canadians that it was their right as Canadians to receive family allowance benefits, and usher in a new era of social security that would see benefits going to those who needed them most.

Lalonde was no stranger to the field of social policy. During the latter part of his term as Trudeau's principal secretary, when opposition to the family income security plan mounted, he had been a member of a small interdepartmental committee to review the policy then being considered. When the major review of Canada's social security began after the election, Lalonde was already familiar with some of the issues. J.W. Willard, the deputy minister of national health and welfare, chaired the committee that also included representatives from the Department of Finance and the Department of National Revenue, the Privy Council Office, and the Prime Minister's Office, but it was clear that the central agencies, like the Prime Minister's Office, wanted a greater hand in making social policy. In addition to re-evaluating the government's position on the family income security plan in light of the various criticisms made of it, Lalonde told the committee that it had to consider the options for the federal government if Quebec announced new initiatives in the income security field. The inter-departmental committee met throughout August and September 1972.

When Lalonde presented the committee's report to the Cabinet, he outlined four options: the reintroduction of the family income security plan, continuation of universal family allowances with security plan-type supplementation, discontinuation of tax deductions for children and payment of non-taxable family allowances, and the continuation of tax deductions for children and payment of taxable but universal family allowances. The committee eventually recommended a variation of the second option, which was referred to as Model 1, though this approach would require an additional $255 million to finance it. As Willard wrote to Munro during the election, this would be the price of placating the spokesmen for the people in families with incomes above $8,000 who had protested their loss of benefits under the income security plan proposal in Bill C-170.

The new proposal called for the retention of family and youth allowances of $6, $8, and $10, and the introduction of a new family income supplement that would have the same income floors and ceilings as proposed under Bill C-170, and the same reduction rate, which would be administered in advance by the family income security plan administration. The amount of the supplement would be $15 for children under twelve, and $20 for those twelve to seventeen, minus the amount of the family or youth allowance paid for them. The committee felt that this approach would meet two criticisms of Bill C-170, since families with incomes above $8,000 would not lose their family allowances, and there would be no stigma in receiving a family allowance cheque. Low-income families would receive higher benefits as proposed in the earlier legislation, but high-income families would also retain their benefits. However, if this proposal were accepted, the extra benefits for low-income families would be financed from general revenues rather than from reduced benefits of well-to-do families. As for the impact on Quebec, the committee believed that the proposal would be acceptable since the federal offer to the provinces to redesign the family income security plan to meet their own priorities could remain unchanged. In sum, the demise of the income security plan and the results of the election in 1972 seemed to indicate a desire of the middle class – and the Liberal government – to retain universality in family allowances. The middle class effectively killed the family income security plan either because they had come to see family allowances as part of their rights as Canadian citizens, regardless of their incomes, or because the greed that we often associate with the decade of the 1980s actually began in the 1970s in Canada.

The Cabinet Standing Committee on Social Policy considered the proposal on 6 December 1972. It noted that while there was probably a greater social need for increased assistance to families than for additional assistance to the aged, a higher priority should be assigned to improvements in the old-age security and/or guaranteed income supplement programs than to increases in family allowances. The Liberals were obviously pandering to the opposition parties as both the New Democrats and the Conservatives had made increases to the old-age security part of their election platforms in the summer campaign. Even so, the committee agreed that any revenue generated from reforms to the Income Tax Act should be used to increase family allowances.[13] Despite the changed political landscape, Lalonde demonstrated a commitment to the fundamental tenants of reform: increasing support to persons on low incomes while maintaining the incentive to work. He also realized, of course, that there was often no relationship between family income and family need. The minister promised that a new family income program would be submitted to Parliament in the spring of 1973.[14]

Given that the Trudeau Liberals had been stung by their first attempt at social welfare reform, they decided on a more cautious approach after the election. At the interprovincial conference of welfare ministers in Victoria, in November 1972, Ottawa asked the provinces to co-operate on a comprehensive review of existing social security systems, recognizing both the tendency of many Canadians to question the effectiveness of the nation's social security programs and wanting to take advantage of the reviews of the welfare system that had already been undertaken by the provinces, voluntary and professional associations, the Senate, and academics. Trudeau had made it clear to Lalonde that he wanted a major review of Canada's social security system when he appointed him to National Health and Welfare. When A.W. Johnson moved to the department as deputy to oversee the process, it was clear that there would be a new approach to social welfare issues.[15] Ottawa's objective was to integrate federal and provincial social security policies, and reform the various programs based on a number of specific principles around which a national consensus of opinion might be formulated. It also indicated the belief in Ottawa that it wanted close federal-provincial collaboration but strong federal leadership role in social security. This approach was designed to avoid the constitutional impasse that had derailed the earlier constitutional agreement in 1971.[16]

In the January 1973 Throne Speech, the federal government promised "that Canada's total social security system – including both federal and provincial elements – [would] be reconsidered and reorganized, and made more sensitive to the needs of people in different parts of the country."[17] Castonguay could have written the words himself, and they showed that Canada had promised a new period of harmonic federalism on social policy. Announcing their review of the social security system, the federal government outlined five broad underlying principles that were to guide the proposed overhaul: 1) the state should ensure a fair and compassionate annual income to all persons unable to work; 2) the social security system, when applied to a person's ability to work, should include work incentives and emphasize the need for the long-term attachment of social welfare recipients to the labour force; 3) a just ratio must be maintained between those who work for minimum wages and those who are guaranteed an income by the state but are unfit to work; 4) the provinces must have the ability to modify social security systems to meet their particular needs; and 5) the review of Canada's social security system must be conducted jointly by the federal and provincial governments. It was also clear that the principle of universality in social programs would not be threatened, especially as long as the Liberals remained in a minority position in Parliament.[18]

In the early months of 1973, Lalonde prepared a working paper on Canada's social security system for release prior to the federal-provincial conference on social security planned for April. The working paper set the agenda and guided the three-year review. Lalonde continually insisted that though the paper would have to be clear to ensure comprehension of the strategies and principles the government proposed, it would not commit the minority Liberal government to any specific set of proposals or bring undue criticism. The Cabinet wanted to avoid putting a series of proposals on the table that would clash with the objectives of the provincial governments, particularly those of Quebec, or appear grandiose to the public.[19] Yet the Cabinet wanted a concrete family allowance proposal put before the provinces at the April meeting of welfare ministers.[20] This effort would reassure Canadians that the Liberal government was committed to substantial and immediate benefits through universal family allowances, as well as provide tangible evidence that the government was indeed serious about meaningful social reform.

Family allowances were an important part of the working paper on social security (the Orange Paper) that Lalonde tabled in the House of Commons on 18 April 1973, just a week before the federal-provincial conference of welfare ministers was scheduled to begin. The paper, which hoped that the process would lead to a more effective and better coordinated system of social security for Canadians within the coming three to five years, was the federal government's contribution toward a joint federal-provincial review of Canada's social security system; the provinces all agreed to participate in this exercise.[21] Ottawa's first strategy in facilitating income security was to provide people with jobs; in this, little had changed since family allowances were introduced in 1944, when Prime Minister King had said that the best social security policy was a successful economic policy and full employment. Thus, the proposed reforms were intended to move people into the job market and keep them there; the state would offer incentives to get people off social assistance or other forms of extended income support and help them equip themselves for employment.

Lalonde wanted the proposal on family allowances immediately adopted for implementation in January 1974, provided, of course, that the provinces and Parliament agreed.[22] That seemed possible in early 1973 when the provinces unanimously agreed at the federal-provincial conference of welfare ministers that the first priority in reforming Canada's social security system should be to increase family allowance benefits.[23]

Specifically, the Orange Paper proposed that family allowances be increased from their average of $7.21 per child per month to an average of $20 per child per month, and be made taxable. Subjecting family allowance benefits to income tax was essentially a way of quietly moving away from universal benefits. The 1970 white paper recommendation to eliminate the universality of family allowances had obviously fallen victim to the political pressures of keeping the minority government in office and the need for provincial approval. Further evidence of the political practicalities was Lalonde's proposal that the level of benefit be periodically reviewed in relation to changes in the consumer price index (as old-age security had been several months earlier). Lalonde suggested that the precise amount paid for individual children would be left to the provinces, as with the proposed family income security plan, but subject to a national minimum and assuming the development of a consensus regarding provincial flexibility and national norms. Provinces could chose to vary the amount paid out either by the age of the child or the size of the family. With an obvious reference to Quebec, Lalonde noted that it was a major constitutional innovation to permit the provinces to determine the benefits paid to individual Canadians by the government of Canada, though within the limits set by Parliament.[24] This flexibility allowed provinces to design their own income support and supplementation programs for families and would mark the introduction of a new – yet much discussed and anticipated – approach to federal-provincial relations in the social security field. As P.E. Bryden has argued for the Quebec and Canada Pension Plans, this shared approach to the administration of family allowances also represented a new method of negotiating with the provinces that served to enhance the role of the federal government while strengthening national unity.[25] When Ottawa accepted a provincial role in a national program like family allowances after spending more than a generation defending its sole prerogative to legislature in the field, it also ensured itself a role in this area for some years to come.

Quebec newspapers saw the change as a decisive step and a major breakthrough for Quebec. *La Presse* wrote, "Fasse le ciel que l'esprit de conciliation dont fait preuve M. Lalonde contribue à mettre un terme aux différends constitutionnels qui ont trop longtemps paralysé l'évolution constitutionnelle du Canada."[26] Most of the English-Canadian media saw the legislation simply as an increase in family allowances, but the *Globe and Mail* described the reforms as "right and proper ... as social welfare is basically a provincial responsibility under the *British North America Act*." While the *Globe and Mail* acknowledged that Ottawa had won its point that recipients of family allowances know where the money for the program comes from, it praised Lalonde for "recognizing that the time had come for reversing the flow of power in his portfolio back to the provinces."[27]

Lalonde maintained that Ottawa had the responsibility to combat poverty through ensuring a fair distribution of income among Canadians, to promote national unity through preventing extremes in income disparities across the country, and to foster a sense of pan-Canadian citizenship and attachment to the federal government in Ottawa. Lalonde insisted that wages did not take into consideration the size of a worker's family, and the income of many Canadians who were gainfully employed was often inadequate to meet their family's needs. The working paper had estimated that it cost between $500 and $700 annually to raise a child, yet the family allowance benefit provided only between $72 and $120 a year per child, and the exemption for dependent children under the tax system took effect only after the family earned more than $3,000. A substantial increase in family allowances was seen as one way to supplement the incomes of the working poor. For those families whose incomes were still inadequate after the proposed increase to family allowances, the government favoured a single, general income supplementation plan, with built-in work incentives.[28] However, family allowances became separated from the wider discussions on a guaranteed annual income plan and the social security review (which has already been considered elsewhere).[29] It is useful to note that besides changes to family allowances, Canada did not implement an income supplementation plan for the working poor.

The Liberal government had clearly responded to the earlier criticism of the family income security plan in its latest proposal and had introduced policies designed to win the support of the NDP in Parliament. The Canadian Council on Social Development immediately praised Ottawa's plan to retain the universality of family allowances and use the tax system to claw back benefits from high-income families. This mix of universal and selective policy instruments with family allowances brought a new meaning to universality in Canada. Reuben C. Baetz, the council's executive director, stated, "The universal aspect of the family allowance proposal is a good thing because it would provide all families with some help for child-rearing expenses."[30]

More important, however, was the agreement of the provincial ministers of welfare to the federal proposal that the national norm for family allowances be set at an average of $20 per child per month. Castonguay had insisted that Ottawa raise the family allowance benefits after it had twice unilaterally increased old-age security payments. Appeasing Quebec was always a consideration. The Alberta government favoured a substantial increase in family allowances as a direct benefit to the working poor with young families, and leaned toward a universal program as it would be a good incentive for parents to work.[31] Similarly, the Honourable Norman Levi, minister of human resources for British Columbia, supported the federal initiative to substantially increase family allowances, noting with approval Ottawa's consultations with the provinces before a final plan was drafted. As with some of the other provinces, British Columbia wanted a universal system, one that was taxable and indexed to the cost of living. And like Quebec, British Columbia expressed a clear preference for administering its own family allowance plan.[32] Ontario, which had wanted income security tied to the tax system, was relatively pleased with Lalonde's latest proposal.[33] However, when the Trudeau government committed itself to the existing universal approach to income supplementation, it meant that further increases to family allowance benefits would be costly and that incremental changes would be difficult because of that. After all, between 1945 and 1973, there had been only one increase to the family allowances.

After he had discussed his working paper's proposals for reform of the family allowances with his provincial counterparts, Lalonde suggested the amendments to the family allowance program to the Cabinet on 11 May 1973. There was no attempt to resurrect the family income security plan. Although there were significant differences between the Canadian and American systems of social welfare, it is noteworthy that Richard Nixon's attempt to establish a family assistance plan in the United States in 1970 also failed. The US plan proposed a guaranteed annual income and it was, like Canada's initiative, premised on the notion that low-income families needed more money to rise out of poverty. After the collapse of his initiative, Nixon decided to raise benefits for the "deserving poor."[34] Lalonde and his officials, on the other hand, had decided that family allowances would be the "essential cog" in what came from the social security review then underway.[35] He reminded his colleagues that family allowances had to be seen as an income supplement that provided the greatest assistance to those families with the greatest need, specifically low-income Canadian families with dependent children. Even so, the proposal would not allow for provinces to vary allowances according to income levels of recipients.

On 17 May, the Cabinet agreed that the government would proceed and introduce legislation to increase the family allowance benefit to $20 per child under age eighteen, though the national minimum could be set as low as two-thirds of the national average ($14 dollars per month per child) if a province introduced legislation to vary the benefits in accordance with the age of the child or the family size. Family allowance cheques would continue to be sent by the federal government directly to families, and the Cabinet insisted that the Parliament of Canada would continue to set norms and national standards in the levels of allowances administered and financed by the government of Canada. It also agreed to make the allowances taxable and provide for the issuance of T4F slips in the name of the mother in receipt of family allowances, including instruction that the allowance be reported by the parent claiming the child's exemption.

The rationale for the new legislation was quite a change from that of the income security plan proposals introduced in 1972, when the government wanted a selective program based on family income and an anti-poverty measure to assist low-income families with children. At that time, the Liberal government had wanted to cease paying family allowances to high-income families and to use the social security program to target benefits to low-income families. The new 1973 proposals were more a continuation of the original program introduced in 1945, when family allowances were a universal program across Canada, paid to parents regardless of their economic status. (In reality, however, the revised allowances were not universal because of the clawback feature.)

Still, there were several significant changes from the 1944 legislation. First, there was no requirement for school attendance under the new legislation, since it was intended as a supplement to the income of Canadian families, regardless of whether or not their children attended school. Second, allowances were to become available to children of immigrants as soon as they legally arrived in Canada, and Ottawa would discontinue the family assistance program for immigrants. Third, and perhaps most important, the new legislation provided for subsequent increases to benefit levels by order-in-council, subject to the approval of the House of Commons, to compensate for changes in the cost of living. This was perhaps not surprising, given that the consumer price index jumped by 4.5% in the first six months of 1973, and Parliament had approved an amendment to the Family Allowances Act and Youth Allowances Act to increase the monthly allowances to a flat $12 per month, effective October 1973, to mitigate the effects of rising prices on Canadian families.[36]

Before the legislation was presented to the House, Lalonde and his officials discussed the proposed legislation with the provinces, though the broad changes had been outlined in the working paper earlier in the year. During these discussions, Ottawa insisted that the provinces ensure that any revision to the level of benefits paid in a province was approved by the legislature of that province rather than through an order-in-council. The discussions also resulted in two significant changes to the proposed legislation.

First, Lalonde agreed to revise his proposed national minimum benefit of $14 per child if the provinces wished to vary the amount of benefits from the $20 Ottawa was proposing for each child. Some of the provinces argued that a lower minimum would afford them greater flexibility to meet their provincial needs. Lalonde agreed to set the minimum at 60% of the average payment or $12 per child, but to ensure that the federal payments in any province that chose to vary the benefits worked out to the national average, he permitted this averaging to be calculated within three consecutive calendar years beginning in 1974. This allowed the provinces to adjust benefits in the second or third year of a three-year period to reflect over- or underpayments in previous years.

Second, Lalonde had insisted in the working paper that the role of family allowances was to supplement the incomes of Canadian families with dependent children. Because it was an income support mechanism, Lalonde had refused family allowances for those children who were maintained by provincial governments or agencies designated by provincial governments. However, when the provinces protested, Lalonde changed his mind and agreed to make provisions in the legislation for a special allowance of $20 per child placed in the care of foster homes and in institutional care. Yet Lalonde made it clear to the provinces that in the new legislation, the minister of national health and welfare had to be satisfied that each provincial configuration met two conditions: that no child would be paid an allowance below the national minimum and that the provincial configuration would result in an average payment per child that was equivalent to the national norm. Otherwise, he warned, the federal government would pay the national norm in that province.[37]

On 16 July 1973, Marc Lalonde introduced in Parliament the new reforms to the family allowance program, claiming that they represented the first phase of a system of family income supplementation, which had been first put forward in the working paper on social security. The minister also told Parliament that these changes were the first concrete step in the overall reform of the Canadian income security system Ottawa and the provinces had begun with their comprehensive two-year review of social security in Canada. Also, the revised family allowance program represented a new formula for federal-provincial co-operation in the area of social security. Yet in many ways, Ottawa had bowed to the pressure to maintain the universality feature of family allowances and permitted every Canadian family the privilege of receiving a monthly cheque, although introducing a measure of income redistribution through the tax system. In a period of rising living costs – and in a minority Parliament – the Liberal government could boast that with its new social security legislation, it added $840 million to the incomes of mainly low- and middle-income families. The total cost for family allowances was now $1.83 billion annually.[38]

Only three provinces took advantage of the federal offer that allowed provinces to vary payments, but with the exception of Saskatchewan, which wanted to retain the universal approach of the existing family allowance program, all of the provinces supported the federal option.[39] Not surprisingly, Quebec was one of them. When Premier Robert Bourassa announced Quebec's family allowance plan on 19 September 1973 – just days before a provincial election – he said that it "constituted an admirable example of a type of federalism which is both flexible and beneficial for Quebec." Social Welfare Minister Claude Castonguay outlined the new Quebec family allowance program that would cover all children up to the age of seventeen, thus eliminating Quebec's schooling allowances that had been created when the province opted out of the federal youth allowance program. The province set the benefits according to the number and age of the children, as provided under the provisions of the bill before Parliament. Federal monthly allowances were pegged at $12 for the first child, $18 for the second, $28 for the third, and $31 for the fourth child and all other children in the family. Additionally, the basic allowance was supplemented by an "age premium" of $5, paid for children between the ages of twelve and seventeen years. The Quebec government would administer and finance a separate Quebec scheme that provided additional monthly allowances of $3 for the first child, $4 for the second, $5 for the third, and $6 for each child after the third.

The Quebec benefits were administered through the Quebec Pension Board, which was already in charge of family and school allowances in the province. Further, the Quebec government decided to make its family allowances tax-free because it felt that middle-income families would have to carry too great a burden if family allowances were taxed, though the federal portion would be subject to federal income tax. Castonguay noted that Quebec had sufficient freedom of action to establish a structure of its own under the proposed federal legislation, and he claimed that the new family allowance program took into consideration the special needs and circumstances of Quebec families – particularly those of large families in the middle- and low-income bracket – whose interest had not been sufficiently considered under the earlier federal schemes.[40] A short time later, Castonguay resigned from the Quebec legislature and became a consultant to Mr. Lalonde. His mission was accomplished. Alberta, on the other hand, varied the benefits according to the age of the children, providing $15 for each child up to and including six years of age, $19 for those aged seven to eleven, $25 for those twelve to fifteen, and $28 for sixteen- and seventeen-year-olds. The government of Prince Edward Island paid an additional $10 per month on behalf of the fifth and each additional child in the family, but included the provincial allowance in the federal cheque.[41]

Given the changes the Liberals had made, there was widespread support for the legislation. However, the Trudeau government had come to realize that significant change to the family allowance program did not come without considerable political cost. David Lewis, who had led the NDP attack on the earlier legislation, took great pride in the belief that his party had forced the Trudeau minority government to introduce the changes. "We will do our best to have the Bill debated and passed quickly," he wrote to J.C. Nicholson, the president of the Children's Aid Society of Cape Breton, "so that Canadian mothers may have the extra benefit as soon as possible."[42] Third reading was given to the new legislation in November 1973, and parents saw the increases in their family allowance cheques in January 1974. Lalonde had inserted a message into the cheques going to Quebec, explaining the main features of the new program. He wanted to make it clear that while the provincial government had asked Ottawa to vary federal payments based on the age and number of children in a family, the federal government paid an average of $20 to each child in Quebec. The insert contained the information reproduced in Table 6.

Clearly, Lalonde wanted to show potential voters that the federal government was still largely responsible for the payment of family allowances in the province. It was not until the February cheques arrived that parents in the other provinces received "An Important Message for Fathers and Mothers" from Lalonde. In that insert, he explained how the benefits were taxable and why the family allowance rates were different in some provinces.[43]

Although the Liberals – and the New Democrats, too – heralded the changes to the 1944 legislation as a major reform of family allowances, the government's changes were far short of what John Munro and Trudeau had wanted when they first considered modifications several years earlier. The Liberals had come

Table 6

Monthly family allowance rate for Quebec, 1974*

	Ages 0-11			Ages 12-17		
	Federal	Quebec	Total	Federal	Quebec	Total
First child	12	3	15	17	3	20
Second child	18	4	22	23	4	27
Third child	28	5	33	33	5	38
Each add'l child	31	6	37	36	6	42

* in dollars.
Source: Library and Archives Canada, Records of the Department of National Health and Welfare, vol. 1609, file 6, "January Family Allowances Insert for Quebec" and "An Important Message for Fathers and Mothers," January 1974.

to the Rubicon but had barely tested the waters and certainly did not cross the proverbial river. In the late 1960s, the Liberals had favoured selectivity over universality in family allowances, but their resolve had crumbled in the face of stiff opposition that wanted to retain the benefits for the middle class. Even within the government and the Department of National Health and Welfare, there was considerable concern that the Lalonde reforms were not particularly effective, especially for those low-income families who during the mid-1970s had to deal with the abnormally high levels of inflation. The National Anti-Poverty Organization criticized the reforms, telling Prime Minister Trudeau that the "increase" had been swallowed up by inflation, and some provinces, particularly Manitoba, New Brunswick, and Newfoundland, had decreased social assistance payments by the gross increase in family allowances, which left low-income families no better off than before.[44]

Because family allowance benefits had been tied to the consumer price index, the government had increased benefits in November 1974, bringing the federal rate to $22.08, effective 1 January 1975. However, this did not last for long, as indexing for the calendar year 1976 was cancelled when the federal government announced its austerity program in December 1975. Forgoing indexing saved Ottawa about $220 million.[45] It was clear that Canada faced a serious financial crisis from the combined effects of a depressed economy and rising inflation that had struck most industrialized states. Between 1973 and 1975, the GDP for the countries in the Organisation for Economic Co-operation and Development (OECD) declined by 5% as industrial output dropped rapidly and international trade plummeted by 14%. More than 15 million workers were out of work in the OECD nations.[46]

In October 1975, Donald Macdonald, the minister of finance, warned the country that Canada was in the grip of serious inflation, and that if the situation continued there was a grave danger that the nation would be subjected to mounting economic stresses and strains.[47] He identified the risks associated with increasing government expenditure, which had risen on a national accounts basis by 28.5% in fiscal 1974-75 and exceeded 18.5% in 1975-76. Macdonald promised to hold spending increases to no more than the increase in the gross national product and to reduce government expenditures where possible. Jean Chrétien, then Treasury Board president, negotiated nearly $1 billion in spending cuts with all departments by 2 July 1975.

Even that proved insufficient and additional cuts were necessary. In those early days of fiscal retrenchment, few programs were eliminated or even reduced because, as Chrétien noted, "an indiscriminate slashing of programs would have disruptive effects on the economy, bear harshly on many people and impair the efficiency of government in providing essential services to the public."[48] However, important reforms were made to the federal contribution to such intergovernmental programs as medicare, hospital insurance, and post-secondary education as the federal government looked for ways to control social welfare spending. In 1977, Ottawa decided that federal contributions to many programs would no longer be tied to provincial expenditures but instead had to be linked to a combination of tax points and per capita cash payments. The change in the federal-provincial fiscal arrangement, formalized with the creation of the Established Program Funding Act that replaced the cost-shared approach for hospitals, medicare, and post-secondary education in favour of a system of financial (cash) and fiscal (tax points) transfers, made the funding mechanism more predictable and saved Ottawa close to another $1 billion in 1977-78.

In 1976, when it became clear that the social security review was destined to fail in the difficult economic climate, Lalonde told the provinces that the federal government remained committed to income supplementation and was willing to proceed unilaterally. He also said that Ottawa would deliver such programs through the tax system.[49] Simon Reisman, the former deputy minister of finance, had steadfastly refused to countenance using the tax system for supplementation purposes when Lalonde began the social security review, but Reisman was replaced by Thomas K. Shoyama, and the minister, John Turner, had resigned to be replaced by Donald Macdonald. The appointments of Macdonald and Shoyama did not signify radical new thinking about social policy in the Department of Finance, but they now seemed willing to support reforms that could be financed through the relocation of the existing welfare budgets.[50] At the same time, Finance agreed in July 1976 to a Task Force on Tax-Transfer Integration – chaired by Mickey A. Cohen, a senior Department of Finance official – that would examine the feasibility of using the tax system to deliver some government programs. The Department of National Health and Welfare, which was represented on the task force, was undoubtedly pleased that the task force report to the Cabinet acknowledged that social programs delivered through the tax system was possible, and that benefits could be assessed in conjunction with the annual tax return and paid either in a lump sum with the tax rebate or spread over several subsequent payments. A restructured child benefit program that reduced monthly benefits while maintaining the universality of family allowances combined with a refundable child tax credit would reflect this approach.[51] The Department of Finance continued to insist that new programs be financed out of savings from reforms in the existing system, but the Cabinet asked the two departments to prepare a memorandum of options for income supplementation.[52] Most of Ottawa understood only too well that the family allowance program was the least redistributive of the federal government's five most expensive income security programs, but it was one that had become intrinsically identified with the rights of Canadian citizenship and, as the government knew, radical change would be difficult.

During the discussions on whether or not to suspend the automatic escalation of benefits, senior officials in the Department of National Health and Welfare again looked at the possibility of redistributing expenditures from high-income families to low-income ones. There appeared to be a continued push among the senior officials for an annual income-tested supplement to low-income families delivered through the tax system, even if it meant the removal of the tax exemption for children and the suspension of escalation of family allowance benefits for all families. An internal discussion paper, "The Alternatives for Income Supplementation," dated 19 July 1977, concluded that a federal tax credit approach to supplementation would be an effective means of addressing the needs of the working poor. Within six months, the department had prepared a report to the deputy ministers of finance and health and welfare, entitled "Tax Transfer Integration: Alternatives for the Child Benefit System." It argued for a refundable tax credit and the de-indexing and income-testing of universal family allowances.[53] However, the consumer price index increase was reinstated in 1977: the federal benefits were raised by 8.2% to $23.89, after Ed Broadbent, the new NDP leader, accused the government of attempting to end all future indexing of family allowance payments. The government increased benefits again in 1978 to $25.68.[54]

From 1977 to 1984, Monique Bégin presided over the Department of National Health and Welfare as minister. Bégin had arrived in Ottawa in 1972 with impeccable credentials as the former executive secretary of the Royal Commission on the Status of Women in Canada from 1969 to 1970, and two years as a research officer at the Canadian Radio and Television Commission. In 1972, she became the first woman from Quebec elected to the House of Commons, as a Liberal. Although she had served as minister of national revenue for nearly two years prior to her appointment as minister of national health and welfare, she was still a junior in the Cabinet. Officials in the policy development branch in the Department of National Health and Welfare noted that the minister herself indicated that she would like to have much more clout in the Cabinet, but they tended to agree with some of the press reports that she was the only genuine Liberal left in the Cabinet.[55]

The Liberals continued to acknowledge that changes to family allowances were necessary. On 23 November 1977, Bégin told Parliament, "We are studying rearrangements which would take away – if I can put it that way – from those who do not need universal programs and would eventually increase the allowances which should be received by families in need." The government clearly wanted to help those most in need but to do so without undermining universality in family allowances.[56] Minister of Public Works Judd Buchanan sent up a trial balloon for the government in a speech in October 1977, when he said that perhaps it was time to re-examine the nation's commitment to universal social programs.[57] The subsequent outburst from both Liberal and opposition members clearly showed the continued support for universal family allowances. Yet many in the government and the Department of National Health and Welfare agreed with Robert Andras, the president of the Treasury Board, when he told Parliament in early 1978, "There is nothing sacred about social programs. They have been revamped before, and they will no doubt be revamped again."[58]

But it was the question of universality and the payment of family allowances to all eligible mothers that most troubled government officials and Liberal politicians. Both the officials and politicians knew that the principle of universality, established in 1945, had created the belief among many in Canada that families with children, regardless of their level of income, were entitled to income security payments for their children. As well, in many cases the allowances still provided the only discretionary income available to mothers who, because they were raising their children, were not in the labour force. This point was made most effectively by the National Action Committee on the Status of Women. Lorna Marshen, president of the committee, wrote Prime Minister Trudeau: "The Family Allowances, being sent to the mother, is a very important aspect of the lives of many Canadian women." She pointed out that the government would be surprised to know how many women had absolutely no cash at all because the husband refused to provide her with any.[59]

Yet these concerns had to be balanced with two other imperatives: the anti-poverty objective of social security programs and the equitable distribution of the tax burden. There were few who disagreed that families with higher incomes should bear more of the tax burden, or that social security spending should be directed toward the poor and low-income families. Even so, entrenched ideas change slowly, and J.E. Osborne, special adviser in policy development at the Department of National Health and Welfare, captured the view of many in the government after canvassing the opinion across the country. In early April 1978, he wrote his assistant deputy minister, T.R. Robinson, that Canadians wanted it both ways: "Universality must be retained for family allowances to meet both the Income Security and the Status of Women objectives. However, selectivity is needed in the system to meet the Anti-Poverty objective."[60]

The reforms in this regard were moved along by Monique Bégin. She had proposed in the final report of the Royal Commission on the Status of Women in Canada in 1970 that cash allowances for children be taxed, and as minister she believed that tax credits were perhaps the best means of introducing a new allowance for the children of the working poor. She also realized that a reduction in current family allowance benefits was necessary to achieve her objectives. Like others in the Trudeau Cabinet, she believed the time had come to eliminate universal programs to provide additional support for those families most in need.[61] The change was made possible only when Trudeau ordered the government to restrain spending in 1978, and family allowances were targeted as one of the programs to be cut. By 1978, the federal expenditure for family allowances had risen to $2.22 billion, nearly a four-fold increase from $559 million in 1964, and costs were expected to rise as benefits were indexed to the cost of living.[62] Allen Lambert, the chair of the federal Royal Commission on Financial Management and Accountability, warned that the income tax burden would become unbearable for Canadians if the costs for income security programs like family allowance continued to climb. He recommended a means test for family allowances as a way to control spending and to direct resources to those most in need.[63]

Yet after the political repercussions of the Liberal attempt to reduce universality in family allowances in the early 1970s, Bégin and Chrétien – indeed, the whole Cabinet – knew that any tampering with family allowances would be potentially damaging to the Liberals. Given the earlier discussions about tax credits to deliver social programs, the Cabinet saw even a modest tax credit as a way to redirect some of the attention away from cuts to universal family allowances. As Robert Andreas, the president of the Treasury Board, noted at the time, the cuts "would not touch payments and services ... to many unfortunate Canadians who are least able to protect themselves against inflation and economic hardship."[64] The Department of Finance obviously agreed, and Shoyama even participated in drafting the memoranda outlining the measure to the Cabinet.

Canada's inflation rate remained at around 10%, and at the economic summit meeting in Bonn in mid-1978, Western leaders agreed that increased government spending was fuelling inflation everywhere. Trudeau returned from these meetings committed to further reducing government expenditure; without informing his ministers, he announced to Canadians that a further $2.5 billion had to be trimmed from federal outflow and that increases in spending had to be curbed. In a nationally televised broadcast on 2 August 1978, he told Canadians that the federal government was spending too much money and also spending it inefficiently.[65] One of the targets of fiscal restraint was the government's child benefits system. In less than three weeks, the Cabinet agreed on a plan to restructure family allowances. On 24 August 1978, Finance Minister Jean Chrétien announced major changes to how the government would provide support to families with children.[66] These changes were driven largely by the fiscal concerns within the government.

For the first time ever, the Canadian government announced plans to make social security more selective. Chrétien subsequently amended the Income Tax Act to provide a refundable child tax credit for children eligible for family allowances. For the first time, the federal income tax system would be used to deliver benefits to low- and middle-income families, including those with incomes below the poverty line and tax-paying threshold.[67] The refundable tax credit allowed a taxpayer to deduct the amount of the credit from the taxes owed or, in the case of low-income persons whose tax was less than the amount of the credit, the difference was paid by the government to the individual.[68] This mechanism allowed the Liberal government to avoid the charge that they were stigmatizing recipients of the benefit by using the means or income test, and since tax credits were treated as a revenue reduction rather than an increase in spending, the government was able to avoid the impression that it had increased its spending. By superimposing the selective program features on an ostensible universal base, these changes accomplished what the earlier 1970s attempts at reform had not: the introduction of the principle of selectivity in the family support program. It should be noted, too, that there had been little discussion with the provinces over the refundable child tax credit program; Chrétien's announcement signalled the return to unilateral action by the federal government after the failed social security review. Ottawa saw no need for discussions with the provinces since family allowances and related programs were clearly within the federal government's authority in terms of making direct payments to Canadian families. Since 1945, Ottawa had jealously protected its prerogative to legislate in the field of income security, and it continued to see programs such as family allowances and children's benefits as "instruments of statecraft."[69]

Because family allowances reached nearly 4 million mothers across Canada, it enhanced the political legitimacy of the federal government and helped it shape citizenship rights in Canada and build a national community, as hoped for.

With the reforms, Canada adopted a two-tier child allowance program. Each Canadian family would be provided with a $200 refundable child tax credit for each child, though the benefits were to be gradually reduced and finally phased out for high-income earners. This had been Trudeau's intention a decade earlier when his government attempted to reform the family allowance program in its first mandate. "A Government Program," a memorandum prepared by Jim Coutts, Trudeau's principal secretary, called for further rationalizing of Canadian social policy to deliver "the money where it [was] needed most." It suggested the redistribution of family allowances in a more efficient, income sensitive manner through the mechanism of refundable tax credits.[70]

To finance the refundable child tax credit, which was slated to begin in early 1979 for the 1978 taxation year, the government proposed three changes to the existing programs: 1) family allowance benefits were to be reduced to an average of $20 per month from $25.68 beginning in January 1979; 2) the higher exemption for the personal income tax for dependent children aged sixteen and seventeen was to be reduced to the same level as that for children under sixteen ($460); and 3) the existing tax reduction of $50 per child was to be eliminated.[71] The proposed changes resulted in increased benefits for families at the bottom of the income scale. Approximately 2 million families would see their benefits rise, while 1.7 million would see a drop in benefits.

Under the system of family benefits and tax exemptions before the changes took effect, families at the top of the income scale received almost $1,000 in family-related benefits while those at the bottom end received $616. The new proposals promised to reverse the situation so that the greatest benefits went to those with the lowest incomes. If the combined income of the parents exceeded $18,000, the basic credit would be reduced by 5 cents for each dollar of family income over $18,000. A low-income family with two children whose primary provider earned the minimum wage would receive $264 more in benefits, while a $30,000-a-year family would receive $52 less. The overall cost of the federal child benefit system was roughly $2.7 billion per annum.

The proposed changes did not represent a net increase in social policy expenditures; rather, they reassigned social expenditures to where they were most needed.[72] However, the program was certainly not intended as a comprehensive anti-poverty initiative; Monique Bégin later wrote a family allowance recipient, "[The] benefits are only intended to supplement the incomes of Canadian families who have undertaken the task of raising children and certainly do not replace the actual expenses incurred."[73] This, as opposed to concepts of anti-poverty effectiveness, was the rhetoric of target efficiency that had become the parlance of the Liberals.[74] It was also thought that the reforms ushered in a more progressive system of child benefits, combining the universality of family allowances with a family-income-tested selectivity of the child tax credit. As Chrétien told Parliament when he introduced the reforms, he did not want to erode the support going to mothers, but he wanted to direct more of the government's resources to those families that needed them most. In his book *The Politics of Public Spending in Canada,* Donald Savoie stated, "Direct spending for family allowances was decreased while the program was enriched through a Child Tax Credit. The estimated net impact on federal revenue was a reduction of $650 million." Had this been provided through direct federal spending rather than revenue loss through the tax system, it would have significantly increased federal spending. Since tax expenditures are not counted in government outlays, tax credits became the preferred subsidy route during the late 1970s.[75] Chrétien also expressed hope that the new tax credit would create additional economic stimulus.[76]

The National Council of Welfare, an advisory body appointed by the governor-in-council to counsel the minister of national health and welfare, welcomed the proposed changes. It had suggested similar modifications to the government earlier in the year, and felt that the changes would bring greater equity to the tax system and improved efficiency to the income security system. The council was under no illusion that the changes would eliminate poverty, but it believed the reforms would increase the incomes of the poor and provide a base on which governments could build in the future. Yet the council was worried that the child tax credit would come under considerable criticism, as had been the case with the family income security plan earlier in the decade, when many of its "intended beneficiaries did not realize what they would gain from it, while many of the organizations concerned about the poor condemned the scheme because it did not solve all problems overnight."[77] Even the New Democrats supported the measure. As T.C. Douglas wrote to one of his supporters, the NDP opposed any reductions to family allowances, but they were convinced that the proposals benefited low- and middle-income families.[78]

However, some groups did oppose the new reforms. The Congress of Canadian Women wrote the prime minister that the federal proposals effectively cut $980 million out of family benefits if they were reduced to $20 from the $28 projected for 1979, and the $50 non-refundable child tax credit and the current exemption for sixteen- and seventeen-year-olds were eliminated. Such cutbacks to family allowances were "a part of the heartless war on social service programs which have been won through decades of struggle to meet human needs." The congress called for an immediate doubling of family allowances.[79] Nevertheless, the changes to family allowances were made without much debate or opposition; the provinces were surprisingly silent.[80]

In the economic climate of the early 1980s, there was increasing concern in Ottawa about the cost of family allowances and other income security programs, and the pivotal question remained how best to spend the limited financial resources committed to programs like family allowances. Concern about Canada's relatively poor economic performance led the government to focus on energy and industrial policy as well as a program of restraint on social spending. Moreover, there was increasing concern over the economic costs of social spending, and considerable attention was being paid to its effect on work incentives, savings, and labour mobility. Clearly, there was a desire to have income security programs promote to non-working parents an attachment to the labour force, and to provide to the working poor benefits that would supplement their incomes. However, the Liberals did not set out a grand design for social policy in the 1980s that articulated those concerns.[81]

Even so, the Liberals signalled a further change in their approach to social policy by retaining the Ministry of State for Social Development (MSSD). Jean Chrétien became its first minister, though he continued to hold the Department of Justice portfolio as well. The short-lived government of Progressive Conservative Prime Minister Joe Clark had created a new ministry of state for the coordination of social programs in August 1979, and Chrétien told the House of Commons on 16 June 1980 that the MSSD was established to assist the government in integrating current social programs and developing more equitable policies for the future. In a lengthy and important speech in the Commons, Chrétien noted that despite the social policy changes throughout the 1960s and 1970s, the distribution of income in Canada was largely unchanged. Further, Canada had more poor children in 1980 than it had a decade earlier. Repeating the promise made in the 1979 election, Chrétien promised to finance, over the long haul, additional social spending by reductions in existing programs or increases in government revenues. He also committed the government to improving the social policy process by moving toward the integration of policy, planning, and expenditure management, and to ensuring that social policy spending was directed to those Canadians most in need.[82]

Chrétien also said the MSSD was to advise the Cabinet Committee on Social Development and help ministers set priorities and integrate social programs to meet the government's social development strategy. The committee eventually dedicated itself to several objectives, including giving priority to social policy initiatives that fostered recipients' attachment to the labour force and helped those most in need.[83] The 1982-83 expenditure plan from the Department of

Supply and Service reinforced the connection between social policy objectives and economic development when it noted, "The distinction between social and economic issues is not always clear cut. The Social Affairs envelope is heavily involved with certain economic issues and will particularly concentrate its effort over the next year on individuals and their contribution to economic growth."[84] This was a clear indication that changes to family allowances and other social programs were imminent as the Liberals attempted to balance compassion to those in need of state assistance with economic development and fiscal restraint.

This inevitably led to further discussions on universality and selectivity in social programs, a topic that had been on Ottawa's agenda since the mid-1960s. As he had since he first became prime minister, Trudeau continued to maintain that family allowances might be more effective if some measure of selectivity were introduced to the program. Most of the senior officials in the Department of National Health and Welfare had been convinced for some time that there was a definite preference for the selective approach internationally and in many of the provinces, but Ottawa was still reluctant to adopt selectivity for its family allowance program. When word leaked out of Ottawa in 1982 – another trial balloon, surely – that the government was once again considering ending universality in favour of a targeted plan, social services agencies, the opposition parties, and Liberal members rushed to condemn the government for contemplating such a change. So worried were some Liberals that they did not press the issue, and Bégin tried to put an end to the discussion when she said in several media interviews that all benefits for children would remain the way they were.[85]

Still, the government announced its plan to suspend full indexation of benefits beginning in January 1983, limiting its increase to a 6% cost of living adjustment in 1983 and 5% in 1984. It raised the child tax credit by $50 for 1983 to compensate low-income families for the capping of family allowances, but as Freda L. Paltiel, senior adviser for the Status of Women, Department of Health and Welfare, had reminded E.M. Murphy, the assistant deputy minister of national health and welfare, in early 1982, the middle class had become increasingly disgruntled that the government was helping the wealthy and the poor at its expense.[86] Bégin told the *Globe and Mail* that changes in family allowances were inevitable: in the years ahead there would be no new money and the problem facing the government would be how to use the available resources most effectively across its various programs; Marc Lalonde remarked to *Le Droit* that he hoped to see a national debate on the reconsideration of the principle of universality of family allowances,[87] and the *Globe and Mail* quoted Lalonde as saying, "The current [fiscal] crisis we're living in makes people think much more deeply about a number of issues than they used to and to realize that there are no free lunches, and that we can't plan on the basis that there's a kind of growing federal pie from which everybody can get an increased share."[88] Flora MacDonald, the Progressive Conservatives' social affairs critic, also called for a comprehensive review of family allowances. The Conservative government of Joe Clark had earlier, in 1979-80, considered abolishing family allowances to redistribute greater benefits to lower income families through better targeting of social programs.[89]

Both the Liberals and Conservatives, it seems, had clearly lost faith in the utility of a universal system of family allowances, but the Trudeau Liberals so feared another political backlash from the middle class that it was very reluctant to radically reform universal demogrants.[90] It continued to support such programs during the final months of its mandate even though many of the officials in the Department of National Health and Welfare – and many politicians themselves – realized that the principle should be seriously considered if not abandoned completely. What had been appropriate at the time of the introduction of family allowances in 1945 no longer pertained.

In the final days of the Liberal mandate, and after John Turner became prime minister, the Department of National Health and Welfare undertook yet another evaluation of family allowances.[91] However, before the initiative could be completed, the Progressive Conservatives under Brian Mulroney swept the country with the promise of change in the election held in September 1984. Universal family allowances would be one of the casualties of change brought by the Mulroney government, but it would soon learn, as the Liberal governments had for more than a decade, that making radical reforms to programs like family allowances, which Canadians had come to regard as theirs by right of their citizenship in Canada, was no easy matter.

The Demise of Family Allowances, 1984-99

PROGRESSIVE CONSERVATIVE leader Brian Mulroney campaigned in 1984 on the promise of change, and Canadians responded, giving his party the largest number of seats ever given to a political party in Canada. The electorate had clearly tired of the Liberals, who had spent nearly two decades in power, and with the economy foundering – the deficit, debt, and interest rates rising – Canadians embraced Mulroney's promise of an era of national reconciliation and renewal. Mulroney and his government came to office believing that Canada was not living up to its potential, and they promised fundamental change that would send Canada along a path that was quite different from that followed by the Trudeau Liberals. Mulroney saw his overwhelming success at the polls in 1984 as a clear mandate for change, not only in policies but in the whole approach to governing Canada.

The Conservatives' approach to government was based on three basic tenets: 1) the privatization of state enterprises, 2) the restructuring of government along market lines, and 3) the reduction in the size of government and the elimination of government deficits by limiting government intervention in the economy and the society.[1] Mulroney would not achieve all of his party's goals by the time he left office in 1993, but during the decade in which he held power, Canada was changed in fundamental ways. Social policy would not escape that change. Despite Mulroney's declaration in 1984 that universality was a fundamental key to social development, the universality of family allowances would continue to be eroded under the Conservative government; the program would be replaced with an income-target child benefit plan.

By the early 1980s, politicians of all stripes had come to realize that seemingly uncontrolled government spending and the resulting deficits had to be brought under control. In fiscal 1968, the federal debt was $18 billion, or 26% of the GDP; in the last year under Trudeau, the debt was $240 billion, or 46% of the GDP. In fiscal 1984 – the year before Mulroney came to office – the federal government expenditures exceeded revenue collected by more than 50% and the federal deficit was $38.5 billion.[2]

Across all industrialized nations, including Canada, there emerged a new political centre, and it was clearly a rightward shift. The dominant political discourse of neo-liberalism embraced a market approach to public policy. There was a definite decline in the belief that the governments and the welfare state had the capacity to redistribute economic and social welfare. By the early 1980s, this issue was not merely the concern of conservative reactionaries. The Liberals, who had presided over an unprecedented rise in public spending in Canada, had finally come to the view that government spending had gotten out of hand, and they made deficit reduction one of their major themes in the 1984 federal election. Even the New Democratic Party, in Canadian politics the major proponent of the interventionist state, had come to recognize the importance of controlling the mushrooming deficit and the necessity of reconfiguring the welfare state.[3]

Influential economists like John Kenneth Galbraith claimed that while the 1960s and 1970s saw the creation of vast economic and social programs, the time had come for governments to "improve the operation [rather] than enlarge and increase its scope." Others, like public-choice economist Doug Hartle, commented, "For many years the forces pushing for more expenditure were overwhelmingly greater ... Now fiscal liberals are being forced into the defensive minority position once occupied by the fiscal conservatives."[4] Writing shortly before the 1984 election, Michael Prince, then at the School of Public Administration at Carleton University, concluded, "The Mulroney Conservative view of social policy is not fundamentally different from the current Liberal view."[5]

Mulroney recognized that universal programs like family allowances were no longer as effective as they had been in 1945 and noted before the 1984 election, "What was good for Mackenzie King is not necessarily good for Canada today."[6] Social policy would no longer be defined in the same way it had been during the 1960s and early 1970s, though it would not be severed from the Canadian notion of social rights. Beginning in the latter part of the 1970s and gaining strength in the 1980s and 1990s, social policy would be balanced first against fiscal responsibility and affordability, and then against the long-term sustainability of what Canadians had come to value as their new social rights, namely, public pensions and a sustainable health care system. What we see emerging in the 1980s, then, is that the role of the state in the policy-making process is determined in large part by the budgetary process. The fiscal capacity of the state emerged to exert a strong influence over social policy decisions. Given the limited resources available at the time, the Canadian state had to make difficult choices in the field of social policy. That the Mulroney government opted for targeted social programs rather than the complete dismantling of the income support programs that had emerged in the postwar consensus suggests that the Conservatives were not ideological about the role of the state in Canadian society; rather, like Canadians in general, they believed that the welfare state had to be changed to help those who needed it most.

When the Conservatives came to power, there were approximately 3.6 million families with children receiving family-related benefits from Ottawa. At that time, family benefits, which included family allowances, the child tax credit, and the child tax exemption, constituted approximately 3.2% of the average family income, a dramatic rise from the 1.8% that such benefits provided in 1971 (but still considerably less than the 4.7% that family allowances contributed in 1945). The gains since 1971 were attributable largely to the decision to tie family allowance benefits to the consumer price index after 1974, and to the introduction of the child tax benefits in 1978.[7]

Basic to any discussion of child benefits in Canada was a review of the fundamental issue of universality and selectivity. Many proponents of the principle of universality borrowed from the work of such scholars as Esping-Anderson, who had formulated the widely accepted typology of welfare regimes that universalistic social policies produced more egalitarian outcomes than those that relied on selectivity or residual welfare programs.[8] The child benefit system cost the federal government $4.3 billion in 1984, comprising $2.4 billion in direct expenditure for family allowances (although a portion of that amount was recovered in income tax) and an additional $1.9 billion in tax expenditures. Family allowances paid average monthly benefits of $29.95 per child, with variations for Alberta and Quebec, which had opted in 1974 to vary the amount depending on the age of children and family size. In addition, special allowances of $44.68 were paid on behalf of children who were in the care of provincial authorities. Family allowance payments were taxable and indexed annually to the cost of living. The child tax credit was a refundable, income-tested credit, which provided $367 per child for the 1984 tax year to mothers with family incomes below $26,330. Above that threshold, benefits were reduced by $5 for every $100 of income, and for a two-child family, ceased at $41,000. When the family's income was too low to have any tax liability, a direct cash payment was made to the mother.

Furthermore, the child tax exemption provided a deduction from income for tax purposes for dependent children, which in 1984 was $710 for a child under eighteen but $1,360 for a dependent child aged eighteen to twenty-one or for those over twenty-one who were infirmed or attending a post-secondary institution. Since the exemption provided higher benefits to those with higher incomes and provided no benefits to those with no taxable income, its value was de-indexed and was to remain at $710 to allow the government to continue targeting the child benefits system to families with low and moderate incomes.[9] In 1985, the Royal Commission on the Economic Union and Development Prospects for Canada recommended that the existing family benefits system –

family allowances, child tax credit, and child tax exemption – be eliminated and replaced with a single large family allowance-type payment or a larger child tax credit, payable monthly where family income was below a certain level.[10]

Shortly after the 1984 election, the Tory government revealed its plans for economic renewal and national growth in a white paper entitled *A New Direction for Canada: An Agenda for Economic Renewal,* frequently referred to as the Agenda Paper. Over the next four years, the Mulroney government pursued a series of initiatives aimed at strengthening the nation through regional and provincial reconciliation, a decentralized federation, debt and deficit reduction, regional equalization, improvement in Canada-US relations, a greater role for free enterprise and the market, and economic renewal. This, the Conservatives believed, was necessary to sustain a strong, united, and prosperous Canada. Finance Minister Michael Wilson wrote in the Agenda Paper, "Refusing change is no longer an option for Canada. If Canadians recoil from the very idea of change ... Canada will be deflected off course in its search for solutions, and for renewal." Social programs were not immune to change, of course, and Wilson repeated the view of many that "wherever possible, and to a greater extent than is the case today, scarce resources should be diverted first to those in greatest need," noting at the same time that the "best income security is a job."[11]

Mulroney had pledged in a major campaign speech in Toronto that if elected, his government would not only restrain government spending but also spend smarter.[12] In his 1985 budget speech, Wilson promised that the government would reduce spending by $15 billion by 1990-91.[13] He also promised an open and frank discussion of the concept of universality. After the reforms that Jean Chrétien, Trudeau's minister of finance, had made to the family benefits in 1978 with the introduction of a refundable child tax credit, the concept of selectivity through the use of the tax system was firmly entrenched, and it would be somewhat easier for the Conservatives to go further and eliminate universality from family benefits altogether. This approach to social policy has been termed the "stealth style" of social policy rationalization by some, a process that "relies heavily on technical amendments to taxes and transfers that are as difficult to explain as they are to understand and thus largely escape media scrutiny and public attention."[14] While the Mulroney government did opt for increased use of tax credits, what the Liberals first found attractive for the targeting of social income security programs like family allowances to low-income Canadians, the adopted policies never escaped public scrutiny and debate, even within the Mulroney government itself.[15] Yet at the end of the Mulroney era, social programs, like so many other things, had been radically transformed, and many of the foundations that had been laid in the mid-1940s with the advent of family allowances had been dismantled. Universality would be replaced with selectivity in family benefits, completing the process first contemplated by the Liberals in the late 1960s.[16]

Like all new governments, the Mulroney Conservatives began their tenure with a major review of government programs to evaluate whether certain expenditures were necessary and effective. In addition to the broad reviews, Wilson subsequently secured Cabinet approval for a series of program reviews that included income security programs; not surprisingly, he wanted the Department of Finance to take the lead in reviewing major social, federal-provincial, and energy programs.[17] The new government had indicated its desire to open discussion on the principles of social and fiscal responsibility in major social programs, but the basic premise as articulated for the review under Mulroney – as under the Trudeau government – was fiscal responsibility and improved efficiency of Canada's social programs, including family allowances. Michael Wilson had wanted all existing social programs examined to ensure that they were sufficiently sensitive to the changing needs of Canadian society and in order to reduce the budget deficit. He favoured spending cuts because he believed that government had become too big: "It intrudes too much ... [and] programs carry on long after the need for them has passed, and are only a fiscal drain."[18]

Still, there were elements in the Tory party, represented by Health and Welfare Minister Jake Epp, who continued to believe that universal social programs were a fundamental principle of Canadian citizenship.[19] Epp was quoted in the Toronto *Globe and Mail* offering his politically convenient definition of universality: "Surely there can only be one workable definition of universality which is also consistent with the principle of fairness. That is that all individuals in the group designated for assistance should receive benefits. At the same time, however, the value of those benefits should surely be greatest for those in greatest need and least for those whose needs are less. No one is excluded from universal programs, but the value of the benefits received should be consistent with the level of need."[20]

Still, in November 1984, shortly after the Conservatives moved into Ottawa, Prime Minister Mulroney hinted about the fate of family allowances when he asked a Vancouver audience, "Does the man who earns $500,000 a year as bank president need to collect family allowances?" The Conservatives made it clear that they wished to reduce universal family allowances in favour of more selective, income-tested ones and to reconsider the whole issue of indexation of selected income security programs that had been intended to protect individuals against rising inflation.[21] In the 1985 Throne Speech, the government clearly stated its intention to reconsider social policy: "Existing programs are not always wholly successful in meeting their objectives: They must be reviewed to ensure they are appropriate to today's circumstances and they must be strengthened if necessary."[22]

Yet Mulroney of course realized that his party was on record as supporting social programs and telling Canadians that universality was a "sacred trust." On 17 December 1984, he told the House of Commons, "All we are trying to do is to share declining resources, modest resources, with those in our society who need it most: the disadvantaged, the widows, those people who need assistance."[23] He later added that his party had to rethink the tax and welfare systems to aid the underprivileged, not reduce the deficit, and stated, "When I said universality was a sacred trust, that is exactly what it is. And there'll be no change." Mulroney and his government had come to realize – as the Liberals had since the mid-1960s – that the whole issue of universality was a thorny one; they were in no hurry to disturb that hornets' nest.[24] Mulroney wanted to reassure Canadians that his government would not follow the lead of the New Right administrations of Margaret Thatcher or Ronald Reagan, which had drastically reduced public expenditures on social programs and the public health system.

Even so, senior officials in the Department of National Health and Welfare had realized that Trudeau's departure was certain to bring major shifts in social policy, and they had prepared a series of studies dealing with what changes might come to the various programs administered by their department in light of the growing fiscal exigencies. So concerned were they about the recommendations in the internal review that was completed in the summer of 1984 that they even kept it from Minister Monique Bégin, for fear that a leak might impact the election results in 1984. One senior official later said, "It has become pretty evident that the whole fiscal position of the government was up for review and possible retrenchment. It was hard to see how social policy would be immune."[25] The studies were not given to Jake Epp until November 1984, after the Conservatives' Agenda Paper confirmed what the internal review at the Department of National Health and Welfare had predicted and the new government had committed itself to a review of existing social programs "to ensure that the government's social policies [were] sensitive to the continually changing needs of Canadian society." The government's policy paper delivered by Finance Minister Michael Wilson promised a "frank and open discussion," and stated, "There is considerable scope for improving and redesigning social programs based on the twin tests of social and fiscal responsibility. *Social responsibility* dictates that wherever possible, and to a greater extent than is the case today, scarce resources should be diverted first to those in greatest need. *Fiscal responsibility* suggests that the best income security is a job, and that government expenditures must be allocated to provide immediate employment opportunities and better ensure sustained income growth."[26]

Wilson clearly had certain notions about social policy, especially when it came to universality in programs like family benefits and applying savings resulting from cutting benefits for middle- and high-income Canadians. However, Jake Epp and Prime Minister Mulroney were opposed to such a strategy, and after a bitter fight in Cabinet, they won the day, arguing that they did not have a mandate from Canadians to tinker with universal payments.[27] Jake Epp subsequently released a consultation paper on child care and elderly benefits in January 1985 that invited Canadians to participate in a consultative process before the government proceeded with its plan to overhaul Canada's social programs.[28]

The paper outlined three basic principles. First, it stated unequivocally that the concept of universality was a keystone of Canada's social safety net. Its integrity could not be called into question. Second, it declared that selective programs such as the child tax credit would be determined on the basis of taxable income and not by a means test. Third, it promised that any savings that might result in changes in the current programs would not be applied to reducing the deficit. Still, there was little doubt about the government's position on family benefits when it asked a series of questions, including: "Is it fair to provide benefits of more than $500 per child to families with income in excess of $45,000 per year ... Should families in the $20,000-$30,000 range receive larger benefits than those with incomes below $10,000 as they do now? Should the Child Tax Credit be increased and be more directly targeted to lower income groups?"

To facilitate the dialogue with Canadians, the government submitted in the paper, for "discussion purposes" only, the proposal that it eliminate the child tax exemption in favour of an increase to the child tax credit from $367 a child to $595 a child and targeting greater resources to low-income families. It also proposed reducing the level of net family income so that the credit began at $20,500 rather than $26,330. The paper argued that this proposal was consistent with the principles enunciated by the government, since it provided additional benefits to the lowest income groups while maintaining the principles of fairness and universality. As an alternative, the consultation paper raised the possibility of improving the outcome for families in the middle-income range with combined incomes between $20,000 and $40,000. Here, it proposed reducing the income tax exemption to $240 from $710 per child, cutting family allowance benefits from $31.27 to $20 per month per child, and increasing the child tax credit to $610 from $367 per child. There was a clear shift here from individual entitlement to family allowances as a right of citizenship to entitlement based on family income or need, which angered many women's groups in particular.[29] The consultation paper was referred to the Standing Committee on Health, Welfare and Social Affairs after it was tabled in the House of Commons. The minister asked the committee to present its report by 31 March 1985.[30]

Many advocacy groups welcomed the review, though most of them did not embrace the options presented by the government. The National Council of Welfare, which was mildly supportive of the government's proposals, welcomed the review as a breakthrough in the history of Canadian public policy.[31] The Social Policy Reform Group, a coalition of six national social policy and women's organizations, presented the minister with their plan for reform. They wanted family allowances left intact and recommended that the child tax exemption be eliminated and funds directed to the refundable child tax credit. They also wanted the child care expense deduction and the equivalent-to-married exemption[32] converted to credits. They claimed that if Ottawa could get the provinces to agree to leave their revenue gains (from abolishing the child's tax exemption) with Ottawa, the proposals could be enacted without any increase in the expenditure for the family benefits.[33] Nearly twenty groups testified before the parliamentary committee and ninety-two briefs were presented.[34]

The Conservatives had to deal with the same criticisms that had been levelled at the Liberals whenever there was any hint that government might end the universal payment of family allowances. One of the most virulent critics in the House of Commons was NDP Member from Vancouver East and social activist Margaret Mitchell. She called the government's intent to redesign universal social programs, particularly family allowances and old-age security, shocking. Universality was sacrosanct, she told the minister, and it was the right of middle-class Canadians to receive universal family allowances. After all, she told the prime minister, the middle class paid "most heavily for these programs through their tax system and certainly expect[ed] to retain some benefits." Even Leader of the Opposition John Turner argued that the middle class should not bear the brunt of any changes in family benefits.[35] Despite the reluctance on all sides to touch universality in social programs for high-income Canadians, the *Globe and Mail* reported on 19 September 1984 that 86% of Canadians in a survey favoured cutting social benefits to high-income earners as a way of reducing the federal deficit.

The Conservative government's approach to social policy reform was more or less set when the government acted in its first budget in February 1985 to end the full indexation of social programs that had been in place for a decade. In a move designed to save Ottawa $2 billion by 1990-91 and limit the growth on social spending, Wilson announced that family allowances and old-age security would be increased only if the annual change in the consumer price index exceeded three percentage points; the Liberals had capped the indexation provisions of both programs in 1983 and 1984.

There was much debate in the Cabinet about Wilson's announcement, and several influential ministers were clearly opposed. Wilson argued that individuals should be expected "to bite the bullet" to aid in deficit reduction,[36] and a national poll found 85% of Canadians were opposed to the full de-indexing of pensions. The *Globe and Mail* captured the mood of seniors and others opposed to the policy when it wrote, "The cost of reducing the real income of elderly who depend on this money to live may be calculated in terms of hunger, forced isolation and increased ill health: it may be entered in the books as a shabby treatment of millions of people who have spent their lives contributing to this country and who deserve better from a nation with an active social conscience."[37]

The opposition to the de-indexation of old-age pensions was so intense that Wilson restored full indexation of pensions on 27 June 1985, though that decision, too, created a serious division within Mulroney's Cabinet.[38] Although the Conservatives had learned a tough lesson on changing social security for seniors, the de-indexing of family allowances had failed to mobilize Canadians to the same degree as had changes to old-age security. Still, Mulroney realized that reforms would have to be evolutionary rather than revolutionary: Canadians held strong views about their right to income security.[39] It has been suggested that the Conservatives' attempt at reform was a "half-hearted attempt to break with the centrist consensus in Canada over social protection."[40] Social policy experts Michael Prince and James Rice characterized the Mulroney policy as "a strategy of containment rather than neo-conservative dismantlement."[41]

The Conservatives also signalled that they would restructure the family benefits system. Wilson maintained that the changes to the child tax credit came as a response to suggestions from individual Canadians and social groups who had appeared before the parliamentary Standing Committee on Health, Welfare and Social Affairs. In an approach remarkably similar to that of the previous Liberal government, the Conservatives introduced a policy to provide greater assistance to families with lower incomes and to make child benefits more progressive, while preserving the universality of family allowances. At the same time, as had been proposed in Epp's consultation paper, benefits for high-income families were reduced: the income level at which the child tax credit began to be phased out was lowered from $26,330 to $23,500. This continued the Liberal approach of using the tax system to effect their intended changes. Given the rising fiscal crisis, Wilson said that scarce funds had to be used more effectively. Beginning in 1986, and implemented fully over the following three tax years, the child tax credit was increased by $140 dollars to $524 per child in 1988 (see Table 7).

While the changes reduced net federal expenditure by $15 million in fiscal 1985-86 and an additional $40 million in fiscal 1986-87, Finance Minister Wilson said that the changes would "ensure that current inequities in the distribution of benefits – whereby benefits increase with income over certain ranges – [would]

Table 7

Net annual child benefits* for one-earner families with two children aged 18 or younger residing in Ontario, 1985-89

Family earnings (Dollars)	Existing	Proposed			
	1985	1986	1987	1988	1989
0	1,484	1,524	1,670	1,740	1,812
10,000	1,484	1,561	1,681	1,745	1,812
20,000	1,673	1,711	1,771	1,790	1,812
30,000	1,621	1,661	1,564	1,584	1,597
40,000	1,177	1,217	1,104	1,114	1,117
50,000	1,048	1,051	921	841	764
60,000	1,048	1,051	921	841	764

* Includes family allowances, child tax credit, and child tax exemption.

be corrected by 1989."[42] The government also moved to reduce the value of the tax exemption for child dependants from $710 in 1985 to $384 in 1989, though Wilson did not go as far as a number of community groups had urged him to do and abolish the exemption.[43]

When Jake Epp introduced Bill C-70 on 16 September to amend the Family Allowances Act, he promised that the government planned over the next three years to increase the support provided to low-income families through a gradual restructuring of benefits delivered through the tax system. Epp pointed out as well that social benefits could not be maintained, let alone improved if the deficit was ignored. Social programs and benefits could not be separated from economic reality.[44] It took $26 billion to service the debt on an annualized basis, an amount roughly equivalent to the budget for Epp's department, and without healthy economic conditions, an adequate social welfare system was impossible.[45] Still, the Conservatives accelerated the shift in expenditures from universal to selective programs: during the first full year of Conservative budgetary control, universal programs grew by 6.8% compared to 39.9% for selective programs.[46]

Not surprisingly, of course, the Liberals severely criticized the government for breaking its promise to not use any savings from reducing social benefits for high-income Canadians to reduce the deficit. The Conservatives had promised to transfer any savings from reform of social spending to programs for low-income Canadians. The Liberal Opposition resorted to the usual arguments about universality, claiming that it should be maintained. Moreover, it warned that the middle class was adversely affected by the new measures and that all families, regardless of income, should receive some recognition for the contribution they made to society by raising children. Once again, the Opposition argued that family allowances and child benefits were often the only independent sources of income for many women. Because such benefits were seen as so significant for women, women's groups vigorously defended the universal programs. The Liberals continued to argue that family benefits stimulated the economy by putting purchasing power into the hands of low- and middle-income Canadians.[47]

The Canadian Council on Social Development opposed the 3% reduction in the indexation of family allowances as well as the proposed changes to family benefits, claiming that $600 million would be lost to Canada's children by 1990-91 if the Tory proposals were implemented. Similarly, the National Council on Welfare opposed the changes, and Sylvia Gold, the director of the Canadian Advisory Council on the Status of Women, claimed, "The economic security of women with children at home is threatened by the de-indexation of family allowances and the child tax credit" and strenuously opposed the change. NDP MP Margaret Mitchell told Epp that women's groups across Canada opposed any reduction to family benefits because they saw it as an "attack on their children and an attack on them." She went on to argue, as the Liberals had, that universal family allowances recognized the value society placed on child rearing, and family benefits were not simply about the money. She said there was no stigma attached to family allowances: "it is one of the few benefits which go to middle income earners who carry the greatest tax burden to pay for our social programs ... Family allowances is a social right." She also charged that the Conservative government was eroding the universality of social programs.[48] Ed Broadbent, NDP leader, told the House that family allowances had an important place in the values most Canadians shared and supported.[49]

There was no backing down on the Conservatives' proposals, however. The government continued to target social spending to low-income Canadians throughout the late 1980s, and it never ceased to link expenditures on social policy with the Canadian debt, which by that time had reached more than $300 billion. All of the Cabinet ministers continued to insist that the debt represented a mortgage on the future of Canadian children, and unless spending was controlled, the government would not be able to afford the social programs that made Canada such a generous country. In the 1989 Throne Speech, Mulroney reaffirmed his government's commitment to social benefits that supported the family and again promised to direct more assistance toward those with low incomes. Subsequently, the government moved closer to ending the universality of family allowances when Michael Wilson delivered his fifth budget on 27 April 1989.

FIGURE 16   This editorial cartoon demonstrates the slow pace of social policy reform in the Mulroney government (*Globe and Mail*, 12 May 1988).
Reprinted with permission of the Globe and Mail

The government was attempting to sever the link between automatic access to some social programs and the rights of Canadian citizenship that had prevailed since 1945 with family allowances. Wilson announced that high-income taxpayers would repay, through the tax system, old-age security and family allowances at the rate of 15% on individual net incomes exceeding $50,000. The measure – the so-called clawback provision – was to be phased in over three years. The clawback would affect about 14% of the 3.8 million recipients of family allowances, but fewer than 10% would repay the full amount of benefits received. Wilson claimed that his reforms maintained the universal character of family allowances, since all families would continue to receive benefits regardless of income, but only those who needed them would keep all they received from the government. He reminded Canadians that the change "preserve[d] the social safety net and help[ed] provide a sound financial basis for social programs into the future."[50]

What it meant was that the Conservatives – just as the Liberals had done since 1978 – were able to maintain the universal delivery mechanism of family allowances while insisting on the fairness of the rich returning those benefits they did not need, which were to be redistributed to those who did. Previously, family allowances had been taxable but middle-income earners were able to keep a portion of their benefits. Wilson's changes meant that any individual with income over $55,240 would forfeit the entire amount of the $786 in family allowance benefit they received. Wilson argued that the clawback had not affected the universality of the program because families still received the benefits, even if the payment was completely recovered for high-income earners.[51] Such an arrangement prompted Marjorie Nichols, a columnist with the *Ottawa Citizen,* to write that Wilson's changes brought the end of universality. She concluded, "Don't trust a Tory to tell the truth about a social program."[52]

The opposition to the government's proposals was as predictable as the Conservative policy itself. The Liberals again attacked Wilson in the House of Commons for destroying universality. They charged that the Conservatives were making Canadian social policy in the American image, even though Wilson was extending the principle the Liberals had introduced in 1978. Albina Guarniere, the Liberal MP for Mississauga East, reflected her party's position when in debate in the House on 5 May 1989 she said, "The principle of universality lies at the heart of a compassionate state. It is the birthright of every Canadian to be provided with not just the basic needs of survival but with the foundation of a meaningful and dignified life." She went on to argue that the family allowance cheque, especially for women, was "a universal right [and] not a gift ... it is an integral part of the Canadian social identity."[53] Later, in debate, John Turner charged, "This is abandonment of the commitments and the social contracts that governments have had with the people in this country." Universality, he claimed, had been a unifying force in Canada. He went on to say, as others argued as well, that once the government set a discretionary limit on what level of income was enough, "nobody is safe and nobody can count on it because it is no longer a right of citizenship." This was the "thin edge of the wedge" argument that so many of the opponents feared would lead to an undermining of the whole social safety net. Turner concluded that the Mulroney government simply did not believe in the universality of social programs. The Liberals also continually tried to make the point that the proposed changes flowed out of the 1989 Canada-United States Free Trade Agreement, charging that the Conservatives were determined to harmonize Canadian social policy with that of the United States.[54]

A number of social-action groups opposed the proposed legislation as well. The National Council on Welfare called on the government to abandon the proposed clawback of both family allowances and old-age security pensions. It considered the move away from universal benefits as one of the most significant and negative changes in social policy in a generation. Moreover, the measure had simply been announced by Finance Minister Wilson without any prior consultation. The council claimed that the government itself had rejected the idea of a clawback on old-age pensions in early 1986 because it would seriously disrupt the retirement income system. The council also charged that the clawback discriminated against one-earner families. The legislation proposed that a single-income family with two children and a net income of $56,000 would lose all of its family allowances, but a two-earner family with one spouse earning $45,000 and the other $35,000, for instance, would escape the clawback despite their combined income of $80,000.[55] There was little discussion in Parliament about the fact that the traditional family of married parents with children had changed radically by the early 1980s. In 1981, the once dominant family form made up only 55% of all families and that number would drop to 45% by 1995. The percentage of lone-parent families and never-married parent families constituted more than 11% of all families, and the vast majority of these families were led by women and many were dependent on government transfers.[56]

But the income security policies of the Conservatives would not be universal. In 1992, Don Mazankowski, the new minister of finance, introduced changes to family allowances that politicians and bureaucrats had first discussed and contemplated more than two decades earlier. In his first budget on 25 February 1992, Mazankowski told Canadians that because of cuts in defence spending – in response to the changing world order – and due to a prudent fiscal restraint program, Ottawa was able to provide a "social dividend" for low-income families. Moreover, Mulroney wanted to demonstrate that he and his government were committed to improving the lives of Canadian children. After all, the prime minister had been the chair of the World Summit for Children and had signed the UN Convention on the Rights of the Child, which Canada subsequently ratified on 11 December 1991. The prime minister had maintained since his election in 1984 that his government's principle was that "the people who need assistance, who need the benefits of this kind [family allowances] – those people most in need – get more from the Government at all times."[57] Mazankowski pointed out as well that the major reforms to the existing system of child benefits were decided on only after Benoît Bouchard, the minister of national health and welfare, had consulted with Canadians on how best to meet the needs of children.

In fiscal 1991, Ottawa had provided $4.5 billion in financial assistance to Canadian families through the payment of family allowances and the tax system. Yet the system that had evolved since 1945 was a patchwork of measures that was neither well targeted nor easily understood and Mazankowski maintained that it was high time the program was simplified, streamlined, and targeted. The Conservative government proposed eliminating universal family allowances in favour of a new child tax benefit that combined some features of the existing family allowance program with the refundable tax credits into a single, tax-free monthly payment determined on the basis on the family income tax returns.

Mazankowski promised to restructure and substantially enrich the existing system. The child tax benefit, unlike family allowances, would not be subject to the income tax. Bill C-80, which enacted the child tax benefit, provided for payments, usually to mothers, for all eligible children under the age of eighteen. It provided $1,020 per child annually, plus $213 if parents or spouses did not claim child care expenses, and another $75 starting with the third child. In addition, the child tax benefit included a working income supplement, which provided benefits of up to $500 per year per family at a cost of $250 million annually. The income supplement recognized the additional costs of working parents and offered limited compensation for the fact that wages did not consider the number of children in the family as social assistance did (so this benefit was not extended to welfare recipients). Families with net incomes less than $25,921 received $1,733 for the first child and $1,233 for each subsequent child, but the benefit was reduced once net family incomes exceeded $25,921 and reached zero at an income of about $66,600 for one- or two-child families.

The government believed that there should be some kind of support to ensure that people were better off financially while working; as Barbara Sparrow, the parliamentary secretary to the minister of national health and welfare, said later in the House of Commons, "Today, there needs to be an incentive for people to get out and work." The reforms were to increase total expenditure for the federal child benefits by $400 million per year and $2.1 billion over the following five years.[58] The child tax benefit was clearly designed to reinforce the incentives for low-income parents to participate in the work force, and it represented for Canada a shift from a horizontal distribution of family allowance benefits to one in favour of greater vertical equity (targeting) in social programs, a trend that had had its beginnings in the late 1970s with Jean Chrétien's child tax credit and one that was more clearly defensible with the rising government deficits and debts of the 1980s and early 1990s.[59] The elimination of family allowances meant that the federal government destroyed the principle that had existed since 1945 that taxpayers who were parents had greater financial responsibilities than those at the same income level who did not have children to support.

Of course, the government realized that it would be criticized for ending universality in family allowances, and it was quick off the mark to defend its reforms. In conjunction with the budget speech, Minister of National Health and Welfare Benoît Bouchard produced "The Child Benefit: A White Paper on Canada's New Integrated Child Tax Benefit," which outlined the changes as well as the rationale for the new program. The minister claimed that a network of social policy groups both inside and outside government had identified five main shortcomings of the existing system.

First, many groups had argued that greater assistance was needed for low-income families, even though they already received the largest child benefits. Second, the existing system that combined family allowances, the child tax credit, and the refundable tax credit was cumbersome and confusing. Moreover, about 600,000 high-income families received benefits, some or all of which were recovered by the government at tax time. Third, family allowances were targeted according to individual incomes, while family income was a better basis for directing assistance to children. Fourth, the existing system did nothing to provide an incentive to work for low-income families that were faced with employment-related expenses and possibly a reduction in social assistance benefits if they returned to the labour force. Fifth, the refundable tax credit was available only after tax returns were assessed, thus failing to meet the immediate needs of modest-income families.

However, the white paper pointed out that the new child tax benefit also had a number of important advantages, including improved benefits, especially for low- and modest-income families. Moreover, the new system directed assistance to those most in need and supplemented the earnings of the working poor while promising to consolidate three programs into one that was simpler and more responsive to changes in family need, such as the birth of a new child or a change in family status through a marriage breakdown.[60]

It was no coincidence, of course, that Bouchard rather than the finance minister led the debate on the government's budget. The Conservatives wanted their policies seen as reforming Canada's income security system and not as an extension of the government's fiscal policies. Bouchard focused his attention on the new child benefit, calling it a "reaffirmation of Canadians' belief in fairness" and the largest and most important social initiative since the child tax credit was introduced in 1978. Quoting extensively from Prime Minister King's speech when he introduced family allowances in July 1944, Bouchard also said, "There is an obligation upon the state to assist in the upbringing of children [since] the family and the home are the foundation of national life." According to Bouchard, the new child benefit resulted from the recommendations of two parliamentary reports – one from a Senate committee entitled *Child Poverty: Towards a Better Future* and another from a Commons subcommittee entitled *Canada's Children: Our Future* – that the government had accepted and was now implementing. The new child benefit was administratively simple, Bouchard maintained; parents had no additional paperwork to complete, the payments were made monthly, and it was tax-free for parents to keep and spend on their children. Unlike the 1989 policy that clawed back 15% of family allowances where individual net incomes exceeded $50,000, the new child benefit was based on the overall net income of the family, an obvious response to earlier criticism. Also, the new benefit package was more generous for low-to-moderate income families that earned less than $50,000. Of course, the Conservatives maintained that the reform was a "fiscally responsive decision." Bouchard noted that "fiscal responsibility is itself a social benefit. Our children must not inherit a Canada that is crippled by debt."[61]

The New Democrats were the first to voice their opposition to the government's plan to eliminate family allowances. The party also criticized the government for not doing enough to help those in poverty. Margaret Mitchell charged that the measure divided and discriminated as it pitted middle-class families against low-income earners, and that the new child tax credit was simply an incentive for parents to move off welfare and into the work place. She claimed that it did nothing to help families on welfare: Bill C-80 provided additional credits for the working poor that the poor who did not work would not receive. She asked the minister, "Are poor kids on welfare less deserving than the children of working parents?" The NDP charged that the reforms were a return to the trend prominent at the beginning of the 20th century to distinguish between the deserving poor and the undeserving poor.[62] Later, in the parliamentary debate on Bill C-80, Chris Axworthy, NDP member for Saskatoon-Clark's Crossing, argued for the retention of universality, saying, "Once you remove universality you begin the process of removing the program altogether."[63] "It seem ludicrous," he said, "that [the government] would so systematically and completely break the ties that bind."[64]

Many social policy organizations and children's advocacy groups attacked the proposals, while others offered support. Those opposed claimed that the proposals offered inadequate protection against inflation (since the new benefits were only partially indexed when inflation moved above 3%). Ken Battle of the Caledon Institute of Social Policy, a non-profit organization committed to fostering effective social policy, said that if the inflation rate were at 3%, for instance, there would be no new revenues coming to welfare recipients and poor families. He argued that if the inflation rate rose to 5%, the child benefit would rise by only 2%, pushing many of the families below the poverty line. Still, he favoured the changes, noting that he did not mourn the loss of universal family allowances, because "they were replaced by fairer and more sustainable income-tested programs."[65] Lise Corbeil of the National Anti-Poverty Organization criticized the legislation because it was inadequate as an anti-poverty measure, and it favoured the working poor at the expense of the non-working poor. She called the proposal a discriminatory package, as it treated working poor families with children as deserving of extra assistance through the earned-income supplement, while the children of families on welfare and not in the work force were treated as undeserving. Gerard Kennedy of the Canadian Association of Food Banks, on the other hand, called it "the most deceptive and cruel thing coming from government that we have seen in a long time. It is a tremendous blow to the hopes of low income people."[66]

Of course, many of the groups also criticized the abolition of universal child benefits. Some of the arguments for universality presented to the legislative committee reviewing Bill C-80 had been used for generations. Paying all parents, they argued, helped ensure broad public support for such social programs in general. If the middle class failed to reap the benefits of such programs and realized that their taxes were used to support those with low incomes or on welfare, support for the welfare state would be eroded. Others claimed that universal social programs developed social cohesion and solidarity in society.

Once again, the connection was also made between child benefits and cheques for mothers. Some women's groups argued that universal family allowances provided many mothers without income who had no access to their spouses' income even where families were relatively affluent. This was the poor wives with rich husbands argument. Micheline Lavoie from the Réseau d'action et d'information pour les femmes said that for an abused woman, family allowance was "a life-saving buoy ... At least she will have the money for a taxi in which to escape with her children in case of assault, and she will be able to cover necessary minimum expenses."[67] Only nine of the forty witnesses were heard by the committee reviewing the bill before the Conservatives moved the bill to a vote, and the voices in opposition did not matter much, it seemed. The government proceeded with the legislation virtually unchanged.[68] When the legislation passed the House of Commons in December 1992, the universal family allowances introduced in July 1945 were eliminated in favour of a selective, income-tested supplement for children. Canada's best known universal social welfare program was gone, replaced by the child tax benefit that provided monthly tax-free payments to nearly 85% of all Canadian families with children. By 1997, Ottawa was expending more than $5.1 billion annually on the new program.[69]

The ending of family allowances and universality represented a major paradigm shift in the history of Canadian social policy; it represented a full break with universality in favour of targeting benefits. With its new policy, the government had challenged the notion that family allowances were a right of *all* Canadian families, and had rejected the principle that the state had to contribute directly to the raising of *all* families in Canada.[70] Still, social spending continued to outpace economic growth during the Mulroney years as it had for much of the period since the end of the Second World War. In the 1950s, for instance, annual social spending grew in real terms by 8.6%, compared to 5.6% for real

GDP. Throughout the 1960s, social spending averaged 8.1% annually compared to 5.6% for GDP, and in the 1970s the rates were 8.9% to 5.2% in favour of social spending. The annual rate for social spending fell to 4.3% in the 1980s when the growth of GDP declined to 2.2%, but the rate of social spending again outpaced economic growth during the Mulroney era.[71] Table 8 offers an overview of rates of expenditure in Canada from 1980 to 2003, and is a good illustration of the approach that governments took to social spending over the past two decades.

In the years following the Conservative reforms to social policy in 1992, following the introduction of similar social policies in Germany and Australia, for instance, there were several attempts to improve children's benefits and a clear effort to integrate federal and provincial programs, an objective largely

Table 8

Rates of change in program spending, 1980-2003

	Average annual growth rates				Cumulative growth rates (base year equal to 100)			
	1980-1983	1984-1993	1994-2003	1980-2003	1980-1983	1984-1993	1994-2003	1980-2003
Real GDP*	−0.2	1.4	2.8	2.1	99.2	114.6	131.4	165.5
Consumer Price Index	7.2	3.5	1.8	3.6	131.9	141.2	119.9	233.4
Social programs								
Transfers to persons	7.0	2.9	0.4	2.5	130.9	133.5	104.4	178.8
Transfers to other levels of government	1.1	0.9	1.0	1.2	104.3	109.7	110.5	134.5
Total social spending	4.3	2.1	0.7	1.9	118.4	123.2	106.7	158.0
Other programs								
Transfers to business	−7.1	−10.1	−0.2	−5.2	74.6	34.4	98.0	27.9
Other transfers	1.7	1.1	0.2	1.1	107.2	112.0	102.5	130.2
Defence	2.5	0.3	−1.6	0.2	110.4	103.2	85.2	104.0
Total program spending	2.3	1.1	0.5	1.2	109.5	111.6	105.1	133.3
Debt charges	7.6	2.8	−3.4	1.6	133.8	132.2	70.6	147.2
Total expenditures	3.2	1.5	−0.3	1.3	113.4	115.8	96.8	135.5

* Real expenditures, constant 1992 dollars (1996 basket).
Source: Michael J. Prince and James J. Rice, "Governing through Shifting Social-Policy Regimes: Brian Mulroney and Canada's Welfare State," in *Transforming the Nation: Canada and Brian Mulroney*, ed. Raymond B. Blake (Montreal and Kingston: McGill-Queen's University Press, 2007), 172.

absent during the Mulroney years. By 1996 (and three years after the Liberals were returned to power and governments in Canada had made considerable progress in controlling their deficits), governments embarked on a series of initiatives to renew the federation. One of the primary objectives of these initiatives was to continue to target social assistance to society's most vulnerable, including children living in poverty. The "Report to Premiers on the Ministerial Council on Social Policy Reform and Renewal," released in March 1996, proposed "the possible consolidation of income support for children into a single national program, jointly managed by both orders of government, with options for either federal or provincial/territorial delivery of benefits."[72]

Momentum for social welfare reform continued to grow and at the June 1996 first ministers' conference, the premiers and the prime minister decided to place child poverty on the national agenda. When the premiers met again a few months later, they (with the exception of the premier of Quebec) asked their ministers to work on an integrated child benefit program with the federal government. In the 1996 Speech from the Throne, Ottawa committed itself to renew and modernize Canadian federalism so that it met the needs of Canadians in the 21st century. An important aspect of that renewal was the enhancement of social solidarity in Canada by "preserving and modernizing the social union so that the Canadian commitment to a caring and sharing society remain[ed] truly Canada-wide in scope."[73] One of the primary areas of concern was to improve the prospects for children in low-income families; the government maintained that children were the future and there was no better place for Canadians to invest. Under the system existing prior to 1997, child benefits were often reduced when parents left social assistance or welfare to enter the workforce. Both levels of government realized that children should not be penalized when their parents took a job.[74] While a variety of government programs provided various forms of support to families with children, they had inadvertently created a "welfare wall" that made it difficult for parents to move from welfare to work. In other words, the existing systems created significant financial disincentives to leave social assistance.

To deal with this dilemma, the federal government introduced a national child benefit initiative.[75] Through this initiative, the federal, provincial, and territorial governments hoped to extend and simplify income support for low-income families with children and invest more in services for children, as well as provide incentive for parents to go to work. This meant moving child benefits out of the welfare system so that when parents left social assistance, they kept these benefits for their children. In 1998, Ottawa created the Canada child tax benefit (this is the federal component of the national child benefit) by combining the existing $5.1 billion child tax benefit and working income supplement,

$250 million committed in the 1996 budget, plus $600 million from the 1997 budget.[76] The new program, totalling $6 billion, provided considerable support to all low-income families across Canada and was billed as a substantial down payment on "an important national project." The Canada child tax benefit amount payable to each family is determined through the income tax system, based on the previous year's family income, and is automatically adjusted in July of each year. However, there are two components to the Canada child tax benefit: the first, a base benefit, is available to families with incomes up to $66,721; the second is the national child benefit supplement, which is available to families with incomes of up to $25,931.[77] When it was introduced, Pierre S. Pettigrew, then minister of human resources development, admitted that the national child benefit system would not eliminate child poverty, but it would improve the living standards of thousands of Canadian children.[78] Ken Battle and Sherri Torjman have argued that in recent years Canada has tripled the amount paid to low-income families in child and family benefits. For instance, measured in constant dollars (for the year 2000), child and family benefits for low-income families have increased from $1,451 in 1947 to $4,456 in 2001 for two children. They have presented their findings in Figure 17.

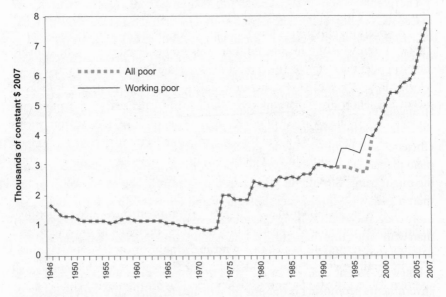

FIGURE 17   Federal child benefits for low-income families, 1946-2007 (constant 2007 dollars)

Source: Reprinted with permission of Ken Battle

Moreover, the national child benefit system was an attempt to implement structural reforms to how governments responded to the needs of low-income families with children. Underlying this, there was an effort to promote attachment to the workforce by ensuring that families would be better off finding work than relying on social assistance. Increased federal expenditure on programs for children and low-income families resulted in substantial savings for most provinces. It allowed them to redirect provincial resources toward improved income support and children's services for low-income working families.

By 1999, the provincial and territorial governments had reinvested more than $450 million in improved benefits and services for low-income families with children, in such areas as income supplements for the working poor, child care support, early intervention programs, and supplementary health benefits.[79] There has been considerable pressure for such programs from public policy think tanks like the Caledon Institute and the C.D. Howe Institute. As the *Globe and Mail* noted regarding the children's agenda, "Just giving poor families more money will not do: helping unprepared parents of any income to understand what good child-rearing practices are, and to support them in the home is essential."[80] Interestingly, this objective is not unlike the one that led to mother's allowance nearly a hundred years earlier.

The recent revisions in social policy for children marked a fundamental change in Canada's welfare state. One can argue that from the end of the Second World War to the late 1960s, Canada's social security system was built on the notion of collective social responsibility, designed to ensure that all Canadians enjoyed a social minimum, even if programs like family allowances served an economic as well as a social public good.[81] In the 1980s and 1990s, state revenue exerted a strong influence over social policy spending and priorities. During this period, the state came to increasingly view social policy as a way of promoting economic efficiency and income growth, and fostering the notion that a greater attachment to market can also be a way of protecting its citizens from the uncertainties life might bring. Social policy has become more a branch of economic policy than it ever was. Employment insurance and job retraining, for instance, are more concerned with helping Canadians respond to marketplace opportunities than with protecting them from the damaging consequences that often accompany economic cycles.

Likewise, recent changes in social policy for children are concerned with governments promoting economic growth and helping citizens participate in the market economy as much as being a protector of children. At the same time, though, the state has retained a measure of social citizenship, even if it is focused more on a selective and residual model rather than a universal one that once applied to family allowances in Canada. That change was driven in the last two decades largely by the fiscal position of the national government. Yet for a government that wished to maintain the welfare state, the cost was simply funnelling most of the income support monies for families to those most vulnerable and most in need of assistance and away from those who did not need state support. The history of family allowances, then, has been a study of a Canadian social program that has evolved from one based primarily on rights to one that had increasingly come to be based on needs.

Conclusion

PETER GZOWSKI, the well-known former CBC journalist and author, observed in one of his many books that Canada's social safety net – which included programs like family allowance – was the product of a variety of factors: our history, our heritage, and our need to huddle together against the cold. Gzowski also proclaimed that because there was not enough private capital in Canada to build the institutions that would define a nation and tie it together, Canada used public capital to do so.[1] While Gzowski's analysis of the emergence of Canada's welfare state might have been a little tongue-in-cheek, he was certainly right on two points: first, there was no single factor that explained the origins of Canada's welfare state, and second, Canada's welfare state has become a defining national characteristic. A variety of factors did indeed come together to create Canada's social security system and then, subsequently, to reform various aspects of it. It was my objective when I began writing this book on the history of family allowances to demonstrate that public policy decisions are rarely the result of a single interest group and hardly ever the result of a single factor; through the case study of family allowances we can see that social policy making in Canada is a complex process and it emanates from a variety of forces. Canada's social security system emerged and developed from a conjunction of interests.

This book, based primarily on original archival research, provides a historical analysis of Canada's national program of family allowances. It covers the period from the time just before the Great Depression in 1930, when the idea of a family allowance was first considered, to the implementation of family allowances for all children in 1945 in the context of the Second World War. The study concludes with the demise of the program in 1992 when it was changed into an income-tested child tax benefit. When adopted in 1945, family allowances were the first social security measure in Canada to be paid to all mothers with children regardless of income. As such, it also marked the beginning of the principle of universality in national social programs; successive federal governments remained committed to that principle for nearly a half century.

Few other Canadian social programs have undergone such a complete transformation from a "rights" to a "needs" based approach over the past quarter century. A history of family allowances, therefore, provides a revealing window into the much larger ideological, fiscal, social, intergovernmental, and political transformations at work in the restructuring of the Canadian welfare state – and, hence, Canada itself – over the past five hundred years. We witness in this period not only a shift from Keynesianism to neo-liberalism within Canadian social policy but also a reordering of the priorities of governments, political parties, the bureaucracy, and citizens themselves on how they came to view the role of income support programs like family allowances in Canada.

I have attempted to argue that social policies are inextricably tied to politics – that is to say, not only are they products of moral, ideological, social, bureaucratic, and fiscal imperatives, but they also reflect the political calculations of governing parties, most often in moments of political crisis. This theme is explored through the analysis of the origins of the family allowance legislation in relation to fears of a crisis in family life and social stability in Canada during wartime in the 1940s; the neglect of the programs for the next quarter century of rapid economic growth; the growing realization of senior government officials, particularly those in the Department of National Health and Welfare in Ottawa and elected politicians in Canada's two major political parties, of the ineffectiveness of the family allowance benefit to assist low-income families; the re-emerging federal interest in the program in response to Quebec's heightened demands for constitutional autonomy over social policy in the 1970s; and, finally, the impact of the deficit and debt reduction strategies of the 1980s and early 1990s on the stripping away of middle-class entitlements to children's benefits as the state directed its dwindling resources to those it saw in greatest need.

We can also see through the history of family allowances in Canada the interplay of politics and policy. Social policy was never simply about creating a kinder, gentler, and more compassionate Canada. Rather, public policy decisions in the field of social policy have been essentially a political process that has responded to a series of political crises. Family allowances were introduced in 1945 to respond to a particular political crisis, and they were modified and reformed in the following five decades largely in response to other political crises. In the 1940s, Prime Minister King believed that a national program of family allowances would aid in bringing stability to the institution of the family and otherwise help ensure a smooth transition from war to peace.

I argued at the beginning of this book that examining the family allowance program historically through extensive archival research would offer an important contribution to the wider discussion on the intriguing question of the origins and subsequent development of the welfare state in Canada. Such an approach would address and engage many of the arguments made by other scholars. This book presents a more nuanced and complete explanation for the origins and development of family allowances than has been presented elsewhere, and it contends that we need to reconsider the history of family allowances, and social policy generally, from what has become the dominant paradigm over the past two decades.

By the 1970s, social scientists had dismissed the notion that social programs emerged from an enlightened state in favour of society-centred models that argued it was the influence of actors within society that prompted state action. Initially, the Marxist and neo-Marxist approach predominated. This model asserts that the state embraced the welfare state as a means to ensure social control and buy peace with labour. In the Canadian example, the Marxist analysis maintains that Prime Minister King embarked on a universal family allowance program because of political and economic pressure from labour and their working-class supporters, notably the Co-operative Commonwealth Federation.

Welfare policy has not proven anywhere to be a very effective mechanism of social control, and I contend here that it does not seem plausible that a radicalized and angry labour movement – as Canada's was in 1943 when one in three workers went on strike – would accept from a Liberal government it had come to distrust the promise of a family allowance program that might pay to married workers with families $8 per child beginning two years down the road. In addition, the Marxist model is not particularly useful in explaining the radical changes that were made to family allowances after the 1970s. What it ignores is that all three of Canada's political parties accepted some form of social security in the postwar period and, in the 1970s, limitations on government spending. The Marxist model also ignores the fact that social security had emerged as the most pressing public policy issue in nation-states throughout much of the industrialized world during the 1940s. Similarly, the difficult fiscal situation of governments became a preoccupation of governments and citizens alike in most industrialized nations after the 1970s. Policy developments in Canada were influenced by the intellectual and social currents in the international community, and it is crucial that as historians we consider global developments when writing about national topics.

The new dominant paradigm in social policy analysis focuses not on class but rather on the gendered origins of the welfare state, another society-centred approach that emerged in the mid-1970s. The gendered approach borrowed heavily from Marxist analysis, but it was concerned primarily with sexual inequalities and the historically disadvantaged role of women in society. Scholars who approached the study of social policy from this perspective have argued that state-sponsored measures like family allowance were designed to force women to remain dependent on the primary male breadwinner, and to perpetuate the traditional role of women as mothers and caregivers. This is the case, as Ruth Roach Pierson contends, even if government officials were silent on the role of women in the development of postwar Canada social policy; silence on women meant the state gave priority to policy issues for men. This study of family allowances acknowledges that cash benefits that were paid to mothers in the name of their children certainly encouraged women's roles as mothers and homemakers. It also contends that gender can function as a key lens of analysis, but the analysis here does not support the argument that other scholars have made that family allowances were *essentially* a wage to keep women at home. Yet it is clear that the state and the most Canadians, including the vast majority of women, too, saw an important role for women in restoring the social institution of the family that had come under considerable stress during the Great Depression and the Second World War that followed it. Admittedly, this role was consistent with the cultural-historical norms of the period. Similarly, proponents of the family allowance program conceived only of heterosexual and two-parent families in the 1940s. But we cannot lose sight of the fact that women across Canada welcomed family allowances, and support for the programs among mothers remained high well into the 1990s. It is interesting, too, that when the Liberal government attempted to increase family allowances in the 1970s to low-income families at the expense of middle-income Canadians, it was middle-class mothers and women who protested such reforms most vigorously. Perhaps family allowances did help empower women and change the nature of Canadian families.

While this study acknowledges that both class and gender are important lenses of social policy analysis, it does not accept the premise that either class or gender alone can fully explain the origins and development of Canada's family allowance program. This study contends above all else that historical developments like the origins of a welfare state – and the origins and demise of the family allowance program – can be explained and understood only through the examination of several different factors and the interplay between them. Each phase of the family allowance program was shaped by different needs, different interest groups, and different political, economic, constitutional, and social events.

Through each phase, the state was an important actor in social policy development and change. This study confirms that policy making within the federal bureaucracy plays an important role in shaping welfare policy in Canada. Policy makers and politicians themselves recognized the importance of social welfare in the 1940s. It was the bureaucrats within the Department of National Health and Welfare who were among the first to recognize in the early 1960s that family allowance benefits were no longer an effective policy, particularly for low-income families. They came to realize as well that a universal program like family allowances was no longer an appropriate mechanism to get money into the hands of the families who needed it most: the state could not afford to pay every family more simply to help those in greatest need. This dilemma led to the acceptance of the principle of selectivity (or targeted funding) within the department by the late 1960s, which lends support to the argument that the role of the state is important in the policy-making process. It also confirms Leslie Pal's argument that social policy is determined in large part by the budgetary process and the fiscal capacity of the state. Given the limited resources available to the state from the mid-1970s onward, policy makers had to make difficult social policy choices, and both the Trudeau and the Mulroney governments opted for targeted social programs. The Liberals reduced the value of the family allowance benefits when they introduced an income-tested child tax credit in 1978.

It is also argued here that the state is additionally important because it considered social policy as a powerful and cohesive national symbol in Canada. Because of their redistributive functions, many social security programs, like family allowances, strengthened the attachment of citizens to a national community that enjoyed a shared set of rights as Canadians. One of the important considerations for the Canadian state as it weighed the impact of replacing the universal family allowance program with one that targeted specific income groups was negotiating the question of citizenship rights. Following the Second World War, there was an expansion of social rights in Canada that quickly became entrenched in the mindset of Canadians; any attempt to reform the family allowance program that would see benefits either reduced or eliminated for any family quickly became intertwined with the rights of Canadian citizenship. When the Trudeau government first proposed a major overhaul of family allowances in favour of increased support to low-income families, there were loud protests from the middle class who argued that they paid their taxes and were entitled to family benefits simply because they were Canadian citizens. Their level of income should not matter in what can be described as a revolution of rising entitlement in the generation after the end of the Second World War. This argument played an important role in the debate over the principles of universality and selectivity in social programs, especially during the period of Liberal rule from 1972 to 1983 and also in the first term of the Mulroney government.

This study also concludes that Canada's federal system had an important impact on the development of family allowances, especially as the two orders of government were attempting to resolve outstanding constitutional issues. When a nationalist Quebec government demanded that Ottawa withdraw from the social policy field and transfer monies expended on such programs to the provinces, family allowance became intricately involved in the minefield of Canadian intergovernmental relations. Because family allowance was one of the few programs shared by all Canadian families and one of the means of building social cohesion across Canada, the federal government initially refused to allow any provincial involvement in the program. By the early 1970s, however, family allowance was elevated from sectoral or "low politics" to the realm of "high politics." The program had rarely been the concern of the first ministers except when it had been introduced in 1945, but during the constitutional negotiations in 1970 and 1971 they moved to the centre of Canadian politics. Prime Minister Trudeau proved willing to make changes to the family allowance program as a means of enticing Quebec Premier Robert Bourassa to amend the British North America Act. In those intergovernmental negotiations to patriate the constitution, family allowances played an instrumental role. Ottawa promised certain reforms to the program to satisfy some of Quebec's social and constitutional objectives and its demands for greater autonomy within the Canadian federation as a way to move the constitutional file to a conclusion. The changes that were made to family allowances to allow the provinces to determine how the benefits were allocated to parents came as a result of the political manoeuvring with Quebec. Even so, Trudeau realized, as had Mackenzie King much earlier, that family allowances served as a link between the federal government and individual Canadian citizens in various regions, especially in Quebec. Even as the program was being reformed, the federal government made certain that family allowances would remain a nation building tool to help foster a pan-Canadian citizenship and attachment to the government of Canada. The federal government, it might be concluded, designed some of their family allowance reforms to counter the province-building project in which the Quebec provincial government was so heavily involved.

It is widely accepted within the academic literature that Brian Mulroney and his Progressive Conservatives arrived in Ottawa in 1984 with an ideological agenda to dismantle Canada's welfare state. Such claims are usually premised on two arguments: the reduction in federal expenditures on social programs and the replacement of universal family allowances for targeted benefits for low-income families. This study of family allowances confirms that the Conservatives came to Ottawa with a clear goal to restructure government to make it more efficient and effective, but it does not support the claim that the Conservatives wanted to dismantle the welfare state, even if they made major reforms to it (see Figure 18). They created a different welfare state, and Gosta Esping-Andersen and others have acknowledged that the social welfare reforms in Canada have been modest. And for good reason: social policy expenditure by all governments in Canada increased not only in absolute terms but also as a share of total program spending and as a share of GDP during the Mulroney years. Moreover, both poverty and income equality declined in Canada during the Mulroney era, a fact that may indeed surprise many people.[2] As this study

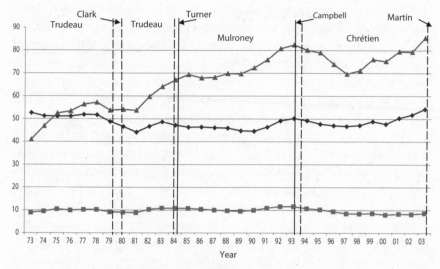

FIGURE 18   Federal social spending in context

Source: Michael J. Prince and James J. Rice, "Governing through Shifting Social-Policy Regimes: Brian Mulroney and Canada's Welfare State," in *Transforming the Nation: Canada and Brian Mulroney*, ed. Raymond B. Blake (Montreal and Kingston: McGill-Queen's University Press, 2007), 170.

demonstrates, the reconsideration of the principle of universality did not suddenly emerge among policy makers in 1984; it had been discussed seriously in the Department of National Health and Welfare and throughout Canada for nearly two decades. The Liberal government had deliberately chosen a targeted approach to family benefits rather than a universal one when it reformed the family allowance program in 1978. Officials in the Department of National Health and Welfare had prepared a major review of family allowances by the summer of 1984, but they kept the report from the Liberal minister because they feared its content might influence the vote in the coming election. The report suggested that the family allowance program could not continue as it had for nearly four decades. It was left to the Mulroney Conservatives to reform the family allowance program to make it more selective. Even so, Mulroney found that there were deep divisions in his party over the principle of universality, and he moved only incrementally in his reforms.

Through the lens of the family allowance program, we were also able to explore the concept of universality versus selectivity as competing approaches to Canadian social policy, and, as this study shows, neither Liberal nor Progressive Conservative governments were simply ideological about the concept. What had emerged in Canada by the later 1980s – largely because of the fiscal difficulties of all orders of government – was a new political consensus among all three of the major political parties, but especially with the Liberals and the Conservatives and among Canadian citizens as well. When the Mulroney government decided to eliminate universal family allowances in favour of targeted funding, Canadians still demanded a safety social net, but in the area of income security for children and families, it was one that was more residual and targeted than the social security system established in the postwar generation. The political consensus that had fostered a universal family allowance program during the time of Mackenzie King in the 1940s had been replaced in the 1970s and 1980s with a new political consensus that had most Canadians readily accepting income support programs that went to those in greatest financial need. That consensus was driven by the realization that the decline in state revenues meant that there had to be a reconsideration of state priorities in social programs.

The fact that universal family allowances were eliminated with little more than a whimper from Canadian families (compared to change to seniors' benefits, for example) suggests that most Canadians did not oppose the change. However, it should be noted that by this time many Canadians had turned their attention to other areas of social policy, particularly public pensions and health care (where universality has been preserved). Canadians wanted those aspects of the welfare state strengthened. The demise of family allowances, then, marked the beginning of a new era in Canadian social policy; it did not mean an end to the welfare state in Canada but rather a change in focus and orientation. Universality was no longer a sacred trust in income support for children at a time when the emphasis in Canadian society moved from collective rights to individual rights and responsibility, marked most notably by the emergence of the Charter of Rights and Freedoms. Social policy remained an important marker of Canadian identity and a tool of nation building and social cohesion, but the focus had shifted from universal family allowances to other types of social security. While some might see the demise of family allowances in 1992 as the end of the welfare state in Canada, the recent changes in income support for families with children might well be regarded as a new approach to social welfare in Canada.

If we can learn anything from a history of family allowances, it is that social policy decision making in Canada since 1945 has been essentially a complex process, and that Canada's social programs have evolved and changed most rapidly in response to political crises. Moreover, this book has shown that there is no simple or single explanation to help us understand the development of social policy in Canada. We can only comprehend the matter by examining the interplay of a variety of forces. Each phase of the family allowance program was shaped by different needs, different interest groups, and different political, economic, constitutional, and social considerations; family allowances emerged and changed when a conjunction of interests was served. There was never any simple explanation for either the introduction or the demise of the family allowance program in Canada, but this history of the family allowance program demonstrates how one Canadian social security program changed from being a right of all Canadian families with children to one based solely on financial need.

Notes

Introduction

1 Library and Archives Canada, The Diaries of Prime Minister William Lyon Mackenzie King, 17 July 1945.

2 Dominique Marshall, *Aux origines sociales de l'État-providence: Familles québécoises, obligations scolaires et allocations familiales 1940-1955* (Montreal: Presses de l'Université de Montréal, 1998).

3 Jane Ursel, *Private Lives, Public Policy: 100 Years of State Intervention in the Family* (Toronto: Women's Press, 1992), especially 175-229.

4 Brigitte Kitchen, "The Introduction of Family Allowances in Canada," in *The Benevolent State in Canada: The Growth of Welfare in Canada,* ed. Allan Moscovitch and Jim Albert (Toronto: Garamond Press, 1987), 235.

5 John Macnicol, *The Movement for Family Allowances, 1918-1945: A Study in Social Policy Development* (London: Heinemann, 1980) also argues for the United Kingdom that the government introduced family allowances as a way to moderate wage demands.

6 Ursel, *Private Lives, Public Policy,* 192.

7 Heron concludes his review of Ursel's book: "In the end, Ursel's relentless effort to squeeze her historical evidence into a rigid, structuralist, theoretical mould rules out the subtler, more nuanced, and more dynamic analysis that the topic cries out for. This is the ultimate disappointment of a book that promised so much." See Craig Heron's review of *Public Lives, Public Policy* in *Canadian Historical Review* 77, 1 (March 1996): 141-42 and at http://www.utpjournals.com/product/chr/771/policy15.html.

8 See Kitchen, "The Introduction of Family Allowances in Canada," 222-41; and Dennis Guest, *The Emergence of Social Security in Canada,* 2nd ed. (Vancouver: UBC Press, 1991), 131-32.

9 On this point, see Alvin Finkel, *Social Policy and Practice in Canada: A History* (Waterloo: Wilfrid Laurier University Press, 2006), especially Chapter 6; and Dennis Guest, *The Emergence of Social Security in Canada,* 131-32.

10 James J. Rice and Michael Prince, *Changing Politics of Canadian Social Policy* (Toronto: University of Toronto Press, 2000).

11 Karl Polanyi, *The Great Transformation: The Political and Economic Origins of Our Times* (Boston: Beacon Press, 1957). Rice and Prince discuss how Polanyi continues to have relevance in understanding recent approaches to Canadian social policy in their book *Changing Politics.*

12 Harold L. Wilensky, *The Welfare State and Equality: Structural and Ideological Roots of Public Expenditure* (Berkeley: University of California Press, 1975).

13 Richard Titmuss, *Problems of Social Policy* (London: HMSO, 1950).

14 Louis Hartz, *The Founding of New Societies* (New York: Harvest Books, 1964); and Roy Lubove, *The Struggle for Social Security* (Pittsburgh: University of Pittsburgh Press, 1986).

15 Internationally, some of the major proponents of this approach are Ian Gough, *The Political Economy of the Welfare State* (London: Macmillan, 1979), and Frances Fox and Richard

Cloward, *Regulating the Poor: The Functions of Public Welfare* (New York: Pantheon Books, 1971). For the Canadian example, see Finkel, *Social Policy and Practice in Canada*, especially Chapter 6. Ursel also argues that "the driving force behind the development of the Family Allowance program was the stalemate between business and labour over wages"; Ursel, *Private Lives, Public Policy*, 191.

16 Dominique Marshall, *The Social Origins of the Welfare State: Quebec Families, Compulsory Education, and Family Allowances*, trans. Nicola Doone Danby (Waterloo: Wilfrid Laurier University Press, 2006).

17 James Struthers, *The Limits of Affluence: Welfare in Ontario, 1920-1970* (Toronto: University of Toronto Press, 1994), 9.

18 Joel F. Handler and Yeheskel Hasenfeld, *The Moral Construction of Poverty: Welfare Reform in America* (Newbury Park: Sage, 1991), 5.

19 See Cynthia R. Comacchio, *"Nations Are Built of Babies": Saving Ontario's Mothers and Children, 1900-1940* (Montreal: McGill-Queen's University Press, 1993).

20 Leslie Pal, "Revision and Retreat: Canadian Unemployment Insurance, 1971-1981," in *Canadian Social Welfare: Federal and Provincial Dimensions*, ed. Jacqueline S. Ismael (Montreal and Kingston: McGill-Queen's University Press, 1985), 85-104; Alvin Finkel, *Business and Social Reform* (Toronto: James Lorimer, 1979); and Carl J. Cuneo, "State, Class and Reserve Labour: The Case of the 1941 Canadian Unemployment Insurance Act," *Canadian Review of Sociology and Anthropology* 16, 2 (1979): 147-70.

21 Mini Abramovitz, *Regulating the Lives of Women: Social Welfare Policy from Colonial Times to the Present* (Boston: South End, 1989); Ursel, *Private Lives, Public Policy*.

22 Maureen Baker and David Tippen, *Poverty, Social Assistance and the Employability of Mothers: Restructuring Welfare States* (Toronto: University of Toronto Press, 1999).

23 Wendy McKeen, *Money in Their Own Name: The Feminist Voice in Poverty Debate in Canada, 1970-1995* (Toronto: University of Toronto Press, 2004), i-ii.

24 Nancy Christie, *Engendering the State: Family, Work, and Welfare in Canada* (Toronto: University of Toronto Press, 2000).

25 Ruth Roach Pierson, "Gender and the Unemployment Insurance Debate in Canada, 1934-40," *Labour/Le Travail* 25 (Spring 1990): 78-79.

26 Jane Lewis, *Should We Care about Family Change?* 2001 Joanne Goodman Lectures (Toronto: University of Toronto Press, 2003), 8-9.

27 Jeffrey A. Keshen, *Saints, Sinners, and Soldiers: Canada's Second World War* (Vancouver: UBC Press, 2004). See also Ann Porter, "Women and Income Security in the Post-War Period: The Case of Unemployment Insurance, 1945-1962," *Labour/Le Travail* 31 (Spring 1993): 111-44.

28 Theda Skocpol, *Protecting Soldiers and Mothers: The Political Origins of Social Policy in the United States* (Cambridge: University of Cambridge Press, 1992), 506.

29 On this point, see Richard Splane, "Social Policy-Making in the Government of Canada," in *Canadian Social Policy*, rev. ed., ed. Shankar A. Yelaja (Waterloo: Wilfrid Laurier University Press, 1987), 224-44; Daniel Patrick Moynihan, "The Professionalization of Reform," *Public Interest* 1 (Fall 1965): 9.

30 T.H. Marshall, *Citizenship and Social Class and Other Essays* (Cambridge: Cambridge University Press, 1950).

31 Keith Banting, "Social Citizenship and the Multicultural State," in *Citizenship, Diversity, and Pluralism*, ed. Alan C. Cairns et al. (Montreal and Kingston: McGill-Queen's University Press, 1999).

32 Janine Brodie, "Citizenship and Solidarity: Reflections on the Canadian Way," *Citizenship Studies* 6, 4 (2002): 377-94.

33 Janet Siltanen, "Paradise Paved? Reflections on the Fate of Social Citizenship in Canada," *Citizenship Studies* 6, 4 (2002): 395-414.

34 J. Frank Strain, "Debts Paid and Debts Owed: The Legacy of Mulroney's Economic Policy," in *The Nation Transformed: Canada and Brian Mulroney,* ed. Raymond B. Blake (Montreal and Kingston: McGill-Queen's University Press, 2007), 53-56.

35 Harold Laski, "The Obsolescence of Federalism," in *The People, Politics and the Politician,* ed. A.N. Christensen and E.M. Kirkpatrick (New York: Holt, 1941), 111-17.

36 Anthony Birch, *Federalism, Finance, and Social Legislation in Canada, Australia, and the United States* (Oxford: Oxford University Press, 1955).

37 Pierre Elliott Trudeau, "The Practice and Theory of Federalism," in *Social Purpose for Canada,* ed. M. Oliver (Toronto: University of Toronto Press, 1967), 371-93.

38 Keith Banting, "Institutional Conservatism: Federalism and Pension Reform," in *Canadian Social Welfare Policy: Federal and Provincial Dimensions,* ed. Jacqueline S. Ismael (Montreal and Kingston: McGill-Queen's University Press, 1985), 48-74.

39 On this point, see Bruno Théret, *Protection sociale et fédéralisme dans le miroir de l'Amérique du Nord* (Brussels/Montreal: P.I.E.-Peter Lang/Presses de l'Université de Montréal, 2002).

40 James P. Mulvale, *Reimaging Social Welfare: Beyond the Keynesian Welfare State* (Aurora, ON: Garamond Press, 2001).

41 Linda McQuaig, *The Quick and the Dead: Brian Mulroney, Big Business and the Seduction of Canada* (Toronto: Penguin Books, 1991), 249-51.

42 Reg Whitaker, "Neo-Conservatism and the State," in *Socialist Registrar,* ed. Ralph Miliband, Leo Panitch, and John Saville (London: Merlin Press, 1987).

43 Rice and Prince, *Changing Politics,* 236.

44 Gosta Esping-Andersen, "After the Golden Age? Welfare State Dilemmas in a Global Economy," in *Welfare States in Transition: National Adaptations in Global Economies,* ed. G. Esping-Andersen (London: Sage, 1996). Gosta Esping-Andersen developed his typology of national welfare states as liberal, conservative-corporatist, and social democratic. He defined the liberal welfare state as one that relied on means-tested benefits that targeted those who had no other means of support. All programs were funded through general taxation, and benefits were usually ungenerous and stigmatized the recipients. The conservative/corporatist welfare was essentially based on social insurance and financed through contributions from workers and employers. The benefits for those attached to the labour force were generous but much less so for those who were not working. The social democratic models provided relatively generous benefits that were available to all citizens regardless of income or labour force attachment. And like those benefits in the liberal model, they were financed through general taxation. He defined Canada's as a liberal welfare state because market forces were predominate and social welfare programs were limited and modest. G. Esping-Andersen, *Three Worlds of Welfare Capitalism* (Princeton: Princeton University Press, 1990).

45 John N. Lavis, *Political Elites and Their Influence on Health Care Reform in Canada,* Discussion Paper No. 26, Commission on the Future of Health Care in Canada, Ottawa, 10 October 2002. The concept of "high politics" is often used in the study of international relations and foreign policy to distinguish, for example, between issues among heads of state and those discussed at the level of officials.

46 Tom Courchene, *Social Canada in the Millennium: Reform Imperatives and Restructuring Principles* (Toronto: C.D. Howe Institute, 1994).

47 Rice and Prince, *Changing Politics.*

Chapter 1: The Dawning of a New Era in Social Security, 1929-43

1 Canada, *House of Commons Debates* (13 February 1929).
2 Library and Archives Canada [LAC], William Lyon Mackenzie King Papers [King Papers], series J4, vol. 211, file 2018, "Notes, re: Social and Industrial Reform," January 1935.
3 James Struthers, "In the Interests of the Children: Mothers' Allowances and the Origins of Income Security in Ontario, 1917-1930," in *Social Fabric or Patchwork Quilt: The Development of Social Policy in Canada*, ed. Raymond B. Blake and Jeff A. Keshen (Peterborough: Broadview Press, 2006), 60. For a discussion of mother's allowance in Canada, see Veronica Strong-Boag, "Wages for Housework: Mothers' Allowances and the Beginning of Social Security in Canada," *Journal of Canadian Studies* 14, 1 (Spring 1979): 24-32.
4 Leon Lebel, "Family Allowances as a Means of Preventing Emigration: A Plea for the Family of Workers so that It May Shape in the General Prosperity of the Nation" (Montreal, 1928). For a fuller discussion of this point, see Brigitte Kitchen, "The Introduction of Family Allowances in Canada," in *The Benevolent State in Canada: The Growth of Welfare in Canada*, ed. Allan Moscovitch and Jim Albert (Toronto: Garamond Press, 1987), 222-41. See also Nancy Christie, *Engendering the State: Family, Work and Welfare in Canada* (Toronto: University of Toronto Press, 2000), 178-95.
5 LAC, King Papers, series J1, vol. 154, Lebel to King, 14 May 1928.
6 Canada, House of Commons, *Select Standing Committee on Industrial and International Relations: Report, Proceedings, and Evidence* (Ottawa: King's Printer, 1929), 19. See also Dominique Marshall, *The Social Origins of the Welfare State: Quebec Families, Compulsory Education, and Family Allowances, 1940-1955*, trans. Nicola Doone Danby (Waterloo: Wilfrid Laurier University Press, 2006), especially 14-19.
7 Canada, House of Commons, *Select Standing Committee on Industrial and International Relations*, 52, 55.
8 Ibid., 56.
9 Ibid. Interestingly, Woodsworth did not push for family allowances throughout his parliamentary career. After the committee reported, he focused on such matters as basic minimum wages, collective bargaining rights, unemployment insurance, etc. Labour's opposition to family allowances might help explain his lack of interest in further pursuing family allowances. On this point, see Mark Edward Palmer, "The Origins and Implementation of Family Allowances in Canada" (MA thesis, Queen's University, Kingston, 1976). For a biography of Woodsworth, see Kenneth McNaught, *A Prophet in Politics: A Biography of J.S. Woodsworth* (Toronto: University of Toronto Press, 1959).
10 Canada, House of Commons, *Select Standing Committee on Industrial and International Relations*, 57.
11 Ibid., 68.
12 Ibid., 72.
13 Ibid., 69.
14 *Labour Gazette* (September 1929): 1011.
15 Ibid. (December 1929): 1359-65.
16 LAC, Department of National Health and Welfare, Acc. 85-86/343, box 12, file 3201-3-3, pt. 3, "Family Allowances – Jurisdiction of the Parliament of Canada," 24 December 1979.
17 LAC, King Papers, series J4, vol. 211, file 2018, "Copy of Hansard," 22 November 1932.
18 For a discussion of the Montpetit commission and social legislation in Quebec in the 1930s, see B.L. Vigod, "'The Quebec Government and Social Legislation During the 1930s': A Study in Political Self-Destruction," in *Social Welfare Policy in Canada: Historical Readings*, ed. Raymond B. Blake and Jeff Keshen (Toronto: Copp Clark, 1995), 153-66.

19 *Labour Gazette* (August 1932): 861-62.

20 LAC, The Diaries of Prime Minister William Lyon Mackenzie King [King Diaries], 15 April 1931.

21 This is largely based on Doug Owram, *The Government Generation: Canadian Intellectuals and the State, 1900-1945* (Toronto: University of Toronto Press, 1986), 160-91, especially 160 and 171.

22 Although it would take more than a decade for many of the ideas discussed from the earlier 1930s to find their way into government policy, Owram concludes that "the movement of the intellectual elite into the 'inner circles' of the parties was a matter of major historical portent." He correctly suggests that all three national parties looked to the intellectual community that "espoused a reform agenda based on the methods of the emerging social sciences and oriented toward the urban middle class." The intellectuals believed in efficiency and justice, and saw the state as the agent of change. On this, Owram argues, "There was little difference in the expression of the new reformism within the three parties." See Owram, *The Government Generation*, 189-90.

23 Nancy Christie and Michael Gauvreau, *A Full-Orbed Christianity: The Protestant Churches and Social Welfare in Canada, 1900-1940* (Montreal and Kingston: McGill-Queen's University Press, 1996).

24 See Michiel Horn, *The League for Social Reconstruction: Intellectual Origins of the Democratic Left in Canada, 1930-1942* (Toronto: University of Toronto Press, 1980).

25 Owram, *The Government Generation*, 177.

26 Ibid., 177-80.

27 Ibid., 189-90.

28 Quoted in Canada, *House of Commons Debates* (27 January 1939).

29 Owram, *The Government Generation*, 255-60.

30 See, for example, entries in the King Diaries for 13 July 1940, 9 and 15 January 1941, and 18 November 1945.

31 Reg Whitaker, *A Sovereign Idea: Essays on Canada as a Democratic Community* (Montreal and Kingston: McGill-Queen's University Press, 1992), 48.

32 *Saturday Night*, 15 August 1942, 12.

33 LAC, Ian Mackenzie Papers [Mackenzie Papers], vol. 41, file G-25-15, "Watchman – What of the Night," address delivered by Ian Mackenzie to the Canadian Club, Quebec City, 20 June 1941.

34 Blair Fraser, *The Search for Identity: Canada, 1945-1967* (Toronto: Doubleday Canada, 1967), 18-19.

35 LAC, Mackenzie Papers, vol. 4, file G-25-9, "Social Security Legislation of Other Countries," prepared by W.S. Woods, associate deputy minister in the department of pensions and health, 18 December 1942.

36 *Saturday Night*, 14 June 1941, 14-15. For a history of family allowance in the United Kingdom, see John Macnicol, *The Movement for Family Allowances, 1918-45: A Study in Social Policy Development* (London: Heinemann, 1980).

37 LAC, Mackenzie Papers, vol. 41, file G-25-15, "Notes from King's Address, The Lord Mayor's Luncheon," London, England, 4 September 1941.

38 LAC, Mackenzie Papers, vol. 41, file G-25-15, "The Rt. Hon. W.L. Mackenzie King, Prime Minister of Canada, Address to the American Federation of Labour 1942 Convention," 9 October 1942.

39 Owram, *The Government Generation*, 279.

40 See Dean Oliver, "When the Battle's Won: Military Demobilization in Canada, 1936-46" (PhD diss., York University, Toronto, 1996), 49-53.

41 LAC, King Papers, series J4, vol. 356, file 3816, Mackenzie to King, 30 October 1939; King to Mackenzie, 1 November 1939.

42 Ian Mackenzie, the minister of pensions and national health, had written King on 30 October 1939 to remind him of the problems the government had faced at the end of the Great War. He suggested that the government begin to plan for the cessation of hostilities. LAC, King Papers, series J4, vol. 856, file 3816, Mackenzie to King, 30 October 1939.

43 Canada, *House of Commons Debates* (6 December 1940).

44 LAC, Privy Council, Order-in-Council. 1218, 17 February 1941.

45 LAC, Privy Council, Order-in-Council. 6874, 2 September 1941.

46 LAC, Mackenzie Papers, "Watchman – What of the Night?" In his speeches throughout 1940 and 1941, Mackenzie never failed to speak about his vision of Canada that included a national system of social security, which he frequently claimed "nurtured and strengthened" democracy. See LAC, Mackenzie Papers, vol. 41, file G-25-15, "National Broadcast," Ian Mackenzie, 16 September 1941. On that particular occasion, Mackenzie said he wanted to reassure soldiers that their government was putting concrete plans in place for a national social security program.

47 LAC, Mackenzie Papers, "Target for Tomorrow," address by Ian Mackenzie to the Canadian Club, London, Ontario, 16 September 1942.

48 LAC, Canadian Association of Social Workers Papers, vol. 10, file 12, "Minutes of Meeting of Committee on Canada in War and Post-war Reconstruction Period," Toronto, 12 November 1942.

49 Leonard Marsh to J.L. Granatstein, 23 March 1972. Dr. J.L. Granatstein kindly allowed me to read a series of correspondence he initiated with Leonard Marsh during 1971-72.

50 LAC, Records of the Department of Finance, vol. 3583, file R-09, "Memorandum – Committee of Reconstruction," 14 June 1941; J.L. Granatstein, *Canada's War: The Politics of the Mackenzie King Government, 1939-1945* (Toronto: Oxford University Press, 1975), 257; Owram, *The Government Generation*, 282.

51 LAC, Mackenzie Papers, vol. 62, file 527-64 (5), "Statement by Dr. F. Cyril James, Chairman of the Committee on Reconstruction, before the Special Committee of the House of Commons on Reconstruction and Reestablishment," 14-15 May 1942.

52 LAC, King Papers, series J4, vol. 415, file 3993, "Report on the Reconstruction Committee's Recommendations regarding Ministerial Responsibility for Reconstruction Planning by W.C. Clark," 28 November 1942.

53 Ibid. J.L. Granatstein makes a similar argument in *The Ottawa Men: The Civil Service Mandarins, 1935-1957* (Toronto: Oxford University Press, 1998), 161-63.

54 LAC, King Papers, series J4, vol. 415, file 3993, "Report on the Reconstruction Committee's Recommendations regarding Ministerial Responsibility for Reconstruction Planning by W.C. Clark," 28 November 1942.

55 Owram, *The Government Generation*, 286.

56 LAC, Mackenzie Papers, vol. 62, file 527-64 (6), Mackenzie to James, 24 December 1942; LAC, King Papers, series J4, vol. 415, file 3993, P.C. 609, 23 January 1943.

57 See Granatstein, *The Ottawa Men*, 161-62.

58 Granatstein, *Canada's War*, 275.

59 LAC, King Diaries, 5 December 1942.

60 Ibid., 6 December 1942.

61 LAC, Mackenzie Papers, vol. 62, file 527-64 (6), Mackenzie to James, 9 December 1942.

62 See LAC, Canadian Association of Social Workers Papers, vol. 10, file 12, "Minutes of a Meeting of the Committee on Canada in the War and Post-War Reconstruction Period," Toronto, 12 November 1942.

63 LAC, Canadian Council on Social Development Papers, vol. 70, file 518 (1941-46), Davidson to Cassidy, 12 March 1943. Davidson also said that if "Mr. King stands still and does nothing for a while, he will be in good company," since neither the British nor the Americans had enacted any major policies after the release of reports in both countries advocating major social security improvements.

64 Canada, House of Commons, *Reconstruction, Social Security and Health Insurance: Two Complimentary Statements before the Special Select Committees of the House of Commons by the Hon. Ian Mackenzie* (Ottawa: King's Printer, 1943), 3. The House of Commons had established its own Special Committee on Reconstruction and Re-establishment in March 1942 and the Senate later followed with its own committee.

65 LAC, Mackenzie Papers, vol. 79, file 567-27(3), "Mackenzie Memo to Deputy Minister," 2 December 1942.

66 LAC, Mackenzie Papers, vol. 40, file G-25-9, "Social Security Legislation of Other Countries," prepared by W.S. Woods, 18 December 1942.

67 LAC, King Diaries, 5 January and 7 January 1943. In *Canada's War*, Granatstein notes that the conversation with Ian Mackenzie was "a crucial one for King, and one that marked the beginning of a new period for the Prime Minister. The issues discussed would dominate King's thinking – and the country's – to an increasing extent through 1943 and 1944. See pages 249-50.

68 LAC, King Papers, series J1, vol. 345, Mackenzie to King, 6 January 1943, 8 January 1943, and 12 January 1943.

69 LAC, King Diaries, 10 January 1943.

70 See LAC, King Papers, series J2, vol. 306, file P-875-1. One such letter came from Howard A. Hall, solicitor for the Corporation of the Township of York, Toronto, 7 December 1942. Mr. Hall reassured King, "Should your Government announce its decision to proceed along these lines [as in the Beveridge Report] it will receive the general and favourable approval of the people throughout the country."

71 LAC, King Diaries, 12 January 1943.

72 See James Struthers, *No Fault of Their Own: Unemployment and the Canadian Welfare State, 1914-1941* (Toronto: University of Toronto Press, 1983).

73 See Granatstein, *Canada's War*, 253.

74 LAC, King Diaries, 24 January, 26 January, and 17 February 1943.

75 LAC, King Diaries, 24 March 1943. In this, King was pretty much following what was happening elsewhere. When he met Churchill in Quebec on 11 August 1943, the British prime minister told him that he had outlined his commitment to social security, and that "it was necessary to devote everything to winning the war first, postponing social programmes till later." See LAC, King Diaries, 11 August 1943.

76 LAC, King Papers, series J4, vol. 415, file 3993, Rogers to King, 20 January 1943.

77 On King's role, see Raymond B. Blake, "Mackenzie King and the Genesis of Family Allowances in Canada, 1939-44," in *Social Welfare Policy in Canada: Historical Readings*, ed. Raymond B. Blake and Jeff Keshen (Toronto: Copp Clark, 1995).

Chapter 2: Family Allowance Comes to Canada, 1943-45

1 James C. Vadakin, *Children, Poverty and Family Allowances* (New York: Basic Books, 1968), 44-72. Many of those programs had features that were dramatically different from the elements of the program Canada would adopt, but those pioneering efforts elsewhere influenced Canadian policy by defining a range of tested alternatives from which Canadian decision makers could select their options. See also Mark Edward Palmer, "The Origins and Implementation of Family Allowances in Canada" (MA thesis, Queen's University, Kingston, 1976).

2 Susan Pedersen, *Family, Dependence, and the Origins of the Welfare State: Britain and France, 1914-1945* (Cambridge: Cambridge University Press, 1993). This book argues that in France the campaign for family allowances was led by a conservative group of paternalist employers, social Catholics, and those concerned about population levels in France.

3 *Saturday Night*, 14 June 1941; *Labour Gazette* (May 1932): 542.

4 *Labour Gazette* (May 1932): 542.

5 *International Labor Review*, August 1943, November 1944, and November 1945, and Provisional Bulletin #1, Inter-American Committee on Social Security, International Labour Organization, February 1943.

6 See John Macnicol, *The Movement for Family Allowances, 1918-45: A Study in Social Policy Development* (London: Heinemann, 1980).

7 Library and Archives Canada [LAC], Canadian Council of Social Development Papers, vol. 59, file 490 (1941-44), "Memorandum by the Chancellor of the Exchequer Presented to Parliament," May 1942.

8 LAC, Records of the Department of Finance [DF], vol. 304, file 101-53-114, vol. 2, Rowat to Mackintosh, 24 December 1943; *International Labor Review*, August 1943, November 1944, and November 1945.

9 See Desmond Morton, *Fight or Pay: Soldiers' Families in the Great War* (Vancouver: UBC Press, 2004).

10 LAC, William Lyon Mackenzie King Papers [King Papers], series J4, vol. 273, file 2753 (2) "Facts regarding Dependents' Allowances," 31 January 1940; LAC, Ian Mackenzie Papers [Mackenzie Papers], vol. 72, file G-25-12, "Canada's Wartime Record in the Field of Social Security," prepared by Mr. Senior, 1943.

11 LAC, Canadian Association of Social Workers Papers, vol. 10, file 8, "Report of the National Committee on Rising Cost of Living," 1942.

12 LAC, King Papers, series J4, vol. 332, file 3551, "Submission from the National Social Security Association of Canada to Prime Minister King and his Cabinet," 1941.

13 The concept of universality has been an important one in the development of Canadian social policy. While Michael Prince and James Rice have pointed out that "the theoretical case for universality does not exist as a well-codified set of hypotheses," there are a number of principles and ideas associated with the concept. For a fuller discussion of universality, see James J. Rice and Michael J. Prince, *Changing Politics of Canadian Social Policy* (Toronto: University of Toronto Press, 2000), 169-75.

14 See Sir William Beveridge, "The Report on Social Insurance and Allied Services in the United Kingdom" (London: Inter-Departmental Committee on Social Insurance and Allied Services, 1942).

15 See *Canadian Welfare* 18, 7 (1943): 3-6. Davidson also wrote, "Its chief value for Canada comes from the impetus that it will give to the development of post-war security in our largely undeveloped country."

16 J.L Granatstein, *Canada's War: The Politics of the Mackenzie King Government, 1939-1945* (Toronto: Oxford University Press, 1975), 257-58.

17 McGill University Archives, Cyril James Collection, container 192, file 2226B, James to Marsh, 8 February 1943, 17 February 1943; James to King, 5 February 1943.

18 Marsh to Granatstein, 23 October 1972. Letter in possession of J.L. Granatstein.

19 See Leonard Marsh, *Report on Social Security for Canada* (Toronto: University of Toronto Press, 1975).

20 LAC, Mackenzie Papers, vol. 41, file G-25D, "Statement by the Honourable Ian Mackenzie, Minister of Pensions and National Health before the Special Select Committee of the House of Commons on Social Security," March 1943.

21 See Toronto *Globe and Mail*, 19 March 1943.

22 See Marsh, "Report of Social Security for Canada" (Ottawa: Committee on Reconstruction, 1943).

23 See Marsh, *Report of Social Security for Canada*, especially 196-208, 1943.

24 LAC, Co-operative Commonwealth Federation Papers [CCF Papers], vol. 183, file Research – Social Security 1943-46, "The Nature and Setting of Social Security Legislation for Canada: Statement by Leonard Marsh to the Senate Special Committee on Economic Reestablishment and Social Security," 9 June 1943.

25 On 10 March 1943, just a few days before the release of the Marsh Report, President Franklin Roosevelt of the United States laid before Congress the broad outlines of an enlarged and expanded program of social security to cover Americans from the cradle to the grave and designed to ensure freedom from want in the postwar period. However, there was little immediate support for the measures in Congress. See Toronto *Globe and Mail*, 11 March 1943.

26 Montreal *Gazette*, 16 March 1943.

27 Vancouver *Province*, 15 and 16 March 1943.

28 Toronto *Globe and Mail*, 17 March 1943.

29 See LAC, Mackenzie Papers, vol. 40, file G-25 [7], "Wartime Information Board, Reports Branch, Press Survey," 15-22 March 1943.

30 LAC, Canadian Association of Social Workers Papers, vol. 65, file S-452, Elizabeth Wallace to John Bracken, 31 March 1943. A similar letter was sent to Prime Minister King.

31 LAC, DF, vol. 1883, file R170/100-1/51, "Brief by the Canadian Association of Social Workers on the Marsh Report," n.d.

32 LAC, John Bracken Papers [Bracken Papers], vol. 65, file Social Security S-452, Whitton to Bracken, 17 March 1943.

33 LAC, Bracken Papers, vol. 65, file Social Security S-452, "Memorandum to Bracken from Whitton," 2 April 1943; "Memorandum for File by R.A. Bell," 13 April 1943.

34 Correspondence between Leonard Marsh and J.L. Granatstein, December 1972 (Granatstein's personal collection). Most of the contemporary affairs journals and magazines provided offered lengthy reviews of the Marsh Report. Most were supportive, but *Public Affairs*, one of the leading journals on contemporary issues in Canada, included a lengthy review of the Marsh Report in its summer 1943 edition. Written by University of Toronto economist Dr. A.E. Grauer, the review was largely critical of children's allowances. It ridiculed Marsh for claiming that a small cash payment to parents would improve the health of Canadian children: healthy children are brought about by health measures, not cash payment to families. Moreover, Grauer claimed that Marsh took a simplistic view of the place of children in social security policy and simply extended to them the notion of social insurance in a form of universal cash benefits. It might have been more effective, if social security initiatives were to function in the very best interests of children, to begin with the educational system as a point of departure. Could not, Grauer asked, educationalists, child psychologists, nursery school experts, and experienced administrators of child welfare devise a more effective approach to solve the problems of childhood? Would not the addition of nursery schools to the public school system have a more efficacious effect, and come more cheaply than family allowances? Still, Grauer noted that the social security plans with the slogan of "cradle to the grave" protection had unusual popular and therefore political appeal. *Public Affairs* 6 (Summer 1943): 181-90.

35 D.H. Stepler, "Family Allowances for Canada," *Behind the Headlines* 3, 2 (March-April, 1943): 1-32.

36 H.M. Cassidy, *Social Security and Reconstruction in Canada* (Toronto: Ryerson Press, 1943). Cassidy's report was published in February, about three weeks before Marsh presented his report to the parliamentary committee.

37 Quoted in Stepler, "Family Allowances for Canada," 12.

38 George F. Davidson, "The Future Development of Social Security in Canada," *Canadian Welfare* 18, 7 (1943): 5.

39 LAC, Canadian Council on Social Development, vol. 59, file 490, McWilliams to Davidson, 30 March 1943; Davidson to McWilliams, 10 April 1943.

40 *Canadian Forum,* January 1943.

41 Ibid.

42 LAC, Mackenzie Papers, vol. 41, file G-25D, "Statement by the Honourable Ian Mackenzie, Minister of Pensions and National Health, before the Special Select Committee of the House of Commons on Social Security," March 1943.

43 LAC, DF, vol. 3976, file E-3-0, Bryce to Clark, 21 March 1943.

44 LAC, DF, vol. 3392, file 04747P-1, "Memorandum for Dr. MacKintosh Re: Your List of Post-War Economic Problems," 27 January 1943.

45 LAC, DF, vol. 3446, file Post-war Planning, "Constitutional Problems of Dominion Post-War Policy, 12 April 1943"; "Comments on Draft by R.B. Bryce," 19 April 1943. It was Bryce who suggested the title for the memo. Skelton commented on the memo: "The need for a comprehensive social security system is perhaps even greater from a social and political point of view if a policy of generous assistance to private business and agriculture is adopted." Bank of Canada Archives, Louis Rasminsky Papers, LR 76-196, Skelton for EAC, 3 April 1943.

46 LAC, King Papers, series J1, vol. 345, 346. Mackenzie to King, 8 October 1943.

47 LAC, King Papers, series J4, vol. 273, file 2753 (2), Robertson to King, 8 June 1943.

48 LAC, DF, vol. 3392, file 04747P-1, "Memorandum for Dr. MacKintosh Re: Your List of Post-War Economic Problems," 27 January 1943.

49 It is worthwhile noting that McTague, who was appointed national chair of the PC party in 1944, later remarked in a speech to the Seigniory Club in Toronto, "There is little use talking glibly about family allowances being a substitute for wages. No one suggests that they are. They represent a measure of social security for people whose status really requires it." See *Toronto Star,* 2 June 1944.

50 Bank of Canada Archives, Graham Towers Papers, Governor's Speeches, 1943, "Speech to CMA," 10 June 1943.

51 LAC, DF, vol. 304, file 101-53-114, vol. 1, Towers to Clark, 13 June 1943, and the enclosed memorandum, "The Case for Children's Allowances."

52 LAC, DF, vol. 304, file 101-53-114, "Memorandum of Information on Children's Allowances," 21 June 1943.

53 Ibid.

54 LAC, Department of National Health and Welfare [DNHW], vol. 1930, file R-230-000, "Eugenic Aspects of Children's Allowances by Sir William Beveridge," 16 February 1943.

55 Bank of Canada Archives, Research Department, vol. 189, file DG 100-9, Gordon to Towers, 25 June 1943, and attachments, including memo by H.R. Kemp, 23 June 1943, and memo by J.R. Beattie, 30 June 1943. Handwritten notation on letter. A copy of the letter and attachments is also in LAC, J.W. Pickersgill Papers, vol. 2, file Reconstruction, Memoranda, Speeches, Lists, 1943-45.

56 LAC, DF, vol. 304, file 101-53-114, "Memorandum of Information on Children's Allowances," 21 June 1943.

57 Bank of Canada Archives, Research Department, vol. 189, file DG 100-9, Gordon to Towers, 25 June 1943.

58 LAC, DF, vol. 498, file 121-0-7, "Draft Report of the Economic Advisory Committee on the Price and Wage Stabilization Program," 16 July 1943.

59 LAC, King Papers, series J4, vol. 415, file 3993, "Report of the Economic Advisory Committee of the Report on the Advisory Committee on Reconstruction," prepared by W.A. Mackintosh, 20 November 1943.

60 Provincial Archives of Ontario, RG 3-17, vol. 446, file 181-0 (McTague), "Public Enquiry of the National War Labour Board to the Honourable the Minister of Labour for Canada, Ottawa, Ontario," 19 August 1943. See especially 14-22.

61 *Labour Gazette* (October 1943): 382-84.

62 *Toronto Daily Star,* 5 October 1943.

63 See LAC, DF, vol. 304, file 101-53-114, unsigned memo, 9 December 1943, in R.B. Bryce's working files.

64 Queen's University Archives, W.C. Clark Papers, box 15, "Report of the Economic Advisory Committee on the National Labour Board Reports," 18 September 1943. In a memorandum on the reports of the National War Labour Board for the minister of labour, Assistant Deputy Minister Vincent C. MacDonald recommended that the government not establish a system of government-paid family allowances. See LAC, Privy Council Office Papers, vol. 46, file D-16-2, "Report to the Minister of Labour from Vincent C. MacDonald," 10 September 1943.

65 LAC, King Papers, "Memorandum for the Prime Minister, Re: War Labour Board Reports," 20 September 1943. The memorandum was also submitted to the Cabinet. Even so, in earlier drafts of the EAC's report, particularly one prepared by J.R. Beattie of the Bank of Canada, he felt strong that the committee should recommend family allowances, though for a variety of reasons; on 8 September 1943, he wrote, "The Committee feels the government should make it as clear as possible that the [family allowance] scheme is not a palliative but a permanent extension of its social policy." See Bank of Canada Archives, Research Department, vol. 184, file 3B-162, "Memo on Suggested Outlines for Report by Economic Advisory Committee," prepared by J.R. Beattie, 8 September 1943.

66 LAC, King Diaries, 14 September 1943.

67 LAC, King Papers, series J1, vol. 339, file Conant, J.B – Cuthburtson, A.D. (291382), Crerar to King, 13 October 1943.

68 LAC, DF, vol. 3448, file EAC-Agenda Material, "Memo prepared by R.B. Bryce," 17 September 1943.

69 See Dominique Marshall, *The Social Origins of the Welfare State: Quebec Families, Compulsory Education, and Family Allowances, 1940-1955,* trans. Nicola Doone Danby (Waterloo: Wilfrid Laurier University Press, 2006), 20-21; and Brigitte Kitchen, "Wartime Social Reform: The Introduction of Family Allowances," *Canadian Journal of Social Work* 7, 1 (1981): 37-45. Marshall writes, "The immediate result of federal family allowances was to quell the discontented workers." It should be noted that at this time the government had not made any public announcement on family allowances. Kitchen claims that King made no mention of family allowances when he announced his labour policy in late 1943 because if he had, family allowances would have been forever associated with low-wage policy and a means to maintain the government's wage and price stabilization policy. This is conjecture on Kitchen's part and not supported by archival evidence. It is clear that family allowances and wage rates were discussed throughout the fall of 1943, but the government (as well as King himself) wanted to move slowly on such an expensive item. The reason King did not mention family allowances in his labour policy speech was that the government had not begun to seriously discuss family allowances at that point and certainly had not made a decision of whether or not they would be introduced. What was clear, however, was that family allowances would not begin, if at all, until after victory in Europe. See also, A.W. Johnson, "Social Policy in Canada: The Past as It Conditions the Present," in

The Future of Social Welfare Systems in Canada and the United States, ed. Shirley B. Seward (Halifax: Institute for Research on Public Policy, 1987).

70 LAC, CCF Papers, vol. 154, file Research – Family Allowances, 1941-56, "Statement by M.J. Coldwell," 14 October 1943.

71 Brigitte Kitchen, "The Introduction of Family Allowances in Canada," in *The Benevolent State: The Growth of Welfare in Canada,* ed. Allan Moscovitch and Jim Albert (Toronto: Garamond Press, 1987), 236.

72 J.W. Pickersgill, *The Mackenzie King Record,* Vol. 1 (Toronto: University of Toronto Press, 1960), 591.

73 LAC, Progressive Conservative Party Papers, vol. 410, file Family Allowances, n.d., "Gallup Poll of Canada," 21 October 1943.

74 Laurel Sefton MacDowell, "The Formation of the Canadian Industrial System during World War Two," in *Canadian Working Class History: Selected Readings,* ed. Laurel Sefton MacDowell and Ian Radforth (Toronto: Canadian Scholars' Press, 1992), 575-93.

75 J.W. Pickersgill, *The Mackenzie King Record,* 599-601; Toronto *Globe and Mail,* 6 December 1943.

76 LAC, Canadian Council on Social Development, vol. 59, file 490, 1941-44, "Response to Mr. MacMillan's Questions," June 1944.

77 LAC, DF, vol. 304, file 101-53-114, "Memorandum for Mackintosh," n.d. However, a note written after 30 November 1943 attached to a memo from Bryce indicates that he was to prepare a memo for Mackintosh on family allowances.

78 Ibid.; "Notes" in Bryce's working files. All the files were passed to Clark on 6-7 January 1943. See file 101-53-114, vol. 2, "Memorandum to Dr. Mackintosh," 7 January 1943.

79 It has been argued by many who have looked at the history of social welfare in Canada that the growing support for the CCF and the labour movements prompted Prime Minister King to embrace a policy of greater social security for Canadians. Allan Moscovitch and Glenn Drover, "Social Expenditures and the Welfare State: The Canadian Experience in Historical Perspective," in *The Benevolent State: The Growth of Welfare in Canada,* ed. Allan Moscovitch and Jim Albert (Toronto: Garamond Press, 1987), 27-28; Robert Bothwell and William Kilbourn, *C.D. Howe* (Toronto: University of Toronto Press, 1979); J.L. Granatstein, *Canada's War;* L.S. MacDowall, "The Formation of the Canadian Industrial Relations System during World War Two," *Labour/Le Travail* 3 (1978): 175-96.

80 *Saturday Night,* 27 March 1943, 5-6.

81 Walter Young, *The Anatomy of a Party: The National CCF, 1932-1961* (Toronto: University of Toronto Press, 1969); Reginald Whitaker, *The Government Party: Organizing and Financing the Liberal Party of Canada 1930-58* (Toronto: University of Toronto Press, 1977).

82 Quoted in Owram, *The Government Generation: Canadian Intellectuals and the State, 1900-1945* (Toronto: University of Toronto Press), 310.

83 LAC, CCF Papers, vol. 179, file Research-Reconstruction, 1941-45, "The CCF Program for Reconstruction," 29 July 1942.

84 LAC, Bracken Papers, vol. 39, file O-150, "Policy of the Progressive Conservative Party," adopted 9-11 December 1942.

85 Owram, *The Government Generation,* 267-68.

86 Whitaker, *The Government Party,* 137-38.

87 LAC, DF, vol. 3402, files 06301 to 06400, "Resolutions Approved by Advisory Council," National Liberal Federation, 27-28 September 1943.

88 See Dean Oliver, "Public Opinion and Public Policy in Canada: Federal Legislation on War Veterans, 1936-46," in *The Welfare State in Canada: Past, Present, and Future,* ed.

Raymond B. Blake, Penny E. Bryden, and J. Frank Strain (Toronto: Irwin Publishing, 1997), 200-1.

89 LAC, Brooke Claxton Papers [Claxton Papers], vol. 2, file Reconstruction, Memoranda, Speeches, Lists, 1943-1945, "Memorandum to the Prime Minister," prepared by Claxton, 5 June 1943; LAC, King Papers, series J4, vol. 415, file 3993, "Memorandum from War Industries Board," April 1943.

90 LAC, King Papers, series J4, vol. 415, file 3994, Heeney to King, 5 June 1943.

91 LAC, CCF Papers, vol. 183, file Research – Social Security, 1943-46, "The Nature and Setting of Social Security Legislation in Canada," statement by Leonard Marsh to Senate Special Committee on Economic Re-establishment, 9 June 1943.

92 Queen's University Archives, R.C. Wallace Papers, box 9, file 13, James to King, 24 September 1943, on submitting Final Report of Advisory Committee on Reconstruction.

93 Quoted in Granatstein, *Canada's War*, 270-71.

94 LAC, King Papers, series J4, vol. 302, file 3123, "Memorandum for the Prime Minister," prepared by Claxton, 7 October 1943. See also Liberal Party, "The Task of Liberalism: Resolutions Approved by Advisory Council, National Liberal Federation, Ottawa, September 27 and 28, 1943," National Liberal Federation, Ottawa.

95 LAC, King Papers, series J1, vol. 339, King to Crerar, 5 December 1943.

96 On 1 October 1943 when the subject was raised, King had written in his diary that to give family allowances to everyone as part of a strategy to deal with the labour issue was "sheer folly" that might create much resentment toward him and his party.

97 LAC, King Diaries, 13 January 1944.

98 *Saturday Night,* 31 October 1942, 6-7.

99 *Saturday Night,* 12 July 1943, 20-21.

100 LAC, Mackenzie Papers, vol. 72, file G-25-12, "Social Security and Liberalism: The Meaning of Social Security."

101 *Saturday Night,* 15 August 1945, 12.

102 LAC, King Diaries, 6 January 1944.

103 One excellent example of gender analysis can be found in Ann Porter, *Gendered States: Women, Unemployment Insurance, and the Political Economy of the Welfare State in Canada, 1945-1997* (Toronto: University of Toronto Press, 2003).

104 Ruth Roach Pierson, "Gender and the Unemployment Insurance Debate in Canada, 1934-40," *Labour/Le Travail* 25 (Spring 1990): 78-79. On this point, also see Carol Pateman, *The Disorder of Women: Democracy, Feminism and Political Theory* (Stanford, CA: Stanford University Press, 1989), 14-17. She maintains that gender was a central but invisible method of maintaining hierarchical structures within society.

105 Jean Dominique, "Family Allowances and Family Autonomy: Quebec Families Encounter the Welfare State, 1945-1955," in *Canadian Family History: Selected Readings,* ed. Bettina Bradbury (Toronto: Copp Clark Pitman, 1992), 405. She argues that one of the "immediate" purposes of family allowances was to "promote the return of married women workers to their homes after the war." In support of this claim, she quotes Paul Martin who said that family allowances were "a long overdue tribute to the mothers of Canada." Several others have made the same claim, notably, Ruth Roach Pierson, *They're Still Women After All: The Second World War and Canadian Womanhood* (Toronto: McClelland and Stewart, 1986).

106 Nancy Christie, *Engendering the State: Family, Work, and Welfare in Canada* (Toronto: University of Toronto Press, 2000), 306-9.

107 Violet Anderson, "Part-time Work for Married Women," *Canadian Forum* 23 (April 1943), 90; Dorothy Anderson, "Feminism, 1943," *Canadian Forum* 22 (March 1943): 352-53; and *Saturday Night,* 5 December 1942, "Women in a Man's World," 28.

108 Marshall, *The Social Origins of the Welfare State,* 26.

109 LAC, National Council of Women of Canada Papers, vol. 84, file 17, "Final Report of the Subcommittee on Post-war Problems of Women of the Advisory Committee on Reconstruction," 30 November 1943.

110 LAC, King Papers, Correspondence series, vol. 345, J.A. MacKinnon to King, 19 November 1943.

111 LAC, King Papers, Correspondence series, vol. 362, Ilsley to King, 4 January 1944.

112 LAC, King Papers, Memorial and Notes series, vol. 371, file F3906, Pickersgill to King, 27 December 1943; file F3906, St. Laurent to King, 18 November 1943; series J1, vol. 342, file 293977, Howe to King, 17 November 1943.

113 LAC, King Diaries, 13 January 1944.

114 Pickersgill, *The Mackenzie King Record,* 632-33.

115 LAC, DNHW, vol. 1933, file R233-100-1-9, pt. 3, "Family Allowances in Canada: A Background Paper," by J.W. Willard, deputy minister of national welfare, 1968, 1-2.

116 LAC, King Papers, Correspondence series, vol. 362, Ilsley to King, 4 January 1944.

117 Since 1918, there had been a system of income tax credits for dependent children of taxpayers.

118 LAC, DF, vol. 304, file 101-53-114, vol. 1, Bryce to Avison, 12 January 1944. Attached is a copy of the memorandum prepared for Ilsley on children's allowances.

119 Ibid.

120 LAC, DF, vol. 304, file 101-53-114, vol. 1, "Children's Allowance," memorandum prepared for Ilsley, 12 January 1944.

121 There are many references to these points in the King Diaries. See, for example, the entries for 5 December 1942, 24 January 1943, 16 November 1944.

122 LAC, DF, vol. 304, file 101-53-114, vol. 1, "Children's Allowance," memorandum prepared for Ilsley, 12 January 1944.

123 Ibid. Emphasis in original.

124 Pickersgill, *The Mackenzie King Record,* 633.

125 LAC, Mackenzie Papers, vol. 72, file, G-25-1, Bengough to Senior, 17 September 1943.

126 In late December 1944, Mackintosh had had D.C. Rowat prepare a memorandum examining what Canada might learn from the various family allowance schemes introduced elsewhere in the world. See DF, vol. 304, file 101-53-114, vol. 2, Rowat to Mackintosh, 24 December 1943.

127 LAC, DF, vol. 304, file 101-53-114, vol. 1, "Children's Allowance," memorandum prepared for Ilsley, 12 January 1944.

128 LAC, DF, vol. 304, file 101-53-114, Clark to Ilsley, memo undated but attached to it was *Labour News,* October 1943.

129 LAC, King Diaries, 13 January 1944; on 27 December, Pickersgill had given him a list of what each minister saw as important for the government's postwar reconstruction policy, so he would know which ones supported family allowances. See LAC, King Papers, series J4, vol. 371, file F3905, "Memorandum on Postwar Reconstruction," 27 December 1943.

130 LAC, King Diaries, 13 January 1944; LAC, Claxton Papers, vol. 62, file J.W. Pickersgill, Claxton to Pickersgill, 12 January 1944.

131 LAC, King Diaries, 13 January 1944.

132 See Granatstein, *Canada's War,* 283.

133 LAC, King Diaries, 19 January 1944.

134 *Saturday Night,* 11 February 1942, 30. That the life insurance industry embraced social security is particularly noteworthy. It was an industry that was a product of individual initiative and was truly a free enterprise institution. In his support for the principle of social security, John G. Parker, president of the Canadian Life Insurance Officers Association,

noted that the various reports on social security in the Allied nations are regarded as an indication of the trend of thought with respect to problems in the postwar world. See *Saturday Night*, 12 June 1943, 38-39.

135　*Canadian Forum* 22 (February 1943): 322.

136　See Oliver, "Public Opinion and Public Policy in Canada," 207.

137　LAC, Mackenzie Papers, vol. 55, file 520-88, Mackenzie to King, 25 May 1943.

138　LAC, King Diaries, 24 January 1944.

139　*Saturday Night*, 5 February 1944, 26. *Canadian Welfare* made many of the same arguments in its editorial on 1 March 1944.

140　*Saturday Night*, 4 March 1944, 28.

141　LAC, King Papers, Memoranda and Notes series, vol. 382, file F3551, "Memorandum for Mr. Pickersgill," 29 January 1944. Robert Weaver makes an interesting argument that the introduction of family allowances in 1945 helps explain the underdevelopment of child care services in Canada. See Robert Weaver, "Understanding the Present by Exploring the Past: An Analysis of Family Allowances and Child Care in Canada" (Master of Social Work thesis, University of Regina, 2000).

142　LAC, DF, vol. 304, file 101-53-114, vol. 2, Bryce to Clark, 29 March 1944.

143　LAC, DNHW, vol. 1934, file R233-100-2, "Mr. Mackenzie King – July 25, 1944."

144　*Toronto Star*, 26 July 1944.

Chapter 3: The 1944 Family Allowance Debate and the Politics of It All

1　Library and Archives Canada [LAC], The Diaries of Prime Minister William Lyon Mackenzie King [King Diaries], 24 March and 11 August 1943.

2　LAC, Prime Minister William Lyon Mackenzie King Papers [King Papers], series J4, vol. 273, file 2753 (2) "A Reply to Mr. Bracken's Statement of June 25th, 1944."

3　Canada, *House of Commons Debates* (27 June 1944).

4　David Jay Bercuson, *True Patriot: The Life of Brooke Claxton, 1898-1960* (Toronto: University of Press, 1993), 119, 123.

5　Canada, *House of Commons Debates* (27 June 1944).

6　LAC, King Diaries, 15 June 1944; J.W. Pickersgill and D.F. Forster, eds., *The Mackenzie King Record*, Vol. 2 (Toronto: University of Toronto Press, 1968), 27-28.

7　Pickersgill and Forster, *The Mackenzie King Record*, Vol. 2, 27-28.

8　Ibid., 34-36. See also Donald Creighton, *The Forked Road: Canada 1939-1957* (Toronto: McClelland and Stewart, 1976), 88-91.

9　The resolution for family allowances was placed on the order paper under King's name. It had been decided that because the proposed legislation was primarily a matter of social security and a "fundamental Government policy," and not a primarily financial measure, King would sponsor the bill. See LAC, Records of the Department of Finance [DF], vol. 304, file 101-53-114, Ilsley to King, 8 June 1944.

10　Canada, *House of Commons Debates* (25 July 1944).

11　LAC, King Papers, series J4, vol. 273, file 2752, "Arguments for Family Allowances." This document was used by King in the parliamentary debate on family allowances.

12　Canada, *House of Commons Debates* (25 July 1944).

13　LAC, King Papers, series J4, vol. 273, file 2752, "Arguments for Family Allowances."

14　Canada, *House of Commons Debates* (26 July 1944).

15　*The Financial Post*, 29 July 1944.

16　See LAC, King Papers, series J4, vol. 273, file 2754, "Children's Allowances."

17　Canada, *House of Commons Debates* (25 July 1944); Canada, House of Commons, "Bill 161, An Act to Provide for Family Allowances," 1 August 1944.

18 LAC, DF, vol. 304, file 101-53-114, Mr. Bryce's Working Papers, "Outlines for a Possible Program of Children's Allowances."

19 LAC, Henry E. Kidd Papers, vol. 10, file Liberal Policy Reference Files, Family Allowances, file 1, "An Explanation of the Sliding Scale," n.d.

20 Canada, House of Commons, "Bill 161, An Act to Provide for Family Allowances"; LAC, King Papers, series J4, vol. 274, file 2752, "Bill No. 161, Detailed Notes on the Sections of the Bill," July 1944.

21 Canada, *House of Commons Debates* (25 July 1944).

22 Ibid.; *Ottawa Citizen*, 26 July 1944.

23 Pickersgill and Forster, *Mackenzie King Record*, Vol. 2, 37-38.

24 See J.L. Granatstein, *The Politics of Survival: The Conservative Party of Canada, 1939-45* (Toronto: University of Toronto Press, 1967), 168-70.

25 See P.T. Rouke and R.L. Schnell, *No Bleeding Heart: Charlotte Whitton, A Feminist on the Right* (Vancouver: UBC Press, 1987).

26 Ibid., 113-15.

27 LAC, John Bracken Papers [Bracken Papers], vol. 65, file Social Security S-452, Whitton to Bracken, 17 March 1943; correspondence between Leonard Marsh and J.L. Granatstein, December 1972. In the possession of J.L. Granatstein.

28 LAC, Bracken Papers, vol. 65, file S-452, "Progressive Conservatism and the Public Welfare," 9 April 1944; LAC, Gordon Graydon Papers [Graydon Papers], vol. 11, file F-100, Stevens to Graydon, 16 May 1944.

29 LAC, Bracken Papers, vol. 17, file F-100, press release, 24 June 1944; vol. 135, file Whitton, Dr. C., Whitton to Bracken, letter (n.d.) and memorandum.

30 LAC, King Papers, series J4, vol. 273, file 2753 (2) "A Reply to Mr. Bracken's Statement of June 25th, 1944."

31 Canada, *House of Commons Debates* (27 June 1944).

32 Canada, *House of Commons Debates* (25 July 1944).

33 LAC, Ian Mackenzie Papers [Mackenzie Papers], vol. 72, file G-25-1, Bengough to Senior, 17 September 1943.

34 *The Canadian Unionist* (July-August 1944): 3. By the fall of 1944, both the Canadian Congress of Labour and the Trades and Labour Congress of Canada came out in support of family allowances.

35 F.R. Scott, "The Constitution and Post-War Canada," in *Canada after the War*, ed. F.R. Scott (Toronto: Macmillan, 1943), 78.

36 Canada, *House of Commons Debates* (25 July 1944).

37 Canada, Dominion-Provincial Conference, 1935, *Record of Proceedings* (Ottawa: King's Printer, 1936), 9.

38 Donald V. Smiley, "The Rowell-Sirois Report, Provincial Autonomy and Post-war Canadian Federalism," in *Canadian Federalism: Myth or Reality*, ed. J. Peter Meekison (Toronto: Methuen Publishers, 1968), 69.

39 André Laurendeau, "Is There a Crisis in Nationalism?" in *French Canadian Nationalism: An Anthology*, ed. Ramsay Cook (Toronto: Macmillan, 1969), 269-70.

40 Canada, *House of Commons Debates* (25 July 1944).

41 LAC, Graydon Papers, vol. 22, file S-542, Esling to Graydon, 22 July 1944.

42 Canada, *House of Commons Debates* (27 July 1944); *Ottawa Citizen*, 28 July 1944. Incidentally, before the debate began in Parliament, King had asked the Canadian High Commissioner in London about the reaction in Britain to family allowances. The High Commissioner wrote King that the question of family allowances had been settled, since "all parties and all shades of public opinion practically accept[ed] the principle of family

allowances." The only matter to be settled, he said, was amount of the cash payments. See LAC, DF, vol. 777, file 334-3, High Commission to Secretary of State for External Affairs, 14 July 1944.

43 See Canada, *House of Commons Debates* (27 July 1944). See also LAC, Graydon Papers, vol. 22, file S-542.

44 See J.L. Granatstein, *The Politics of Survival*, 168-69. Granatstein suggests that at least nine MPs opposed the bill and two more had doubts, but they all realized that voting for the bill was good politics.

45 Graydon Papers, vol. 11, file F-100 Family Allowances Material, Meighen to Graydon, 20 July 1944. Senator John T. Haig also wrote Graydon that he considered Bill 161 unconditional, though he supported family allowances in principle. Haig said that because many of the taxpayers would receive little or no benefit from family allowances, the program would have little impact where Conservative candidates had a chance of success. See Graydon Papers, vol. 22, file S-542, Haig to Graydon, 22 July 1944.

46 See Herbert Bruce, *Varied Operations: An Autobiography* (Toronto: Longmans, Green, 1958); Donald Creighton, *The Forked Road: Canada, 1939-57* (Toronto: McClelland and Stewart, 1976), 90.

47 LAC, King Papers, series J4, vol. 273, file 2752, "Family Allowances." This was a memo prepared for Liberal Cabinet members during the parliamentary debate on family allowances.

48 LAC, Graydon Papers, vol. 22, file S-542, Bruce to Graydon, 20 July 1944.

49 Canada, *House of Commons Debates* (26 July 1944).

50 *Financial Times*, 4 August 1944.

51 See Mark Edward Palmer, "The Origins and Implementation of Family Allowances in Canada," (MA thesis, Queen's University, Kingston, 1976), 196-97.

52 Canada, *House of Commons Debates* (26 July 1944). See also *Toronto Daily Star*, 29 July 1944.

53 Canada, *House of Commons Debates* (26 July 1944).

54 *Toronto Star*, 26 July 1944.

55 Canada, *House of Commons Debates* (26 July 1944).

56 Toronto *Globe and Mail*, 27 July 1944.

57 LAC, Graydon Papers, vol. 81, file Family Allowances, "Memo, Progressive Conservatism and Bill 161," no date but clearly written in July 1944.

58 LAC, King Papers, series J4, vol. 273, file 2753 (2), "Memorandum for the Prime Minister," prepared by Brooke Claxton, 29 July 1944.

59 Canada, *House of Commons Debates* (31 July 1944).

60 See *Toronto Telegram*, 1 August 1944.

61 Pickersgill and Forster, *Mackenzie King Record*, Vol. 2, 39-40. A few days later, King received a letter from Mrs. Irving E. Robertson, the president of the Canadian Mothercraft Society, congratulating him on family allowances and telling him that it would make a great deal of difference to mothers. "In doing this for other mothers," she wrote, "you honor your own mother." That must have pleased him immensely. See King Papers, series J1, vol. 369, Robertson to King, 2 August 1944.

62 LAC, DF, vol. 304, file 101-53-114, Pickersgill to King, 14 June 1944.

63 LAC, King Papers, series J4, vol. 273, file 2753 (2), Claxton to King, 6 July 1944.

64 James Struthers, *The Limits of Affluence: Welfare in Ontario, 1920-1970* (Toronto: University of Toronto Press, 1994).

65 LAC, King Papers, series J1, 356, file June-July, 1944, Casselman to King, 30 June 1944.

66 Canada, *House of Commons Debates* (1 August 1944).

67 Vancouver *Daily Province,* 2 August 1944.

68 LAC, Mackenzie Papers, vol. 40, file Family Allowances, 1944, Vancouver broadcast, week of 7 August 1944.

69 LAC, Mackenzie Papers, vol. 40, file Family Allowances 1944. Casselman to Mackenzie, 19 July 1944.

70 LAC, King Papers, series J4, vol. 245, file F2515, "What Family Allowances Will Mean to You," broadcast by Claxton, 11 August 1944.

71 LAC, Co-operative Commonwealth Federation Records [CCF], vol. 154, file Research: Family Allowances, "Miss Whitton on Children's Allowances," n.d.

72 LAC, Progressive Conservative Party of Canada Papers, vol. 323, file Whitton, "Digest of Address by Dr. Charlotte Whitton," 27 January 1944.

73 LAC, Bracken Papers, vol. 65, file S-452, "Priorities in Child Care and Development: Are Cash Grants for Children First or Feasible?" address by Charlotte Whitton, 10 April 1944.

74 *Ottawa Citizen,* 26 June 1944.

75 *Public Welfare* 20, 4 (September 1944): 159.

76 *Canadian Forum* (September 1944): 123.

77 LAC, Canadian Council on Social Development, vol. 88, file Charlotte Whitton, 1945-52, Lea to Whitton, 8 September 1945; "Extract from Minutes of the Second Meeting, 1944-45, Board of Governors," Montreal, 31 July 1944. The Canadian Welfare Council had circulated a questionnaire to all board and committee members of the council to ascertain their views on family allowances. Of the forty replies returned, twenty-eight supported family allowances, six were opposed, and six were noncommittal. Based on these results, the board agreed that if the council were asked, it would state its support for family allowances.

78 LAC, Canadian Association of Social Workers, vol. 39, file 39-25, Family Allowances, "Excerpt from Minutes of Board of Directors," 19 July 1944.

79 *Ottawa Citizen,* 13 July 1944.

80 LAC, King Papers, series J4, vol. 427, file P.C.O. War Comm. Memo, 1944, W.I.B. Survey, 30 June and 29 July 1944.

81 Findings of poll reported in the *Edmonton Journal,* 3 August 1944. See Montreal *Gazette,* 18 October 1944. A letter to the editor commented on the fact that women had been remarkably silent on the issue. The writer asked, "Are women hopeless, filled with apathy or ignorant, that this most vital piece of legislation does not stir them to utterance and action either for or against the proposals of the King government?"

82 These polls were taken by the Canadian Institute of Public Opinion.

83 LAC, Bracken Papers, vol. 81, file Family Allowances, "Memorandum from George Drew, Re: Family Allowances," 19 July 1944.

84 LAC, George Drew Papers, vol. 305, file 182, "Premier George Drew, Speaking to Progressive Conservative Rally at Richmond Hill," 2 August 1944; *Ottawa Journal,* 3 August 1944.

85 LAC, George Drew Papers, vol. 305, file 1893b, "Address by Premier George Drew, Eastern Progressive Conservative Association," General Meeting, Ottawa, 29 September 1944; *Winnipeg Free Press,* 24 August 1944.

86 Text of Drew's speech appeared in the *Financial Post,* 24 August 1944 and Toronto *Globe and Mail,* 10 August 1944.

87 Toronto *Globe and Mail,* 13 October 1944.

88 LAC, Bracken Papers, vol. 81, file Family Allowances, Lamont to Bell, 4 October 1944.

89 *Winnipeg Free Press,* 23 August 1944.

90 *Winnipeg Free Press,* 1 August 1944; *Toronto Star,* 10 August 1944.

91 Toronto *Globe and Mail,* 14 August 1944.

92 *Winnipeg Free Press,* 10, 18, and 21 August 1944.

93 On this point, see Alvin Finkel, *Social Policy and Practice in Canada: A History* (Waterloo: Wilfrid Laurier University Press, 2006), 134-44.

94 Montreal *Gazette,* 25 September 1944. Garson introduced the Manitoba Health Plan in the legislature in 1944. Garson had conceived the health plan on what he described as a "carefully considered" and "very economic basis." Two basic goals underlay the health proposals: first, the prevention of disease, and second, the provision of a variety of services, including curative medical services, hospitalization, dental care, and nursing services, to all residents of Manitoba. The plan proposed the provision of full-time public health service as a cost that the population could afford. This would assist in the prevention of illness and the promotion of health. The plan also included the provision of diagnostic facilities, such as X-ray and laboratory services, without cost to the patients. The third basic principle of the Health Service Plan was to provide a family doctor for all Manitobans. Yet Garson believed that the plan would not be complete with the provision of hospital facilities in rural communities. The program, he maintained, could not be delivered unless the federal government provided much of the funding. As Garson told the Dominion-Provincial Conference in 1945-46, "The first and most important grants that should be made by the Federal Government are those having to do with Public Health and Preventive Medicine, and of these the most urgent is a grant to assist the provinces to establish throughout their rural areas proper preventive services." Archives of Manitoba, GR 3151, Attorney General's Department, Deputy Minister's Office, box N-14-5-18, Dominion-Provincial Conference, April 1946, and Dominion-Provincial Conference, 1945, *Dominion and Provincial Submissions and Plenary Conference Discussions* (Ottawa: King's Printer, 1946), 157-58.

95 Toronto *Globe and Mail,* 29 August 1944.

96 Toronto *Globe and Mail,* 3 and 4 October 1944.

97 Montreal *Gazette,* 30 September 1944.

98 *Ottawa Journal,* 11 August 1944.

99 LAC, Stanley Knowles Papers, vol. 428, file 51-B(2), "Family Allowances: National Need or Political Football," radio address by Edward B. Jolliffe, 13 September 1944; LAC, CCF, vol. 50, file Ontario Council and Executive Minutes, "Minutes, Provincial Council," 10 September 1944.

100 LAC, King Papers, series J1, vol. 341, November-December 1943. Godbout to King, 1 December 1943. On the Quebec contributory plan, see Dominique Marshall, *The Social Origins of the Welfare State: Quebec Families, Compulsory Education, and Family Allowances, 1940-1955,* trans. Nicola Doone Danby (Waterloo: Wilfrid Laurier University Press, 2006), 18 and 29.

101 LAC, King Papers, series J1, vol. 359, June-July 1944. "Wartime Information Board," 31 July 1944.

102 LAC, King Papers, series J1, vol. 369, August-September 1944, "Quebec Board of Trade to King," 1 August 1944.

103 *Ottawa Journal,* 8 October 1944.

104 *Ottawa Journal,* 25 July 1944; Toronto *Globe and Mail,* 24 June 1944; Montreal *Gazette,* 26 June 1944; Winnipeg *Tribune,* 29 July 1944; Vancouver *Daily Province,* 28 June 1944; *Toronto Daily Star,* 17 July and 9 September 1944.

105 Grant Dexter, *Family Allowances: An Analysis* (Winnipeg: Free Press, 1944); and *Winnipeg Free Press,* 1 August 1944.

106 LAC, King Papers, vol. 356, file 3816, Claxton to King, 21 December 1943.

107 LAC, King Papers, vol. 301, file 3112, Claxton to King, 28 June 1944.
108 LAC, H.E. Kidd Papers, vol. 1, file July 1944, Kidd to Claxton, 17 July 1944.
109 LAC, H.E. Kidd Papers, vol. 10, file 1, Kidd to Fortin, 28 July 1944, and attachment; LAC, King Papers, vol. 273, file 2753 (2), Claxton to King, 29 July 1944.
110 LAC, Liberal Party Papers, vol. 606, file 13, Kidd to McLean, 19 September 1944; Kidd to Hale, 22 September 1944.
111 LAC, King Papers, series J2, vol. 256, file 450, Tweed to Pickersgill, 15 August 1944.
112 *The Canadian Unionist* (July-August 1944): 3.
113 LAC, King Papers, series J1, vol. 360, Fenwick to King, 9 August 1944.
114 LAC, King Papers, series J1, vol. 356, file July-August, 1944, Alfred Charpentier, president of the Canadian and Catholic Confederation of Labour, to Humphrey Mitchell, minister of labour, 31 July 1944.
115 LAC, King Papers, series J1, vol. 368, file August, 1944, Parkin to King, 3 August 1944.
116 LAC, DF, vol. 497, file 121-0-7-7-1 to 25, vol. 1, "Memorandum of the Canadian and Catholic Confederation of Labour to the Federal Cabinet," March 1945, and "Memorandum Presented to the Dominion Government by the Trades and Labour Congress Canada," 25 February 1945.
117 See J.L. Granatstein, *The Politics of Survival*, especially 176-97.
118 LAC, King Diaries, 30 July 1944.

Chapter 4: Sharing the Wealth

1 Claxton became the first minister of the newly created department. See David Jay Bercuson, *True Patriot: The Life of Brooke Claxton, 1898-1960* (Toronto: University of Toronto Press, 1993).
2 Library and Archives Canada [LAC], William Lyon Mackenzie King Papers [King Papers], series J4, vol. 273, file 2753 (2), Claxton to King, 27 July 1944; LAC, Records of the Department of Finance [DF], vol. 304, file 101-53-114, vol. 2, Bryce to Claxton, 26 July 1944.
3 LAC, DF, vol. 304, file 101-53-114, "Implications of Social Security Measures for Vital Statistics," prepared by the Department of Finance in collaboration with the Dominion Bureau of Statistics, 1945.
4 LAC, DF, vol. 304, file 101-53-114, "An Agreement between the Government of the Dominion of Canada and the Governments of the Several Provinces of Canada regarding the Registration of Births, Marriages and Deaths," no date but notes that meeting was held 28 September 1944.
5 LAC, Brooke Claxton Papers [Claxton Papers], vol. 167, file Family Allowances, "Statement regarding Possibilities of Obtaining Birth Certificates and Death Lists in Each Province," n.d.
6 LAC, King Papers, series J1, vol. 381, 31 January-3 May 1944, Duplessis to King, 31 January 1945; King to Duplessis, 3 February 1945.
7 Montreal *Gazette*, 21 February 1945.
8 *Ottawa Citizen*, 22 December 1944.
9 LAC, H.E. Kidd Papers, vol. 10, file Liberal Policy Reference, "National Health and Welfare Registration Campaign," 7 February 1945.
10 *Montreal Star*, 15 December 1944; LAC, Canadian Council on Social Development, vol. 111, file 778, Maines to Claxton, 23 December 1944; LAC, Canadian Association of Social Workers, vol. 39, file 39-25, Taylor to Maines, 21 December 1944, and Davidson to Maines, 27 December 1944.
11 See http://www.collectionscanada.gc.ca/women/002026-823-e.html.
12 J.W. Pickersgill and D.F. Forster, *The Mackenzie King Record*, Vol. 2 (Toronto: University of Toronto Press, 1968), 420.

13 LAC, Canadian Federation of Business and Professional Clubs, vol. 8, file Family Allow-ances, Thornton to Davidson, 19 April 1945, and Davidson to Thornton, 23 April 1945.

14 LAC, King Papers, series J1, vol. 379, Microfilm C9872, Casgrain to King, 8 June 1945. After the government announced that it would pay Quebec mothers, Casgrain wrote King, "I want to thank you with all my heart for having spared the women of Quebec from a most humiliating and most unnecessary discrimination"; Casgrain to King, 3 July 1945.

15 *Ottawa Citizen,* 3 July 1945.

16 LAC, Department of National Health and Welfare [DNHW], Acc. 85-86/343, box 38, file 3301-3-516, "Gallup Poll of Canada," 18 August 1999.

17 LAC, King Papers, series J1, vol. 381, Finlayson to King, 3 August 1945.

18 Montreal *Gazette,* 10 January 1945.

19 *Ottawa Journal,* 6 February 1944.

20 LAC, Claxton Papers, vol. 167, file Family Allowances, "Speech by Honourable Brooke Claxton, Minister of National Health and Welfare to the Rotary Club," Charlottetown, 19 February 1945; *Ottawa Citizen,* 6 February 1945; LAC, H.E. Kidd Papers, vol. 10, file Liberal Party Reference Files, Family Allowances, vol. 1, "Registration Campaign," 7 February 1945.

21 LAC, Claxton Papers, vol. 195, file Speeches – Election, 1945, "Speech by the Honourable Brooke Claxton, Minister of National Health and Welfare, to the Canadian Club," Van-couver, 12 March 1945.

22 For a discussion of the Declaration of the Rights of Children, see C.M.S McGlynn, *Families and the European Union: Law, Politics and Pluralism* (Cambridge: Cambridge University Press, 2006).

23 LAC, DNHW, vol. 1933, file R233-100-1-9, pt. 1, Claxton to King, 15 February 1945. Similar letters were sent to all Members of Parliament. See LAC, Claxton Papers, vol. 167, file Family Allowances, "Family Allowances: A Children's Charter."

24 LAC, Claxton Papers, vol. 196, file Speeches – Election 1945, "Family Allowances," May 1945.

25 LAC, Canadian Council on Social Development, vol. 111, file 778, Family Allowance Regis-tration Form and accompanying guide.

26 LAC, H.E. Kidd Papers, vol. 10, file 4, "Proofs for the Announcements Which Will Appear throughout Canada in Connection with the Registration of Children for Family Allowances."

27 LAC, Claxton Papers, vol. 196, file Speeches – Election 1945, "Speech by the Honourable Brooke Claxton, Minister of National Health and Welfare, over the National Network of the CBC," 22 March 1945; Montreal *Gazette,* 22 March 1945.

28 The deputy minister of national revenue for taxation subsequently prepared a memoran-dum for all employers explaining the changes and a form for all employees to complete so that the necessary adjustments to their income tax deductions could be made at source on the pay-as-you-earn program. See LAC, Canadian Council on Social Development, Department of National Revenue, vol. 59, file 490, "Income Tax Deductions and Family Allowance Payments," June 1945.

29 LAC, DNHW, Acc. 86-87/049, box 2, file 180-14-1, Boutin to Claxton, 6 April 1945.

30 LAC, King Papers, series J1, vol. 381, Wartime Information Board, "Wartime Information Board Reports," 26 March and 9 April 1945.

31 *New York Times,* 25 April 1945.

32 LAC, DNHW, Acc. 86-87/049, box 1, file 180-14-1, P.C. 3180, 1 May 1945.

33 LAC, National Liberal Federation Papers, vol. 604, "Radio Speech by Mrs. S.C. Tweed," no date, but sometime after 20 May 1945.

34 LAC, DNHW, Acc. 85-86/343, box 38, file 3301-3-516, "Gallup Poll of Canada," 30 May 1945.

35 LAC, Claxton Papers, vol. 196, file Speeches – Election 1945, "Speech by the Honourable Brooke Claxton, Minister of National Health and Welfare, over the National Network of the CBC," 17 July 1945.

36 Ibid.

37 LAC, Claxton Papers, vol. 167, file Family Allowances, "Advertisement Issued by the Department of National Health and Welfare."

38 See LAC, Claxton Papers, vol. 167, file Family Allowances, "Broadcast by Honourable Brooke Claxton," 19 April 1945; vol. 196, file Speeches – Election 1945, "Address on Family Allowances."

39 LAC, DNHW, vol. 537, file 135-0-167, "Proposals of the Government of Canada," Dominion-Provincial Conference on Reconstruction, August 1945.

40 For a discussion of Indian welfare policy, see Hugh E.Q. Shewell, *"Enough to Keep Them Alive": Indian Social Welfare in Canada, 1873-1965* (Toronto: University of Toronto Press, 2004).

41 LAC, DNHW, vol. 1934, file R233-100-2, "Family Allowances Regulations," 3 August 1945.

42 Montreal *Gazette*, 22 March 1945.

43 LAC, DNHW, vol. 1934, file R233-100-2, "Family Allowances Regulations," 3 August 1945.

44 P.G. Nixon, "The Welfare State North: Early Developments in Inuit Security," *Journal of Canadian Studies* 25, 2 (1990): 144-54. See also Ronald Manzer, *Policies and Political Development in Canada* (Toronto: University of Toronto Press, 1985), 335.

45 LAC, DNHW, vol. 2361, file 264-3-1, "Memo Prepared by Director of Indian Affairs Branch, Department of Mines and Resources, re: School Attendance," 16 April 1945.

46 LAC, DNHW, vol. 1934, file R233-100-2, "Family Allowances Regulations," 3 August 1945.

47 Canada, National Energy Board, *The Report of the Mackenzie Valley Pipeline Inquiry,* Vol. 1 (Ottawa: Queen's Printer, 1977), 85-87.

48 LAC, The Diaries of William Lyon Mackenzie King [King Diaries], 12 April 1945. Premier George Drew of Ontario had already called a provincial election for 11 June, but Liberal Party strategists believed that having the Ontario provincial election and the federal election concurrently would work to the advantages of the Liberal Party.

49 Quoted in J.L. Granatstein, *Canada's War: The Politics of the Mackenzie King Government 1939-45* (Toronto: Oxford University Press, 1975), 403.

50 LAC, King Papers, series 1, vol. 382, Microfilm C9874, Address, *Mackenzie King to the People of Canada* (Ottawa, 16 May 1945), 5-18.

51 Quoted in Granatstein, *Canada's War,* 406; *Mackenzie King to the People of Canada,* 39.

52 LAC, Progressive Conservative Party Papers, vol. 306, file Family Allowances, 1945, Bell to Hargreaves, 10 April 1945.

53 *Toronto Star,* 2 May 1945.

54 LAC, Claxton Papers, vol. 196, file Speeches – Election 1945, "Broadcast by Honourable Brooke Claxton, Minister of National Health and Welfare, over Radio Station CKPR, at Fort William," May 1945.

55 LAC, Claxton Papers, vol. 167, file Family Allowances, "Building a New Social Order in Canada" leaflet, prepared by the National Liberal Federation.

56 Ibid.

57 LAC, DNHW, vol. 3402, file 06301, "Opportunities for All," prepared by the National Liberal Federation, 1945.

58 LAC, King Papers, series J1, vol. 387, 5 March-15 March 1945, MacLean to King, 6 March 1945.

59 LAC, H.E. Kidd Papers, vol. 10, file Liberal Policy Reference: Family Allowances, file 1, "Family Allowances."

60 LAC, National Liberal Federation Papers, vol. 604, file Family Allowances, 1945, "Family Allowances, A Suggested 14-Minute Radio Talk."

61 This was prepared in the DNHW at Claxton's request for the National Liberal Federation. See LAC, Claxton Papers, vol. 44, file Kidd, H.E., Claxton to Kidd, 2 April 1945.

62 LAC, Claxton Papers, vol. 152, file Speech Material, "Bulletins to Candidates and Speakers from the National Liberal Committee, Ottawa," nos. 13 and 15, 2 May 1945. The Ontario Liberal Association also used family allowances as an item in the provincial campaign that overlapped with the federal election. In one of its campaign bulletins, it provided estimates of monthly family allowance payments to the federal constituencies in Ontario. See LAC, King Papers, series J4, vol. 273, file 2753 (2), "Bulletin No. 10 Sent to Provincial Candidates from the Ontario Liberal Association," 14 May 1945.

63 LAC, King Papers, series J4, vol. 273, file 2753 (2), Claxton to all senators, Members of Parliament and candidates, 10 May 1945.

64 LAC, King Papers, series J6, vol. 110, file 10, "Quotable Quotes for Editorial Page Fillers," compiled by the National Liberal Committee, Ottawa, 15 May 1945.

65 LAC, John Bracken Papers [Bracken Papers], vol. 128, file Speech – Gen. Election 1945, "Text of Speech by Honourable John Bracken, Kenora, Ontario," 19 May 1945.

66 The Family Allowances Act reduced payments for each child beginning with the fifth child in each family.

67 LAC, Progressive Conservatives Party Papers, vol. 436, file Social Security, "Here Is Your Plan for Social Security," prepared by PC Party, 1945.

68 See *Public Opinion Quarterly* IX (Summer 1945): 237.

69 See J.L. Granatstein, *The Politics of Survival: The Conservative Party of Canada, 1939-45* (Toronto: University of Toronto Press, 1967), 196-97.

70 LAC, King Papers, series J4, vol. 98, file, Confidential Memo to Cabinet, "Memorandum to Cabinet," 18 June 1945. For an overview of the 1945 election, see Granatstein, *Canada's War*, 382-418.

71 Except in Charlottetown and Fredericton, which did not have such organizations. In Charlottetown, the Red Cross Administrative Corps was enlisted instead.

72 LAC, DNHW, vol. 913, file National Registration – Family Allowances, Davidson to Ross, 31 January 1945; Claxton to LaFleche, 16 January 1945; Davidson to West, 13 February 1945.

73 LAC, King Papers, series J1, vol. 380, Microfilm C9872, Claxton to King, 20 August 1945.

74 Joseph W. Willard, "Family Allowances in Canada," in *Children's Allowances and the Economic Welfare of Children*, ed. E. Burns (New York: Citizen's Committee of New York, 1968), 64-65.

75 LAC, DF, vol. 304, file 101-53-114, vol. 2, Davidson to McIntyre, 30 July 1945.

76 LAC, Bracken Papers, vol. 17, file F-100, Brunet to Bracken, 20 September 1945; Bracken to Brunet, 10 October 1945; LAC, King Papers, series J1, vol. 387, Microfilm C9877, Marion to King, 28 September 1945; King to Marion, 24 September 1945; vol. 378, Microfilm C9877, Vanier to Claxton, August 1949.

77 LAC, King Papers, series J1, vol. 397, Microfilm C9887, Wilson to King, August 1945.

78 LAC, Claxton Papers, vol. 167, file Family Allowances, extracts from letters, 15 November 1945; *Toronto Daily Star*, 20 December 1945.

79 LAC, Bracken Papers, vol. 17, file F-100, Stephen to Bracken, 29 September 1945, and enclosed copy of North American Life Assurance Company brochure "For the Children."

80 LAC, Canadian Association of Social Workers, vol. 10, file 18, "The Baby Bonus and Savings Accounts," by Charlotte Whitton, September 1945.
81 *Toronto Daily Star,* 20 December 1945.

Chapter 5: The Impact of Family Allowances up to the 1960s

1 On this point, see Dominique Marshall, *The Social Origins of the Welfare State: Quebec Families, Compulsory Education and Family Allowances, 1940-1955,* trans. Nicola Doone Danby (Waterloo: Wilfrid Laurier University Press, 2006), 71-94.
2 Library and Archives Canada [LAC], Brooke Claxton Papers, vol. 167, file Family Allow- ances, "Address by the Honourable Brooke Claxton, Minister of National Health and Welfare, to the National Catholic Welfare Conference at Washington, DC," 6 February 1946.
3 The biggest change in social security (aside from family allowances) came in 1951 with the enactment of the national and universal pension paid under the Old Age Security Act, supplemented by the means-tested, cost-shared benefits made available under the Old Age Assistance Act. These two acts replaced the 1927 Old Age Pension Act and came into force on 1 January 1952.
4 One of the best studies of the impact of family allowances (and compulsory education) in Quebec is Dominique Marshall, *Aux origines sociales de l'État-providence: Familles québécoises, obligations scolaire et allocations familiales, 1940-1955* (Montreal: Presses de l'Université de Montréal, 1998).
5 See LAC, Records of the Department of National Health and Welfare [DNHW], vol. 1283, file 266-5-45, "Annual Report of the Family Allowance Division of the Welfare Branch of the Department of National Health and Welfare for the Year Ending 31 March 1946," 1-10, 1 April 1946; Regina *Leader-Post,* 16 March 1946; LAC, Canadian Council on Social De- velopment, vol. 59, file 490 (1943-48), "Synopsis of Ontario Farm Radio Forum Findings, 4 February 1946."
6 LAC, DNHW, vol. 1283, file 266-5-45, "Annual Report of the Family Allowance Division of the Welfare Branch of the Department of National Health and Welfare for the Year Ending 31 March 1946," 1 April 1946.
7 See Veronica Strong-Boag, "Wages for Housework: Mothers' Allowances and the Begin- ning of Social Security in Canada," *Journal of Canadian Studies/Revue d'études canadiennes* 12, 1 (1979): 24-34.
8 See LAC, Canadian Council on Social Development, vol. 58, file 490 (1944-64), R.H. Par- kinson, assistance national director of family allowances, to George Caldwell, associate executive secretary, Canadian Welfare Council, 15 April 1964.
9 LAC, DNHW, vol. 1283, file 266-5-45, "Annual Report of the Family Allowance Division of the Welfare Branch of the Department of National Health and Welfare for the Year Ending 31 March 1946," 1 April 1946; Statistics Canada, W67-93, "Total Enrolment and Percentage of Average Daily Attendance in Public and Secondary Schools, 1920-75."
10 Marshall, *The Social Origins of the Welfare State,* 61-69.
11 LAC, Brooke Claxton Papers, vol. 167, file Family Allowances, "Address by the Honourable Brooke Claxton, Minister of National Health and Welfare, to the National Catholic Welfare Conference at Washington, DC, 6 February 1946"; and Statistics Canada, W67-93, "Total Enrolment and Percentage of Average Daily Attendance in Public and Secondary Schools, 1920-1975."
12 Regina *Leader-Post,* 16 March 1946.
13 LAC, Canadian Council on Social Development, vol. 59, file 490 (1943-48), Jackson to Lichstein, 3 May 1946.

14 LAC, Canadian Council on Social Development, vol. 59, file 490 (1943-48), "Synopsis of Ontario Farm Radio Forum Findings," 4 February 1946.

15 LAC, Prime Minister William Lyon Mackenzie King Papers [King Papers], series J1, vol. 403, Microfilm C9169, Estey to Matte, 5 April 1946. The article was eventually published in the magazine *Health* and it provided the source for an editorial in the *Ottawa Citizen* on 27 August 1947.

16 LAC, Canadian Council on Social Development, vol. 59, file 490 (1943-48), "Notes on Speech Made by Dr. George Davidson at Children's Aid Annual Meeting," 27 May 1946.

17 Many parents informed the regional office when their children reached their sixteenth birthdays and hence became ineligible for family allowances. One parent from Toronto so informed the department in October 1963 just after her son turned sixteen, noting her appreciation for the monthly cheques. See LAC, DNHW, vol. 2357, file 260-1-1, pt. 1.

18 It must be recognized that factors other than the payment of family allowances may have also played a role in the increased consumption of milk. For instance, there was a serious shortage of soft drinks immediately after the war. The repatriation of increased numbers of servicemen from Europe also caused a rapid increase in milk consumption.

19 *Toronto Evening Telegram*, 1, 8, and 18 February 1947.

20 *Canadian Home Journal* (June 1947): 11-13.

21 See, for example, LAC, Canadian Council on Social Development, vol. 59, file 490 (1943-48), Tousel to Krughoff, 19 January 1949. Bessie Tousel, assistant executive director of the Canadian Welfare Council, had obviously discussed this with George Davidson, the deputy minister of national health and welfare. She wrote, "Both George and I feel that an article done by an American visitor will be preferable than one done by someone in government. Reports by the departmental people themselves could not, I think, carry the value in reports that outsider's [sic] writing might do." LAC, Louis St. Laurent Papers [St. Laurent Papers], vol. 11, file 50-D, copy of "Family Allowances in Canada"; *Canadian Welfare* (December 1946): 11-12.

22 LAC, DNHW, Acc. 85-86/343, box 38, file 3303-3-516, "Canadian Institute of Public Opinion," 2 July 1947; "Gallup Poll of Canada," 15 May 1948; "Gallup Poll of Canada," 17 May 1950.

23 See *Toronto Star,* 12 March 1953. In the same poll, 57% agreed that the age limit for family allowances should be raised from sixteen to eighteen years.

24 T.H. Marshall, "Citizenship and Social Class," in *Citizenship and Class* [1950], ed. T.H. Marshall and T. Bottomore (London: Pluto Press, 1992); Keith Banting, "Social Citizenship and the Multicultural State," in *Citizenship, Diversity, and Pluralism,* ed. Alan C. Cairns et al. (Montreal and Kingston: McGill-Queen's University Press, 1999). For a more recent essay on these ideas, see Janine Brodie, "Citizenship and Solidarity: Reflections on the Canadian Way," *Citizenship Studies* 6, 4 (December 2002): 377-94.

25 Raymond B. Blake, *Canadians At Last: Canada Integrates Newfoundland as a Province* (Toronto: University of Toronto Press, 1994, 2004), chap. 3, "Sharing the Wealth."

26 Edward E. Schwartz, "Some Observations of the Canadian Family Allowances Program," *Social Service Review* 10, 4 (December 1946): 1-23.

27 See LAC, Canadian Council on Social Development, vol. 58, file 490 (1944-46), Elinor Barnstead, "The Experience of Private Family Agencies in Regard to Family Allowances during the First Year of their Operation," presented at the Canadian Conference of Social Work, Halifax, 28 June 1946.

28 Schwartz, "Some Observations," 1-23.

29 Ibid.

30 See LAC, St. Laurent Papers, vol. 11, file 50-D, Field, executive assistant to Paul Martin, to Bernier, 13 August 1947.

31 LAC, Ian A. Mackenzie Papers [Mackenzie Papers], vol. 41, file G-25-A, press release: "Family Allowances," issued by Paul Martin, 1 July 1947.

32 See LAC, St. Laurent Papers, vol. 11, file 50-D, Family Allowances, 1946-47.

33 George F. Davidson, "Canada's Family Allowances in Retrospect," *Children* 4, 3 (May-June, 1957): 15-28; R.H. Parkinson, "Ten Years of Family Allowances," *Canadian Welfare* (November 1955): 195-200.

34 Canada. Report of the Department of National Revenue for the fiscal year ended 31 March 1954 (Ottawa, Queen's Printer, 1954).

35 LAC, DNHW, vol. 1931, file R233/100, pt. 1, "Ten Years of Family Allowances," by R.H. Parkinson, 1 November 1955.

36 Ibid. This essay was also published in *Canadian Welfare* in November 1955. The view that family allowances had proven beneficial was shared by the *Toronto Star*. In its editorial on 7 July 1955, it asserted, "All the good predicted for family allowances has been realized, none of the woes forecast by its opponents has come to pass."

37 Davidson, "Canada's Family Allowances in Retrospect." See also LAC, Richard A. Bell Papers [Bell Papers], vol. 22, file Family Allowances, 1958-68. The Union of Electors in Montreal circulated a petition in 1958 calling for the doubling of family allowances to restore to the program their original purchasing power.

38 Statistics Canada, Historical Statistics of Canada, H19_34(1) "Federal Government Expenditure by Category, 1867-1975."

39 LAC, Records of the Department of Finance [DF], vol. 304, file 101-53-114, vol. 2, Davidson to Clark, 23 March 1948; Clark to Bryce, 4 May 1946. Louis St. Laurent had said during the debate on the family allowance bill: "We believe that strangers should not benefit from the allowances simply by having crossed our borders. A certain amount of time must pass as proof of their intention to stay in our country." Cited in Marshall, *The Social Origins of the Welfare State*, 77.

40 LAC, Records of the Privy Council Office, vol. 1934, file R-233-100-3, pt. 2, "Memorandum to Cabinet," 29 November 1948; LAC, DF, vol. 304, file 101-53-114, vol. 2, "An Act to Amend the Family Allowances Act, 1944," assented to 30 April 1949; Paul Martin, *A Very Public Life*, Vol. 2 (Toronto: Deneau, 1985), 62-63.

41 Toronto *Globe and Mail*, 4 February 1949.

42 LAC, Bell Papers, vol. 78, file I-2-50B, "Memo Prepared for Deputy Minister in Department of Citizenship and Immigration," 17 June 1958.

43 LAC, J.W. Pickersgill Papers, vol. 53, file I-2-4103A, Martin to Pickersgill, 23 September 1954. In his letter, Martin quotes from the one he had sent to Harris on 5 March 1952.

44 LAC, Canadian Council on Social Development, vol. 58, file 490, "Note Prepared in the Department of National Health and Welfare," 1 October 1954, signed by B.G.

45 Statistics Canada, Historical Statistics of Canada, A350, "Immigrant Arrivals in Canada, 1852-1977."

46 LAC, Bell Papers, vol. 78, file I-2-50B, "Memo Prepared for Deputy Minister in Department of Citizenship and Immigration," 17 June 1958.

47 LAC, Canadian Council on Social Development, vol. 58, file 490 (1944-64), "Resolutions on Family Allowances to Immigrants Passed by Various Organizations," 9 June 1955; LAC, Bell Papers, vol. 78, file I-2-50B, Richard E.G. Davis, executive director, Canadian Welfare Council, to J. Waldo Monteith, minister of national health and welfare, 20 May 1958. Other organizations included the Canadian Citizenship Council Catholic Women's League of Canada, the Canadian Red Cross Society, National Seminar on Citizenship, Welfare Council of Toronto, Canadian Congress of Labour, Canadian Federation of Agriculture, Confédération des travailleurs catholiques du Canada, and the New Canadians and Citizenship of Regina.

48 LAC, J.W. Pickersgill Papers, vol. 53, file I-2-4103A, Martin to Pickersgill, 23 September 1954.

49 LAC, Privy Council Office Papers, Acc. 90-91/154, box 80, file 5-60-4, Pickersgill to Martin, 31 October 1955. Letters were also sent to other Cabinet ministers.

50 LAC, J.W. Pickersgill Papers, vol. 53, file I-2-4103A, "Memorandum for Cabinet," prepared by J.W. Pickersgill, 24 January 1956.

51 Canada, *House of Commons Debates* (19 March 1956).

52 LAC, J.W. Pickersgill Papers, vol. 53, file I-2-4103A (1956-57), "Information to Be Included on the Reverse of the Application Form for Family Assistance," 22 March 1956; "Family Assistance for Immigrants and Settlers," approved by Pickersgill, 27 April 1956; LAC, Bell Papers, vol. 78, file I-2-50B, "Memo prepared for deputy minister in department of citizenship and immigration," 17 June 1958.

53 LAC, Records of Secretary of State, Acc. 1986-87/319, box 3, file Cb-1-4-2/3-1, "Children's Family Allowances for Immigrants," 16 February 1960.

54 LAC, Bell Papers, vol. 78, file I-2-50B, Richard E.G. Davis, executive director, Canadian Welfare Council, to J. Waldo Monteith, minister of national health and welfare, 20 May 1958.

55 Statistics Canada, Historical Statistics of Canada, A350 "Immigrant Arrivals in Canada, 1852-1977." http://www.statcan.ca/english/freepub/11-516-XIE/sectiona/A350.csv.

56 LAC, J.W. Pickersgill Papers, vol. 78, file I-2-50-B, "Memorandum to Cabinet, 'Family Assistance for Immigrants and Settlers,'" 26 October 1961; "Statement by the Minister to the House of Commons," 29 March 1962; press release, 29 March 1962.

57 LAC, DNHW, vol. 1933, file R233-100-1-6, Davidson to Willard, 1955. See also Marshall, *The Social Origins of the Welfare State.*

58 Cited in Marshall, *The Social Origins of the Welfare State,* 167.

59 LAC, Paul Martin Papers, vol. 210, file Pensions, Family Allowances (1), press release, 17 September 1957; LAC, DNHW, vol. 1932, file R233-100-1-2, pt. 2, Davidson to Trainor, 18 March 1959.

60 *Financial Post,* 23 March 1957; and Statistics Canada, Historical Statistics of Canada, C27-39, "Family Allowances, Federal Payments, for Canada and by Province, Fiscal Years Ending 31 March, 1946 to 1976."

61 Blair Fraser, *The Search for Identity: Canada, 1945-1967* (Toronto: Doubleday Canada, 1967), 165.

62 For a discussion of the reforms in social security in the late 1950s and early 1960s, see James Struthers, *The Limits of Affluence: Welfare in Ontario, 1920-1970* (Toronto: University of Toronto Press, 1994), 182-230; Rodney S. Haddow, *Poverty Reform in Canada, 1958-1978: State and Class Influences on Policy Making* (Montreal and Kingston: McGill-Queen's University Press, 1993), 20-45.

63 LAC, Canadian Council on Social Development, vol. 58, file 490 (1944-64), Weiss to Willard, 23 June 1964.

64 Carl M. Brauer, "Kennedy, Johnson, and War on Poverty," in *Poverty and Public Policy in Modern America,* ed. Donald T. Critchlow and Ellis W. Hawley (Chicago: Dorsey Press, 1989), 232-35.

65 LAC, DNHW, vol. 2357, file 260-1-1, pt. 1, Blais to all regional directors, 6 August 1964.

66 Richard Splane, "Social Policy-Making in the Government of Canada," in *Canadian Social Policy,* rev. ed., ed. Shankar A. Yelaja (Waterloo: Wilfrid Laurier University Press, 1987), 224-44. Splane served in the Department of National Health and Welfare from 1952 to 1972, including twelve years as deputy minister.

67 LAC, DNHW, vol. 2357, file 260-1-1, pt. 1, Green to Blais, 26 August 1964; Davis to Blais, 18 August 1964. Marcel Caron, the regional director in Quebec, noted that family allowances

in rural areas like the Gaspé Bay, where cash incomes were seasonal, were very important. See Caron to Blais, 11 August 1964; Bone to Blais, 25 August 1964; Mitchell to Blais, 12 August 1964; Blais to Willard, 7 October 1964.

68 See LAC, DNHW, vol. 1933, file R233-100-1-9, pt. 1, "Family Allowances in Canada: A Background Paper," by Joseph Willard, 1968. A letter to the editor of the Toronto *Globe and Mail* on 21 January 1964 raised the question of whether it was necessary to pay family allowances to all children in Canada when many did not need it or if it might be more effective use of government revenues to establish priorities in the field.

69 On this point, see Andrew Armitage, *Social Welfare in Canada: Ideals and Realities* (Toronto: McClelland and Stewart, 1975), Richard Splane, "Social Policy-Making," 224-44; for the American experience, see Daniel Patrick Moynihan, "The Professionalization of Reform," *The Public Interest* 1 (Fall 1965): 6-16.

Chapter 6: Poverty, Politics, and Family Allowances, 1960-70

1 *Le Devoir,* 20 November 1965.

2 One of the most comprehensive overviews of social security in Quebec for this period is Yves Vaillancourt, *L'évolution des politiques sociales au Québec, 1940-1960* (Montreal: Presses de l'Université de Montréal, 1988).

3 *Le Devoir,* 20 November 1965. Lévesque's proposal for family allowances was shaped, in part, by Jacques Henripin, a professor of demography at L'Université de Montréal and an adviser to the minister, who had published his ideas in *Socialisme.* He maintained that family allowances fell under provincial jurisdiction. Lévesque clearly agreed with Henripin that the province should not wait for Ottawa to make changes before it reformed its social security program. He believed that it was necessary for the state to rectify the social inequality between parents with several dependent children and others by transferring income from the latter group to the former.

4 Gouvernement du Québec, *Rapport du Comité d'étude sur l'assistance publique (Rapport Boucher),* juin 1963 [Quebec, *Report of the Study Committee on Public Assistance*] (Quebec City, 1963). For a discussion of the Boucher Report, see B.L. Vigod, "History According to the Boucher Report: Some Reflections on the State and Social Welfare in Quebec before the Quiet Revolution," in *The Benevolent State: The Growth of Welfare in Canada,* ed. Allan Moscovitch and Jim Albert (Toronto: Garamond Press, 1987), 174-85.

5 Quebec had pioneered the idea of youth allowances in 1961, a demogrant program that Canada adopted for the whole country in 1964. Youth allowances were merely an extension of the family allowance program to include children up to the age of eighteen, provided they were in full-time attendance at school. The program was a recognition that the years of a child's dependency had increased since 1945, when most children were in the workforce in their mid-teens. Moreover, youth allowances were an attempt by the governments to deal with the growing need for educational preparation for Canada's growing technology-based workforce. Quebec opted out of the federal scheme but incorporated the objectives of the new federal measure into its existing program. Ottawa compensated Quebec through a tax abatement adjusted to equal the amount that the federal government would otherwise have paid in allowances to Quebec residents. For a detailed description of youth allowances, see Dennis Guest, *The Emergence of Social Security in Canada,* 2nd ed. (Vancouver: UBC Press, 1991), 15.

6 See Judy LaMarsh, *Memoirs of a Bird in a Gilded Cage* (Toronto: McClelland and Stewart, 1969), 123-24; and *Ottawa Evening Citizen,* 25 November 1965. Lesage told the Southam News Services that Quebec wished to take over the whole field of social security under a "particular status" in Confederation. One could make the argument that the province had first established its basic economic framework through the nationalization of the

power companies and after that had turned its attention to social issues ranging from medicare to urban renewal. This shift in emphasis was signalled in part by the appointments of Lévesque as minister of family and social welfare and Eric Kierans to health.

7 Library and Archives Canada [LAC], Records of the Department of National Health and Welfare [DNHW], vol. 2361, file 264-1-8, Willard to LaMarsh, 25 November 1965.

8 Montreal *Gazette*, 27 November 1965.

9 LaMarsh, *Memoirs of a Bird in a Gilded Cage*, 124.

10 See P.E. Bryden, *Planners and Politicians: Liberal Politics and Social Policy, 1957-1968* (Montreal and Kingston: McGill-Queen's University Press, 1997), especially 127.

11 *Toronto Telegram*, 26 November 1965.

12 LAC, Papers of Prime Minister Lester B. Pearson, vol. 200, file 631, LaMarsh to Pearson, 17 December 1965.

13 LAC, DNHW, vol. 2361, file 264-1-8, Willard to MacEachern, 23 December 1965.

14 LAC, DNHW, vol. 2361, file 264-1-8, "Brief of the Province of Quebec for the Federal-Provincial Conference on the Canada Assistance Plan," Ottawa, 7-8 January 1966. Lévesque proposed redistributing benefits to larger families by reforming the existing system of family allowances. As a first step, Lévesque wanted the family allowances for students sixteen and seventeen years old doubled to $20 per month and extended to include those aged eighteen and attending educational institutions. If Ottawa were not willing to participate in such a scheme, Quebec would forge ahead alone as soon as it was financially possible to do so. Similarly, allowances for children aged thirteen to fifteen who were the third and subsequent children in the family, should be doubled to $16 monthly. He told the federal-provincial meeting that Quebec wanted allowances eliminated over time for the first child in a family to direct greater benefits to these families with larger burdens.

15 LAC, DNHW, vol. 2361, file 264-1-8, "Brief of the Province of Quebec for the Federal-Provincial Conference on the Canada Assistance Plan," Ottawa, 7-8 January 1966; "Note of Quebec's Proposal to Revise the Family and Youth Allowances Programs," prepared by Research and Statistics Division, 10 January 1966.

16 Toronto *Globe and Mail*, 15 January 1966.

17 John Saywell, ed., *Canada Annual Review for 1966* (Toronto: University of Toronto Press, 1967), 49.

18 Ibid., 51.

19 LAC, DNHW, vol. 2361, file 264-1-8, Lévesque to MacEachern, 11 February 1966.

20 *Montreal Star*, 18 February 1966.

21 LAC, DNHW, vol. 1932, file 233/100-1-2, pt. 2, MacEachern to Lévesque, 24 January 1966; Willard to Roger Marier, deputy minister, Department of Family and Social Welfare (Quebec), 4 March 1966.

22 LAC, DNHW, vol. 1934, file R233-100-3, "Memorandum Prepared on Family Allowances," 17 February 1966.

23 LAC, DNHW, vol. 1517, file 201-11-2, pt. 2A, Bryce to Willard, 18 February 1966; vol. 1932, file R233-100-1-2, pt. 2, Osborne to Gorman, 21 March 1967; vol. 2081, file 20-1-1, pt. 2, Willard to MacEachern, special assistant to the minister, 24 August 1967; Blais to Bill MacEachern, 28 March 1967. Blais told MacEachern that Hart Clark of the Department of Finance had in turn told him about what Sharp had said to Bryce. Newfoundland was the only other province to have a similar program, which it called the parents' allowance, though it was frequently referred to as a school allowance. Introduced in 1966, the benefit of $15 was annually paid in October and April to help defray the cost of books and clothing for children attending school. The only test of eligibility was school registration.

24 LAC, Robert Winters Papers, vol. 74, file Family Allowances, 1967-68, Cloutier to MacEachern, 7 September 1967.

25 LAC, DNHW, vol. 2361, 264, Willard to MacEachern, 26 September 1967.

26 LAC, Robert Winters Papers, vol. 74, file Family Allowances, 1967-68, MacEachern to Cloutier, 9 November 1967, and "Memorandum to the Cabinet," 14 November 1967. Robert Winters, the minister of trade and commerce, had written MacEachern that he "was reluctant to see services such as these [family allowances] assigned to the provinces." See Winters to MacEachern, 5 January 1968.

27 LAC, DNHW, vol. 2081, file 20-1-1, pt. 2, "Record of Cabinet Decision," 21 November 1967.

28 In Canada, many commentators and academics have associated selectivity with cutbacks in social spending and an attempt to dismantle the welfare state. As an example, see Allan Moscovitch, "The Welfare State since 1975," *Journal of Canadian Studies* 21, 2 (Summer 1986): 83. He wrote, "One means of eroding social welfare has been through the use of more selectivity, or means testing benefits." During the 18-19 January 1968 Federal-Provincial Conference, Minister of National Health and Welfare Allan J. MacEachern told the ministers of welfare who met in Ottawa that the shift from a flat-rate universal payment, like the old-age security pension, to a selective type of payment geared to income and as exemplified by the guaranteed income supplement in 1967 represented a significant reassessment and change of course in the Canadian approach to social security.

29 LAC, Grace MacInnis Papers, vol. 12, file Social Security 1966-74, "A Social Policy for Canada," 1969 (no day or month given). The memo attributes the quote from Trudeau to the CMA's *Industry*, May 1968. In January 1969, the principle of selectivity was introduced into the family allowance program in the United Kingdom. See J.I. Clark, "Recent Trends and Developments in Guaranteed Income," paper prepared for Nuffield Canadian Seminar on Guaranteed Annual Incomes: An Integrated Approach, Canadian Council on Social Development, April 1972.

30 Quoted in Rodney S. Haddow, *Poverty Reform in Canada, 1958-1978: State and Class Influences on Policy Making* (Montreal and Kingston: McGill-Queen's University Press, 1993), 92.

31 Toronto *Globe and Mail*, 13 May 1969.

32 *Ottawa Citizen*, 13 November 1969.

33 LAC, Pierre Elliott Trudeau Fonds [Trudeau Fonds], vol. 406, file 631 1968-1975. There are many letters and telegrams in this volume warning Trudeau to leave family allowances alone.

34 See http://www.swc-cfc.gc.ca/pubs/0662322177/200206_0662322177_7_e.html.

35 See Ian Adams, William Cameron, Brian Hill, and Peter Penz, *The Real Poverty Report* (Edmonton: M.G. Hurtig Limited, 1971); Canada, Economic Council of Canada, *Fifth Annual Review* (Ottawa: Queen's Printer, 1968); Canada, Senate, Special Committee on Aging, *Final Report* (Ottawa: Queen's Printer, 1966); Canada, *Poverty in Canada: Report of the Special Senate Committee on Poverty* (Ottawa: Queen's Printer, 1971); and Canada, *Report of the Royal Commission on the Status of Women in Canada* (Ottawa: Queen's Printer, 1970).

36 See Archives of Ontario, Ministry of Community and Social Services, RG 29-138-0-69, box 6, Government of Quebec, "Statement by the Honourable Jean-Paul Cloutier, Minister of Family and Social Welfare and Minister of Health at Federal-Provincial Conference of Welfare Ministers," 16-17 January 1969.

37 The cost of family allowances had risen considerably since 1945, as the following table illustrates:

1945-46	$172,632,147
1950-51	$309,465,461

```
1955-56    $382,535,026
1960-61    $506,191,647
1965-66    $615,746,762 (includes youth allowances)
1966-67    $612,642,182
```

38 See LAC, DNHW, Acc. 84-85/548, box 1, file R230/100-3, "Family Allowances in Canada," prepared by research and statistics directorate, August 1967.

39 LAC, DNHW, Acc. 85-86/343, box 38, file 3301-3-S11, "Notes for Report to Cabinet Committee on Income Security (Green Book) proposals," 7 January 1970; box 84, file 3201-3-3, pt. 3, "Memorandum on Development of the Family Income Security Plan," prepared by John Clark, 4 January 1980.

40 LAC, DNHW, vol. 3354, file 2101-3-4, pt. 2, Osborne to Willard, 2 May 1969, and attachment "Comments on Memorandum of Department of Finance, 'Family Allowances, Youth Allowances, and the Income Tax System.'" Emphasis in original.

41 LAC, DNHW, Acc. 85-86/343, box 32, file 3301-3-F4, "Program Review," 29 August 1969.

42 Ibid.

43 LAC, DNHW, vol. 1934, file R233-100-3, "Special Tax Recovery Allowances Scheme," 30 October 1968, and "Supplementary Family Allowances Scheme," 31 October 1968.

44 LAC, DNHW, Acc. 85-86/343, box 38, file 3301-3-516, "The Gallup Report," 8 and 12 November 1969.

45 LAC, Trudeau Fonds, MG 26 O7, vol. 117, file 312.4 1968, "Memorandum to the Prime Minister, Re: Future Work of the Cabinet Committee on Social Policy and Its Review of the Willard Report," 12 September 1969; vol. 397, file 600, "Memorandum to the Prime Minister," 13 November 1969.

46 LAC, Trudeau Fonds, MG 26 O7, vol. 117, file 312.4 1968-1975, Trudeau to MacEachern, 20 November 1969; vol. 397, file 600 1968-1969, Munro to Trudeau, 25 September 1969.

47 LAC, DNHW, Acc. 85-86/343, box 39, file 3301-3-W3, "Memorandum to Cabinet, White Paper on Social Security," 28 November 1969.

48 Don Jamieson, *A World unto Itself: The Political Memoirs of Don Jamieson,* ed. Carmelita McGrath (St. John's: Breakwater Books, 1991), 41-42.

49 LAC, DNHW, Acc. 85-86/343, box 28, file 3301-3-C14, "Memorandum to Cabinet," 29 July 1970, and "Memorandum to Cabinet," 1 September 1970; box 39, file 3301-3-W28, "Memorandum to Cabinet, Report of the Officials' Committee on White Paper on Social Security," 2 November 1970.

50 Jamieson, *A World unto Itself,* 45.

51 LAC, Privy Council Office Papers, vol. 6359, "Cabinet Conclusions," 16 and 23 April 1970; Jamieson, *A World unto Itself,* 46-47.

52 Jamieson, *A World unto Itself,* 42.

53 On this point, see Haddow, *Poverty Reform,* especially 97-99; and Richard Splane, "Social Policy-Making in the Government of Canada," in *Canadian Social Policy,* rev. ed., ed. Shankar A. Yelaja (Waterloo: Wilfrid Laurier University Press, 1987), 229.

54 For an overview of Johnson's career, see http://www.awjohnson.net/about/index.html.

55 Haddow, *Poverty Reform,* 98; A.W. Johnson, "The Treasury Board of Canada and the Machinery of Government in the 1970s," *Canadian Journal of Political Science* 4, 3 (1971): 346-66; Richard French, *How Ottawa Decides: Planning and Industrial Policy-Making 1968-1984* (Toronto: James Lorimer, 1980).

56 See LAC, DNHW, Acc. 85-86/343, box 38, file 3301-3-S11, "Memorandum to Prime Minister from A.W. Johnson," January 1970; see "Comments Prepared by J.I. Clark," 3 February 1970.

57 Splane has suggested that the white paper process has diminished the role of the bureaucracy in policy making because the ministers usually brought outsiders in on special assignment to be a part of their staff during the process. See Splane, "Social Policy-Making," 230.

58 LAC, DNHW, Acc. 85-86/343, box 39, file 3301-3-W28, "Memorandum to Cabinet, Report of the Officials' Committee on White Paper on Social Security," 2 November 1970. Don Jamieson confirms this in his published memoir. There he claims that the white paper was delayed during the summer of 1970 as "[the government] still had not decided with clarity what our general philosophy towards social security and the myriad of related issues should be." Jamieson, *A World unto Itself,* 46.

59 The federal government had also prepared white papers on tax reform and unemployment insurance. The Toronto *Globe and Mail* wondered in an editorial on 30 January 1971 why the government was handling each of the issues in isolation rather than together. After all, it noted, the problems they wanted to tackle were all related.

60 LAC, DNHW, Acc. 85-86/343, box 28, file 3301-3-C14, "Privy Council Office, Record of Cabinet Decision," 19 November 1970.

61 LAC, Stanley Knowles Papers, vol. 39, file 3, Munro to Gelinas, 16 December 1970.

62 LAC, Robert L. Stanfield Papers, vol. 193, file Social Welfare, July 1969-May 1973, news release: "White Paper on Income Security," 30 November 1970.

63 LAC, DNHW, Acc. 85-86/343, box 40, file 3301-3-431, pt. 2. "Cabinet Memorandum," prepared by John Munro, 22 July 1970. This matter arose as a problem again in the summer of 1971, when Ottawa planned to extend coverage of the family income security plan to include dependants aged sixteen and seventeen. The Federal-Provincial Fiscal Revision Act, 1964, which had given Quebec a three-point special abatement when it opted out of the national youth allowance program, had created a discrepancy between the yield from the abatement and the cost to Quebec for the program. While the actual cost for the program to Quebec in 1971-72 was about $24 million, the yield from the three tax points was $57.9 million. In a letter to J.W. Willard, the deputy minister of national welfare, T.K. Shoyama, the deputy minister of finance, suggested several options for eliminating the discrepancy, though he noted, "In the present sensitive context of relations with Quebec, we feel we should avoid initiating confrontations on questions which may not be really significant in substance." LAC, DNHW, vol. 1937, file R234/100, Shoyama to Willard, 12 August 1971.

64 LAC, DNHW, vol. 1937, file R234/100, "Summary of the Steps That Have Been Taken to Accommodate Quebec's Point of View," 15 June 1972.

65 The Quebec plan was designed to function in three phases: in the first phase it would supplement the incomes of the working poor whose incomes failed to keep them above the poverty line; the second phase was designed to work with other income security plans when the worker ceased to be employed; the third phase would provide a taxable family allowance to aid families with children where incomes were below the basic minimum. See Toronto *Globe and Mail,* 29 January 1971.

66 *Ottawa Journal,* 29 January 1971, and Toronto *Globe and Mail,* 29 January 1971.

67 LAC, DNHW, Acc. 85-86/343, box 28, file 3301-3-C6, "Memorandum to Cabinet," 2 February 1971; and vol. 1932, file R233/100-1-2, pt. 2, Munro to Brenda Robertson, minister of youth responsible for welfare, government of New Brunswick, 21 January 1971.

68 Leonard Shifrin, "Income Security: The Rise and Stall of the Federal Role," in *Canadian Social Welfare Policy: Federal and Provincial Dimensions,* ed. Jacqueline S. Ismael (Montreal and Kingston: McGill-Queen's University Press, 1985), 24.

69 LAC, T.C. Douglas Papers, vol. 24, file 12-7, Douglas to Lane, 15 December 1970; Wynter to Douglas, 17 December 1970; Douglas to Wynter, 6 January 1971.

70 LAC, DNHW, Acc. 85-86/616, box 10, file 1600-P1-6, "White Paper – Public Reaction," 20 January 1971.

71 Munro later said that he had disbanded a secretariat he had created in the department to answer questions about the plan because of the lack of queries it had received. *Winnipeg Free Press,* 20 September 1972.

72 LAC, Trudeau Fonds, MG 26 O7, vol. 117, file Memorandum to the Prime Minister, "Meeting of Cabinet Committees on Federal-Provincial Relations," prepared by E. Gallant, 2 February 1971. It is noted here that there was "a certain amount of annoyance shown that Mr. Munro [had] come forward with major [social policy] proposals at the last minute. Mr. Munro's only active support came from Mr. Andras."

Chapter 7: Family Allowances and Constitutional Change, 1968-72

1 A version of this chapter has been published as "Intergovernmental Relations Trumps Social Policy Change: Trudeau, Constitutionalism, and Family Allowances," *Journal of the Canadian Historical Association,* New Series 18, 1 (2007): 207-39.

2 Canada. Exchequer Court. *Canada Law Reports:* Exchequer Court of Canada, 1957 (Ottawa: Queen's Printer, 1958), 83-87. After his claim for the $300 exemption for his children was denied by the Income Tax Board, François Albert Anger, a Quebec taxpayer, took the matter to court, claiming that the board's decision constituted "an attack upon the legislative attributes of the Province in the matter of civil rights and family authority." The court ruled that the act was within the legislative competence of the Parliament of Canada: it was "a national benevolent measure assimilated in the good government of Canada clause."

3 See R.A. Young, Philippe Faucher, and André Blais, "The Concept of Province-Building: A Critique," *Canadian Journal of Political Science/Revue canadienne de science politique* 17, 4 (December 1984): 783-818.

4 Maureen Baker, "Advocacy, Political Alliances and the Implementation of Family Policies," in *Child and Family Policies: Struggles, Strategies and Options,* ed. Jane Pulkingham and Gordon Ternowetsky (Halifax: Fernwood Publishing, 1997), 159.

5 Provincial Archives of New Brunswick, Records of the Department of Finance, file 01-01-00, "Ottawa – Conférence constitutionelle 1969, Summary of Proceedings," 18 March 1970.

6 Peter H. Russell, *Constitutional Odyssey,* 3rd ed. (Toronto: University of Toronto Press, 2004), 85-91; Kenneth McRoberts, *Misconceiving Canada: The Struggle for National Unity* (Toronto: Oxford University Press, 1997), 146.

7 Library and Archives Canada [LAC], Department of National Health and Welfare [DNHW], Acc. 85-86/343, box 28, file 3301-3-C8, pt. 1, "Memorandum to Cabinet from Mitchell Sharp," 1 February 1971. On 7 May 1970, in a discussion on the Quebec situation and national unity, Sharp had said in the Cabinet that "the government had to do everything possible to assist the new Premier of Quebec [Robert Bourassa] because it might well be the last chance to solve the problems in Quebec." LAC, Privy Council Office Papers, vol. 6359, "Cabinet Conclusions," 7 May 1970.

8 LAC, DNHW, Acc. 85-86/343, box 28, file 3301-3-C8, pt. 1, "Memorandum to Cabinet from Mitchell Sharp," 1 February 1971.

9 John Saywell, ed., *Canadian Annual Review of Politics and Public Affairs, 1971* (Toronto: University of Toronto Press, 1972), 42.

10 LAC, DNHW, Acc. 85-86/343, box 28, file 3301-3-C8, "Memorandum for the Prime Minister," prepared by Gordon Robertson, 4 February 1971. The memorandum was based on Robertson's telephone conversation with Chouinard.

11 On this point, see Alvin Finkel, *Social Policy and Practice in Canada: A History* (Waterloo: Wilfrid Laurier University Press, 2006), especially 266-70.

12 LAC, DNHW, Acc. 85-86/343, box 29, file 3301-3-C6, "Memorandum for the Prime Minister, Re: Quebec's Proposals in Social Policy," prepared by R.B. Bryce, 5 February 1971. Bryce also reminded the prime minister that if an arrangement on social policy were worked out with Quebec and then announced to the other provinces without any prior notice, it would cause trouble in getting them to agree on a package to patriate the constitution, "which most of them believe[d] they [were] doing in order to help Mr. Bourassa."

13 LAC, DNHW, vol. 1937, file R234/100, "Summary of the Steps That Have Been Taken to Accommodate Quebec's Point of View," 15 June 1972.

14 Provincial Archives of New Brunswick, Records of the Department of Finance, file 01-03-00, "Ottawa – Conference – Constitutional, 1971, Statement of Conclusions." 9 February 1971.

15 Saywell, *Canadian Annual Review*, 44.

16 See LAC, Pierre Elliott Trudeau Fonds [Trudeau Fonds], MG 26 O7, vol. 117, "Memorandum to the Prime Minister, Meeting of Cabinet Committees on Federal-Provincial Relations," prepared by E. Gallant, 16 February 1971.

17 Ibid.

18 LAC, DNHW, Acc. 85-86/343, box 28, file 3301-3-C6, "Memorandum to Cabinet," prepared by Bryce, 1 March 1971.

19 LAC, DNHW, Acc. 85-86/343, box 28, file 3301-3-C8, pt. 1, Bryce to Willard, 24 March 1971.

20 LAC, DNHW, Acc. 85-86/343, box 28, file 3301-3-C8, pt. 2, "Memorandum to Cabinet, Report on Initial Discussions with Minister of Social Affairs of Quebec," prepared by Bryce, 30 March 1971.

21 Don Jamieson, *A World unto Itself: The Political Memoirs of Don Jamieson,* ed. Carmelita McGrath (St. John's: Breakwater Books, 1991), 44.

22 LAC, DNHW, vol. 1629, file 1, "Memorandum, Allocation of $150 Million Additional Funds for FISP [family income security plan]," 7 April 1971.

23 LAC, Privy Council Office Papers, Cab Doc 416/71.

24 LAC, DNHW, Acc. 85-86/343, box 28, file 3301-3-C8, pt. 2, "Memorandum to Cabinet, Negotiating Positions on Social Policy with Quebec," submitted by John Munro, 26 April 1971.

25 LAC, DNHW, vol. 1629, file 1, "Memorandum to Cabinet, Quebec Proposal to Amend the Constitution Concerning Family Allowances, 4 May 1971," submitted by John Turner, and accompanying Appendix A, "Inclusion of Family Allowances in Section 94A." Emphasis in original.

26 Ibid.

27 LAC, DNHW, Acc. 84-85/085, box 12, file 2100-1-9, "Memorandum to Cabinet," submitted by John Munro, 11 May 1971. The memorandum included the *aide-mémoire.*

28 LAC, DNHW, vol. 1629, file 1, "Memorandum to Cabinet, Federal-Provincial Discussions on Income Security with Atlantic and Western Provinces," submitted by John Munro, 31 May 1971.

29 LAC, DNHW, vol. 1629, file 2, "Memorandum to Cabinet, Federal-Provincial Discussions on Income Security with Ontario," 31 May 1971.

30 LAC, DNHW, vol. 1629, file 1, "Memorandum to Cabinet, Federal Provincial Discussions on Income Security with Quebec," 31 May 1971.

31   John Saywell and Paul Stevens, "Parliament and Politics," in *Canadian Annual Review of Politics and Public Affairs, 1971,* ed. John Saywell (Toronto: University of Toronto Press, 1972), 51-52.

32   LAC, DNHW, vol. 1605, file 6, "Constitutional Conference, 3rd Working Session, February 8-9, 1971: Statement of Conclusions," 8-9.

33   Saywell and Stevens, "Parliament and Politics," 56.

34   Quoted in ibid., 58-79.

35   Ibid., 48-49, 63. The Victoria Charter can be found at http://www.solon.org/Constitutions/Canada/English/Proposals/Victoria_Charter. html.

36   Author's interview with Peter Meekison, Calgary, AB, 17 October 2003.

37   Quoted in Saywell and Stevens, "Parliament and Politics," 61.

38   LAC, Trudeau Fonds, MG 26 O7, vol. 117. "Memorandum to the Prime Minister, Meeting of Cabinet Committees on Federal-Provincial Relations," prepared by E. Gallant, 16 February 1971.

39   LAC, DNHW, Acc. 85-86/343, box 28, file 3301-3-C8, pt. 2, "Memorandum, Re: Provincial Options to Modify Federal Family Income Security Plan, 20 June 1971," prepared by Bryce. Bryce noted that the proposals should be put to Premier Bourassa on 23 June "if it appears that such action is needed and has a good chance of success in gaining Quebec's approval to the Charter." Bryce added, "[There seems to be] a reasonable chance of reaching a conclusion on this proposal by Monday, June 28, the deadline for governments to approve the Charter."

40   See Richard Simeon, *Federal-Provincial Diplomacy* (Toronto: University of Toronto Press, 1972), 66-68. Simeon also suggests that Trudeau's vision of federalism had three other components: Ottawa's insistence that it would respect the constitution, the respect for firm lines between federal and provincial responsibilities, and Ottawa's right to spend in matters of federal jurisdiction.

41   LAC, DNHW, vol. 1629, file 1, "Record of Cabinet Decision," 18 June 1971.

42   Saywell and Stevens, "Parliament and Politics," 48-49, 63. See also Jeremy Webber, *Reimaging Canada: Language, Culture, Community, and the Canadian Constitution* (Montreal and Kingston: McGill-Queen's Press, 1994), 97-99; and Rodney S. Haddow, *Poverty Reform in Canada, 1958-1978: State and Class Influences on Policy Making* (Montreal and Kingston: McGill-Queen's University Press, 1993), 94-96.

43   Saywell and Stevens, "Parliament and Politics," 63-64, 68.

44   LAC, DNHW, vol. 1937, file R234/100, "Announcement by Honourable John Munro," 29 June 1971; Canada, *House of Commons Debates* (29 June 1971).

45   Jamieson, *A World unto Itself,* 187-88.

46   LAC, DNHW, vol. 1629, file 1, "Memorandum to Cabinet, Three Aspects of Canada-Quebec Relations on Income Security," prepared by Munro, 22 July 1971; "Record of Cabinet Decision," 29 July 1971.

47   LAC, DNHW, vol. 1610, file 9, Gallant to Willard, 20 August 1971.

48   LAC, DNHW, vol. 1629, file 1, "Record of Cabinet Decision," 9 September 1971; see also Acc. 85-86/343, box 2, file 2101-4-1, pt. 2 "Basis of Federal Approach," September 1971.

49   LAC, DNHW, vol. 1629, file 1, "Record of Cabinet Decision," 1 September 1971; "Record of Cabinet Decision," 29 July 1971. Interestingly, Allan J. MacEachern, the president of the Privy Council, had told John Munro on 28 July 1971 that he did not think it was possible to have the family income security plan legislation introduced in the third session as Munro wanted, though it could be done early in the fourth session of Parliament. See LAC, DNHW, vol. 2367, file 264-16-1, MacEachern to Munro, 28 July 1971.

50 LAC, DNHW, Acc. 85-86/343, box 37, file 3301-3-A16, Bourassa to Trudeau, 2 September 1971, and Trudeau to Bourassa, 17 September 1971 (unofficial translation of both letters); and vol. 1629, file 1, "Memorandum to Cabinet," 14 October 1971. Prime Minister Trudeau tabled the letter from Premier Bourassa in the House on 15 September 1971; Montreal *Gazette*, 14 September 1971.

51 Arrangements that had been made with Quebec regarding youth allowances would continue.

52 LAC, Stanley Knowles Papers [Knowles Papers], vol. 39, file 51-B-FISP, "Speech for the Minister on FISP before the House Standing Committee on Health, Welfare, and Social Affairs," March 1972.

53 The maximum income in one-child families beyond which no benefits were paid was to be $10,560 if the child was in the twelve to seventeen age group, and $9,045 if younger than twelve. Corresponding ceilings for families with two children were $11,060 and $9,545, respectively. For families with three children, the ceilings were $11,560, $10,045, and so on by $500 intervals.

54 LAC, DNHW, Acc. 85-86/343, box 37, news release, 13 September 1971; LAC, Knowles Papers, vol. 39, file 51-B-FISP, "Speech for the Minister on FISP before the House Standing Committee on Health, Welfare, and Social Affairs," March 1972.

55 Minister of the Department of National Health and Welfare John Munro and his officials consulted with the provinces on several occasions in preparing the family income security plan. One month after the "White Paper on Income Security for Canadians" was released in November 1970, the minister and his officials visited all of the provinces to discuss the nature and scope of the federal proposals with their provincial counterparts. In January 1971, the proposals were further examined in a federal-provincial conference of welfare ministers. Changes were made in Ottawa, and in the early spring of 1971, the minister and his officials made another round of the provinces. Following that, the welfare ministers gathered again to discuss matters relating to income security. After Munro's announcement in Parliament on 29 June 1971, there were further discussions with some of the provinces. LAC, Liberal Party of Canada Papers, vol. 1149, file Family – Income Security, Munro to all Members of Parliament, "Background to Family Income Security Plan Proposals prepared for MPs," no date, but clearly this document was circulated in the fall of 1971.

56 LAC, Knowles Papers, vol. 39, file 51-B-FISP, "Speech for the Minister on FISP before the House Standing Committee on Health, Welfare, and Social Affairs," March 1972.

57 LAC, DNHW, Acc. 85-86/343, box 27, file 3301-3-A16, "Responses to the Criticisms Made by Ontario of the Family Income Security Plan," 30 August 1971.

58 LAC, DNHW, vol. 1610, file 9, "Family Income Security Plan – Fact Sheet," 18 August 1971; Acc. 85-86/343, box 37, news release, 13 September 1971.

59 Ibid. In the material prepared in Munro's office at the DNHW, one draft copy of a speech for Members of Parliament included the following paragraph: "Universal payments ... or, as we call them, demogrants, ... such as Family Allowances ... have been ineffective over the years ... Between 1946 and 1969, the cost of living has increased over 100 percent while Family Allowances benefits have remained virtually the same. Payment per child of $72 to $120 per year does not come near the annual cost of maintaining a child. Similarly, Family Allowances have been inefficient in directing funds to where they are most needed. As an example, in 1971 it is estimated that 24 percent of Family Allowances benefits will be paid to families with incomes under $5,000 and 76 percent with incomes above." See LAC, Liberal Party of Canada Papers, vol. 1149, file Family – Income Security, Munro to all Members of Parliament, "Drafts of Speech Materials for MPs," n.d.

60 LAC, Knowles Papers, vol. 39, file 3, "FISP in relation to Income Security in General," DNHW, 13 September 1971.

61 Toronto *Globe and Mail*, 14 September 1971.

62 *Toronto Star*, 24 September 1971.

63 LAC, Liberal Party of Canada Papers, vol. 1149, file Family Income Security, Munro to Fellow Members, n.d.

64 Quoted in Jane Pulkingham and Gordon Ternowetsky, eds., *Child and Family Policies: Struggles, Strategies and Options* (Halifax: Fernwood Publishing, 1997), 30.

65 Montreal *Gazette*, 23 September 1971; LAC, DNHW, vol. 1937, file R234/100, John E. Osborne to Joseph Willard, 22 September, 1972; Acc. 85-86/343, box 84, file 3201-3-3, pt. 3, "Policy Considerations Underlying the Design and Development of the Family Income Security Plan," January 1980.

66 LAC, DNHW, Acc. 85-86/343, box 32, file 3301-3-D4, "Address Delivered by Mr. Claude Castonguay in Montreal, 7 February 1972 before the St. Laurent Richelieu Club."

67 LAC, DNHW, vol. 2367, file 264-16-1, "Family Income Security – Key Factors."

68 LAC, DNHW, vol. 1629, file 1, "Memorandum to Cabinet," 14 October 1971.

69 Ibid.

70 LAC, DNHW, Acc. 85-86/343, box 27, file 3301-3-P15, "Summary of the Steps That Have Been Taken to Accommodate Quebec's Point of View," March 1972.

71 LAC, Trudeau Fonds, MG 26 07, vol. 332, file 363.44, Marc Lalonde to Trudeau, "Conversation téléphonique avec l'honorable Bourassa," 6 December 1971; DNHW, Acc. 85-86/343, box 28, file 3301-3-C1, "Memorandum to Cabinet," 10 December 1971.

72 LAC, Trudeau Fonds, MG 26 07, vol. 332, file 363.44 Marc Lalonde to Trudeau, with report on Lalonde's conversation with Julien Chouinard, 2 December 1971.

73 LAC, Trudeau Fonds, MG 26 07, vol. 105, file 306.4, "Memorandum from Marc Lalonde to Trudeau, 3 March 1972; LAC, DNHW, Acc. 85-86/343, box 28, file 3301-3-C1, "Memorandum to Cabinet," 10 December 1971.

74 Toronto *Globe and Mail*, 18 February 1972.

75 LAC, DNHW, vol. 1610, file 6, Trudeau to Bourassa, 9 March 1972; Acc. 85-86/343, box 84, file 3201-3-3, pt. 3, "Memorandum on Policy Consideration Underlying the Design and Development of the Family Income Security Plan," 4 January 1980.

76 LAC, Trudeau Fonds, MG 26 07, vol. 332, file 363.44, Marc Lalonde to Trudeau, "Rencontre avec l'honourable Bourassa," 17 January 1972.

77 LAC, Trudeau Fonds, MG 26 07, vol. 105, file 306.4, Trudeau to Bourassa, 9 March 1972; LAC, DNHW, vol. 1610, file 6, Trudeau to Bourassa, 9 March 1972; Acc. 85-86/343, box 84, file 3201-3-3, pt. 3, "Memorandum on Policy Consideration Underlying the Design and Development of the Family Income Security Plan," 4 January 1980. On the issue of the federal definition of income, Claude Castonguay had emphatically stated in September 1971 that Quebec required that the determination of income reside with its department of revenue. This issue was important because income levels determined the level of allowance. See Montreal *Gazette*, 16 March 1972.

78 LAC, Trudeau Fonds, MG 26 07, vol. 105, file 306.4, Bourassa to Trudeau, 17 March 1972; LAC, DNHW, Acc. 85-86/343, box 27, file 3301-3-A16, "Telex to the Prime Minister from Robert Bourassa," 17 March 1972. Bourassa wrote in the telex, "I think that the proposals in your letter are in keeping with the talks we have been having on this matter for some months and that they make an appropriate framework within which we shall be able to draw up the specific terms and conditions for an agreement at further meetings." (Translation in the Trudeau Fonds.) See also *Journal de Montréal*, 14 March 1972.

79 LAC, Trudeau Fonds, MG 26 07, vol. 332, file 363.44, Marc Lalonde to Trudeau, "Rencontre avec l'honourable Bourassa," 17 January 1972.

80 LAC, Trudeau Fonds, MG 26 07, vol. 105, file 306.4, Trudeau to W.A.C. Bennett, 9 March 1972. The same letter was sent to all of the premiers with the exception of Quebec; LAC, DNHW, vol. 1610, file 6, Trudeau to premiers, 9 March 1972. This is not to suggest that the provinces other than Quebec had not been involved in the discussions over the family income security plan; indeed, they had been. Both Munro and his officials had met with provincial ministers and their officials on numerous occasions since the release of Munro's white paper. See Acc. 85-86/343, box 27, file 3301-3-A16, "Consultations with the Provinces," 16 March 1972.

81 A number of newspapers, including the *Ottawa Citizen, Ottawa Journal, Toronto Star, Toronto Globe and Mail, Windsor Star, La Presse, Le Soleil,* and *Le Devoir,* carried major stories and editorials on the development in the period from 13 March to 18 March 1972.

82 See LAC, DNHW, Acc. 85-86/343, box 27, file 3301-3-P15, "Basis of Federal Approach," March 1972; see for example the Montreal *Gazette,* 14 March 1972, and *Le Devoir,* 14 and 15 March 1972. In early March, the Joint Parliamentary Committee on the Constitution, which had been appointed a year earlier, issued its report. It recommended major changes to demogrants like family allowances. It also recommended concurrent jurisdiction with limited provincial paramountcy as to the scale of benefits and allocation of federal funds among the various income support programs. This meant that the province could switch federal funds between programs, subject to a limitation on the amount they could reduce the benefits of any particular individual. See LAC, Trudeau Fonds, MG 26 O7, vol. 107, file 307.74, "Constitution, Memorandum for the Prime Minister," 17 March 1972. Copy of report attached and marked as "Seen P.M."

83 LAC, DNHW, Acc. 85-86/343, box 84, file 3201-3-3, pt. 3, "Memorandum on Policy Consideration Underlying the Design and Development of the Family Income Security Plan," 4 January 1980.

84 LAC, Knowles Papers, vol. 38, file 3, "Bill C-170 Background for the Caucus Discussion," 13 April 1972.

85 LAC, Knowles Papers, vol. 39, file 4, "Notes for a Speech to Be Delivered by NDP Leader David Lewis, Toronto," 30 May 1972.

86 *Ottawa Citizen,* 8 May 1972; LAC, Knowles Papers, vol. 39, file 3, "Bill C-170 Background for Caucus Discussion," 19 April 1972; LAC, David Lewis Papers, vol. 91, file Legislation: Family Allowance-Income and Security Program, news release, 19 April 1972, 20 April 1972.

87 LAC, DNHW, Acc. 81-82/184, box 14, file 5-10-3, pt. 9, Oshanek to Munro, 23 June 1972; Whelan to Munro, 20 June 1972.

88 *Toronto Star,* 22 April 1972.

89 LAC, Robert L. Stanfield Papers, vol. 196, file 631, Geoffrey T. Molyneux, director, research office of the official Opposition, to Stanfield, 20 April 1972, and "Rationale for Voting on Bill C-170," 25 April 1972.

90 See LAC, Grace MacInnis Papers, vol. 4, file Family Allowances, Grace MacInnis to LeRoux, 8 June 1972.

91 LAC, DNHW, Acc. 85-86/343, box 84, file 3201-3-3, pt. 3, "Memorandum on Policy Consideration Underlying the Design and Development of the Family Income Security Plan," 4 January 1980. The legislation did not include a method of automatic escalation of benefits, but it did provide authority for the governor in council, on receipt of a report from the minister of Department of National Health and Welfare, to order an increase in maximum benefits to reflect changes in consumer prices and increase the amounts of the basic family income thresholds to reflect changes in the general levels of wages and salaries.

92   LAC, DNHW, vol. 1937, file R234/100, Osborne, assistant deputy minister, research, planning and evaluation (DNHW), to Willard, 15 June 1972.

93   Montreal *Gazette,* 13 May 1972; *Toronto Star,* 13 May 1972.

94   Toronto *Globe and Mail,* 8 June 1972.

95   LAC, DNHW, Acc. 85-86/343, box 28, file 3301-3-C12, "Draft Statement by the Honourable John Munro," 28 July 1972.

96   Alexander B. Campbell, acting chair of the Council of Maritime Premiers, wrote Trudeau that the stipulation that the provinces provide at least 15% of total outlays for family allowances meant that the economically challenged provinces would not be able to participate in the new arrangement. He wrote, "Your proposal would further tend to perpetuate and increase the disparity in income security and social assistance payment levels across the country." He also said that the three maritime provinces did not contemplate the establishment of their own family allowance programs. See LAC, DNHW, vol. 1610, file 4, Campbell to Trudeau, 6 July 1972; LAC Trudeau Fonds, MG 26 07, vol. 105, file 306.4, Campbell to Trudeau.

97   LAC, Trudeau Fonds, MG 26 07, vol. 105, file 306.4, Trudeau to Bourassa, 9 June 1972; LAC, DNHW, vol. 1610, file 4, Trudeau to Bourassa, 9 June 1972.

98   LAC, DNHW, vol. 1610, file 4, "Memorandum for Mr. Lalonde," prepared by F.A.G. Carter, 16 June 1972.

99   Montreal *Gazette,* 17 May 1972; *La Presse,* 18 and 22 July 1972.

100   LAC, DNHW, vol. 2081, file 20-1-1, pt. 3, "Statement by the Honourable John Munro," July 1972. See *La Presse,* 22 July 1972.

101   *Le Devoir,* 24 July 1972.

102   LAC, DNHW, vol. 2081, file 20-1-1, pt. 3, Castonguay to Munro, 25 July 1972; Munro to Castonguay, 28 July 1972. The statement unofficially translated reads: "The statement makes me realize once again how little the objectives pursued by the Province of Quebec in the field of income security and, more particularly, family allowances, seem to have been understood or evaluated in their perspective by the government to which you belong."

103   *Le Devoir,* 24 July 1972.

104   LAC, Trudeau Fonds, MG 26 O7, vol. 406, file 631 1968-1975, Thompson to Trudeau, 26 September 1972, and enclosure.

Chapter 8: Wrestling with Universality, 1972-83

1   Library and Archives Canada [LAC], Department of National Health and Welfare [DNHW], Acc. 85-86/343, box 36, file 3301-3-06, "Memorandum to the Cabinet," 21 November 1972.

2   LAC, Pierre Elliott Trudeau Fonds [Trudeau Fonds], MG 26 O7, vol. 406, file 631 1968-1975, Dan Jones to Trudeau, 19 July 1972.

3   Cited in Keith Banting, *The Welfare State and Canadian Federalism,* 2nd ed. (Montreal and Kingston: McGill-Queen's University Press, 1987), 112. See LAC, DNHW, vol. 1937, file R234/100, "The Gallup Report," 27 March 1971. This report found that 66% of Canadians approved of the government's plan to reduce the payments of family allowances to the well-to-do in order to increase payments to those with low incomes.

4   LAC, DNHW, vol. 1628, file 3, "Participation in Social Policy Decision Making," memo prepared by L. Shifrin, 7 November 1972.

5   LAC, Trudeau Fonds, MG 26 O7, vol. 406, file 631 1968-1975, Norman Cafik to Trudeau, 15 August 1972. Cafik wrote that many other MPs were quite concerned over the family allowances legislation.

6 LAC, Trudeau Fonds, MG 26 O7, vol. 117, file 312.4 July 1971-March 1972, "Memorandum for the Prime Minister, Family Income Security Plan Timing," 2 November 1971.

7 Leonard Shifrin, "Income Security: The Rise and Fall of the Federal Role," in *Canadian Social Welfare Policy: Federal and Provincial Dimensions*, ed. Jacqueline S. Ismael (Montreal and Kingston: McGill-Queen's University Press, 1986), 24.

8 On the point, see Richard Splane, "Social Policy-Making in the Government of Canada," in *Canadian Social Policy*, rev. ed., ed. Shankar A. Yelaja (Waterloo: Wilfrid Laurier University Press, 1987), 237

9 LAC, DNHW, Acc. 85-86/343, box 36, file 2102-5-1, pt. 1, "Memorandum to Cabinet," 1 December 1972. Don Jamieson claims that Trudeau "felt it might be wise to move John Munro from Health and Welfare" during the summer of 1970. Don Jamieson, *A World unto Itself: The Political Memoirs of Don Jamieson*, ed. Carmelita McGrath (St. John's: Breakwater Books, 1991), 182.

10 Quoted in Banting, *The Welfare State*, 112-13. See also Toronto *Globe and Mail*, 21 December 1972.

11 See LAC, DNHW, vol. 1937, file R234/100, "The Gallup Report," 27 March 1971.

12 Quoted in James Rice and Michael Prince, *Changing Politics of Canadian Social Policy* (Toronto: University of Toronto Press, 2000), 169-75, 179.

13 LAC, DNHW, Acc. 85-86/343, box 28, file 3301-3-C3, "Memorandum to Cabinet," 1 December 1972, and "Reconsideration of FISP," prepared by J.W. Willard, 6 September 1972; box 84, file 3201-3-3, pt. 3, "Memorandum on Policy Consideration Underlying the Design and Development of the Family Income Security Plan," 4 January 1980; box 26, file 3303-3-A3, pt. 1, "Memorandum for the Cabinet," 6 December 1972.

14 LAC, Grace MacInnis Papers, vol. 15, file Social Security, 1966-74, "Speech Delivered by the Honourable Marc Lalonde to the Montreal Chamber of Commerce on Canada's Social Security Policy," 5 February 1973.

15 A.W. Johnson, "Social Policy in Canada: The Past as It Conditions the Present" (Institute for Research on Public Policy, Montreal, September 1987), 24; and Splane, "Social Policy-Making in the Government of Canada," 236.

16 On the point, see Splane, "Social Policy-Making in the Government of Canada," 237.

17 John Saywell and Paul Stevens, "Parliament and Politics," in *Canadian Annual Review of Politics and Public Affairs, 1971*, ed. John Saywell (Toronto: University of Toronto Press, 1972), 105.

18 LAC, Grace MacInnis Papers, vol. 15, file Social Security, 1966-74, "Speech Delivered by the Honourable Marc Lalonde to the Montreal Chamber of Commerce on Canada's Social Security Policy," 5 February 1973.

19 LAC, DNHW, Acc. 85-86/343, box 26, file 3301-3-A3, pt. 2, A.W. Johnson to Lalonde, 26 March 1973.

20 LAC, Trudeau Fonds, MG 26 O7, vol. 117, file 312.4 January-May 1973, "Memorandum for Prime Minister," prepared by F.A.G. Carter, 10 April 1972. The memo was a briefing note for the meeting of the Cabinet Committee on Federal-Provincial Relations, 10 April 1973; DNHW, Acc. 85-86/343, box 26, file 3301-3-A3, pt. 2, A.W. Johnson to Lalonde, 26 March 1973. John Turner wrote to Marc Lalonde on 23 March 1973, suggesting that a family allowance proposal be put to the provinces in April.

21 The joint review of Canada's social security system turned out to be a long and complicated process and its final outcome is beyond the scope of this study. The reform of family and youth allowances and the decision to integrate the federal family allowance program with the provincial schemes were a part of the review, but family allowance reforms were

completed by the end of 1973. Family allowances did not figure prominently in the review after that date.

22   LAC, DNHW, Acc. 85-86/343, vol. 31, file 3301-3-C47, news release: "Health and Welfare Canada," 18 April 1973, and Marc Lalonde, "Working Paper on Social Security in Canada" (Ottawa: Department of Department of National Health and Welfare, 18 April 1973), 2.

23   LAC, DNHW, Acc. 85-86/343, box 32, file 3301-3-D4, news release: "Health and Welfare Canada: Speech by the Honourable Marc Lalonde, Second Reading of Bill C-211, Family Allowances," 15 October 1973.

24   LAC, DNHW, Acc. 85-86/343, vol. 31, file 3301-3-C47, news release: "Health and Welfare Canada," 18 April 1973.

25   P.E. Bryden, *Planners and Politicians: Liberal Politics and Social Policy* (Montreal and Kingston: McGill-Queen's University Press, 1997).

26   *La Presse*, 20 April 1973.

27   Toronto *Globe and Mail*, 22 September 1973.

28   LAC, DNHW, Acc. 85-86/343, vol. 31, file 3301-3-C47, news release: "A Credo of Social Security Values, and Strategies for a New Social Security System, Health and Welfare Canada," 18 April 1973.

29   See especially Rodney S. Haddow, *Poverty Reform in Canada, 1958-1978: State and Class Influences on Policy Making* (Montreal and Kingston: McGill-Queen's University Press, 1993), especially Chapters 6 and 7; and Clifford J. Williams, "The Social Services Story in Ontario, 1970-1987," unpublished paper.

30   LAC, DNHW, Acc. 85-86/613, box 4, file 1600-P1-7, "Communiqué, Canadian Council on Social Development," 24 April 1973. The council called this idea "selectivity within universality," and saw no contradiction in a universal program that was selective in favour of low-income people.

31   LAC, DNHW, Acc. 85-86/547, box 1, file 100-19, "Income Security in Canada: Alberta's Position," Hon. Neil Crawford, minister of health and social development, 25 April 1973.

32   LAC, DNHW, Acc. 85-86/547, box 1, file 90-99, "Working Paper on Income Security," by the Honourable Norman Levi, April 1973.

33   Provincial Archives of Ontario, Ministry of Social Development, RG 75-19, box 26, file 1973- Family Allowances, "Cabinet Committee on Social Development," 17 April 1973.

34   Nancy Altman, *The Battle for Social Security: From FDR's Vision to Bush's Gamble* (Hoboken, NJ: John Wiley and Sons, 2005), 209-11.

35   LAC, DNHW, Acc. 85-86/343, box 42, file 3302-1-6, pt. 3, "Notes on Cancellation of FA Escalation," prepared by John E. Osborne, 9 March 1976.

36   LAC, DNHW, Acc. 85-86/343, box 12, file 3201-3-1, pt. 1, "Memorandum to Cabinet," 11 May 1973; vol. 67, file 3401-4/73-2, pt. 2, "Amendments to the Family Allowance and Youth Allowance Acts," 17 May 1973.

37   LAC, DNHW, vol. 2081, file 20-1-1, pt. 3, Lalonde to Honourable Alex Taylor, minister of social services, government of Saskatchewan, 11 July 1973. The same letter was sent to all provincial ministers of welfare.

38   LAC, DNHW, vol. 2081, file 20-2-2, pt. 3, news release: "Minister Introduces New Family Allowance Legislation," July 1973. It was estimated that the tax recovery for the federal Treasury would be $350 million and a further $115 million for the provincial treasuries.

39   LAC, Trudeau Fonds, MG 26 O7, vol. 330, file 360.4 1968-1972, Haney to Willard, "Memorandum on Conference of Provincial Premiers," 3-4 August 1972.

40   LAC, DNHW, Acc. 84-85/085, box 2, file 2106-71-6, pt. 1, press release: "Government of Quebec, Executive Branch," 19 September 1973. Bourassa also said there would be reform in the province's welfare program in light of the changes to the family allowance program,

so that family allowances and welfare benefits were never greater than the income from employment calculated on the basis of the minimum wages. This was to encourage individuals to work.

41 LAC, DNHW, vol. 1609, file 6, "Family Allowance Insert," n.d.

42 LAC, David Lewis Papers, vol. 54, file 12-7, Lewis to Nicholson, 20 August 1973.

43 LAC, DNHW, vol. 1609, file 6, "January Family Allowances Insert for Quebec" and "An Important Message for Fathers and Mothers," January 1974.

44 LAC, Trudeau Fonds, MG 26 O7, vol. 406, file 631 1968-75, Marjorie Hartling, executive director, National Anti-Poverty Organization, to Trudeau, 25 September 1974. "A Critique of the New Family Allowances," prepared by the organization, was also sent to the prime minister.

45 LAC, DNHW, vol. 1931, file R233/100, pt. 3, Osborne to Johnson, 23 November 1974; Acc. 85-86/343, box 42, file 3302-1-6, pt. 3, "Notes of Cancellation of FA Escalation," John E. Osborne, 9 March 1976.

46 Ian Gough, *The Political Economy of the Welfare State* (London: Macmillan, 1979), 132.

47 Canada, "Attack on Inflation: A Program of National Action." Tabled in the House of Commons, 14 October 1975, by Donald Macdonald. See also Donald J. Savoie, *The Politics of Public Spending in Canada* (Toronto: University of Toronto Press, 1990), 149.

48 Quoted in Savoie, *The Politics of Public Spending,* 151.

49 LAC, DNHW, vol. 1296, file 5619-2-762, "Meeting of the Federal and Provincial Ministers of Welfare, 1-2 June 1976, Summary Minutes." It was clear that John Turner, the minister of finance, was concerned through the whole social security review with the financial implications of any major initiatives in the social security field. See in particular LAC, Trudeau Fonds, MG 26 O7, vol. 117, file 312.4, "Note pour le premier ministre," 8 November 1974. See also Haddow, *Poverty Reform,* 148-49.

50 Quoted in Haddow, *Poverty Reform,* 145.

51 LAC, DNHW, Acc. 85-86/343, box 84, file 2101-3-1, pt. 3, "Chronology of Policy Development Leading to Child Benefit Proposals of 1978," no author.

52 LAC, DNHW, Acc. 85-86/343, file 3203-16-1, pts. 3 and 4, "The Tax-Transfer Integration Task Force," March 1977 and January 1978.

53 LAC, DNHW, Acc. 85-86/343, box 84, file 2101-3-1, pt. 3, "Chronology of Policy Development Leading to Child Benefit Proposals of 1978," no author; box 31, file 3301-6-1, "Memo Re: Family Allowances," prepared by John E. Osborne, 26 October 1977.

54 LAC, DNHW, Acc. 85-86/343, box 91, file 3201-3-3, pt. 2, "Provincial Flexibility in Setting Federal Family Allowances Rate," prepared by Guy Fortier, 15 April 1977; MG 32 C59, vol. 29, file 51-B-73, news release, 27 September 1976; Acc. 85-86/616, box 43, file 1637-77-166, news release, 30 November 1977. The National Anti-Poverty Organization examined the impact of the amendment to family allowances that took effect on 1 January 1974 and concluded four years later that the increase had had little impact on families because it had been swallowed up by inflation. See LAC, Robert L. Stanfield Papers, vol. 196, file 631-1-C, "Critique of Family Allowances," September 1974.

55 LAC, DNHW, Acc. 85-86/343, box 78, file 3102-18, "Selectivity vs Universality," prepared in policy development branch by E.J. van Goudever, 8 January 1979.

56 Canada, *House of Commons Debates* (23 November and 19 December 1977).

57 LAC, DNHW, Acc. 85-86/343, box 78, file 3102-18, "Selectivity vs Universality," prepared in policy development branch by E.J. van Goudever, 8 January 1979.

58 Canada, *House of Commons Debates* (22 February 1978).

59 LAC, Trudeau Fonds, MG 26 O7, vol. 569, file 190305 1976, Marsden to Trudeau, 25 March 1976.

60 LAC, DNHW, Acc. 85-86/343, box 84, file 3201-3-3, pt. 3, Osborne to Robinson, 7 April 1978. A year later, Freda Paltiel, chair of the department advisory committee on the status of women in the Department of National Health and Welfare, wrote to Osborne (who passed her concerns along to Deputy Minister Pamela D. McDougall), again expressing concern that the government might eliminate the universality of family allowances and direct the funds to low-income families. She expressed fear about alienating the middle class, who were asked to bear an inordinate share of taxes to support the poor, and about taking money away from mothers. See Paltiel to Osborne, 9 November 1979.

61 On this point, see Haddow, *Poverty Reform*, 150-51, Canada, *House of Commons Debates* (23 November 1977); DNHW, Acc. 85-86/343, box 78, file 3102-18, "Selectivity vs Universality," prepared in policy development branch by E.J. van Goudeover, 8 January 1979.

62 Statistics Canada, *National Income and Expenditure Accounts, 1964-1978;* http://www. statcan.ca/english/freepub/11-516-XIE/sectionf/sectionf.htm#Nat%20Income and Banting, *The Welfare State*, 17-18.

63 On this point, see Andrew F. Johnson, "Restructuring Family Allowances: Good Politics at No Cost?" in *Canadian Social Welfare Policy: Federalism and Provincial Dimensions*, ed. Jacqueline S. Ismael (Montreal and Kingston: McGill-Queen's University Press, 1985), 106; Canada, "Royal Commission on Financial Management and Accountability, Final Report" (Ottawa, 1979).

64 Quoted in Haddow, *Poverty Reform*, 151.

65 On this point, see Savoie, *The Politics of Public Spending*, 151-55.

66 See Johnson, "Restructuring Family Allowances," 105-19.

67 This was now an approach that had been adopted in the mid-1970s in many countries, including the Federal Republic of Germany, Israel, Australia, and the United Kingdom. The changes made to similar programs in those countries were to achieve coordination between family allowances and the tax system to simplify the system of financial assistance for families whose incomes were below the tax threshold. See LAC, DNHW, Acc. 85-86/343, box 84, file 3201-3-3, pt. 3, "Recent Changes in Family Allowances – International," 19 April 1978.

68 Refundable tax credits did not provide the same benefits to all families. If the government wished to provide greater benefits to those with low and moderate income, this could be done through a diminishing refundable tax credit, a credit whose value is reduced by some percentage of income beyond a certain level. See LAC, Stanley Knowles Papers [Knowles Papers] (MG 32 C59), vol. 38, file 51-B Family Allowances (1), National Council of Welfare, "The Refundable Child Tax Credit," 4.

69 On this point, see Keith Banting, *The Welfare State.*

70 LAC, Trudeau Fonds, MG 26 O7, vol. 682, file 140612.4 1978, "Memo to the Prime Minister from Jim Coutts," 10 July 1978.

71 LAC, Trudeau Fonds, MG 26 O7, vol. 711, file 190305, Bégin to Mary Dennis, president, Congress of Canadian Women, 22 September 1978; LAC, Knowles Papers, vol. 38, file 51-B Family Allowances (1), National Council of Welfare, "The Refundable Child Tax Credit: What It Is ... How It Works."

72 LAC, DNHW, Acc. 84-85/085, box 12, file 2100-1-9 (senior policy adviser), 25 August 1978; LAC, Knowles Papers, vol. 38, file 51-B Family Allowances (1), National Council of Welfare, "The Refundable Child Tax Credit: What It Is ... How It Works." See also news release, 24 August 1978.

73 LAC, DNHW, Acc. 85-86/343, box 32, file 3301-F2, "Evaluation Assessment Study Report: Family Allowance Program, Draft," June 1984.

74 LAC, DNHW, Acc. 85-86/343, box 78, file 3102-18, "Selectivity vs. Universality," prepared in policy development branch by E.J. van Goudeover, 8 January 1979.

75 Quoted in Savoie, *The Politics of Public Spending*, 162.

76 Canada, *House of Commons Debates* (31 October 1978).

77 LAC, Knowles Papers, vol. 38, file 51-B Family Allowances (1), National Council of Welfare, "The Refundable Child Tax Credit: What It Is ... How It Works."

78 LAC, T.C. Douglas Papers, vol. 46, file Health and Welfare, pt. 4, Douglas to Rodd, 2 October 1978.

79 LAC, Knowles Papers, vol. 428, file 51B, "Brief on Family Allowance Cuts and Proposed Child Tax Credits," presented by Congress of Canadian Women to prime minister and Members of Parliament, October 1978.

80 This is a subject that requires further investigation, and a good starting point is Johnson, "Restructuring Family Allowances."

81 See, for example, LAC, DNHW, Acc. 84-85/085, box 12, file 2100-1-9, "Social Policy in the 1980s: A Department of National Health and Welfare Perspective," January 1980. The file also contains a number of responses to the document.

82 Canada, *House of Commons Debates* (16 June 1980). See also Michael J. Prince, "What Ever Happened to Compassion? Liberal Social Policy 1980-84," in *How Ottawa Spends, 1984: The New Agenda*, ed. Allan M. Maslove (Toronto: James Lorimer, 1984), 81-85.

83 This is discussed briefly in Prince, "What Ever Happened to Compassion?" 86-87.

84 Ibid., 95.

85 *Winnipeg Free Press*, 22 October 1982; *Ottawa Citizen*, 22 October 1982; CP Wire Service, 4 November 1982. See Allan Moscovitch, "The Welfare State since 1975," *Journal of Canadian Studies* 21, 2 (Summer 1986): 83.

86 LAC, DNHW, Acc. 85-86/343, box 78, file 3102-18, "Universality and Selectivity," prepared by John I. Clark, senior advisory; box 89, file C3101-8-4, Paltiel to Murphy, 2 Feb 1982.

87 Toronto *Globe and Mail*, 5 November 1982; *Le Droit*, 4 November 1982.

88 Toronto *Globe and Mail*, 6 November 1982 and 28 December 1983.

89 Canada, *House of Commons Debates* (28 October 1982), and Toronto *Globe and Mail*, 6 November 1982.

90 Banting has described demogrants as "universal, flat-rate payments made to individuals or families solely on the basis of demographic characteristics, such as age, rather than on the basis of proven need as in the case of social assistance, or previous contributions as in the case of social insurance." Banting, *The Welfare State*, 7.

91 LAC, DNHW, Acc. 85-86/343, box 32, file 3301-F2, "Evaluation Assessment Study Report: Family Allowances Program," June 1984.

Chapter 9: The Demise of Family Allowances, 1984-99

1 See Colin Campbell and William Christian, *Parties, Leaders, and Ideologies in Canada* (Toronto: McGraw-Hill Ryerson, 1996); Michael J. Prince, "What Ever Happened to Compassion? Liberal Social Policy 1980-84," in *How Ottawa Spends, 1984: The New Agenda*, ed. Allan M. Maslove (Toronto: James Lorimer, 1984), 53-54 and 81-85.

2 During the Mulroney period, the government failed to eliminate the annual deficit. It was still $30 billion in 1993, but that amount did not go to new government spending. In fact, the $300 billion that was added to the debt during Mulroney's term went to cover interest charges on the debt. The Mulroney government balanced public spending and revenue collection near the end of its term in office. The government was able to do this because it increased taxes (including the introduction of surtaxes) – which disappointed many

who had hoped for lower taxes with the Tories – phased out a number of programs, sold a number of Crown corporations, and substantially reduced grants and subsidies to business.

3 See Donald J. Savoie, *The Politics of Public Spending in Canada* (Toronto: University of Toronto Press, 1990), 17-18. James Laxer recommended a reorientation for the New Democratic Party in his 1984 book, *Rethinking the Economy* (Raleigh: NC Press, 1984).

4 Quoted in Savoie, *The Politics of Public Spending*, 17; Douglas G. Hartle, *A Theory of the Expenditure Budget Process in the Government of Canada* (Toronto: Ontario Economic Research Studies, 1984). In 1978, Prime Minister Trudeau announced that $2 billion would be cut from federal expenditures: "We must have a major re-ordering of Government priorities. We must reduce the size of Government," and if the deficit was not curbed, "Canadians within several years would almost certainly be faced with a fiscal crisis." Quoted in Savoie, *The Politics of Public Spending*, 152. See also Toronto *Globe and Mail*, 3 August 1978. When John Crosbie became the minister of finance in Joe Clark's short-lived government, he and Sinclair Stevens, the president of the Treasury Board, issued a statement on government spending that read: "Our government feels we cannot tolerate the spending level inherent in past actions, and we intend to face up to the problem of taking some hard decisions which are necessary to get government spending in this country under control." See LAC, Department of Finance [DF] and the Treasury Board, "Briefing on Federal Expenditures," 20 July 1979, 1.

5 Prince, "What Ever Happened to Compassion?" 80.

6 Quoted in Clare Hoy, *Friends in High Places: Politics and Patronage in the Mulroney Government* (Toronto: Key Porter Books, 1987).

7 Ken Battle, "Child Benefits in Decline," *Policy Options* (January 1988): 3-7.

8 Gosta Esping-Andersen, *The Three World of Welfare Capitalism* (Princeton: Princeton University Press, 1990).

9 Library and Archives Canada [LAC], Department of National Health and Welfare [DNHW], Acc. 85-86/343, box 32, file 3201-3-4-1, "Child Benefit System," discussion paper, 23 November 1984.

10 Canada, *Royal Commission on the Economic Union and Development Prospects for Canada Report*, Vol. 2 (Ottawa: Supply and Services Canada, 1985), 771-803.

11 LAC, DF, "A New Direction for Canada: An Agenda for Economic Renewal," presented by Finance Minister Michael Wilson, Ottawa, 8 November 1984. See Peter C. Newman, *The Canadian Revolution: From Deference to Defiance* (Toronto: Penguin Books of Canada, 1996), especially 215-64.

12 "Background Notes for an Address by Brian Mulroney," Toronto, Ontario, Progressive Conservative Party, 28 August 1984. Personal copy of author.

13 LAC, DF, "Budget Speech," 23 May 1985. Ottawa: Supply and Services, 1985.

14 See particularly Grattan Gray, "Social Policy by Stealth," *Policy Options* 11, 2 (March 1990): 26; Ken Battle, *The Politics of Stealth: Child Benefits under the Tories*, in *How Ottawa Spends: A More Democratic Canada ... ? 1993-1994*, ed. Susan D. Phillips (Ottawa: Carleton University Press, 1993). James J. Rice and Michael J. Prince examine social policy in the Mulroney era in "Lowering the Safety Net and Weakening the Bonds of Nationhood: Social Policy in the Mulroney Years," in *How Ottawa Spends: A More Democratic Canada ... ? 1993-1994*; see Chapter 6, "A Sacred Trust," in David Bercuson, J.L. Granatstein, and W.R. Young, *Sacred Trust? Brian Mulroney and the Conservatives in Power* (Toronto: Doubleday Canada, 1986) for an overview of social policy in the early years of Mulroney's government. Battle had argued that the Mulroney government "accomplished its changes to child benefits and other social programs through the skilful exercise of 'the politics of stealth'

which has not only siphoned growing billions out of social spending at virtually no political cost, but also neutralized opposition from social advocates and stifled the informed and open public debate that is so badly needed as Canadian social policy wanders through the wilderness."

15 On this point, see Bercuson, Granatstein, and Young, *Sacred Trust?* especially 93-120.
16 Paul Pierson has argued that reform to universal programs are common since "an ideologically committed and consistent conservative government would object most strongly to governmental provisions for the middle class ... [C]onservatives are very concerned with reducing spending, and it is hard to squeeze much spending out of marginal, means-tested programs. The largest potential targets are bound to be those that include the middle class [i.e., universal programs]; budget cutters will find their attention drawn to universal programs." *Dismantling the Welfare State? Reagan, Thatcher and the Politics of Retrenchment* (New York: Press Syndicate of the University of Cambridge, 1994), 101-2.
17 Savoie, *The Politics of Public Spending*, 163-64.
18 "A New Direction for Canada: An Agenda for Economic Renewal," presented by Finance Minister Michael Wilson, 8 November 1984 (Ottawa: Department of Finance, 1985), 15. Prime Minister Mulroney appointed Deputy Prime Minister Eric Nielsen to head a ministerial task force to review existing programs with a view to "eliminating those that no longer served a purpose and consolidating others in the hope that not only savings, but also better government would result." When the task force reported in March 1986, it recommended one-time expenditure and tax reductions of between $7 billion and $8 billion, but the government did not implement many of Nielsen's recommendations. On this point, see Savoie, *The Politics of Public Spending*, 132-42.
19 Campbell and Christian, *Parties, Leaders, and Ideologies in Canada*, 53. Many of the regional ministers as well as Conservative MPs opposed many of the cuts that Nielsen, Wilson, and de Cotret suggested. On this point, see Savoie, *The Politics of Public Spending*, 140-42 and Chapter 7.
20 Toronto *Globe and Mail*, 18 December 1984.
21 In response to a question in the House of Commons on 9 November 1984, Mulroney again raised the "$500,000 income" issue, when he said that it was a "legitimate question" to ask if high-income earners needed social security benefits or "could they not be added to the benefits of those who need them most in our society, the poor, the disadvantaged, and people on welfare." He added that the government was seeking a "more effective delivery of dollars to the people in our society who need them most." See Canada, *House of Commons Debates* (9 November 1984).
22 "Speech from the Throne," 1 October 1986. http://www2.parl.gc.ca/Parlinfo/Documents/ThroneSpeech/33-02-e.pdf.
23 Canada, *House of Commons Debates* (17 December 1984).
24 Toronto *Globe and Mail*, 19 January 1985.
25 Quoted in Bercuson, Granatstein, and Young, *Sacred Trust?* 98.
26 "A New Direction for Canada: An Agenda for Economic Renewal," presented by Finance Minister Michael Wilson, 8 November 1984. Ottawa: Department of Finance, 1985. Emphasis in original.
27 See Toronto *Globe and Mail*, 23 January 1985.
28 DNHW, "Child and Elderly Benefits – Consultation Paper," (Ottawa: Supply and Services, January 1985).
29 Ann Porter, "Constrained and Redefined: Women's Issues in the Mulroney Era," in *Transforming the Nation: Canada and Brian Mulroney,* ed. Raymond B. Blake (Montreal and Kingston: McGill-Queen's University Press, 2007), 180-81, 187.

30 LAC, DNHW, "Child and Elderly Benefits – Consultation Paper," January 1985.

31 See James J. Rice, "Restitching the Safety Net: Altering the National Social Security System," in *How Ottawa Spends, 1987-88: Restraining the State,* ed. Michael J. Prince (Toronto: Methuen, 1987), 218.

32 The equivalent-to-married exemption allowed single parents an income tax exemption for one of their children equal to the exemption for married taxpayers who supported a spouse not in the work force.

33 Social Policy Reform Group, "Child Benefit Reform," Ottawa, March 1985. The groups in the coalition included the Canadian Advisory Council on the Status of Women, the Canadian Association of Social Workers, the Canadian Council on Social Development, the National Action Committee on the Status of Women, the National Anti-Poverty Organization, and the National Council of Welfare. See also Battle, "The Politics of Stealth."

34 Battle, "The Politics of Stealth," 424.

35 Canada, *House of Commons Debates* (19 November 1984 and 29 January 1985).

36 Canada, Department of Finance, "Budget Speech," 23 May 1985; Savoie, *The Politics of Public Spending,* 167.

37 Toronto *Globe and Mail,* 11 and 18 June 1985.

38 Rice, "Restitching the Safety Net," 211-36. See also John C. Crosbie, *No Holds Barred: My Life in Politics* (Toronto: McClelland and Stewart, 1997), 290-91.

39 Rice, "Restitching the Safety Net," 219-20.

40 R. Mishra, *The Welfare State in Capitalist Society: Policies of Retrenchment and Maintenance in Europe, North America, and Australia* (Toronto: University of Toronto Press, 1990), 75.

41 Michael J. Prince and James J. Rice, "Governing through Shifting Social-Policy Regimes: Brian Mulroney and Canada's Welfare State," in *Transforming the Nation: Canada and Brian Mulroney,* ed. Raymond B. Blake (Montreal and Kingston: McGill-Queen's University Press, 2007), 167. For a view from 1990, see Alan Moscovitch, "Slowing the Steam Roller: The Federal Conservatives, the Social Sector, and the Child Benefit Reform," in *How Ottawa Spends, 1990-91: Tracking the Second Agenda,* ed. Katherine Graham (Ottawa: Carleton University Press, 1990). Prince and Rice suggest that the changes made during the Mulroney period now appear much more modest given the reforms that came after the Liberals were returned to power in 1993.

42 Canada, Department of Finance, "Budget Speech," 23 May 1985; "Budget Papers," Ottawa: 1985. In 1986, Wilson took additional measures with "Bill C-11: An Act to Amend the Income Tax Act," to help the poorest families when he moved to advance the payment of $300 of the child tax credit to families whose income in 1985 was $15,000 or less.

43 Dennis Guest, *The Emergence of Social Security in Canada,* 3rd ed. (Vancouver: UBC Press, 1997), 221.

44 See Jack Tweedie, "Resources Rather than Needs: A State-Centred Model of Welfare Policymaking," *American Journal of Political Science* 38, 3 (August 1994): 651-72.

45 Canada, *House of Commons Debates* (16 September 1985). See also comments by Pierre Blais, the parliamentary secretary to the minister of agriculture in debate on 17 September 1985.

46 Rice, "Restitching the Safety Net," 222.

47 See Canada, *House of Commons Debates* (16 September 1985).

48 Ibid. In the debate on 17 September 1985, Cyril Keeper, NDP Member for Winnipeg North Centre, said that "family allowance continues to be a way for the Canadian Government to recognize the value of the unpaid work of women in our society."

49 Canada, *House of Commons Debates* (20 January 1986).

50 Canada, "Speech from the Throne," 3 April 1989, http://www2.parl.gc.ca/Parlinfo/ Documents/ThroneSpeech/34-02-e.pdf; Department of Finance, "Budget Speech," 27 April 1989 and "Budget Papers," 27 April 1989 (Ottawa, 1989).

51 Ken Battle, "Clawing Back," *Perceptions* 14, 3 (1990): 35-36.

52 *Ottawa Citizen*, 29 April 1989. The president of the Senior Citizens Federation wrote Prime Minister Mulroney on 23 June 1989: "We view this proposal as a serious breach of faith by our government and an insidious effort to undercut the social security programs that you have on numerous times stated are a sacred trust." The Coalition of Quebec Seniors similarly criticized the legislation. See Canada, *House of Commons Debates* (11 October 1989).

53 Canada, *House of Commons Debates* (5 May 1989).

54 Canada, *House of Commons Debates* (11 and 17 October 1989).

55 National Council of Welfare, news release, 13 September 1989, quoted in Canada, *House of Commons Debates* (18 October 1989).

56 Jane Pulkingham and Gordon Ternowetsky, eds., *Child and Family Policies: Struggle, Strategies and Options* (Halifax: Fernwood Publishing, 1997), 18-19. It should also be noted that this book is part of an extensive and important literature on family policy in Canada. Much of that literature argues that the principle of universality has been abandoned by social policy groups on the left and right because such programs are "too expensive." This is only part of the explanation: there has been a desire among some activists and the state that government expenditures be directed to where they do the greatest public good.

57 See Canada, *House of Commons Debates* (9 November 1984). The government's initiative was also presented in *Brighter Futures: Canada's Action Plan for Children*, published by the DNHW in 1992.

58 Department of Finance, "Budget Speech," 25 February 1992, Ottawa, Department of Finance, 1992; and Canada, *House of Commons Debates* (1 June 1992). This program was remarkably similar to that recommended in 1985 by the Macdonald Commission (the Royal Commission on the Economic Union and Development Prospects for Canada) that called for family allowances, the child tax credit, and the child tax exemption to be replaced by a single large family allowance-type payment or a larger child tax credit, payable monthly for low-income families.

59 Some of the critics of the new initiative pointed out that there was no new money in the new plan. What this fails to recognize is that the total expenditure would be distributed to a fewer number of families, thus increasing the amount that went to low-income families.

60 LAC, DNHW, "The Child Benefit: A White Paper on Canada's New Integrated Child Tax Benefit," Ottawa, 1992.

61 House of Commons *Debates* (26 February 1992).

62 Ibid. (11 March 1992).

63 Ibid. (1 June 1992).

64 Press release: "The New Democrats," 10 May 1991.

65 See Ken Battle, "Back to the Future: Reforming Social Policy in Canada," in *In Pursuit of Public Good: Essays in Honour of Allan J. MacEachern*, ed. Tom Kent (Montreal and Kingston: McGill-Queen's University Press, 1997), 53.

66 Quoted in Canada, *House of Commons Debates* (15 September 1992). Kennedy was elected to the Ontario legislature as a Liberal in 1996.

67 Reseau d'action et d'information pour les femmes, "Federal Government Threatens Demise of Children's Safety Net: A Brief Condemning the New Integrated Child Tax Benefit as Dangerous and Inequitable," Montreal, 16 July 1992; Battle, "The Politics of Stealth," 431-32.

68 *Vancouver Sun,* 10 October 1992.
69 Department of Finance, *Working Together towards a Child Benefit System* (Ottawa: Queen's
    Printer, 18 February 1997), 4.
70 For a discussion of comparative policies for children, see Maureen Baker, *Canadian Family
    Policies: Cross-National Comparisons* (Toronto: University of Toronto Press, 1995), especially
    Chapter 4.
71 Battle, "Back to the Future," 56.
72 The "social union" initiative is the umbrella under which government indicates it will
    concentrate its efforts to renew and modernize Canadian social policy. Under this view,
    children in poverty are one of the first priorities of building a strong social union.
73 LAC, Privy Council Office Papers, "Renewing the Canadian Federation: A Progress Report,"
    Ottawa, 1996, 2.
74 Department of Finance, *Working Together towards a Child Benefit System,* 1.
75 Douglas Durst, ed., *Canada's National Child Benefit: Phoenix or Fizzle* (Halifax: Fernwood
    Publishing, 1999).
76 As an interim step toward the new benefit system, the 1997 budget promised to enrich
    and restructure the working income supplement by providing benefits for each child
    rather than a single benefit per family. The maximum benefit was increased from $500
    per family to $605 for the first child, $405 for the second, and $330 for each additional
    child.
77 Government of Canada, "National Child Benefit Progress Report: 1999," (Ottawa, National
    Child Benefit, 1999), 4-5.
78 Department of Finance, *Working Together towards a Child Benefit System,* 1-2.
79 See Toronto *Globe and Mail,* 15 May 1999. In 1997, for instance, the combined provinces
    funded various social assistance programs, providing approximately $2 billion in benefits
    for children.
80 Toronto *Globe and Mail,* 21 May and 9 October 1999.
81 See Keith Banting and Ken Battle, eds., *A New Social Vision for Canada? Perspectives on
    the Federal Discussion Paper on Social Security Reform* (Kingston: School of Policy Studies,
    1994).

Conclusion

1 Peter Gzowski, *The Private Voice: A Journal of Reflection* (Toronto: McClelland and Stewart,
   1988).
2 J. Frank Strain, "Debts Paid and Debts Owed: The Legacy of Mulroney's Economic Policies," in *The Nation Transformed: Canada and Brian Mulroney,* ed. Raymond B. Blake
   (Montreal and Kingston: McGill-Queen's University Press, 2007), 44-45.

Bibliography

Primary Sources

Bank of Canada Archives
Graham Towers Papers

Library and Archives Canada

Government Records
Department of Finance
Department of Industry Trade and Commerce
Department of Labour
Department of National Health and Welfare
Privy Council Office
Records Relating to Indian Affairs
Royal Canadian Mounted Police
Treasury Board

Manuscript Collections
Bell, Richard A.
Bracken, John
Canadian Association of Social Workers
Canadian Council on Social Development
Canadian Federation of Business and Professional Clubs
Claxton, Brooke
Co-operative Commonwealth Federation
The Diaries of Prime Minister William Lyon Mackenzie King
Douglas, T.C.
Drew, George
Graydon, Gordon
Kidd, Henry E.
King, William Lyon Mackenzie
Knowles, Stanley
Liberal Party of Canada
MacInnis, Grace
Mackenzie, Ian
National Council of Women of Canada
Pearson, Lester B.
Pickersgill, Jack
Progressive Conservative Party
St. Laurent, Louis
Stanfield, Robert L.
Trudeau, Pierre Elliott

McGill University Archives
Cyril James Collection

Provincial Archives of New Brunswick
Records of the Department of Finance

Provincial Archives of Ontario
Ministry of Community and Social Services
Ministry of Social Development

Queen's University Archives
W.C. Clark Papers
R.C. Wallace Papers

Newspapers and Magazines

Canadian Forum
Canadian Home Journal
Canadian Unionist
Canadian Welfare
Edmonton Journal
Financial Post
International Labour Review
La Presse
Labour Gazette
Le Devoir
Le Soleil
Montreal *Gazette*
Montreal Star
New York Times
Ottawa *Citizen*
Ottawa *Journal*
Public Affairs
Public Opinion Quarterly
Regina *Leader-Post*
Saturday Night
Toronto Daily Star
Toronto *Globe and Mail*
Toronto Star
Vancouver *Province*
Winnipeg Free Press
Winnipeg *Tribune*

Published and Secondary Sources

Abramovitz, Mimi. *Regulating the Lives of Women: Social Welfare Policy from Colonial Times to the Present.* Boston: South End, 1989.

Adams, Ian, William Cameron, Brian Hill, and Peter Penz. *The Real Poverty Report.* Edmonton: M.G. Hurtig Limited, 1971.

Altman, Nancy. *The Battle for Social Security: From FDR's Vision to Bush's Gamble.* Hoboken, NJ: John Wiley and Sons, 2005.

Armitage, Andrew. *Social Welfare in Canada: Ideals and Realities*. Toronto: McClelland and Stewart, 1975.

Baker, Maureen. *Canadian Family Policies: Cross-National Comparisons*. Toronto: University of Toronto Press, 1995.

Baker, Maureen, and David Tippen. *Poverty, Social Assistance and the Employability of Mothers: Restructuring Welfare States*. Toronto: University of Toronto Press, 1999.

Banting, Keith. "Institutional Conservatism: Federalism and Pension Reform." In *Canadian Social Welfare Policy: Federal and Provincial Dimensions*, ed. Jacqueline S. Ismael, 48-74. Montreal and Kingston: McGill-Queen's University Press, 1985.

–. "Social Citizenship and the Multicultural State." In *Citizenship, Diversity, and Pluralism*, ed. Alan C. Cairns, John C. Courtney, Peter MacKinnon, Hans J. Michelmann, and David E. Smith, 108-36. Montreal and Kingston: McGill-Queen's University Press, 1999.

–. *The Welfare State and Canadian Federalism*. 2nd ed. Montreal and Kingston: McGill-Queen's University Press, 1987.

Banting, Keith, and Ken Battle, eds. *A New Social Vision for Canada? Perspectives on the Federal Discussion Paper on Social Security Reform*. Kingston: School of Policy Studies, 1994.

Battle, Ken. "Back to the Future: Reforming Social Policy in Canada." In *In Pursuit of Public Good: Essays in Honour of Allan J. MacEachern*, ed. Tom Kent, 35-64. Montreal and Kingston: McGill-Queen's University Press, 1997.

–. "Child Benefits in Decline." *Policy Options* (January 1988): 3-7.

–. "The Politics of Stealth: Child Benefits under the Tories." In *How Ottawa Spends: A More Democratic Canada...? 1993-1994*, ed. Susan D. Phillips, 267-95. Ottawa: Carleton University Press, 1993.

Beiner, Ronald, and Wayne Norman, eds. *Canadian Political Philosophy: Contemporary Reflections*. Toronto: Oxford University Press, 2001.

Bercuson, David Jay. *True Patriot: The Life of Brooke Claxton, 1898-1960*. Toronto: University of Toronto Press, 1993.

Bercuson, David Jay, J.L. Granatstein, and W.R. Young. *Sacred Trust? Brian Mulroney and the Conservatives in Power*. Toronto: Doubleday Canada, 1986.

Beveridge, William. *The Report on Social Insurance and Allied Services in the United Kingdom*. London: His Majesty's Stationery Office, 1942.

Birch, Anthony. *Federalism, Finance, and Social Legislation in Canada, Australia, and the United States*. Oxford: Oxford University Press, 1955.

Blake, Raymond B. *Canadians at Last: Canada Integrates Newfoundland as a Province*. Toronto: University of Toronto Press, 1994, 2004.

–. "Mackenzie King and the Genesis of Family Allowances in Canada, 1939-44." In *Social Welfare Policy in Canada: Historical Readings*, ed. Raymond B. Blake and Jeff Keshen, 244-54. Toronto: Copp Clark, 1995.

Bothwell, Robert, and William Kilbourn, *C.D. Howe*. Toronto: University of Toronto Press, 1979.

Bothwell, Robert, Ian Drummond, and John English. *Canada since 1945: Power, Politics and Provincialism*. Toronto: University of Toronto Press, 1981.

Brauer, Carl M. "Kennedy, Johnson, and War on Poverty." In *Poverty and Public Policy in Modern America*, ed. Donald T. Critchlow and Ellis W. Hawley, 26-47. Chicago: Dorsey Press, 1989.

Brodie, Janine. "Citizenship and Solidarity: Reflections on the Canadian Way." *Citizenship Studies* 6, 4 (December 2002): 377-94.

Bruce, Herbert. *Varied Operations: An Autobiography*. Toronto: Longmans, Green, 1958.

Bryden, P.E. *Planners and Politicians: Liberal Politics and Social Policy, 1957-1968*. Montreal and Kingston, McGill-Queen's University Press, 1997.

Campbell, Colin, and William Christian. *Parties, Leaders, and Ideologies in Canada*. Toronto: McGraw-Hill Ryerson, 1996.

Canada. Department of Finance. "A New Direction for Canada: An Agenda for Economic Renewal." Presented by Finance Minister Michael Wilson, Ottawa, 8 November 1984.

–. "Budget Speech," Ottawa, 23 May 1985.

Canada. Department of National Health and Welfare. "The Child Benefit: A White Paper on Canada's New Integrated Child Tax Benefit," Ottawa, 1992.

Canada. Dominion-Provincial Conference, 1935. *Record of Proceedings*. Ottawa: King's Printer, 1936.

Canada. Economic Council of Canada. *Fifth Annual Review*. Ottawa: Queen's Printer, 1968.

Canada. Exchequer Court. *Canada Law Reports:* Exchequer Court of Canada, 1957. Ottawa: Queen's Printer, 1958.

Canada. House of Commons. *Select Standing Committee on Industrial and International Relations: Report, Proceedings, and Evidence*. Ottawa: King's Printer, 1929.

Canada. *Poverty in Canada: Report of the Special Senate Committee on Poverty*. Ottawa: Queen's Printer, 1971.

Canada. *Report of the Royal Commission on the Status of Women in Canada*. Ottawa: Queen's Printer, 1970.

Canada. *Royal Commission on the Economic Union and Development Prospects for Canada Report,* Vol. 2. Ottawa: Supply and Services, 1985.

Canada. Senate, Special Committee on Aging. *Final Report*. Ottawa: Queen's Printer, 1966.

Cassidy, H.M. *Social Security and Reconstruction in Canada*. Toronto: Ryerson Press, 1943.

Christie, Nancy. *Engendering the State: Family, Work, and Welfare in Canada*. Toronto: University of Toronto Press, 2000.

Christie, Nancy, and Michael Gauvreau. *A Full-Orbed Christianity: The Protestant Churches and Social Welfare in Canada, 1900-1940*. Montreal and Kingston: McGill-Queen's University Press, 1996.

Clark, J.I. "Recent Trends and Developments in Guaranteed Income." Paper prepared for Nuffield Canadian Seminar on Guaranteed Annual Incomes: An Integrated Approach. Canadian Council on Social Development, April 1972.

Cloutier, J.E. *The Distribution of Benefits and Costs of Social Security in Canada, 1971-1975*. Discussion Papers Nos. 1-8. Ottawa: Economic Council of Canada 1978.

Comacchio, Cynthia R. *"Nations Are Built of Babies": Saving Ontario's Mothers and Children, 1900-1940*. Montreal and Kingston: McGill-Queen's University Press, 1993.

Courchene, Tom. *Social Canada in the Millennium: Reform Imperatives and Restructuring Principles*. Toronto: C.D. Howe Institute, 1994.

Creighton, Donald. *The Forked Road: Canada, 1939-57*. Toronto: McClelland and Stewart, 1976.

Crosbie, John C. *No Holds Barred: My Life in Politics*. Toronto: McClelland and Stewart, 1997.

Cuneo, Carl J. "State, Class and Reserve Labour: The Case of the 1941 Canadian Unemployment Insurance Act." *Canadian Review of Sociology and Anthropology* 16, 2 (1979): 147-70.

Dale, Jennifer, and Peggy Foster. *Feminists and State Welfare*. London: Routledge and Kegan Paul, 1986.

Davidson, George F. "Canada's Family Allowances in Retrospect." *Children* 4, 3 (May-June, 1957): 15-28.

–. "The Future Development of Social Security in Canada." *Canadian Welfare* 18, 7 (1943): 195-200.

Dexter, Grant. *Family Allowances: An Analysis*. Winnipeg: Free Press, 1944.

Durst, Douglas, ed. *Canada's National Child Benefit: Phoenix or Fizzle?* Halifax: Fernwood Publishing, 1999.

Esping-Andersen, Gosta. "After the Golden Age? Welfare State Dilemmas in a Global Economy." In *Welfare States in Transition: National Adaptations in Global Economies*, ed. G. Esping-Andersen, 1-31. London: Sage, 1996.

–. *Three Worlds of Welfare Capitalism*. Princeton: Princeton University Press, 1990.

Evan, Patricia M., and Gerda R. Wekerle, eds. *Women and the Canadian Welfare State: Challenges and Change*. Toronto: University of Toronto Press, 1997.

Finkel, Alvin. *Business and Social Reform in the Thirties*. Toronto: James Lorimer, 1979.

–. *Social Policy and Practice in Canada: A History*. Waterloo: Wilfrid Laurier University Press, 2006.

–. "The State of Writing on the Canadian Welfare State: What's Class Got to Do with It?" *Labour/Le Travail* 54 (2004): 247-61.

Fox, Frances, and Richard Cloward. *Regulating the Poor: The Functions of Public Welfare*. New York: Pantheon Books, 1971.

Fraser, Blair. *The Search for Identity: Canada, 1945-1967*. Toronto: Doubleday Canada, 1967.

French, Richard. *How Ottawa Decides: Planning and Industrial Policy-Making, 1968-1984*. Toronto: James Lorimer, 1980.

Gleason, Mona. *Normalizing the Ideal: Psychology, Schooling and the Family in Postwar Canada*. Toronto: University of Toronto Press, 1999.

Gordon, Linda. *Pitied but Not Entitled: Single Mothers and the History of Welfare, 1890-1935*. New York: Free Press, 1994.

Gough, Ian. *The Political Economy of the Welfare State*. London: Macmillan, 1979.

Granatstein, J.L. *Canada's War: The Politics of the Mackenzie King Government, 1939-1945*. Toronto: Oxford University Press, 1975.

–. *The Ottawa Men: The Civil Service Mandarins, 1935-1957*. Toronto, Oxford University Press, 1982.

–. *The Politics of Survival: The Conservative Party of Canada, 1939-45*. Toronto: University of Toronto Press, 1967.

Guest, Dennis. *The Emergence of Social Security in Canada*, 2nd and 3rd eds. Vancouver: UBC Press, 1991, 1997.

Gzowski, Peter. *The Private Voice: A Journal of Reflection*. Toronto: McClelland and Stewart, 1988.

Haddow, Rodney S. *Poverty Reform in Canada, 1958-1978: State and Class Influences on Policy Making*. Montreal and Kingston, McGill-Queen's University Press, 1993.

Handler, Joel F., and Yeheskel Hasenfeld, *The Moral Construction of Poverty: Welfare Reform in America*. Newbury Park: Sage, 1991.

Hartle, Douglas G. *A Theory of the Expenditure Budget Process in the Government of Canada*. Toronto: Ontario Economic Research Studies, 1984.

Hartz, Louis. *The Founding of New Societies*. New York: Harvest Books, 1964.

Heron, Craig. Review of *Public Lives, Public Policy* in *Canadian Historical Review* 77, 1 (March 1996): 141-42.

Horn, Michiel. *The League for Social Reconstruction: Intellectual Origins of the Democratic Left in Canada, 1930-1942.* Toronto: University of Toronto Press, 1980.

Hoy, Claire. *Friends in High Places: Politics and Patronage in the Mulroney Government.* Toronto: Key Porter Books, 1987.

Jamieson, Don. *A World unto Itself: The Political Memoirs of Don Jamieson.* Edited by Carmelita McGrath. St. John's: Breakwater Books, 1991.

Jean, Dominique. "Family Allowances and Family Autonomy: Quebec Families Encounter the Welfare State, 1945-1955." In *Canadian Family History: Selected Readings,* ed. Bettina Bradbury, 401-37. Toronto: Copp Clark Pitman, 1992.

Jenson, Jane, and Mariette Sineau, eds. *Who Cares? Women's Work, Childcare, and Welfare State Redesign.* Toronto: University of Toronto Press, 2001.

Johnson, Andrew F. "Restructuring Family Allowances: 'Good Politics at No Cost?'" In *Canadian Social Welfare Policy: Federal and Provincial Dimensions,* ed. Jacqueline S. Ismael, 105-19. Montreal and Kingston: McGill-Queen's University Press, 1985.

Johnson, A.W. "Social Policy in Canada: The Past as It Conditions the Present." In *The Future of Social Welfare Systems in Canada and the United States,* ed. Shirley B. Seward, 1-26. Halifax: Institute for Research on Public Policy, 1987.

–. "The Treasury Board of Canada and the Machinery of Government in the 1970s." *Canadian Journal of Political Science* 4, 3 (1971): 346-66.

Keshen, Jeffrey A. *Saints, Sinners, and Soldiers: Canada's Second World War.* Vancouver: UBC Press, 2004.

Kitchen, Brigitte. "The Introduction of Family Allowances in Canada." In *The Benevolent State in Canada: The Growth of Welfare in Canada,* ed. Allan Moscovitch and Jim Albert, 221-41. Toronto: Garamond Press, 1987.

–. "Wartime Social Reform: The Introduction of Family Allowances." *Canadian Journal of Social Work* 7, 1 (1981): 37-45.

Lalonde, Marc. "Working Paper on Social Security in Canada." Department of National Health and Welfare, Ottawa, 18 April 1973.

LaMarsh, Judy. *Memoirs of a Bird in a Gilded Cage.* Toronto: McClelland and Stewart, 1969.

Laski, Harold. "The Obsolescence of Federalism." In *The People, Politics and the Politician,* ed. A.N. Christensen and E.M. Kirkpatrick, 111-17. New York: Holt, 1941.

Laurendeau, Andre. "Is There a Crisis in Nationalism?" In *French Canadian Nationalism: An Anthology,* ed. Ramsay Cook, 257-75. Toronto: Macmillan, 1969.

Lavis, John N. *Political Elites and Their Influence on Health Care Reform in Canada.* Discussion Paper No. 26. Commission on the Future of Health Care in Canada, Ottawa, 2002.

Laxer, James. *Rethinking the Economy.* Raleigh: NC Press, 1984.

Lebel, Leon. "Family Allowances as a Means of Preventing Emigration: A Plea for the Family of Workers so that It May Shape in the General Prosperity of the Nation." Montreal, 1928.

Lewis, Jane. "Family Change and Family Politics in the UK." *Journal for the Study of British Cultures* 9, 2 (2003): 209-22.

–. "Gender and Welfare State Change." *European Societies* 4, 4 (2002): 331-57.

–. *The Politics of Motherhood: Child and Maternal Welfare in England, 1900-1939.* Montreal and Kingston: McGill-Queen's University Press, 1980.

–. *Should We Care about Family Change?* 2001 Joanne Goodman Lectures. Toronto: University of Toronto Press, 2003.

Lewis, Jane, and Rebecca Surender, eds. *Welfare State Change: Towards a Third Way?* Oxford: Oxford University Press, 2004.

Little, Margaret. "The Leaner, Meaner Welfare Machine: The Harris Government's Ideological and Material Attack on Single Mothers." In *Making Normal: Social Regulation in Canada*, ed. Deborah Brock, 235-58. Toronto: University of Toronto Press, 2003.

–. *No Car, No Radio, No Liquor Permit: The Moral Regulation of Single Mothers in Ontario, 1920-1997*. Toronto: Oxford University Press, 1998.

Lubove, Roy. *The Struggle for Social Security*. Pittsburgh: University of Pittsburgh Press, 1968.

MacDowall, L.S. "The Formation of the Canadian Industrial Relations System during World War Two." *Labour/Le Travail* 3 (1978): 175-96.

Macnicol, John. *The Movement for Family Allowances, 1918-45: A Study in Social Policy Development*. London: Heinemann, 1980.

Manzer, Ronald. *Policies and Political Development in Canada*. Toronto: University of Toronto Press, 1985.

Marsh, Leonard. *Report on Social Security for Canada*. Toronto: University of Toronto Press, 1975.

Marshall, Dominique. *Aux origines sociales de l'État-providence: Familles québécoises, obligations scolaires et allocations familiales, 1940-1955*. Montreal: Presses de l'Université de Montréal, 1998.

–. *The Social Origins of the Welfare State: Quebec Families, Compulsory Education, and Family Allowances, 1940-1955*. Translated by Nicola Doone Danby. Waterloo: Wilfrid Laurier University Press, 2006.

Marshall, T.H. *Citizenship and Social Class and Other Essays*. Cambridge: Cambridge University Press, 1950.

–. "Citizenship and Social Class." In *Citizenship and Class* [1950], ed. T.H. Marshall and T. Bottomore, 3-51. London: Pluto Press, 1992.

Martin, Paul. *A Very Public Life*, Vol. 2. Toronto: Deneau, 1985.

McDowell, Linda. "Life without Father and Ford: The New Gender Order of Post-Fordism." *Transactions of the Institute of British Geographers* 16 (1991): 400-19.

McKeen, Wendy. *Money in Their Own Name: The Feminist Voice in Poverty Debate in Canada, 1970-1995*. Toronto: University of Toronto Press, 2004.

McNaught, Kenneth. *A Prophet in Politics: A Biography of J.S. Woodsworth*. Toronto: University of Toronto Press, 1959.

McQuaig, Linda. *The Quick and the Dead: Brian Mulroney, Big Business and the Seduction of Canada*. Toronto: Penguin Books, 1991.

McRoberts, Kenneth. *Misconceiving Canada: The Struggle for National Unity*. Toronto: Oxford University Press, 1997.

Mishra, R. *The Welfare State in Capitalist Society: Policies of Retrenchment and Maintenance in Europe, North America, and Australia*. Toronto: University of Toronto Press, 1990.

Morton, Desmond. *Fight or Pay: Soldiers' Families in the Great War*. Vancouver: UBC Press, 2004.

Moscovitch, Allan. "Slowing the Steam Roller: The Federal Conservatives, the Social Sector, and the Child Benefit Reform." In *How Ottawa Spends, 1990-91: Tracking the Second Agenda*, ed. Katherine Graham, 427-82. Ottawa: Carleton University Press, 1990.

–. "The Welfare State since 1975." *Journal of Canadian Studies* 21, 2 (Summer 1986): 77-95.

Moscovitch, Allan, and Glenn Drover. "Social Expenditures and the Welfare State: The Canadian Experience in Historical Perspective." In *The Benevolent State: The Growth of Welfare in Canada*, ed. Allan Moscovitch and Jim Albert, 13-46. Toronto: Garamond Press, 1987.

Moynihan, Daniel Patrick. "The Professionalization of Reform." *Public Interest* 1 (Fall 1965): 6-16.

Mulvale, James P. *Reimaging Social Welfare: Beyond the Keynesian Welfare State*. Aurora, ON: Garamond Press, 2001.

Newman, Peter C. *The Canadian Revolution: From Deference to Defiance*. Toronto: Penguin, 1996.

Nixon, P.G. "The Welfare State North: Early Developments in Inuit Security." *Journal of Canadian Studies* 25, 2 (1990): 144-54.

Norrie, Ken, Douglas Owram, and J.C. Herbert Emery. *A History of the Canadian Economy*, 3rd ed. Toronto: Harcourt Brace Canada, 2002.

Oliver, Dean. "Public Opinion and Public Policy in Canada: Federal Legislation on War Veterans, 1936-46." In *The Welfare State in Canada: Past, Present, and Future*, ed. Raymond B. Blake, Penny E. Bryden, and J. Frank Strain, 193-214. Toronto: Irwin Publishing, 1997.

–. "When the Battle's Won: Military Demobilization in Canada, 1936-46." PhD diss., York University, Toronto, 1996.

Owram, Doug. *The Government Generation: Canadian Intellectuals and the State, 1900-1945*. Toronto: University of Toronto Press, 1986.

Pal, Leslie. "Revision and Retreat: Canadian Unemployment Insurance, 1971-1981." In *Canadian Social Welfare: Federal and Provincial Dimensions*, ed. Jacqueline S. Ismael, 75-104. Montreal and Kingston: McGill-Queen's University Press, 1985.

Palmer, Mark Edward. "The Origins and Implementation of Family Allowances in Canada." MA thesis, Queen's University, Kingston, 1976.

Parkinson, R.H. "Ten Years of Family Allowances." *Canadian Welfare* (November 1955): 195-200.

Pateman, Carol. *The Disorder of Women: Democracy, Feminism and Political Theory*. Stanford, CA: Stanford University Press, 1989.

Pedersen, Sucan. *Family, Dependence, and the Origins of the Welfare State: Britain and France, 1914-1945*. Cambridge: Cambridge University Press, 1993.

Pickersgill, J.W. *The Mackenzie King Record*, Vol. 1. Toronto: University of Toronto Press, 1960.

Pickersgill, J.W., and D.F. Forster, eds. *The Mackenzie King Record*, Vol. 2. Toronto: University of Toronto Press, 1968.

Pierson, Paul. *Dismantling the Welfare State? Reagan, Thatcher and the Politics of Retrenchment*. New York: Press Syndicate of the University of Cambridge, 1994.

Pierson, Ruth Roach. "Gender and the Unemployment Insurance Debate in Canada, 1934-40." *Labour/Le Travail* 25 (Spring 1990): 78-90.

–. *They're Still Women After All: The Second World War and Canadian Womanhood*. Toronto: McClelland and Stewart, 1986.

Polanyi, Karl. *The Great Transformation: The Political and Economic Origins of Our Times*. Boston: Beacon Press, 1957.

Porter, Ann. "Constrained and Redefined: Women's Issues in the Mulroney Era." In *Transforming the Nation: Canada and Brian Mulroney*, ed. Raymond B. Blake, 178-204. Montreal and Kingston: McGill-Queen's University Press, 2007.

–. *Gendered States: Women, Unemployment Insurance, and the Political Economy of the Welfare State in Canada, 1945-1997.* Toronto: University of Toronto Press, 2003.

–. "Women and Income Security in the Post-War Period: The Case of Unemployment Insurance, 1945-1962." *Labour/Le Travail 31 (Spring* 1993): 111-44.

Prince, Michael J. "What Ever Happened to Compassion? Liberal Social Policy 1980-84." In *How Ottawa Spends, 1984: The New Agenda,* ed. Allan M. Maslove, 79-121. Toronto: James Lorimer, 1984.

Prince, Michael J., and James J. Rice. "Governing through Shifting Social-Policy Regimes: Brian Mulroney and Canada's Welfare State." In *Transforming the Nation: Canada and Brian Mulroney,* ed. Raymond B. Blake, 164-77. Montreal and Kingston: McGill-Queen's University Press, 2007.

Pringle, Rosemary, and Sophie Watson. "Fathers, Brothers and Mates: The Fraternal State in Australia." In *Playing the State: Australian Feminist Intervention,* ed. Sophie Watson, 229-43. London: Verso, 1990.

Pulkingham, Jane, and Gordon Ternowetsky, eds. *Child and Family Policies: Struggles, Strategies and Options.* Halifax: Fernwood Publishing, 1997.

Quebec. *Report of the Study Committee on Public Assistance.* Quebec City, 1963.

Réseau d'action et d'information pour les femmes. *Federal Government Threatens Demise of Children's Safety Net: A Brief Condemning the New Integrated Child Tax Benefit as Dangerous and Inequitable.* Montreal, 16 July 1992.

Rice, James J. "Restitching the Safety Net: Altering the National Social Security System." In *How Ottawa Spends 1987-88: Restraining the State,* ed. Michael J. Prince, 211-36. Toronto: Methuen, 1987.

Rice, James J., and Michael J. Prince. *Changing Politics of Canadian Social Policy.* Toronto: University of Toronto Press, 2000.

–. "Lowering the Safety Net and Weakening the Bonds of Nationhood: Social Policy in the Mulroney Years." In *How Ottawa Spends: A More Democratic Canada ... ?* ed. Susan D. Phillips, 356-78. Ottawa: Carleton University Press, 1993.

Rouke, P.T., and R.L. Schnell. *No Bleeding Heart: Charlotte Whitton, A Feminist on the Right.* Vancouver: UBC Press, 1987.

Russell, Peter H. *Constitutional Odyssey.* 3rd ed. (Toronto: University of Toronto Press, 2004).

Savoie, Donald J. *The Politics of Public Spending in Canada.* Toronto: University of Toronto Press, 1990.

Saywell, John, ed. *Canada Annual Review for 1966.* Toronto: University of Toronto Press, 1967.

–. *Canadian Annual Review of Politics and Public Affairs, 1971.* Toronto: University of Toronto Press, 1972.

Saywell, John, and Paul Stevens, "Parliament and Politics." In *Canadian Annual Review of Politics and Public Affairs, 1971,* ed. John Saywell, 3-102. Toronto: University of Toronto Press, 1972.

Schwartz, Edward E. "Some Observations of the Canadian Family Allowances Program." *Social Service Review* 10, 4 (December 1946): 1-23.

Scott, F.R. "The Constitution and Post-War Canada." In *Canada after the War,* ed. F.R. Scott, 209-12. Toronto: Macmillan, 1943.

Shewell, Hugh E.Q. *"Enough to Keep Them Alive": Indian Social Welfare in Canada, 1873-1965.* Toronto: University of Toronto Press, 2004.

Shifrin, Leonard. "Income Security: The Rise and Stall of the Federal Role." In *Canadian Social Welfare Policy: Federal and Provincial Dimensions,* ed. Jacqueline S. Ismael, 21-28. Kingston and Montreal: McGill-Queen's University Press, 1985.

Siltanen, Janet. "Paradise Paved? Reflections on the Fate of Social Citizenship in Canada," *Citizenship Studies* 6 (4) 2002: 395-414.

Simeon, Richard. *Federal-Provincial Diplomacy*. Toronto: University of Toronto Press, 1972.

Skocpol, Theda. *Protecting Soldiers and Mothers: The Political Origins of Social Policy in the United States*. Cambridge: University of Cambridge Press, 1992.

–. *Social Policy in the United States: Future Possibilities in Historical Perspective*. Princeton: Princeton University Press, 1995.

Smiley, Donald V. "The Rowell-Sirois Report, Provincial Autonomy and Post-War Canadian Federalism." In *Canadian Federalism: Myth or Reality*, ed. J. Peter Meekison, 259-79. Toronto: Methuen, 1968.

Splane, Richard. "Social Policy-Making in the Government of Canada." In *Canadian Social Policy*, rev. ed., ed. Shankar A. Yelaja, 222-64. Waterloo: Wilfrid Laurier Press, 1987.

Stepler, D.H. "Family Allowances for Canada." *Behind the Headlines* 3, 2 (March-April, 1943): 1-32.

Strain, J. Frank. "Debts Paid and Debts Owed: The Legacy of Mulroney's Economic Policy." In *The Nation Transformed: Canada and Brian Mulroney*, ed. Raymond B. Blake, 42-60. Kingston and Montreal: McGill-Queen's University Press, 2007.

Strong-Boag, Veronica. "Home Dreams: Women and the Suburban Experience in Canada, 1945-1960." *Canadian Historical Review* 72, 4 (December 1991): 471-504.

–. "Wages for Housework: Mothers' Allowances and the Beginning of Social Security in Canada." *Journal of Canadian Studies/Revue d'études canadiennes* 12, 1 (1979): 24-34.

Struthers, James. "In the Interests of the Children: Mothers' Allowances and the Origins of Income Security in Ontario, 1917-1930." In *Social Fabric or Patchwork Quilt: The Development of Social Policy in Canada*, ed. Raymond B. Blake and Jeff A. Keshen. Peterborough: Broadview Press, 2006.

–. *The Limits of Affluence: Welfare in Ontario, 1920-1970*. Toronto: University of Toronto Press, 1994.

–. *No Fault of Their Own: Unemployment and the Canadian Welfare State, 1914-1941*. Toronto: University of Toronto Press, 1983.

Théret, Bruno. *Protection sociale et fédéralisme dans le miroir de l'Amérique du Nord* (Brussels/Montreal: P.I.E.-Peter Lang/Presses de l'Université de Montréal, 2002).

Titmuss, Richard. *Problems of Social Policy*. London: HMSO, 1950.

Trudeau, Pierre Elliott. "The Practice and Theory of Federalism."/ In *Social Purpose for Canada*, ed. M. Oliver, 371-93. Toronto: University of Toronto Press, 1967.

Ursel, Jane. *Private Lives, Public Policy: 100 Years of State Intervention in the Family*. Toronto: Women's Press, 1992.

Vadakin, James C. *Children, Poverty and Family Allowances*. New York: Basic Books, 1968.

Vaillancourt, Yves. *L'évolution des politiques sociales au Québec, 1940-1960*. Montreal: Presses de l'Université de Montréal, 1988.

Vigod, B.L. "History According to the Boucher Report: Some Reflections on the State and Social Welfare in Quebec before the Quiet Revolution." In *The Benevolent State: The Growth of Welfare in Canada*, ed. Allan Moscovitch and Jim Albert, 175-85. Toronto: Garamond Press, 1987.

Weaver, Robert. "Understanding the Present by Exploring the Past: An Analysis of Family Allowances and Child Care in Canada." MA thesis, University of Regina, Saskatchewan, 2000.

Webber, Jeremy. *Reimaging Canada: Language, Culture, Community, and the Canadian Constitution*. Kingston and Montreal: McGill-Queen's University Press, 1994.

Weir, Margaret, Ann Orloff, and Theda Skocpol, eds. *The Politics of Social Policy in the United States*. Princeton: Princeton University Press, 1988.

Whitaker, Reginald. *The Government Party: Organizing and Financing the Liberal Party of Canada 1930-58*. Toronto: University of Toronto Press, 1977.

–. "Neo-Conservatism and the State." In *Socialist Registrar*, ed. Ralph Miliband, Leo Panitch, and John Saville, 121-35. London: Merlin Press, 1987.

–. *A Sovereign Idea: Essays on Canada as a Democratic Community*. Montreal and Kingston: McGill-Queen's University Press, 1992.

Wilensky, Harold L. *The Welfare State and Equality: Structural and Ideological Roots of Public Expenditure*. Berkeley: University of California Press, 1975.

Willard, Joseph W. "Family Allowances in Canada." In *Children's Allowances and the Economic Welfare of Children*, ed. E. Burns, 54-72. New York: Citizen's Committee of New York, 1968.

Williams, Clifford J. "The Social Services Story in Ontario, 1970-1987." Unpublished paper.

Young, R.A., Philippe Faucher, and André Blais, "The Concept of Province-Building: A Critique." *Canadian Journal of Political Science/Revue canadienne de science politique* 17, 4 (December 1984): 783-818.

Young, Walter. *The Anatomy of a Party: The National CCF, 1932-1961*. Toronto: University of Toronto Press, 1969.

Index